THE LONDON SCHOOL OF ECONOMICS
AND POLITICAL SCIENCE
PAPERS IN SOVIET AND EAST EUROPEAN
LAW, ECONOMICS AND POLITICS

General Editor
LEONARD SCHAPIRO

2

ASPECTS OF PLANOMETRICS

Aspects of
Planometrics

by

ALFRED ZAUBERMAN

With contributions by A. BERGSTROM,

T. KRONSJÖ, and E. J. MISHAN,

and editorial assistance by M. J. ELLMAN

NEW HAVEN

YALE UNIVERSITY PRESS

1967

Published in Great Britain by
THE ATHLONE PRESS
UNIVERSITY OF LONDON
at 2 Gower Street, London WC1

Printed in Great Britain by
WILLIAM CLOWES AND SONS, LIMITED
LONDON AND BECCLES

To my wife

Preface

Most of the essays in this volume are appearing in print for the first time. The few—five out of twenty—which have been previously published (some of them in non-English journals) have now been thoroughly revised. I have tried to systematise and integrate the essays around one central theme: the impact on Soviet theoretical thinking and planning techniques of the emerging mathematical school; or, to use the name coined by V. S. Nemchinov, the focus is on 'planometrics'; hence our title. As my work proceeded I thought it useful to widen the scope so as to allow for developments in the same domain in other normatively planning countries. I can only hope that a reasonable degree of unity of matter has been achieved.

Once the 'planometric' school emerged its progress proved remarkably fast. At least to indicate what has happened during the inevitably long gestation of the book, appendices have been added to some chapters and the apparatus of footnotes has been greatly expanded. My apologies are offered to the reader for inconvenience thereby caused.

Debt incurred for advice has been acknowledged in individual chapters to Dr Bergstrom, Dr Morton, Professor Nove and Professor Phillips. Professor Nove also read the draft of this book, and I am grateful for his sympathetic appreciation and comment. My sincere thanks for help in my research for the chapter on normative and indicative planning go to Mr Michael Kaser, Professor Massé, the Commissaire-Général du Plan, Professor Malinvaud, Professor Nataf, Professor Phelps Brown and Professor Tinbergen. I wish to thank Professor Wiles for advice offered. I benefited greatly from my conversations on some subjects of this book with the late Academician Nemchinov. I also gratefully acknowledge the help of Academician Fedorenko, Director of the Central Economic-Mathematical Institute, the Academy of Sciences of the USSR, in providing me with valuable material. Needless to say none of them bears any responsibility whatsoever for anything in my work. I am happy to be able to include two joint contributions, one with Professor Bergstrom and another with Dr Mishan, in the fields in which their authority is recognised; and also gratefully acknowledge the collaboration with Dr Kronsjö who has contributed an important, rigorous addendum to my exposition of problems of foreign-trade planning. This list would certainly be incomplete if it failed to mention the Editor of the Series, Professor Schapiro: the volume could not have appeared without his invaluable help and advice and kind understanding.

After the first draft was completed Mr Michael Ellman and Mr Patrick Davis assisted me in editing and revising it; Mr Ellman also assisted me in my research. I wish to thank them both, and also to thank Mr A. M. Wood and the staff of the Athlone Press, for giving to this book more care than the author can usually expect from the Publisher. Mrs H. Parkes helped me greatly in indexing the book. Finally thanks are due to the editors of the journals in which some of the essays originally appeared.

London School of Economics   Alfred Zauberman
and Political Science

Contents

CONTENTS

B. Profit Guidance

C. Efficiency of Investment

D. Efficiency of Foreign Trade

E. A Comparison of Planning Techniques under Imperative and Indicative Planning

Introduction: The New Soviet Economics

OVER the last decade and a half Soviet economic thinking has experienced a noteworthy change, and I felt that it might be of help to a Western reader if he was offered, *in lieu* of an introduction, some perspective for an assessment of the road it has travelled. Perhaps brief excerpts from two surveys of Soviet economics, published by me at the end of the 1940s and at the beginning of the 1960s, could be of some use for this purpose.

AS SEEN IN THE LATE 1940s[1]

The Contrast between Soviet and Western Economics

'The reader who crosses the East/West frontier in economic writing has to leave behind much of his usual professional luggage. He would find that the major part of his habitual box of tools would be of little, if any, use to him. His dexterity in applying the marginal analysis would be of no avail. He would have to forget his inclination to an equilibrium approach although the empirically developed system of "economic balances" has at least some characteristics of this approach.[2] He would be faced with declared hostility towards any micro-economic approach: any attitude but the macro-economic is anti-social and therefore banned. Utility calculus is anathema. Great problems hotly debated in the West for the last two or three decades

---

[1] This is an excerpt from 'Economic Thought in the Soviet Union: I. Economic Law and the Theory of Value', published in *Review of Economic Studies*, vol. xvi/i, 1948–49, no. 39.

[2] Planning technique has gradually developed an interrelated system of what are termed 'balances'. The balances are supposed to dovetail with each other. At least one writer maintains that as the economy grows the system is becoming more and more cumbersome. It seems that the ghost of 'innumerable equations' has actually begun to haunt the Soviet planner. (Cf. G. G. Kosiatchenko in *Planovoye Khoziaistvo*, 1938, no. 6.)

A few years ago an attempt to construct an interesting general National Economy Balance by the prominent economist, Professor S. Strumilin, was condemned as an endeavour to revive the moving equilibrium approach to the reproduction problem. Cf. S. Strumilin, *Planovoye Khoziaistvo*, 1936, nos. 9–10; and criticism by Prof. A. Notkin and N. Tsagolev, *Planovoye Khoziaistvo*, 1937, no. 4. The Editors of the *Planovoye Khoziaistvo* (same issue) admitted their blunder in publishing Strumilin's paper, which they described as counter-revolutionary.

are only of remote interest to Soviet economists, as most of these questions refer to the market economy. There is no discussion, for instance,
of such questions as imperfect or monopolistic competition, saving ÷ investment in the particular context of a mature economy, full employment and the trade cycle; no mention of *pontes asinorum* like the
multiplier, acceleration principle, cobweb theorem and so on.

'All this should hardly be surprising to the Western reader. What is
surprising is the scarcity of analytical work on the Soviet model itself.
This model still awaits its General Theory—a fact stressed time and
again by the Soviet Academy of Sciences. Several explanations may
be put forward for this anaemia in theoretical analysis. The simplest
seems to be the fascination which practical problems have had for
Soviet economists during the last thirty years. It may also be the fact
that the very circumscribed acceptance of economic law is a real
handicap to theoretical thinking. It may also be that the stringent
demands of orthodoxy discourage such thinking. A habit of constantly
looking for corroboration of one's theoretical viewpoint in the words
of the Master seems to support this suggestion, although the words of
the Master do not always afford sanctuary to the more independent
thinkers.

Economic Law in Soviet Thought

'At the end of the war the Western economic world was stirred by an
apparent revival of the concept of economic law in Soviet economic
thinking. Hopes were expressed that a bridge between East and West
in economic thought was under construction. Some visualised the
Soviet official doctrine as on its way "From Marx to Menger".[1] The
subsequent development of this doctrine has hardly justified such
hopes. True, the notion of economic law has been re-incorporated in
the body of doctrine. However, the content was sterilised to the extent
of depriving it of any significance.

'A notable authority of Marxism, A. Leontiev, has expounded the
accepted teaching on economic law broadly as follows:[2] Economic

[1] Cf. *American Economic Review*, vol. xxxiv, September 1944, 'Some Questions of
Teaching Political Economy', and in the same issue a comment by Raya Dunayevskaya;
and cf. also Oscar Lange, 'Marxian Economics in the Soviet Union' (vol. xxxv, March
1945), and Carl Landauer, 'From Marx to Menger' (vol. xxxiv, June 1944) and other
contributions on the subject in the same volume. Cf. also John Sommerville, *Soviet
Philosophy, A Survey of Theory and Practice*, N.Y., 1946, pp. 10 ff.

[2] A. Leontiev, *Planovoye Khoziaistvo*, 1947, no. 6.

law is an expression of "objective necessity" in any socio-economic structure. Its modus operandi, is, however, different in different socio-economic milieux. Under capitalism the "objective necessity" manifests itself in the economic laws which (a) operate autonomously independent of human will and consciousness; (b) are expressions of the exploitation of an overwhelming majority of the society by a minority. Under socialism the "objective necessity" operates as a "conscious" necessity, i.e. as one "which makes its way through the consciousness and will of the community as a whole". Thus, e.g. under any socio-economic system there must be some method of allocating scarce resources. In any socio-economic set-up there must also be a correlation between the growth of output and that of consumption. All these are the "objective necessities" of social production. Under capitalism, "objective necessity" acts via the law of value, operating through the mechanism of competition, market fluctuations, the capitalist pursuit of profit and the flow of capital from one industry to another. Under socialism the abolition of private property in the instruments of production makes it "objectively necessary" to replace the natural laws of the market by planning the national economy.

'A closer analysis of Leontiev's reasoning reduces his "objective necessities" to propositions which hardly state more than is already implied in their logical assumptions. It would be erroneous to think that Soviet economic thought has moved during the last five years any nearer to the tenets of the "genetic school" which met its tragic end at the threshold of the thirties.[1,2]

'The theory of value has remained at the stage which it reached on

[1] The question whether and how economic laws operate under socialism was one of the foci of the Great Debate of the twenties. It was a striking transposition of a political struggle into the field of abstract theory. Two schools of thought were struggling for supremacy. The one (the genetic school), whose protagonist was Bukharin, contended that under socialism, the *modus operandi* of economic law was extrapolated from the trend, the plan being thought of as a sort of technical instrument for following this trend in a rational way (while under capitalism the trend followed an accidental course). The other school of thought either rejected the logical validity of economic law under socialism entirely or maintained that it not only changed its *modus operandi*, but even its very content.

As N. Bukharin (cf. *Criticism of the Economic Platform of the Opposition*, Moscow, 1926, p. 48) put it, the latter school saw in the 'plan, planning principle, manœuvre plan, etc., a panacea for economic and consequently all evils'.

B. Khmielnitskaya (cf. *Ekonomicheskoye Obozrienie*, 1925, no. 3, who was close to this school asserted that in the dialectical process of transformation of the chaotic market economy into an 'organised' one—the essence of the economic law would change in such a way as to produce 'norm of economic conduct', and accordingly economics

its re-admission five years ago. At that time it was believed that Soviet economists had set out on a route which led to the conclusion that the labour theory of value was untenable, and must be replaced by a theory explaining values as expressions of utility. These predictions have been falsified. Those socialist economists of the West who, like Professor Lange,[1] have pointed out that Soviet economic theory could provide adequate guidance for the management of the economy only by incorporating the method and technique of the marginal analysis, must find the theoretical developments of the last few years most disappointing.

The Labour Theory of Value

'As one climbs up the ladder of the Soviet planning apparatus, a calculus in physical terms prevails. With a given set of scarce factors and,

would change from what she termed an 'ideographic' into a 'normographic' discipline. Much of this teaching seems to be accepted by the doctrine at present in vogue.

On the extreme wing of the school, Professor E. Preobzazhenskiy (cf. *New Economics*, Moscow, 1926, ch. 3) argued that even at that time, i.e. at the time of the mixed economy of the NEP period—the process of disintegration of economic law as such, had actually begun. According to him the corresponding but antagonistic categories of the capitalist and the socialist economy are: commodity ÷ product; commodity production ÷ socialist planning; the market ÷ socialist accountancy; value and price ÷ labour expenditure in production.

In practical policies the crucial issue dividing the schools of thought was the problem of the rate of industrialisation of the country and of the collectivisation of agriculture. The right wing favoured pro-peasant tendencies, and fought what was called 'the colonial' attitude of the proletariat towards the peasantry: there was much talk of the 'law of primary accumulation' through exploitation of the peasant: price and taxation policies towards the peasant were violently debated. (Cf. Bukharin, *ibid.*, particularly the chapter, 'A New Revelation on Soviet Economics, or How to Wreck the Workers' and Peasants' Alliance'.) The 'extremists' of both schools were routed, and some of the recalcitrants had to pay the supreme penalty. The Party condemned both the left and right deviation, but eventually its general line steered towards the 'leftist' doctrine, in its essence though not in its tactics.

[2] As pointed out by I. Anchishkin in a recent report to the Institute of Economics of the USSR—in the first post-revolutionary years economics as such was considered to be a doomed science. Since, it was assumed, there were no objective economic laws—there would be no scope for theoretical economic analysis under socialism. (This view, we believe, was shared by many classical economists.) The practical effect of this attitude, was that in the Soviet universities, only the theory of economics under capitalism was taught, while problems of the socialist economy were treated from a purely practical approach. Only since Stalin's 'discovery that a law of value operates in a socialist community' has economic theory as such regained respectability as a subject for study and research in the universities.

[1] O. Lange, *The Economic Theory of Socialism*, Minneapolis, 1938, p. 141.

in particular, with given equipment, a general pattern of combination of resources develops, tending to their full employment. From this *point de départ* adjustments and correctives—very often by a trial and error—are made by the planners to accord with the accepted coefficient of growth. In practice this reduces to the problem of a national man-power budget parallel to those now used in the Western semi-planned economies. In the past some Soviet Marxists regarded this method as a confirmation of the thesis that a socialist economy can proceed without reference to the concept of value. Now they want to interpret it as a confirmation of the thesis that a socialist economy proceeds under the rule of the labour theory of value.

'The operation of the labour theory of value in the Soviet Union still awaits its formulation as a self-sufficient and coherent doctrine. This is also true of its correlation with price theory.

'According to a well-known Marxist proposition labour is "social" in its essence whatever the socio-economic structure, provided that division of labour prevails. In this sense it is "social" also under capitalism; it is only the private ownership of the means of production which under capitalism accounts for this property being hidden behind the curtain of "private", i.e. privately appropriated, labour. The social labour of the producer becomes in this way—according to Marxist teaching, the "abstract labour", which is the essence of the value of the commodity. There is by now a consensus among the Soviet Marxists that under socialism, when private ownership of the means of production has been done away with, the actual amount of social labour is identical with the "socially necessary labour".[1] Some say simply: "The socialist transformation of the economy has led to the abolition of the antithesis (between concrete and abstract socially necessary labour) in the U.S.S.R."[2] Others try to be more precise, and their argument is slightly more sophisticated: in the socialist economy labour appears already in the process of production directly, as socially necessary labour. But they qualify, "direct, socially necessary labour" is itself an historical category which passes through different phases; in the present phase of socialism it is still a heterogeneous category: the skilled labourer creates in a unit of time greater value than the unskilled. "That is why the natural calculus of social labour, directly in production units or units of time, is unsatisfactory, and that is why

[1] N. Vozniesienskiy, *The War Economy of U.S.S.R.*, Moscow, 1947, p. 149.
[2] L. Gatovskiy, *Planovoye Khoziaistvo*, 1948, no. 2.

5

it appears necessary to preserve the money calculus, which reduces dissimilar, heterogeneous . . . forms of social labour to . . . the uniform abstract labour."[1] In other words—in the opinion of these writers—"concrete" social labour, although it appears under socialism "directly" in production, still cannot be given direct expression. But this view begs the next question. If "abstract" labour is the true essence of value, admittedly possessing the property of being expressible in money, what is the principle of its money expression, i.e. what is the principle of wage and price expression of value? Thus, the argument of these writers merely extends the chain of reasoning but still lacks the final link.

'Pricing, it is asserted in Soviet economic literature, is "based" on the law of value, though this law does not "dictate" prices. In fact, prices are determined by the Plan which is drawn up on a broad economic perspective of economic growth. However, as Soviet authors usually remark, the law of value "influences" prices in the sense that, on the one hand, growing efficiency of labour tends to lower costs which in the long run tends to lower prices, while on the other, value itself is influenced by the Plan, according to the way in which its elements, i.e. labour efficiency, and, generally speaking, factor costs are planned.[2] In the productive apparatus, the essential function of price is to act as a stimulus for expanding output at a given level of social costs. "The price of a commodity in the Socialist society of the U.S.S.R.", as recently restated by Prof. Vozniesienskiy, "is based on its value or production costs. But it is the Soviet State itself which determines the concrete price of every commodity in the interest of strengthening socialism and raising the standard of living of the workers . . . and which consequently [determines] the degree of deviation . . . from its true value."[3] All such and similar statements are enigmatic and vague, and one cannot help feeling that their authors are at pains to explain away the obvious fact that the current theory of value fails to yield any quantitative formula for the "true" value ÷ price relationship.

'It is customary with Western observers to emphasise the elasticity of the Soviet State in the doctrinal field, and its inclination to estimate dogmas by their bearing on practical affairs. Some reason is required

---

[1] K. Ostrovitianov, *Voprosy Ekonomiki*, 1948, no. 1.
[2] A. Gordin, *Sovietskiye Finansy*, 1945, no. 8.
[3] N. Vozniesienskiy, *op. cit.*, pp. 121–2.

6

as to why it continues to show no sign of wavering in its attachment to a doctrine which, in its accepted ossified version, is not only unwieldy as the theoretical basis for interpreting the working principles of economics, but is demonstrably a real handicap to the policy of the Soviet economic bureaucracy? There is certainly a complex of historical, psychological and political reasons behind the still unchallenged sway of the labour theory of value in Soviet economics. As the basis of the surplus value concept, it has been logically and historically connected with the Marxian theory of exploitation, hence its great emotional significance. Psychologically it harmonises well with the ideology of a proletarian State, and of a community in process of industrialisation. These advantages will probably outweigh the disadvantages for a long time to come. There seems but little probability that the authorised theory may be in a foreseeable future contaminated by ideas borrowed from the Western economists. It need hardly be emphasised that the present phase inaugurated by the now famous condemnation of G. F. Alexandrov's *History of Western European Philosophy*, (June 1947) is not propitious for the reception of Western ideas in any field of research and thought in the Soviet Union.'

AS SEEN AT THE BEGINNING OF THE 1960s[1]

'The field of Soviet economic thought, so distressingly arid for decades, has suddenly begun to bear some interesting fruit. It is fertilised by extensive borrowing from the West. The change is due and confined basically to an assimilation of mathematical concepts and methodologies. Two books of quite exceptional importance which have appeared during the past few months, one a study by the famous mathematician Professor Kantorovich,[2] the other a symposium edited by an untiring though prudent protagonist of new ideas, the distinguished Academician Nemchinov,[3] form a benchmark in these remarkable developments. They provide a focus for the present remarks.

[1] This is an excerpt from 'New Winds in Soviet Planning', published in *Soviet Studies*, vol. xii, July 1960, no. 1.

[2] L. V. Kantorovich, *Ekonomicheskiy raschet nailuchshego ispolzovaniya resursov*, Moscow, 1959. This will be hereafter referred to as *Ekonomicheskiy raschet*. The English translation has the title *The Best Use of Economic Resources* (edited by G. Morton), London, 1965.

[3] V. S. Nemchinov, ed., *Primeneniye matematiki v ekonomicheskikh issledovaniyakh*, Moscow, 1959. This will be hereafter referred to as *Symposium*. The English translation has the title *The Use of Mathematics in Economics* (edited by A. Nove), London, 1964.

7

'An inquiry with a wider horizon would probably have related the happenings in Soviet economics to the more general subject of changes in the Soviet intellectual climate. In our far more modest treatment it is rather the concern for a re-tooling of the planning and control mechanism with imported foreign instruments and certain repercussions of the techniques of their use on economic theory that will come to the forefront. But how far are they foreign?

'One of the explicitly stated aims of Nemchinov's symposium is to "establish priority" (utverdit prioritet),[1] to prove that concepts and methods now in great fashion in the West are either Soviet born or rooted in some early Soviet pioneering work. His own contribution reproduces, in a slightly modernised shape, the Soviet overall 'chess-board' balance of the national economy for 1923/4,[2] first of the kind compiled. It is this work, rudimentary as it was, that gave inspiration, so it is argued, to the then young Leontief to evolve later, in the West, his input-output methodology. Certainly legitimate, I think, is the claim to Soviet parenthood of linear programming. It is said to have been conceived in the late thirties, in the traditionally excellent Mathematics and Mechanics Institute of Leningrad University, where it was employed for planning the utilisation of machine-tool capacities and solving other similar tasks. Kantorovich's paper, first published at the end of the thirties and reprinted in the symposium,[3] will dispel, in his favour I think, any doubts as to the chronology of the "invention": we seem to face here one of the cases where in exploring new avenues minds of genius converge at the same points without knowledge of each other.[4] The remarkable thing, however, is that for two decades

[1] *Symposium*, p. 3.

[2] *Ibid.*, pp. 10 ff.; see W. Leontief's review in *Volkswirtschaftliches Archiv*, 1925.

[3] L. V. Kantorovich, *Matematicheskiye metody organizatsii i planirovaniya proizvodstva* (Mathematical methods of the organisation and planning of production), Leningrad, 1939; *Symposium*, pp. 251 ff.

[4] See the generous tribute to Kantorovich by George B. Dantzig in *Linear Programming and Extensions*, Princeton, 1963, pp. 22 ff.

As Professor Dantzig points out Kantorovich was first to see (in his paper first published in 1939, *Matematicheskiye metody organizatsyi i planirovanya proizvodstva*) that some important broad classes of production problems possess a well-defined mathematical structure permitting numerical evaluation and lending themselves to numerical solution.

Subsequent contributions, in the 1940s, offer a theory of the relation between the primal and the dual, also of the trans-shipment problem and of capacitated 'networks (L. V. Kantorovich, 'O peremeshchenyi mass', *Doklady*, USSR Academy of Sciences, vol. 37, no. 7–8, 1942; L. V. Kantorovich and M. K. Gavurin, 'Primenenye matematicheskikh metodov v voprosakh analiza gruzopotokov' in *Problemy Povyshenya Effektivnosti Raboty Transporta*, Moscow, 1949).

Kantorovich's invention left no impact whatsoever on Soviet economics and economy; that it remained, as it were in the underground of Soviet economic science, a notable pointer, if one were needed, to the powers of obstructive forces. Be that as it may, not only does the unearthing of the Soviet contribution gratify Soviet pride, but it facilitates the osmosis of ideas and allays the acute Soviet touchiness on the point of independence of "bourgeois" thought. It accounts for a new-found readiness to acknowledge some intellectual debts.

'Why are eminent Soviet economists so eager to graft the "new" methods on to Soviet planning? They point to the benefits of resorting to mathematics. They insist on the advantages to be derived from expressing economic life in a system of equations amenable to treatment by high-speed computing equipment. Kantorovich makes no bones about the present state of Soviet planning: it is, he somewhat sarcastically remarks, "qualitative" rather than quantitative—it is practised on a more-of-this and less-of-that basis. (Is it not a contradiction in terms to talk of non-quantitative planning?) Hence plan components are ill-fitted, choices accidental, planning decisions badly outdated, "best solutions only rarely adopted".[1] The results are chronic rigidities and bottlenecks. The crudity of Soviet planning techniques accounts, in Kantorovich's view, for a waste of perhaps as much as a quarter or a third of the potential optimal output.

'The enthusiastic response which the mathematical "novelties" have met in Soviet economics is indeed a measure of the urgency felt in the task of overhauling and modernising the techiques of Soviet planning.

'However, many Soviet economists see the limitations of the new techniques, including their indefatigable elaborators and proponents. Professor Kantorovich himself warns his readers that algebraic equations yield at best only a rather "abstract" picture of an economy.

'Speaking generally, the mathematical methods come up in practice against very formidable technical and computational obstacles and difficulties; something of what one can gain in precision on the swings one is bound to be lost on the roundabouts. But how much? Only practice can given an answer.

'Technical problems apart, the new methodologies in general, and linear programming in particular, have stumbled against certain more

---

[1] *Symposium*, p. 11.

fundamental theoretical obstacles which touch upon ideology. I indicated some of these obstacles—idiosyncrasies and allergies—when discussing Lange's piloting study. The highest hurdle which remains to be taken is the problem of price and of the underlying theory of value. And the problem of price is central to the new methodologies. In a sense they stand or fall with it.

'While much of Kantorovich's attention is of necessity centred on the computational aspect of his price, a fuller theoretical elaboration of it—indeed lifted to the level of philosophy—will be found in Professor Novozhilov's contribution to the symposium,[1] which reproduces in the main the ideas he put forward in the early and middle forties. His point of departure is an inquiry into the continuous tug of war between the practice of Soviet pricing and costing and the theory of value adhered to.

'Novozhilov starts his argument from a superior-type economic environment. Did not Marx, he recalls, recommend the study of the anatomy of man as the key to that of a monkey? A peep into the human future leads him to a bold rejection of the accepted eschatology. As against the romantic vision of a scarcity-free millenium, his hypothesis of Communism assumes the persistence of scarcities. In the first place, he argues, there will always remain in this world the limiting factor of time. On the economic plane this takes the form of time-lags in production and distribution. Further, even if we set the value of the stocks in the capital-abundant society at zero, this would still not entitle us to treat products as free gifts. There will always be disparities in the efficiency of the natural wealth at man's disposal; and there will always remain inequality in the efficiency of man-made instruments of production. Hence the warning: "technological progress cannot do away with these differences because it creates them".[2] Now, if these differences are to continue, so must the need for the calculation of

---

[1] V. V. Novozhilov, 'Izmereniye zatrat i ikh rezultatov v sotsialisticheskom khozyaistve', *Symposium*, pp. 42 ff.

There is an excellent analysis of the Novozhilov optimisation framework by H. Chambre in his introduction to the French translation of the work, in *Cahiers de l'ISEA*, February 1964. Note also that Professor Frisch showed how the selection method developed by Academician Novozhilov in the publications of 1939 and 1946 can be restated in terms of the modern programming language. Cf. V. V. Novozhilov's 'Method of Process Selection and its Transformation into a Linear Programming Problem', *Memorandum*, Sosialokonomisk Institutt Universitetet i Oslo, 27 September 1959, *mimeo*.

[2] *Ibid.*, p. 164.

"differential cost" cost, the rationing of resources by means of efficiency norms (normy effektivnosti). This, Novozhilov contends, creates the pre-conditions of "democratic centralism" or, as we would say, devolution in operational management and centralisation in planning and control.

'Now, from the anatomy of man back to that of a monkey. If the efficiency calculus cannot be dispensed with in the milieu of plenty, it is still more imperative in a socialist society far more constrained by deficiencies. This path of logic, *a majori ad minus*, leads Novozhilov to his conception of the socialist price. This is the "efficiency norm" (norma effektivnosti) in its various "concrete forms"—those of price, thus called, for reproducible intermediate goods ("objects of labour") construed on the principle of feedback relationship, rental charge for man-made fixed productive resources with due allowance for wear and tear and obsolescence, differential rent for natural resources, including land, "normative efficiency" (or simply interest) for capital. All these "forms" are evolved from the "balance". (We would say that they emerge as the value "dual" of a technologically optimal programme.)

'In the forties Professor Novozhilov was effectively silenced by the charge of being dangerously close to "subjective" value theories and to Western marginalism. He was, incidentally, also accused of being tainted with Keynesianism. It may be taken as a sign of some change in mood that he has now been permitted to restate his views. Have his views been thus rehabilitated? The disturbing fact is that in the meantime the same charge has been levelled on the same count against Kantorovich, although the latter couched his ideas in doctrinally less challenging terms. The ideologues have not been inclined to let the sleeping dogs lie! At a conference called to discuss Western econometrics, Kantorovich was charged with "slipping down the vicious path of marginal utility theories and all kinds of marginal solutions".[1] That became the cue for the critique of Kantorovich's work when it crystallised. A review in the organ of the State Planning Commission by the noted mathematical economist Professor Boyarski legitimately pointed out that Kantorovich "substitutes cost relations of the 'last' unit of this or that product for value in its Marxist sense and unwittingly reproduces certain propositions of so-called 'marginalism'". Yet, Professor Boyarski goes on to say, "Marxist criticism demonstrated

[1] See especially Ya. A. Kronrod's contribution to this discussion, *Vestnik Statistiki*, 1959, no. 9, p. 62.

long ago that the marginalist conceptions are built on sand. . . ."[1] Particularly disturbing to the critics, and not unexpectedly so, have been the implications of Kantorovich's approach to wages: "It is known", Boyarski goes on, "that the application of this marginalist conception to wages leads directly to John B. Clark's apologetic theory whose fallacy has been also fully exposed by Marxist criticism."[2] To quote Boyarski for the last time—"A book by a brilliant mathematician (Kantorovich) which contains a brilliant solution of a number of practical problems has suffered from an evident disregard for economic science".[3] The dilemma of economic science is, thus, how to save the mathematician's "brilliant solutions" for economic practice. Perhaps a way out from the impasse will be found in some acceptable semantic patch-up. One cannot exclude, however, that eventually Soviet economics will try to reconcile Marx with marginalism in a fundamental way, perhaps on the lines attempted by Brus[4] and other economists in Poland.[5]

'To sum up. There is today in the Soviet search for superior methods of planning a spirit of Great Adventure, but the proof of the pudding will be in the eating. The extent to which mathematical tools and techniques may add to efficiency in Soviet economic planning and control can only be established empirically. The testing is in too early a stage to warrant even a provisional judgement. It seems, however, that at the very least the experimenting may open the theoreticians' and practitioners' eyes to some possible improvements in the present very rough techniques of "material balances". A study recently published in the West, by Dr Montias, provides a very interesting clue in this direction.[6] Assimilation of mathematical methodologies is also of immediate importance in its impact on the Soviet quest for rational price.

[1] A. Boyarskiy, *Planovoye khozyaistov*, 1960, no. 1, p. 95.   [2] *Ibid.*, p. 96.
[3] *Ibid.*, p. 96.   [4] W. Brus, *Ekonomista*, 1958, no. 3, pp. 563 ff.
[5] When this book was in proof I read Murray Wolfson's *A Reappraisal of Marxian Economics* (New York-London, 1966). I have noted the point about the mis-translation of the oft-quoted operative passage in the standard English edition of the third volume of *Capital*. I have also noted with interest the submission that while it is true that in many passages Marx does speak of prices fluctuating around market values without realizing that the latter cannot be the mean value of market prices and at the same time have prices determined at the margin, yet 'in his careful writing' he gives up the idea that average price be equal to unit value and accepts that price (rather than value) is determined by production at the margin (p. 64). The argument is plausible and bears out the conceptual confusion; it may indicate a possible path of reconciliation of Marxian theory and 'marginalism'.
[6] J. M. Montias, *American Economic Review*, vol. xlix, December 1959, pp. 977 ff.

There again I would hesitate to predict whether the U.S.S.R. is really this time on the way to sounder costing and pricing. But a by-product of that assimilation is at least that the problem of price has been put in a way that would have seemed unthinkable only two years ago when the Great Debate on value and price faded out in an impasse.[1] The two books discussed have especially affected the tone of economic thought and set it at an important theoretical and doctrinal crossroad. Where will it go from here? This is the third point on which I plead inability to foresee.'

More than half a decade has passed and the answer to the questions posed becomes gradually discernible. Looking back from around the mid-1960s, it seems safe to say that obstacles to change in Soviet thought are being overcome at a faster pace and with greater ease than expected by most students, including this writer: an explanation may lie, at least in part, in the stimulus of a changed economic environment and type of growth, to use Academician Novozhilov's terminology, the shift from 'extensive' to 'intensive' growth.[2] The present volume attempts primarily to indicate, even if only very tentatively, some aspects of what one can call by now—with good reason —the *new* Soviet economics.

[1] See A. Zauberman, 'The Soviet Debate on the Law of Value and Price Formation', in G. Grossman, *Value and Plan*, Berkeley, 1960.

[2] V. V. Novozhilov, 'Razvitye sistemy upravlenya sotsyalisticheskim khoziaystvom', in *Ekonomika i Matematicheskiye Metody*, no. 5, 1965, p, 645.

Part I: Fundamental Framework

1 Rethinking the Marxist Model[1]

EXACTLY one hundred years ago a model of economic growth was born that was to make a unique career—well beyond the realm of economic theory. In a letter written to Engels in 1863 Marx set out the substance of his schema of 'expanded reproduction' which was to be embodied later in the second volume of *Capital*. 'Do look up carefully [he said there] the enclosed *Tableau Economique* which I am substituting for Quesnay's, and let me know of any doubts it may arouse in you. It combines a complete process of reproduction.'[2] Such was the claim made for the construct by its author. The letter itself pointed to an implied critique of the Smith-Ricardian tradition in the treatment of profit. But in contrast with the great issue that exercised the minds and emotions of contemporaries, the model would seem to have been originally conceived as a refutation of the dismal Malthusian law of a linear growth of resources in a world with population growing exponentially. The specific context lost its relevance and instead the model's significance for society's class organisation came into focus. It is not surprising that it was a theoretician-revolutionary that devoted his efforts to lending it greater rigour. When the model was thirty years old, Lenin elaborated his own variant in a paper 'On the so called Market Question'[3] (the immediate impulse was given by the polemic with the *narodniki* as to whether capitalism—the 'market'—could develop in Russia and reach full maturity). In the pre-Keynesian world Marx's model provided the unique theoretical frame for Soviet growth-oriented policy. It is now fascinating to watch how, against a changing economic and intellectual landscape, Soviet-Marxist planning theory is today probing into the formal construction and the area of its validity. These remarks, will deal only with such re-thinking in so far as guidance is sought for growth strategy.

[1] This is a revised part of an article which appeared, in French, under the title 'Le Centenaire du Modèle Marxiste de la Reproduction: Le Réexamen Sovietique de ses Aspects Strategiques' in the *Bulletin* of the Centre d' Etude des Pays de l'Est, Université Libre de Bruxelles, 1963. I am grateful to Professor Waelbroeck for his interest and advice. Responsibility for any defects is entirely mine.

[2] Letter of 6 July 1863; see *Karl Marx–Friedrich Engels Ausgewaehlte Briefe*, Moscow-Leningrad, 1934, p. 127.

[3] First published in 1937 in *Bolshevik*, no. 21; English translation available in vol. i of *Collected Works*, Moscow, 1960, pp. 79 ff.

Some of the technical flaws of the original Marxian scheme have been noted in Soviet literature in recent times by several students. To mention one important methodological point, the telescoping of 'expanding reproduction' into a single 'cycle' obscures in the dynamic process what is inherently essential to it—the time horizon. (This has been a cause of a good deal of confusion in Soviet-Marxist writing, as has been pointed out by Vaag in the debate of the 1950s on the theory of value and price.[1]) A more substantial weakness is the absence in the construct of what in Marx's own conception is the motive force of the system. The path of expansion is uniquely determined by the legacy from the past and the rate of capital formation. Between them, history plus accumulation propel an exponential growth, in Marx's celebrated numerical example, at the pace of 9·53 per cent per annum. (Note the implication for the exorcised Malthusian nightmare.) Marx's equilibrium of 'expanded reproduction' rests on his 'Law of Value' which (through the condition of realisation) links up his two 'departments' —those of producer and of consumer goods—and secures an equalised pace of progress throughout the system for ever and ever.

So, in fact, seen against his own order of ideas, Marx's model of growth was 'Hamlet' without the Prince of Denmark: it was Lenin who built into it the impact of technical change as deduced from the argument in the first volume of *Capital*. Growing capital intensity of the production process is conceived in Marx as reflecting a labour-displacing trend in techniques, itself promoted by social-economic forces, the 'relations of production'. In this reasoning competition equalises throughout the system and, in a secular trend, lowers the rate of profit: the ratio of the m, the unpaid-for labour to total capital engaged, that is $m/(c+v)$. (In the denominator c stands for constant capital as defined by Marx. This is one of the cases where lack of time-dimension in the structure has caused some confusion. The c represents material inputs per time-period rather than stocks, including depreciation of fixed capital through wear and tear or obsolescence; i.e. the economy's capital divided by Marx's turn-over period. The v stands for variable capital, or wage bill tending towards the reproduction cost of the economy's labour force.) The rate of profit would be depen-

---

[1] The crucial importance of the hidden assumption in a Ricardian-type model that the period of production is uniform in all industries was pointed out by L. Pasinetti in his 'A Mathematical Formulation of the Ricardian System', *Review of Economic Studies*, February 1960, p. 92.

dent on the 'rate of exploitation' of labour, a certain constant m/v; it would be pushed down by the tendency to raise the volume of capital per worker. In a circular causation, competition makes the capitalist resort to more and more efficient techniques which entails what Marx defined in the first volume of *Capital* as the rising 'organic composition of capital', that is, the rising ratio of constant to variable capital: the c/v, in other words—a rise in the value of plant and materials employed relative to wages. In still other words—capital intensity is an increasing function of investment, and innovation has a labour-saving bias. True, higher organic composition lowers the rate of profit but, by providing the scope for larger scale of production, helps to increase total return on capital—hence the incentive for the capitalist.[1]

Having (*a*) brought into Marx's scheme the law of rising 'organic composition of capital'—of the rising supply to the system of capital goods and materials as against wage goods—and (*b*) having broken down his producer goods department into two subsectors, Lenin mapped out the movement of the system in these terms:

. . . growth in the production of means of production as means of production is the most rapid; then comes the production of means of production of means of consumption; and the slowest is the rate of growth in the production of means of consumption.[2]

This indeed he took as a self-evident consequence—in his own words as a 'mere paraphrase' of the law according to which constant capital tends to grow faster than variable capital.[3] Although in Marx-Lenin the character of advance in technique is connected with the mode of operation of capitalism, it has been axiomatically held by Soviet

---

[1] I shall not presume to examine within these remarks the consistency or otherwise of the system, nor shall I refer to the voluminous literature of the subject.

May I simply draw attention to P. Sweezy's valid point that the assumption of constancy of the 'rate of exploitation' is in conflict with that of rising productivity and Marx's tenet that higher productivity is accompanied by growing exploitation (*Theory of Capitalist Development*, New York, 1942). The logic of the argument has been questioned also by Joan Robinson in *An Essay in Marxian Economics*, London, 1957. Both show that once the assumption of a constant rate of exploitation is rejected the tenet of continuously declining rate of profit becomes indefensible.

There is an admirable discussion of the system set against other growth models in a recent work by Irma Adelman, *Theories of Economic Growth and Development*, Stanford U.P., 1962, ch. 5.

[2] *Lenin, Collected Works*, Moscow, 1960, vol. i, p. 87.

[3] *Ibid.*

economic theory to be universal, independent of socio-economic 'relations of production'. In this way from the 'law' based on the Marxist-Leninist view of the nature of technological progress, Soviet planning theory rationalised its postulate of preferential development of the producer goods sector, a posulate empirically evolved and, under some assumptions defensible as a strategy rule for a given economic environment. As a matter of expedience Soviet planning doctrine has reformulated the rule to call for faster growth in heavy—the 'A'—industries embracing energy, minerals, metals, chemical and building materials, metal-working and construction (the two classifications are in fact not fully identical: for instance many durable consumer goods though produced in the 'A' group belong to the second 'department'; some Soviet economists, notably Notkin, have suggested separating in the Marxist-Leninist model a third 'department', of armaments, in consideration of their specific effect of the growth process).

Now, to re-state in terms of the planner's elbow-room the dynamics of the Leninist variant, it is steered by two, or rather two sectoral pairs of parameters. In addition to those of 'organic composition' he can manœuvre with the sectoral rates of accumulation, the rates that is of 'surplus product' channelled into capital formation (the rate of surplus product is the original rate of 'exploitation' of labour; its emotive connotation was reversed in Soviet economic writing by Stalin[1] who defined it as reflecting—for socialism—the division of net product between 'oneself and the society'). This is in fact the direction of a recent noteworthy investigation pursued by two Soviet econometricians, Plyukhin and Nazarova,[2] to which we intend now to invite the reader's attention.

In the first phase of their argument Plyukhin and Nazarova investigate the growth of the two departments, 1 and 2, taking some parameters as constants. These are, for the i-th sector, the three coefficients: (1) ratio of surplus product to variable capital in the i-th sector $Q_i = M_i/V_i$ (fixed *a priori*); (2) incremental ratio of fixed capital to surplus-product, $R_i = M_{ci}/M_i$ (determined by the planner); (3) incremental ratio of fixed to variable capital, $P_{mi} = M_{ci}/M_{vi}$ (this too is fixed by the planner). It will be noted that $P_i = C_i/V_i$, the ratio of fixed

---

[1] In his *Economic Problems of Socialism*, published in 1953.

[2] B. I. Plyukhin, P. N. Nazarova, 'Upravlayemaya tsepnaya reaktsya rasshirennogo proizvodstva v odnosektornoy i dvusektornoy modelyakh', in *Primenenye matematiki v ekonomicheskikh issledovanyakh*, V. S. Nemchinov, ed., vol. ii, pp. 342 ff.

to variable capital—'the organic composition of capital'—is an endogenous variable.

Now, Plyukhin and Nazarova assume that the 'law of value' has been suspended, meaning broadly that a sector can obtain products from another without equivalent counter-supply. In that case the growth rate of variable capital, $S_{vi} = R_i Q_i / P_{mi} T$, could differ as between the 'departments' (T denotes the production cycle equal throughout the system). These ratios—which are constant because so are all the four elements—are termed *sectoral accelerators*.

It is then shown that if P_{i0} = value of R_i at the time interval $t = 0$, at each time-point $P_i = P_{mi} - (P_{mi} - P_{i0}) e^{-S_{vi}t}$, and hence P_i tends towards P_{mi}. It follows that the growth rate of fixed capital $S_{ci} = R_i Q_i / P_i T$ tends towards $R_i Q_i / P_{mi} T = S_{vi}$.[1] Finally, it is easy to show that the growth rate of production S_i tends itself towards the value of the sectoral accelerator.

At the second stage of the argument, the model is transformed so as to allow for the law of 'proportionate development'. Very vague or tautological in the doctrine, it is formulated here in a significant way: Plyukhin and Nazarova adopt Nemchinov's interpretation which is that in a closed system output of the two departments is partly a function of availabilities of producer and consumer goods produced during the preceding cycle.

Hence they define the system's 'proportionality coefficients' as partial derivatives of the two departments' outputs with respect to inputs of fixed and variable capital $\epsilon_{ik} = X_i(t) / d_{ik} X_k(t - T)$ where X_i is output of the i-th department, d_{ik} is the fraction of output of department k supplied to the i-th department in the following period.

The fundamental equations of the new system appear thus as

$$X_1(t) = a_1(t) + \epsilon_{11} d_{11} X_1(t - T) + \epsilon_{12} d_{12} X_2(t - T)$$

$$X_2(t) = a_2(t) + \epsilon_{21} d_{21} X_1(t - T) + \epsilon_{22} d_{22} X_2(t - T)$$

This sytem of difference equations is first approximated by one of

---

[1] By definition incremental organic composition

$$P_{mi} = \frac{dc_i}{dv_i} > P_i$$

At any given moment the composition of existing capital can be expressed in relation to what it was at some zero moment as

$$P_i = e^{-\int_0^t S_{vi} \, dt} \left(P_{i0} + \int_0^t S_{vi} P_{mi} \, e^{+\int_0^t S_{vi} \, dt} \, dt \right)$$

linear differential equations whose solution defines the two departments' output as a sum of exponentials

$$X_1 = X_{10} + c_{11}/\lambda_1(e^{\lambda_1 t} - 1) + c_{12}/\lambda_2(e^{\lambda_2 t} - 1)$$
$$X_2 = X_{20} + c_{21}/\lambda_1(e^{\lambda_1 t} - 1) + c_{22}/\lambda_2(e^{\lambda_2 t} - 1)$$

Eventually for such an approximation, on the Lyapunov-Poincaré
theorem, the $S_{xi} \to \max(\lambda_1, \lambda_2) = \lambda_1$: relative sectoral growth rates
tend towards both convergence and stability. Relative inter-sectoral
acceleration fades out from the system.

It is arguable that the findings of the second stage of the argument
may seem to be empirically verified. The Soviet Union's industrial
growth has been characterised for years by a remarkable steadiness
and at the same time has displayed a detectable inclination towards
narrowing the gulf between tempi of the two grand sectors.[1] Indeed,
this characteristic stands out in the official projection reaching out to
the threshold of fully-fledged communism.

The reader should not be left with the impression that the Plyuhin-
Nazarova handling of the Marxist-Leninist schemas of expanded
reproduction has come to the Soviet-Marxist economics as a *deus ex
machina*. The 1920s saw attempts at their formal reinterpretation by
Starovskiy and others;[2] but the suspicion of heterodoxy that heavily
weighed upon such treatment halted it for two decades. Attempts
were renewed when the opprobrium on mathematical methods and
techniques was gradually lifted (from about the latter years of the
fifties onwards), and a 'planometric' school emerged in Soviet
economics.[3]

By the way of digression, one may note that in Poland, Minc[4] and
Kalecki argued that progress in techniques was accompanied by secular trends of rising capital-intensity and of productivity of labour. It

---

[1] Keeping to the Soviet dichotomy of industry Academician Strumilin noted that
between 1928 and 1958 the share of the B group in total Soviet industrial output dropped
from 72 to 40 per cent; and that were this tendency to continue indefinitely with the
same vigour this share would be negative by the beginning of the twenty-first century. (In
actual fact the percentage decline noted for the 30 post-1928 years amounted to 19 per
cent, 10 per cent and 4 per cent for each of the three successive decades respectively.)

[2] V. Starovskiy, *Sotsyalisticheskoye Khoziaystvo*, 1928, no. 5–6; see also V. Pogonkin,
Problemy Ekonomiki, 1929, no. 10–11.

[3] See below, pp. 154 ff.

[4] See B. Minc, *Ekonomista*, 1956, no. 5, especially pp. 54 ff. and his *Zagadnienia
ekonomii politycznej socializmu*, Warsaw, 1957, especially chapter v; M. Kalecki, *Ekonomista*, 1956, no. 5; see also *Note* to this chapter, p. 25.

could be capital-saving or capital-absorptive or, from this angle, neutral: clearly it is the latter property of technological advance that was decisive for relative growth rates of the production sphere and consumption sphere of the economy. Minc in particular insisted that faster rate in the output of producer goods depended on a multitude of factors as often as not working in conflicting directions: that historically it was observable during periods when man was being displaced by machines but not when superior machines were substituted for inferior ones, as was the case in the era of automation. He argued further that in a *closed economy* (one should, we suggest, place the emphasis here) with a constant ratio, or still more with a falling ratio of net to global product, in physical terms[1] (in Marx notation $(v+m):(c+v+m)$), faster growth of the first 'department' would require a continually accelerated rate of investment in the shape of producer-goods; since in no society could this go on for ever and ever the hypothesis was reduced to absurdity. (The young Lenin, Minc suggests, was impressed by and had illegitimately generalised the changes in technology typical of an early phase of industrial development such as witnessed by him in the late nineteenth and early twentieth centuries in Russia, and before him by Marx and Engels in England). The immediate reaction in Soviet literature to these views was highly critical; but the critique confined itself largely to invoking *verba magistri*. An oft-referred to paper by Pashkov pointed to Lenin's emphatic statement that the theorem of faster growth of the first department follows automatically from Marx's teaching on the organic structure of capital and on its continuous rise resulting from technical advance.[2]

One may note that the Kalecki-Minc stand found support in the formalised argument by Oskar Lange.[3] In his theory of reproduction and accumulation Lange shows that the condition for the growth equilibrium of a system is:

$$P_1/P_2 = (a_{2c} - \alpha_{2c}):(1 - a_{1c} - \alpha_{1c})$$

In Lange's notation this means that the equilibrium output-ratio of the two Marxian 'departments', the P's, depends on both the sectoral

---

[1] *Ekonomista*, 1956, no. 5, *loc. cit.*

[2] A. Pashkov, *Voprosy Ekonomiki*, 1959, no. 6. For a recent critique of the Minc and Lange stand see however M. R. Eidelman, *Mezhotraslevoy Balans Obshchestvennogo Produkta*, Moscow, 1966, especially pp. 61 ff.

[3] O. Lange, *Teoria Reprodukcji i Akumlacji*, Warsaw, 1961, esp. pp. 44 ff.; also formalization of dynamic equilibrium in his *Ekonomia Polityczna*, vol. ii, Warsaw, 1966, pp. 236 ff.

parameters of capital formation, the α's, and the sectoral parameters of efficiency of capital, the a's.

By now ideas akin to those of Minc and Kalecki have penetrated into Soviet economics, though they have been expressed there with less emphatic articulation. Notkin in particular,[1] points to the structure of the capital/labour ratio: output/labour = capital/output. He at least hints at the strategic role of the latter for the growth process; and by the same hint calls in question Marx's implied tenet of a continuous growth in the organic composition of capital. There is now a discernible tendency in Soviet economics to approach the issues involved in a more empiricist spirit.

To return for a while to the Plyukhin-Nazarova, in some respects they do not go as far as Minc and Kalecki in refuting the Marxist-Leninist conception of technological advance. On the other hand, in their ultimate inferences they show—as we have seen—that even when this vision of progress is accepted the Marxist-Leninist 'law' of the sectoral pace of growth wanes from the model.

Still more noteworthy is perhaps their accent, without precedent in Soviet literature, on the technical rudimentarity, on the very high degree of abstraction from reality and the specificity of assumptions which rob the Leninist variant—to say nothing of Marx's original model—of reliability in guiding a strategy-shaping planner. They are worth quoting on this point: 'although Lenin's variant of the expanded-reproduction schema is substantially nearer to real conditions than the Marxist, yet even that variant is highly simplified and fails to take account of a variety of factors: moreover, it has been severely restricted (by its assumptions). Hence conclusions derived from it cannot be mechanically applied to real reproduction. Its regularities can be taken as a tendency rather than literally, *a tendency overlaid by the counter-action of many non-allowed for and yet essential factors*. (Our italics.) Consequently all one can expect is only a qualitative or semi-quantitative statistical validation of inferences—as is in fact observed in reality.'

So, rather unexpectedly for students of Soviet economic thought, as Marx's model celebrates its centenary, its rank in Soviet economics tends to change from that of a definitive formulation of immutable laws to the status of a, doubtless important, help to insight into the nature of economic growth.

[1] A. Notkin, *Voprosy Ekonomiki*, 1961, no. 11, especially pp. 23 ff.

NOTE TO CHAPTER 1

KALECKI has revisited more recently the problem of sectoral patterning of investment for growth in his theory of growth for a socialist system (*Zarys teorii wzrostu wzrostu gospodarki socialistycznej*, Warsaw, 1963), perhaps so far the most important contribution to the literature of the subject. The Kalecki two-product growth model differs from that of Marx in many respects: (1) Marx's division into two 'departments' is replaced by a dichotomy of an investment (capital-goods) and a non-investment sector, each assumed to be vertically integrated, embracing that is production of materials to feed it; (2) the principal variables in the focus are the r, the rate of growth of what we can define as real gross domestic material product ('gross national income' in constant prices), D and the analogous rate r_i for the investment sector, I, identified with the output of fixed-investment goods (gestating investment is included in consumption; net changes in inventories are assumed to be proportionate to I); (3) a set of parameters is brought into the picture: a and u, reflecting the impact on national income of depreciation and of 'independent' improvement in techniques, respectively, and m—incremental capital-output ratio; of these the latter is assumed to be constant over time and sectorally differentiated and the two others—to be constant as well as uniform; further—at some stage when the assumption of a closed system is relaxed an additional parameter d is brought in to denote the impact of structural shifts in external trade entailed in raising the investment ratio; moreover this portmanteau parameter is made to denote any further adjustments of the system. It is within this scaffolding that Kalecki observes an acceleration manœuvre in which the two strategic ratios, the capital-formation ratio (I/D) and the share of the investment sector in the national investment total (I_i/I) becomes variable; where, we think, he is unconvincing is his contention that values for both must go up: this is not necessarily so since in his parametric framework that would depend on how the national over-all output/capital ratio (the reciprocal of m and the analogous ratio for the investment sector ($1/m_i$) are related to each other[1]. When at the final stage of the argument foreign trade is taken into account by Kalecki (with an assumed export-import balance) the share of the incremental investment required in the speed-up phase appears as

$$\Delta I = 1/m_i \cdot I_i - (a-u) - d \cdot (r_i - r) \cdot I$$

[1] The acceleration process of a socialist economy has been analysed, with conclusions broadly analogous to those of Kalecki, by W. Sadowski, 'Acceleration of Long-Run Growth in the Socialist Economy', in A. Nove and A. Zauberman, eds., *Studies on the Theory of Reproduction and Prices*, Warsaw, 1964.

and the share of the investment sector in the investment total as

$$I_i/I = m_i/m \cdot I/D - m_i \cdot (1-d) \cdot (r_i - r)$$

The adjustments adumbrated by Kalecki's d may involve variations in input-output coefficients and parameters of production functions with possible changes in the product-mix.

A tentative analysis of the Kalecki model has been offered by me elsewhere[1]. In the present context I would only note the indication of the inconclusiveness of a general precept for acceleration strategy derived within the Marxian framework.

[1] A. Zauberman, 'A Few Remarks on Kalecki's Theory on Economic Growth under Socialism', *Kyklos*, July 1966.

2 Assimilating von Neumann

Professor Champernowne[1] concluded his companion-notes to the English version of von Neumann's paper on the general-equilibrium model[2] by pointing to its significance for a planner seeking to make the best use of resources. The passage of a quarter of a century and a profound change of mood were needed remarkably to vindicate this suggestion in Soviet economics. J. von Neumann's growing impact on Soviet thought currents is strikingly reflected in a model recently produced by the protagonist of the mathematical-economic school, Academician V. S. Nemchinov.[3]

The Nemchinov two-sector flow model is a construction of austere design. It has a column-vector X denoting total (global) production and an X_{ij} technological matrix $(i, j = 1, 2)$ of conventional type describing inputs of the product of one of the sectors per output unit of the other; the coefficients are implied to be constant. Matrices $M = M'$ indicate respectively material cost including depreciation of capital stock, and intermediate production, including physical replacement of its use-up. The model is completed by a column-vector of national product or income, Y showing 'physical expansion of the production sphere', and a row-vector, D, denoting net output—the 'productive effectiveness' ('*rezultativnost*')—of a given economic system: for the system as a whole, by definition $Y = D$. Linearity is assumed: scales of production are not considered. Hence a pair of rates-(sectoral) coefficients-describing the mutual impact of main variables: one, $X_j/M_j = \alpha_j$, of '*effectiveness*', and the other, $X_i/M'_i = \beta_i$, of '*expansion*'.

Since Nemchinov argues, for the economy as a whole $M_1 + M_2 = M'_1 + M'_2$ there must be $\alpha_0 = \beta_0$. At a further step he easily proves that they are tied through sectoral structures of material inputs, with corresponding sectoral pairs that is α_i and β_i; and that the latter in turn are completely determined by sectoral material—'intensities', ξ and ξ', the value-term one row-wise, and the physical-term one

---

[1] D. G. Champernowne, 'A Note on J. von Neumann's Article', *Review of Economic Studies*, vol. xiii, 1945–46, no. 1, p. 18.

[2] John von Neumann, 'A Model of General Economic Equilibrium', *Review of Economic Studies*, vol. xiii, 1945–46, no. 1.

[3] V. S. Nemchinov, *Ekonomiko-matematicheskiye metody i modeli*, Moscow, 1962, p. 300.

column-wise ($1 + \alpha_i = 1/\xi_i$ and $1 + \beta_i = 1/\xi_i'$). The basic proportions of the main model components, which determine the physical and value-term sectoral structures of national income and the sectoral composition of net output are thus fully determined by sectoral material—'intensity' ξ_j and weight of intermediate product ξ_i' on the one hand, and by the share of material inputs in total production (ξ_0) on the other.

Nemchinov's emphasis is on differences between his own and the von Neumann models.[1] Certainly there are some, as will appear in the course of our discussion. To begin with, it will be remembered, in von Neumann's circular system, households are an 'industry' absorbing inputs of necessities of life and producing the commodity-labour: labour in this closed circuit appears as output of an 'activity' rather than a primary factor; wages as factor remuneration have no place in it. By contrast, in Nemchinov's model, workers' consumption is not an inter-sectoral flow: it is a part of the final bill Υ, and wages form a component of income D. This changes the values of the denominators of the alphas and betas, which to this extent differ in Nemchinov and von Neumann. Nemchinov's construction is somewhat closer to the Kemeny-Morgenstern-Thompson[2] and the Morishima[3] variants in so far as they bring into von Neumann's model extraneous final consumption. This, however, leaves the fundamental kinship with the latter unaffected (Nemchinov relies on von Neumann's well-known proof of the existence of an equilibrium solution for his system)[4]. It is the affinity rather than the differences that merit recognition.

---

[1] Nemchinov, *op. cit.*, p. 302.

[2] John G. Kemeny, Oksar Morgenstern, Gerald L. Thompson, 'A Generalisation of the von Neumann Model of an Expanding Economy', *Econometrica*, vol. xxiv, April 1956, no. 2.

[3] Michio Morishima, 'Economic Expansion and Interest Rate in Generalised von Neumann Models', *Econometrica*, vol. xxviii, April 1960.

[4] von Neumann provided a proof that for a system with a technological horizon of processes in which competition brings about their selection and shapes prices and profits, there is at least one price constellation Υ^0 and at least one process P^0 which meets the conditions.

$$(P^0, \Upsilon^0) \geqslant (P, \Upsilon^0); \qquad (P^0, \Upsilon^0) \leqslant (P^0, \Upsilon)$$

for any $P \in H$ and for any Υ (H denotes technological horizon). N. Georgescu-Roegen provided an alternative simplified proof in a generalised form—without a postulate of a finite number of processes. See his 'The Aggregate Linear Production Function and its Applications to von Neumann's Economic Model', in *Activity Analysis of Production and Allocation*, New York—London, 1951, pp. 109 ff.

Indeed the mechanisms of the two systems are the same in substance. With a reservation to which we shall return, in both von Neumann and Nemchinov the beta is the maximum 'purely technically possible' rate of expansion of the system, and the alpha its corollary, the minimum still compatible productivity.

In both, in equilibrium—the state of 'balance' in Nemchinov's terminology—the rate of growth is, at its maximum, the fastest that is technologically feasible (elsewhere Nemchinov elaborates his related concept of a structural 'potential of expanded reproduction').[1] This rate can secure in the Nemchinov system, as it does in that of von Neumann, steady as well as smooth and optimal expansion.

A few words about the alpha-beta equality (for the system as a whole) which is the common, signal feature of both the von Neumann and the Nemchinov models. It rests in both on essentially the same reasoning. In the state of equilibrium the value-term margin of output over input must tend to equality throughout the system in all processes adopted—the *modus operandi* familiar to a Marxist from the 'law' of equalisation of the rate of profit (surplus product) which, in Marx's analysis, shapes the *Produktionspreis* of the capitalist mechanism of reproduction. In this context one has to spell out an assumption made in both models, but not explicit in that of Nemchinov. The equilibrium is an ideally competitive one: in von Neumann it is secured by an assumed market free-enterprise, institutional framework; for Nemchinov it can be conceived as simulated in the planner's office. It is the competitive mechanism which acts as the profit leveller. At the same time it is the levelled-out margin of value-term output over inputs that measures the pace—von Neumann's 'velocity'—of expansion: hence in both models the $\alpha_0 = \beta_0$ is the common factor 'multiplying' all adopted processes. It sets the organic rhythm of growth, one by which, to use Champernowne's expressive simile, 'the economic system expands like a crystal suspended in a solution of its own salt'.[2]

In both models the pace-setter is the commodity with the slowest tempo. The one whose output grows faster, becomes in the specific sense a free-zero price-good, with an idle surplus in the system.

Something more about the profit element. Once again one must be

---

[1] V. S. Nemchinov, 'Statistical and Mathematical Methods in Soviet Planning', in *Structural Interdependence and Economic Development*, T. Barna, ed., London, 1963.

[2] *Op. cit.*, p. 16.

reminded of the prevailing state of competitive equilibrium. It is characterised by zero profits, in a conventional sense, that is after primary factors have been compensated. The handling of capital goods is somewhat different in the two models. Depreciation of worn-out equipment is treated similarly as a separate commodity at each stage. Each of the adopted processes is in this sense of a unit-time duration although this is not assumed in Nemchinov as explicitly as it is in von Neumann: the problem of gestation of investment is by-passed as well as that of its life-span. In the latter's model, output of the period (t) absorbs completely that of the $(t-1)$: thus input-cost of production is 'capital' as in Marx's reproduction scheme (and input/output-ratio is the capital coefficient of the system). In both models the excess value of output over 'capital' appears then as the supply-price of waiting over the production cycle, as 'remuneration' of a factor related to the time-unit. It thus becomes in von Neumann, as noted by Georgescu-Roegen, the only social cost, the interest factor. Time-discounted revenue from processes operated is the ceiling above which the unit cost cannot rise: under the assumed perfect competition profitable processes would be enlarged over the time-unit and consequently relative prices of input and outputs would shift so as to eliminate profit; processes operated can thus afford to 'pay off' only interest, which competition depresses to its minimum (activities with negative profit remain unused). The logic of this argument is not changed if the restrictive assumption of one time-unit is discarded; nor is it affected by bringing into the system labour as the second factor, as is the case in the Nemchinov construction. (One can understand Nemchinov's hesitation in following this logic, and preferring the less committing concept of his *rezultativnost'* to that of interest on capital.)

In shifting the wage-goods component from the intermediate input flow to net output and making wages an explicit element of the income vector, Nemchinov has lent greater generality to his model than von Neumann. He has made it also closer to Soviet reality, for which the assumption of living standards at the bare subsistence level (shared by Marx's and von Neumann's models) is, of course, not warranted.

Dropping this assumption adds to the model's relevance for the theory of planning. The uniqueness of the von Neumann's equilibrium solution vanishes and the planner gains control over a strategic variable. In von Neumann's model expansion proceeds at a constant rate with the structure of the economy unchanged for ever: in Nemchinov's it will be shaped, within limits, by planning authorities who prescribe the ratios of consumption and capital formation, so as to secure the desired rate of growth of the system. In the last instance then what is gained by the planner is one degree of freedom—by setting real wages.

Abandoning the assumption of subsistence wages is yet another feature which brings the Nemchinov system closer to the Kemeny-Morgenstern-Thompson and Morishima framework. Had Nemchinov followed their line of exploration he would have found—with Kemeny-Morgenstern-Thompson—the range of the 'allowable' alphas from which the planner would choose the greatest technically possible. And he could have arrived with Morishima at the tenet that so long as it is positive, the rate of expansion is a product of two rates, those of profit and of capital accumulation, another formulation familiar from Marxian analysis.

The treatment of this point in Nemchinov has insufficient rigour. There are only broad suggestions to the effect that, from the macro-economic point of view, a rate of profit could be considered 'normal' if the sum total of profit 'secured a volume of investment necessary to expand the whole sphere of material production at postulated pace'. Nor does Nemchinov tackle the subject of factor substitution although in Nemchinov—unlike von Neumann—labour becomes a factor of production. The matter is not pursued although it is of obvious relevance for the Soviet quest of the criterion of inter-temporal efficiency in capital formation.[1] It is also relevant for the Soviet quest of principles of rational pricing. The precept in Nemchinov is that the price system must be 'profitable', meaning that the row-vector D, in addition to the reward to labour, must include 'sufficient' profit, sufficient that is to safeguard 'the necessary profitability to a normally working enterprise and to cover, for a branch as a whole, the losses in the poorly working ones'.[2] Nemchinov's main focus in analysing the efficient price constellation is on relating prices of final and intermediate products in a state of equilibrium, and the important general moral offered by him to the Soviet planner is that price structure should be built on price ratios of the final bill-of-goods derived from cumulative input coefficients.

The rather unsatisfactory aspect of his price equations is the inexplicitness of the rate of interest. Nor is this rate related to the vector

---

[1] See below, pp. 139 ff.   [2] See below, pp. 59 ff.

of over-all weighted price of the j-th product, intermediate, final and total, $p_j = p_1, p_2, \ldots, p_n$ with which the Nemchinov works. The von Neumann price rule, with the interest factor barring profits, could be restated for Nemchinov (intensities ignored) as

$$\sum_{j=1}^{n} b_{ij} p_j = \beta \sum_{j=1}^{n} a_{ij} p_j - d_j p_j$$

where the a_{ij}'s denote, as before, the input coefficients of the i-th commodity and b_{ij}'s, the output 'quotas'.[1] This agrees with the formulation by Morishima (who refines it by bringing in time-lags between input and output, and works with remuneration to labour rather than the whole of the final product as does Nemchinov).

The fundamental common characteristic of the two models can now be summarised to mean that for both the von Neumann's equation $\alpha = \beta = \phi(X, Y)$ holds good (the X and Y are process intensities and prices). In von Neumann these are the four unknowns of the system with the values of a_{ij} and b_{ij} taken as given. In Nemchinov they are key parameters for decision-making. He hints at the duality of the nexus between the monetary and the technical variables in optimisation, and at the intimate link of his model with a linear-programming set-up. Indeed, his coefficients of *rezultativnost'* and expansion correspond to the same theoretical saddle-point of the output-to-input value ratio, as do the von Neumann analogous factors: at this (maximin-minimax) point optimal strategies of players of a matrix game maximise the ratio, along the columns, with regard to processes, and minimise it, along the rows, with regard to prices. These are, in von Neumann, the 'normal' prices which bring about the technically most efficient intensities in production.

It may be noteworthy that von Neumann's handling of price has, at least as a first theoretical introduction, special attraction for the traditional Soviet-Marxian mode of thinking. True, in so far as his price is derived from the calculus of variations it is 'marginalist'. However, the implied assumption of constant returns to scale brings into the model a constancy of marginal cost: its equality that is with average cost. Further, due to certain simplifications in the assumptions of the von Neumann model, attention is concentrated on supply rather than demand.[2] There is in it no problem of consumer's prefer-

[1] The Kemeny-Morgenstern-Thompson proof (that prices, and production, can be adjusted to any of the 'allowable' rates of expansion) will then hold for the system.
[2] Cf. Champernowne, *op. cit.*, p. 12.

ences: consumer demand is unresponsive to either price or income; the question of the shape of utility functions does not arise; welfare economics, to which Soviet doctrine was traditionally allergic, is by-passed. Since it is the elasticity of supply rather than demand that is thus observed, values placed on commodities appear as cost prices. Price is seen as the average sum total of values of goods absorbed in production plus interest; and the average-cost-plus approach of this kind to pricing is precisely the one congenial to the Soviet economist.

This and a few more elements—some of which we noted in passing —make von Neumann's model relatively assimilable to the intellectual framework of Soviet economics.[1,2]

[1] Professor Morishima has published an illuminating restatement of the von Neumann model in a Marxian framework. Of the basic assumptions of the model three are relaxed so that (1) the working population is taken to grow at a finite rate, (2) capitalists consume a constant proportion of their income, (3) workers' demand for consumption goods depends on prices as well as wages; thus consumers' choice is being explicitly introduced subject to an assumption of income elasticity. Cf. M. Morishima, *Equilibrium, Stability and Growth*, Oxford, 1964, pp. 136 ff.

[2] Since this essay was written, interest in the von Neumann model has grown in Soviet economics. Kantorovich and Makarov have turned to it in their fundamental study of dynamic-planning models ('Optimalnye Modeli Perspektivnogo Planirovanya', in V. Nemchinov, ed., *Primenenye Matematiki v Ekonomicheskikh Issledovanyakh*, vol. 3, Moscow, 1965). They, too, see the limitations of the von Neumann construct for practical 'modelling' of plans: creating labour and some other resources by means of linear technologies and absence of technologically non-reproducible factors are patently unrealistic assumptions; a real-life economy hardly lends itself to description as a mathematically closed system; nor is it realistic to postulate optimality of the economy's initial state rather than, for a general case, of its state 'inherited' from the past. They recognize, however, the importance of the von Neumann model for investigation of the asymptotic behaviour of dynamic processes and from this derive certain indications as to the build-up of an optimality criterion for a very-long-term-'perspective' plan. (We shall come back to it in appropriate contexts). The dynamic nature of the von Neumann model thus helps in finding an approach to one of the trickiest issues of formalised planning.

3 Reconciling Leontief with Marx

RECONCILIATION of Marx's schema of reproduction with Leontief-type input-output analysis is in its own right a legitimate point of theoretical interest. It has assumed special significance for Marxist economics ever since the practical potentialities of the Leontief methodology for Soviet-type planning gained wide recognition. First to address himself to harmonising the two models was Professor Oskar Lange in an important contribution originally published in *Sankhya*[1] some years ago and elaborated in his subsequent writings (the appearance of its Russian translation marked the birth of the Soviet 'planometric' school).[2] A critique by Academician Nemchinov has made it a subject of continuing controversy.[3]

Whether, as some Soviet students insist, Marx's schema did give some kind of general inspiration to Leontief, or did not, is clearly of little relevance for the issue. There are however some fundamental structural features in the two systems which at some high level of abstraction may make them reducible to each other. These are the foci in the balance of flows on inter-sectoral dependencies; and on gross outputs as formed in a process of absorption of material inputs in which values accrue and which feeds itself and yields some net outputs (final bill of goods). This being so it was only a matter of design of tables and matrices to arrive at a formal proof of certain underlying identities. Indeed, nothing could be simpler than to treat in such an exercise Marx's two 'departments' as two inter-dependent 'industries' and to arrange the Leontief-type tableau in such a way that outputs would appear as refunding cost and providing value added. (In pointing this out we do not intend to denigrate Professor Lange's merit: it

[1] *Sankhya* Calcutta, vol. xvii, February 1957; for the latest elaboration see O. Lange, *Teoria reprodukcji i akumlacji*, Warsaw, 1961, pp. 67 ff.

[2] *Balans zatrat i vypuska produktsii*, Moscow, 1958. I wrote at the time: 'The appearance in Moscow of Oskar Lange's study on the input-output method, under the auspices of the Academy of Sciences and with a preface by Academician Nemchinov, is a major event in Soviet economics. Indeed, it looks like the first open breach in the wall by which Soviet economics has isolated itself over the decades from Western thought.' (*Soviet Studies*, April 1959.)

[3] V. S. Nemchinov, ed., *Primenenye matematiki v ekonomicheskikh issledovanyakh*, Moscow, 1959, editorial preface, and his 'Ispolzovanye matematicheskikh metodov vekonomicheskoy rabotye'*ibid.*, pp. 88 ff. For the latest elaboration see V. S. Nemchinov, *Ekonomiko-matematicheskiye metody i modeli*, Moscow, 1962, pp. 88 ff. and 212 ff.

is the simplest discoveries that are the most difficult to make.) By following this tempting line, Lange could translate the familiar elements of Leontief equations into Marx's concepts and notation so that x_{ij} is turned into c_i (the c's stand here for flow, not for stocks—a point which Lange makes usefully explicit to help his operation) and x_{0i} becomes v_i, the difference between total (gross) output and the two $(x_i - c_i - v_i)$ forming a certain m_i. To call this residuum surplus value (or surplus product) rather than profit is then a question of terminological convention dependent on social philosophy rather than a principle of economic calculation.

The inter-industry balance equation of values absorbed and distributed will appear in any case as $x_{01} + x_{11} + x_{21} + m_1 = x_{11} + x_{12} + x_1$.

Under conditions of a hypothetical stationary equilibrium—Marx's simple reproduction—with no capital formation and no final output in 'department' 1 and, of course, no flows from the consumer-goods industry to the producer-goods industry, that is with $x_{21} = 0$, $x_1 = 0$ (and after due reduction), the last equation will become $x_{01} + m_1 = c_2$ in a Leontief dress. In both guises this is indeed but a common sense proposition: where you have only two 'industries', one of which produces exclusively non-consumables, to keep the system in static balance the whole of the surplus of the one must be passed over, in the shape of equipment and materials, to the other in which consumer goods are being fabricated.

The business of reconciliation of the two schemas becomes trickier once the hyper-aggregation of the productive system into two 'industries' is abandoned. It is indeed Nemchinov's main charge against Lange's *tour de force* that in its course, for a multi-sectoral system, the basic dichotomy of the system into the two 'spheres' would get lost.

In what can be read as a rejoinder Lange shows convincingly that a balance condition for any specialised pair taken at random from among the Leontief-table industries holds for Marx's 'departments', and vice versa. The output ratio is $X_1 : X_2 = a_{12} : (1 - a_{11})$; the a's with subscripts are 'directional' coefficients of the use-up of total outputs. Once again then for a stationary system what is not re-used by industry number one within itself, that is $1 - a_{11}$, must be, for the sake of preservation of the balance, channelled into the other industry as a_{12}. Thus the still finer apparatus helps to establish no more than what we called the common-sense proposition.

In turn Nemchinov himself has tried his hand at the reconciliation of the two models by bringing in a concept of the growth ('expanded reproduction') potential. This denotes the excess of value-added in the first 'department' over its re-use in the second, some $M = v_1 + m_1 - c_2$. Another of his devices, a 'balance coefficient', correlates this 'potential' with the invested part of surplus product m, certain q and z, in the producer and consumer-goods production respectively. The case of $(q + z) \, m/M$ equalling a unit would be one of balance; otherwise the fraction would measure the degree disequilibrium. However, when testing numerically these tools on an actual input-output balance (i.e. on Barna's 1935 and 1950 tables for United Kingdom), Nemchinov contented himself with re-arranging quadrants of the Leontief standard table into two 'spheres'—those of producer and of consumer goods. Into the first he put the inter-industrial use-up and his $(q + z)m$, capital formation in fixed assets and inventories; into the second, private consumption (allowance made for exports); and he related each of these 'spheres' to material cost (allowance made for imports) and value-added. To succeed in his attempt Nemchinov would have to *start* from grouping industries into two separable areas of production of producer goods and of consumer goods, and then to show how the inter-change flows between result in the Marxian equilibrium. No less than Lange did he fail in grafting the Marxian dichotomy onto the Leontief system. The obstacle which has not and could not be overcome is not merely technical—one of difficulty in matrix design—but of substance: it is the nature of the Leontief inter-dependence of industries that precludes the disentangling of Marxian departments. Indeed it does so because industries of real life evade it. Today's Soviet mathematical-economic writing points to the 'balance' of national economy of forty years ago, constructed by the Soviet statistical administration, as the precursor of input-output analysis. It may be recalled that its text carried a statement of relevance for our point: 'Since the computation of the balance of national economy deals with the concrete Soviet economy, the schema of the balance will differ from that offered by Marx. . . . It is impossible to group production according to Marx's schema in its pure shape.'[1]

Let us recall that although he had not concerned himself with the Marxist model, Professor Leontief did handle, in an appendix to his

[1] Central Statistical Administration of the USSR, *Balans narodnogo khoziaystva SSSR* 1923/24', Collection of works, *Trudy*, vol. xxix, 1926, p. 27.

fundamental work,[1] a static two-sector model of consumer-goods and producer-goods industries plus households.

Of the sets of equations which he formulated there, the one of interest in our context, is the value-term one:

$$(1) \quad -X_1P_1 + x_{12}P_2 \qquad = 0;$$
$$(2) \quad x_{21}P_1 - X_2P_2 + X_{23}P_3 = 0;$$
$$(3) \quad x_{31}P_1 - X_3P_3 \qquad = 0$$

where the X's stand for the industries' physical-term outputs, the x's for inter-industry flows, the P's for prices and the subscript numbers 1, 2, 3, household, consumer-goods and producer-goods industries in this order. Consumer-goods industry absorbs part of labour services, being here the output of the household 'industry'; the rest of its services goes to the producer-goods industry in which they make the only intake. The third equation of the set would mean that the total output of the producer-goods industry is channelled into the consumer-goods industry; thus if we tried to translate Leontief's set into Marx's terms, X_3P_3, the whole output of the producer-goods sector, transferred for re-use as a means of production in the consumer-goods sector, would correspond to c_2. The $x_{31}P_1$ transfer to households from the producer-goods sector would correspond to the value of the input of (reward to) the only primary factor employed in that sector. Under the assumed ideal competitive equilibrium profit in Leontief's system equalling zero, this term $x_{31}P_1$ should be then re-interpreted as total value added in the production of producer goods, that is Marx's $v_1 + m_1$. Thus the last of the three Leontief equations, i.e. $x_{31}P_1 - X_3P_3 = 0$ will be re-written as $v_1 + m_1 - c_2 = 0$, which is again our old friend the balance condition (for the special case of simple reproduction). So, we suggest, Lange's point can be in fact deduced straight from Leontief's own analysis. Leontief makes this clear, however, that while it might facilitate acquaintance with certain formal features of the theoretical system, his set-up of the two aggregate industries has hardly any practical significance. This warning has been well borne out, we suggest, by the results of experiments in reconciliation of his system with Marx's model, which too can be useful as a drastically simplifying first-step heuristic device (the history of the tenet of preferential development of 'department 1' as a condition of growth derived from it is

[1] W. W. Leontief, *The Structure of American Economy*, 1919–1939, Appendix 1.

one of the lessons which point, though, to the care required in handling
it if pitfalls are to be avoided).[1]

[1] See above, ch. 1. It is fair to note that as early as the 1930s Leontief paid a hand-
some tribute to the Marxian scheme of the two-sector interrelationship as a fundamental
exercise though 'far from being the ultima ratio of this line of analysis', cf. 'The
Significance of Marxian Economics for Present-day Economic Theory', *American
Economic Review*, vol. xxviii, March 1938, Supplement.

4 Resurrection of the Concept of Consumers' Choice

E. J. Mishan and A. Zauberman

WITHIN the last two or three years a marked shift of emphasis has taken place in Soviet planning techniques from concern with gross transactions to concern with the final bill of goods, or net national product.[1] It was during this period, in which procedures of systematic optimisation were being assimilated, that Nemchinov proposed that planning models employ as the objective function a collective consumption function 'characterising the objective economic behaviour of the whole mass of consumers as a single statistical entity'.[2] About the same time Volkonskiy and Pugachev were developing a formal mathematical model[3] purporting to indicate the optimal growth path of the economy employing consumers' preferences with respect to goods and time.[4,5]

Empirical studies since the late fifties also began to move the consumers to the centre of the picture. Cross-section data were being analysed in order to determine quantitative relationships between consumption and price and income variation for a wide range of goods.

It was perhaps inevitable in the less inhibiting atmosphere of recent years, that the theoretical and empirical studies should culminate in a rediscovery of the theory of consumers' choice. The appearance of two papers, by L. M. Dudkin and I. V. Girsanov, in a Moscow University symposium on optimal planning is a noteworthy break-through.

---

[1] See p. 251.

[2] V. S. Nemchinov, *Ekonomiko-matematicheskiye metody i modeli*, Moscow, 1962, p. 390.

[3] A paper produced in the Laboratory of Mathematical-Economic Methods of the Academy of Sciences, referred to *ibid.*; see below, ch. 15.

[4] See A. G. Aganbegyan and V. D. Belkin, *Primenenye matematiki i elektronnoy tekhniki v planirovanyi*, Moscow, 1961, part III; also V. S. Nemchinov, 'The Use of Statistical and Mathematical Methods in Soviet Planning', in T. Barna, ed., *Structural Interdependence and Economic Development*, London, 1963, p. 174.

[5] Note a statement by the Director of the Gosplan Scientific Research Institute, A. Efimov: 'Considerable research work is in progress in the USSR to investigate the dependence of the structure of consumption on the level and structure of the population's incomes, on incomes and prices, on the total level of consumption and other factors influencing the structure of the consumption fund. . . . The solution of all these problems of the planning of consumption becomes one of the central tasks of Soviet economic science because *planning now enters the stage at which the economy's development will be increasingly determined by the volume and structure of consumers' demand and by the dynamics of social consumption.*' *Planovoye Khoziaistvo*, 1963, no. 5, p. 18 (our italics).

Dudkin,[1] elaborating an input-output model whose novel feature was the explicit introduction of a set of demand functions, formalises the consumers' behaviour by means of a demand function which he writes as[2]

$$q_{ij} = q_{ij}(w_j, p_1, \ldots, p_n)$$

when q_{ij} is the average quantity of the i-th good demanded by the j-th category of workers per man-hour; w_j designates the average wage of the j-th category of wage-earners and $p_1, \ldots, p_n$ are the prices of the n finished goods available in the economy. Though something of a novelty in Soviet literature, the Dudkin function is hardly new to Western economists, in particular if we bear in mind that wages and wage-type payments in the USSR are virtually the only source of remuneration, so that w_j may be properly regarded as the individual's income.

The function above is employed in solving the problem of allocative efficiency, being the maximand of Dudkin's optimised input-output system. Indeed, such a function, it is asserted, implements the 'basic economic law of socialism' in its traditional Soviet-Marxist formulation as the maximum satisfaction of the working people's needs.

While neither conceptually nor technically original,[3] Dudkin's procedure of optimisation—starting with an analysis of the surface of the production frontier, and imposing thereon a map of the community's orderings evolved from individual orderings—is unfamiliar to the new generation of Soviet students. For this reason he quotes Uzawa as proving that the existence of a preference function is implied by existence of an individual's demand set as a function of prices and incomes.[4] And he infers (apparently without discussing the problems of aggregation) that the community's preference map, or 'working people's function of consumer preferences', is the counterpart of these

---

[1] L. M. Dudkin, *Problemy optimalnogo planirovanya, proyektorovanya i upravlenya proizvodstvom*, Moscow, 1963.

Regrettably, no copy of this work was available in this country at the time of writing. We have relied on a summary by Professor Montyas and wish to acknowledge our great debt to him.

[2] We have made some changes in symbols to follow the more familiar convention.

[3] 'Of all the points of the feasible surface constrained by conditions . . . it is sufficient to consider only the points on the upper boundary. . . . If we choose any of these points as the most preferred . . . then we shall obtain a plan satisfying the basic economic law of socialism, Dudkin, *op. cit.* (Professor Montyas's translation), p. 43.

[4] The reference is to H. Uzawa's 'Preference and Rational Choice in the Theory of Consumption', in *Mathematical Methods in Social Sciences*, Stanford, 1959, pp. 129 ff.

demand functions. In this way he tries to vindicate the use of this concept of a community preference map, or ordering—hitherto unacceptable in Soviet economics—in determining an optimal position when the former is imposed on the locus of production possibilities. Calling for more research into consumption data he categorically affirms that no planning organ is able better to evaluate the consumer's requirements than the consumer himself.[1]

Dudkin's contribution is taken somewhat further by I. V. Girsanov who considers the 'reasonable' restrictions on the former's demand functions necessary to yield an economically meaningful solution. Some of the restrictions are conventional, adopted for the sake of mathematical convenience: the functions are taken to be determinate and continuously differentiable for all variations in positive prices and wages. A sensible economic solution requires further that quantities demanded are finite for zero prices. However, two very strong axioms are added: one of them postulates a negative relation between the quantity demanded of a good and its price, and the other that all goods be gross substitutes.[2] These restrictive axioms clearly ensure great simplification of the analysis, but they do so by circumventing familiar problems that arise in connection with income effect and complementary goods.

The Western student may be inclined to say that, indeed, too much is being assumed in this way in order to make aggregation easier. In particular the universality of a downwards sloping market demand curve is one of these desirable inferences that has as yet eluded all rigorous theorising. Nevertheless, for the planner in the Soviet environment the negative price-quantity relationship may be a permissible simplification. The assumption that all goods are gross substitutes, on the other hand, may prove more serious in misguiding the planner.[3]

At all events, it is by using these restrictions that Girsanov proves the possibility of an economically meaningful solution sought for by

---

[1] See below, p. 43.

[2] These restraints may be expressed respectively as:

$$\frac{q_{ij}}{p_i}(w_j, p_1, \ldots, p_n) < 0; \quad \frac{q_{ij}}{p_k}(w_j, p_1, \ldots, p_n) \geqslant 0; \qquad i \neq k$$

[3] Note, however, Frish's hypothesis of 'want-independence' in the procedure of aggregation under which elasticities with respect to price are obtained from the knowledge of budget proportions and Engel's elasticities. Cf. R. Frisch, *Econometrica*, vol. xxvii, April 1959.

Dudkin.[1] In order to interpret it as maximising the community's satisfaction, Girsanov introduces the conventional relationship of an individual's utility as a function of quantities of goods consumed. (Incidentally, he also assumes, though the precise relationship is not made clear, that wages themselves are a function of the prices of finished goods—a rather doubtful assumption we shall return to presently.) But since Dudkin has already indicated the dependence of the quantities demanded on wages and prices, he perforce elaborates this utility function as

$$U\{q_{ij}[w_j(p_1, \ldots, p_n); \ p_1, \ldots, p_n], \ldots, q_{nj}[w_j(p_1, \ldots, p_n); \ p_1, \ldots, p_n]\}$$

Thus the utility of the j-th category of wage-earners depends on the quantities of the finished goods, which quantities depend on wages and prices (and in which wages are related to the prices of finished-goods). This is the objective function of the model.

Girsanov envisages the problem facing the planner in terms of an input-output model in which there are, say, n consumer goods, m intermediate goods and k capital goods. The object of the planner is to find a price set that will clear the market, and, subject to given resources and a distribution constraint, yield the community ('all labour groups') a maximum level of satisfaction.

To the Western economist the procedure we have outlined will appear somewhat awkward, if not questionable. The conventional sequence in positive economics is to start from the notion of utility depending upon quantities of finished goods: to introduce a budget constraint in order to derive price-quantity relationships: and to proceed from there to demand functions. As has been noted, Dudkin reverses this sequence. Even Girsanov, who begins with utility as a function of quantities, goes on to incorporate Dudkin's equations (in which quantities demanded depend on prices and wages) into this utility function. However, it is not hard to think of reasons to explain these different inelegances.

Firstly, since notions of consumers' preference maps were familiar to Soviet economic thought only to the extent of them being long suspect, it must have appeared more circumspect to justify them indirectly and by reference to the recently established and inescapable quantitative relationships between income, prices and the purchases of consumer

---

[1] The existence of a solution for any feasible plan is shown where points of the polyhedron generated by the constraints belong to the set of points of possible aggregate demand.

goods.[1] Nor need the drastic assumption of the crucial negative price-demand relations detain us once it is appreciated that these economists were not interested at all in deducing general properties of demand functions; indeed in their papers they were interested only in establishing an allocative economy in which consumers' preferences were to count. (Incidentally, a significant pointer to the new enthusiasm for mathematics in Soviet economics is Dudkin's argument in defence of one of his functions, that a rejection of it would amount to a rejection of mathematical methods.)[2] Nevertheless, as a secondary consideration, an impatience with the all-too-familiar pitfalls of the utility approach—arising from changes in the marginal utility of money income, or, in ordinal utility, from negative income effects and complementarity—is not unknown in the West,[3] and is not necessarily indicative of lack of sophistication.

One may note in passing that the Soviet writers are not explicit about the kind of utility they work with; further that they tend to concentrate on the 'size' aspect of the net product to the neglect of the 'distributional' aspect.[4] (Or rather any prescription concerning the distribution of purchasing power is avoided. Indeed, the tacit assumption appears to be that consumers' preferences are weighted by the distribution of purchasing power in such a way as to conform with the planner's system of preferences.) Again, Pareto optimum—defined as a position in which with given resources, techniques and tastes, nobody's welfare may be increased further without reducing the welfare of others—is not overtly mentioned. But this omission is of no formal significance: any maximisation of the community's utility, subject to given resources, entails a Pareto optimum.[5]

[1] For a useful discussion of the attitude towards Western concepts of utility and social rationality of economic activities see O. Lange, *Political Economy*, vol. i, Warsaw, 1963 (in English), esp. pp. 235 ff. and 317 ff.

[2] '. . . the working peoples' function of consumer preferences is nothing else but the counterpart of their demand function and is really only its other mathematical expression. . . . Consequently, those who speak out against the use of the apparatus of consumer preferences, without objecting to the use of demand functions, are in fact opposing the legitimacy of applying mathematics to economic research, and withal to economics.' Dudkin, *op. cit.*, p. 45.

[3] See Gustav Cassel's '*Theory of Social Economy*', vol. i, London 1932, ch. 80 ff. For a recent appraisal of the literature which reaches conclusions supporting Cassel's theories see E. J. Mishan, 'Theories of Consumer's Behaviour: A Cynical View', *Economica*, February, 1961.

[4] Mishan, *ibid.*, p. 43.

[5] Cf. on these concepts E. J. Mishan, *Economic Journal*, June 1963, pp. 346 ff.

Finally, unequal tastes could be inferred if categories received more or less equal remuneration since the average quantity demanded is a function of the particular category (note in this context that nothing is said about the aggregating of categories).

Thirdly—and here we link up with our first point—though Soviet economics may be seen as turning toward theories of consumer's choice, its orientation is still strongly qualified. The models discussed are, in effect, offered as affording guidance to planners working within the established Soviet institutional framework. In particular the planners are envisaged as paying increased attention to the existing data on consumption.

Though the Dudkin model does rely on consumer's preferences, there is also in its formal description a reservation to reconcile it with the established doctrine of the role of the Soviet State in shaping the course of the economy. Broadly, then, the planner follows his own scale of preference (including time preference) in aiming not only at an overall equilibrium, but also at an equilibrium in each basic good. In so far as excess demands or excess supplies arise in the various goods, Dudkin's model may be interpreted as urging the planner to take action only in close consultation with consumption statistics which he regards as providing us with a 'rationality peg'.[1]

The Soviet planner's approach may also justify Girsanov's handling of the wage-price relationship. As noted earlier, the wage of each of the labour group is taken to be dependent on the prices of all consumer goods, suggesting that wages are structured by the planner with the view to clearing the market at given prices. This interpretation is open to objection. A wage-price relation would suggest, more plausibly, that the level of wages is related to the *level* of prices. In order to cope with excess demand in general, the relationship may be altered by reducing the wage level relative to prices of finished goods, conversely if there is a general over-supply of goods.

Notwithstanding these reasonable conjectures, Soviet planning does, occasionally, deal with particular surpluses and shortages by altering

---

[1] '. . . it is more suitable to start off from the revelation of the actual preference of consumers in as much as there is not a single planning and scientific organ at the present time that is in a position to evaluate better than the consumers themselves the relation among their complex and variegated material and cultural needs . . . *and then only to make corrections for individual products.*' Dudkin, *op. cit.*, p. 45. In our submission the emphasis would be on the last sentence which we have italicised.

44

both the level and the *structure* of wages. For Soviet conditions the postulated wage-price relationship of this kind corresponds to the usual constraint on the utility function requiring equality of purchases of goods and sales of factors. Incidentally, while disutility of labour as such does not appear in the function as written by Dudkin and Gir-sanov, the work-leisure choice (within the bounds drawn by Soviet social-economic organisation) is implied by their relating it to the supply of labour per unit of time.

Before concluding it may be of interest to have a look at the way this problem has been broached in Poland by Professor Kalecki in a recent paper.[1] In the context of planning with variable prices, he employs the concept of 'consumption equivalence'. As drawn by him the curve of this 'equivalence' is convex to the origin, its tangent gradient through a point q_1, q_2 is $-p_1/p_2$ (the q's and p's being quantities and prices respectively); its differential equation is $dq_2/dq_1 = f(q_1, q_2)$. For n commodities points of the n-dimension surface corresponding to the 'equivalent' sets would be found in Kalecki's exposition on the $(n-1)$ dimensional surfaces. (The generality of the latter formulation may be legitimately questioned; surely there is no reason why, say, the case of three goods should be confined to three combinations of these goods?) In short, Kalecki's 'equivalence' curve displays all the relevant properties of an indifference curve. Indeed, it is not easy to see what is gained by bringing in the new notion. Kalecki dissociates his curve, however, from the indifference curve emphatically, and the reason seems to be that he also wishes to dissociate it from the postulate of consumer's choice—or, specifically, consumer's free choice—which might be implied in the former.[2] In that case the notion of consumption equivalence itself is ambiguous both theoretically and from the point of view of planning practice; it would require a definition: in what sense are the commodity-sets 'equivalent'? The abandoning of consumer's choices by Kalecki does not reduce the usefulness of his

[1] Michal Kalecki, *Gospodarka Planowa*, 1963, no. 7, pp. 3 ff.; see also below.

[2] Kalecki stresses that 'the indifference curve as applied in the West' rests on premises different from his own 'equivalence' curve since the former '. . . is treated as a collection of sets of two consumer-goods q_1, q_2 considered *by the consumer* to be equivalent. The fact that at the q_1, q_2 point the tangent has the $-p_1/p_2$ gradient . . . is deduced from the consumer's *optimal choice*. This conception raises various reservations of a fundamental nature', *ibid.*, p. 5. The italics—which are those of the original—would seem to justify our interpretation of Kalecki's reservations.

technical apparatus but it surely does affect the concept of market equilibrium which his curves are supposed to portray. In any case Professor Kalecki leaves the problem of the planner's rationality 'peg' —so strongly underscored by Dudkin[1]—untouched.

NOTE TO CHAPTER 4

SINCE this essay was written Dudkin has designed a planned economy's 'optimal material balance'. The perspective-plan problem is written:

$$\sum_i a_{ij}\,(x_j)x_j + y_i + f_i = x_i; \quad \sum_i b_{si}(x_i) \leqslant R_s$$

$$y_i \geqslant 0; \quad y_i = y_i(v); \quad \sum_i p_i y_i = v$$

(i and s—no. of commodity and scarce resource; x—output; a and b, input/output and resource–use/output coefficients respectively; f—non-productive investment and public consumption; R—available resources; y—households' demand; p—consumer-good price (fixed); v—households' income.) The v, households' income, is now *the maximand*. (L. M. Dudkin, *Optimalnyi Materialnyi Balans Narodnogo Khoziaystva*, Moscow, 1966; see also his analysis of criteria in L. E. Mints, Ed., *Ekonomiko-Matematicheskiye Modeli Narodnogo Khoziaystva*, Moscow, 1966; also reference p. 187 ftn. 1 below.[2])

[1] Dudkin, *op. cit.*, p. 45, passage quoted above.

[2] The reader of this chapter and of the excursus on pp. 71 ff. might find of help an incisive remark in P. Maslov's survey in *Voprosy Ekonomiki*, no. 3, 1967, p. 123 n.: "with us one and the same thing—the function of indifference or utility—is given various names: "the hyperplane of constant living standards" by A. A. Konyus . . ., "the objective function of consumption" by V. Volkonskiy . . ., "the preference function" by L. M. Dudkin and V. S. Vaksman. . . .""

5 Link-up with Russian Thought of the Early 1900s[1]

ONE of the significant symptoms of a search for certain links with Russian, and through it with pre- and post-Marxian Western thought, is the spectacular posthumous career made during the last three years or so in Soviet literature by V. K. Dmitriev, a Russian mathematical economist who wrote at the turn of the century, was little known in his lifetime, and completely forgotten after his death.

Perhaps a few words on Dmitriev's theoretical filiation may help a better understanding of his role in the present-day re-orientation of Soviet economics.

The first volume of *Capital* appeared in Russian in 1872 (this was incidentally its first translation into any foreign language—a rather significant pointer to the interest in its theme). In the prevailing intellectual climate its seed fell on receptive soil: from the very start it exercised a profound influence on Russian minds: in the first place, in economics. Almost immediately a Marxist school sprang up, which was soon to become dominant. The noteworthy characteristic was a strong emphasis on the continuity of classical thought, from Smith through Ricardo to Marx: it has been suggested, not without good reason, that the Russians evolved their own specific brand of Ricardian Marxism.[2] But within a decade or so a reaction set in against pure 'objectivism'. Towards the end of the century a distinct 'subjectivist' trend spread well beyond the realm of economics proper. In philosophy it produced a blend of Marxist dialectical materialism with the Kantian categorical imperative. In economics the syncretist tendencies focused on problems of price and value. A Russian marriage of the labour theory of value with Austrian marginalism is usually identified with with the names of Mikhail Tugan-Baranovsky and Peter Struve. Already in his first printed work—in 1890—Tugan-Baranovsky argued that when properly understood, far from mutually excluding each other, the marginal utility and labour theories of value are comple-

---

[1] This is an abbreviated version of an article which appeared under the title 'A Few Remarks on a Discovery in Soviet Economics', in *Bulletin of the Oxford University Institute of Statistics*, November, 1962.

[2] G. Markelov, *Mir Bozhiy*, 1907, quoted in H. J. Seraphim, *Neue russissche Wert-und Kapitalzinstheorien*, Berlin-Leipzig, 1925. The reader will find a very useful discussion of this phase of Russian economics in Seraphim's work.

mentary.[1] A decade later Struve summed up his own standpoint in the following characteristic passage:

> As I see it, as far as the problem of value is concerned, our critical direction turns back to the careful realism of Ricardo and at the same time tries to combine his teachings with those achievements which economic theory owes to Gossen, Walras, Jevons and to the Austrian school of Menger, Wieser and Böhm-Bawerk. To place this realistic theory of economic phenomena within the wide and grandiose frame of Marx's sociological system—that is, I think, a task which by itself deserves the greatest interest.[2]

The proposition is characteristic of the general attitude: while Marx is the inspiration for the broad sociological sweep, 'realistic' interpretation of value is sought rather in the Ricardian version of the labour theory of value reconciled with the modern 'subjectivists'. Of special interest from the angle of our subject is the methodological link up of the new school with Quesnay: Tugan-Baranovsky gives credit to Marx for borrowing from the *Tableaux*, in the second volume of *Capital*, the formal framework for an analysis of growth processes,[3] and criticises him for consistently failing to stick to it in further argument, let alone to develop it.

This is then the stream of Russian economic thought which engulfed the young Dmitriev—then in his twenties—when he wrote his remarkable *Ekonomicheskie orcherki*, a collection of three essays[4] ('D. Ricardo's Theory of Value'; 'The competition theory of A. Cournot, the great forgotten economist' and 'The marginal utility theory'). His intellectual kinship was soon recognised by both the *prominenti* of the school, but on the whole of the two he was closer to Struve, who hailed him as a 'logically and mathematically thought-out and tested Ricardo'.[5] Illness and death cut short the work of the brilliant Russian. Within a few years of the appearance of his work attention was drawn to it in the West by Ladislaus von Bortkiewicz, who borrowed from Dmitriev a good deal of apparatus for his own critique of the value and price

---

[1] In *Yuridicheskiy Vestnik*. 1890, re-stated by him a quarter of a century later in *Osnovy politcheskoy ekonomii*, Petrograd, 1915, p. 66.

[2] In *Zhizn*, vol. ii, 1900, p. 305, quoted in Seraphim, *op. cit.*, p. 87.

[3] M. I. Tugan-Baranovsky, *Osnovy Politcheskoy Ekonomii*, p. 549.

[4] V. K. Dmitriev, *Ekonomicheskiye ocherki*, Series I; *Opyt organicheskogo sinteza trudovoy teorii tsennosti i teorii predelnoy poleznosti*, Moscow, 1904.

[5] P. Struve, *Russkaya Mysl*, 1913, no. 10, as quoted in Seraphim, *op. cit.*, p. 87.

calculus in the Marxist system,[1] and whose appreciation is worth quoting: 'Considering that the author (that is, Dmitriev) resorts to algebraic tools of exposition and proof, it is hardly surprising that his work (as it would seem, his first work) has elicited little attention (I mean of course, from the Russian side) although it betrays an extraordinary theoretical talent and brings in something really new'.[2] Bortkiewicz's judgement did not save Dmitriev from oblivion for half a century.

The claims made in Soviet literature on behalf of Dmitriev have now culminated in a significant theorem. This has been formulated by three Soviet economists, V. D. Belkin, D. M. Grobman and A. L. Lunts, who offer a rigorous proof of 'correlation of two ways of determining full inputs'.[3] It seeks to establish the identity of full-input coefficients arrived at on either the Leontief or Dmitriev route, inputs of a commodity 'on itself' excepted. We shall now turn our attention to this theorem.

Dmitriev's fundamental equation—the one to which we have already referred here—describes the total labour 'content', the quantity of labour x_A which under the present technological conditions would go '*directly or indirectly*' into production of a unit of commodity A as:[4]

$$x_A = n_A + \frac{1}{m_1} x + \frac{1}{m_2} x_2 + \cdots + \frac{1}{m_M} x_M$$

where n_A stands for labour used up directly, the reciprocals of $(m_1, m_2, \ldots, m_M)$ and $(x_1, x_2, \ldots, x_M)$ stand respectively for fractions

---

[1] L. v. Bortkiewicz, *Archiv fur Sozialwissenschaft und Sozialpolitik*, vol. xxv, Tübingen, 1907. It was on the basis of Bortkiewicz's discussion that Alec Nove and I wrote a note published in *Soviet Studies*, July 1961; no copy of Dmitriev's work was at that time available in the West.

[2] Bortkiewicz, *op. cit.*, p. 18 n. Note the kinship between Dmitriev and P. Sraffa's *Production of Commodities by Means of Commodities*, (Cambridge, 1960).

[3] See V. D. Belkin, 'Natsionalnyi dokhod i mezhotraslevoy balans', in *Primenenie matematiki i elektronnoy tekhniki v planirovanii*, A. G. Aganbegyan and V. D. Belkin, eds., Moscow, 1961. *op. cit.*, pp. 28 ff. We have reproduced the proof in a somewhat shortened form from this source with changes of algebraic argument on a few points where, we believe, it is distorted by misprints. Otherwise only minor changes in symbols have been made.

[4] Dmitriev, *op. cit.*, pp. 7 ff. (notation of the original). This is similar to Sraffa's reduction to dated quantities of labour. In the Sraffa equation representing production of a commodity, the wage and prices are expressed in terms of the standard commodity; subsequently different means of production employed are replaced with a series of quantities of dated labour; *op. cit.*, especially ch. VI.

of 'technical capitals' $(k_1, k_2, \ldots, k_M)$ successively absorbed by the A commodity unit, and for total quantities of labour spent in production of these 'capitals'. The burden of the arguments is that the cumulated labour cost can always be established 'without excursions into the pre-historic time of the first creation of capital'.[1] Since the n's and the m's are technical data, with equal numbers of equations and unknowns, Dmitriev's linear system provides a unique solution in the x's.

Now it is by arguing from *analogy*—we italicise this for reasons which will become clear in the course of our argument—that the authors of the theorem write down for Dmitriev an equation of full inputs c_{ik} of any i-th commodity per unit of a k-th product:

$$c_{ik} = a_{ik} + \sum_{j=1}^{n} c_{ij} a_{jk} \quad (i, k, j = 1, 2, \ldots, n)$$

With a fixed i we have a soluble system of n equations in n unknown c's (The a's describe direct inputs; j-th products are 'intermediate'). The c_{ik} are next related to the familiar Leontief-derived equation for full inputs, expressed as:

$$b_{ik} = \sum_{j=1}^{n} a_{ij} b_{jk} + \delta_{ik} \quad (i, k, j = 1, 2, \ldots, n)$$

where δ is Kronecker delta (that is, zero except for $i=k$ when it is unity). The theorem is then that:

$$b_{ik} = c_{ik} \text{ if } i \neq k \quad \text{and} \quad b_{ik} = c_{ik} + 1 \text{ if } i = k$$

In matrix notation with $A = (a_{ik})$; $B = (b_{ik})$; $C = (c_{ik})$ and, by definition, unit matrix $\mathscr{I} = (\delta_{ik})$, the proof proceeds as follows:

From the above $B = \mathscr{I} + AB$. Note: the product of the two matrices AB is the matrix whose elements are the inner product $\sum_{j=1}^{n} (a_{ij} b_{jk})$; and analogously $C = A + CA$. Solving the two equations:

$$B - AB = \mathscr{I}; \quad (\mathscr{I} - A)B = \mathscr{I}; \quad B = \mathscr{I}(\mathscr{I} - A)^{-1}$$

similarly

$$C - CA = A; \quad C(\mathscr{I} - A) = A; \quad C = A(\mathscr{I} - A)^{-1}$$

Hence the difference of the two matrices

$$B - C = \mathscr{I}(\mathscr{I} - A)^{-1} - A(\mathscr{I} - A)^{-1} = (\mathscr{I} - A) . (\mathscr{I} - A)^{-1} = \mathscr{I};$$

$$B = C + \mathscr{I}; \quad \text{Q ED}$$

[1] Dmitriev, *op. cit.*, p. 9.

In other words a Leontief and an analogous Dmitriev matrix of full coefficients would differ only along the leading diagonal. On the Leontief route full coefficients are computed per unit of output passing into final uses; on the 'analogous' Dmitriev route they would be computed per unit of produced outputs. The economic sense of the basic identity of results is that ultimately outputs always pass, of course, beyond the productive sphere and this is bound to emerge when the cumulation of successive inputs is pursued all along the line. However, on Leontief's route full inputs do also include that part of production which passes into consumption and accumulation, while on Dmitriev's they do not, although they show inputs involved.

When this has been said one should, we think, look to the difference in the very purpose of the two. The authors of the Soviet theorem overlook the fact that Leontief's aim is to provide a theoretical basis of methodology for a practicable analysis of inter-industry flows and for a handy operational mathematical apparatus, suitable for empirical use. Therein lies the immense importance of his path-breaking invention for contemporary economics and potential significance for a Soviet-type centrally planned economy. By contrast, Dmitriev was interested exclusively in the abstract problem of the 'true' cause and source of value. His fundamental equation was actually built up as a didactic device for the exposition of the labour theory of value rather than as a tool of empirical relevance. It is true that in so far as labour is assumed in it to be the only primary input the focus of the Leontief model too—at least in its original static variant—is on labour as *the* social cost. In this sense one formulates in Leontief something that could be called the quasi-historical total cost-coefficient in terms of labour directly used plus all its indirect contributions to a given commodity, obtained from a set of simultaneous equations as did Dmitriev for his x_A in his fundamental equation. But for Dmitriev his abstract exercise of wide sweep settles the question of labour-capital relation, since nothing more was the object of his inquiry.

Unlike Dmitriev, Leontief is concerned of course in specifying inputs of primary factors (in the simple model reduced to labour) and all the various intermediate products compatible with a postulated bill of goods. It has been stressed here that in fact only by resorting to '*analogy*' have Belkin-Grobman-Lunts formulated the equation for a generalised case of c_{ik}, which is indeed *theirs*, not Dmitriev's (though, of course, in Dmitriev a system of *labour-capital* equations does suggest itself as $x_A = n_A + 1/m.x$). It is only in fact in this way that they set their proof going. The Dmitriev approach is remarkable and, we believe, noteworthy for the historian of economic thought. His basic equation as an expression of *direct and indirect* inputs—though confined to a prime factor input only—broadly anticipates by several decades the line of development of theory. But there ends its immediate significance for this theory and also for the Soviet planometrician's box of tools. Yet by now the fundamental input-output equation $X_i = \sum a_{ij} X_j + Y_i$ is being referred to in Soviet literature as the Dmitriev formula.

Some Soviet economists now also look to Dmitriev for rescue from their perennial theoretical embarrassment: the inability to make use, still today, a quarter of a century since the establishment of a fully socialist society, of Marx's precept for economic accounting. Academician Nemchinov argues[1] that by dividing money-term national income of an optimal plan by its labour-time 'content' calculated on the principle of Dmitriev's fundamental equation, the money-expressed, planned unit of value can be found (value *pure et simple* in the Marxist sense, as distinct from Marx's use value; *stoimost* in the accepted Soviet-Marxist terminology, which is however a rather ambivalent term considering that the same word in Russian means 'cost').[2] Then, multiplying by this value-unit, total *optimal* labour-time expenditures on individual commodities or sectors—which per unit of output measures socially necessary labour—would yield their 'true', money-expressed 'value'. It is thus by redefining the concept of 'socially necessary labour' to mean amounts of labour 'congealed' in an *efficient*[3] plan that the will-o'-the-wisp of Soviet-Marxist economics is

---

[1] V. Nemchinov, *Voprosy Ekonomiki*, 1960, no. 12, p. 90.

[2] Dmitriev himself uses another Russian term for value—*tsennost*.

[3] Professor Novozhilov will agree only that a system of Dmitriev equations will yield 'actual' (*fakticheskaya*) value, since they do not allow for the limitations of productive resources which constrain a realistic programme.
These equations, Novozhilov argues, are in fact insufficient for computing any feasible, let alone optimal, plan variant. If the equations were used for calculation of 'reproduction values' those for commodities no longer produced would fall out of the set. Yet values of these commodities may remain as unknowns in equations of goods still produced. However (Novozhilov qualifies his argument) both value and 'full cost' could be established by bringing in limitations of 'reproduction'. In fact, the unknown 'reproduction values' of those means of production which are no longer produced can be taken as equal their past value of production, or zero. In either case the numbers of equations and unknowns will become equal. See 'Ischislenye zatrat v sotsyalisticheskom khoziaystve', *Voprosy Ekonomiki*, no. 2, 1961.

hoped to be captured. (It will be granted that Dmitriev's fundamental equation does imply social optimality: in this sense it is a kind of rudimentary linear programme with choices of technology made behind the scenes, no substitution, no joint production, etc.) So let us examine somewhat more closely Dmitriev's stand in these matters.

Now, as we have seen, it is true that Dmitriev is concerned with 'labour' as the ultimate source of value, but he is so within the Ricardian tradition and framework: indeed, his fundamental equation was evolved by him to corroborate Ricardo. His tenet is that Ricardo does give a correct analysis of the 'law' which governs values of commodities produced at different costs. But he insists that 'this analysis does not prove at all, as Ricardo believes, that the value of such products does not depend ultimately on conditions of demand and supply, and tends towards some level depending exclusively on conditions of production'.[1] On the contrary, he contends further, '. . . it is evident that any change in demand-supply conditions (which in the last instance reduce themselves to shifts in the consumption sphere, as follows from . . . analysis of the demand curve) inevitably leads to a change in the production price (= value in terms of a certain product whose own value is taken as constant), even if all conditions of production (dependent on the state of techniques and on availability of different natural factors of production rather than on economic accounting, *khoziay-stvennyi raschet*), remained unchanged'. All this is, in Dmitriev, holds for a value-theory based on 'socially necessary labour' since it is precisely 'nothing else but conditions of demand and supply that in each case determine what amount of labour is socially necessary'.[2] In substance his may be the case of an optimum discussed by Professor Hicks:[3] with the labour theory of value reduced to the proposition that where labour is assumed to be the only scarce factor prices of production would be proportional to labour costs.

In this reasoning Dmitriev takes initially the demand curve as an 'empirical datum'. In investigating it at a subsequent stage he builds his own bridge between Ricardo and marginal utility theories. (The purpose of his work is explicitly stated in its sub-title as 'An attempt at an organic synthesis between the labour theory of value and the marginal utility theory'.) This is the theme of the second essay on the

---

[1] Dmitriev, *op. cit.*, p. 55; see also p. 149.
[2] Dmitriev, *op. cit.*, p. 55.
[3] J. R. Hicks, 'Linear Theory', *Economic Journal*, December 1960, p. 683.

progress of these theories from Galliani's *Della Moneta* to the Austrians, whose role incidentally Dmitriev is inclined to under-estimate. As noted, the essay is preceded by another one on Cournot, the real hero of Dmitriev's story. This largely historical disquisition brings Dmitriev eventually to the formulation of a system of simultaneous equations describing general competitive equilibrium.[1] Mathematically it is a considerably simplified Walrasian model with a 'utility curve' borrowed from Auspitz-Lieben.[2,3] (The equilibrium is stated in probabilistic terms with reference to Bernoulli's Theorem.)

One final remark. Curiously enough, in Dmitriev, Marxist economics is not even mentioned by name. It would seem that by the time *Ekonomicheskie ocherki* went to the printers Marx had no longer the kind of 'sociological' spell over Dmitriev that he still exercised over Struve himself and his school generally. There is, in Dmitriev, a rather pointed reference to a 'developed' form of labour theory of value (the ironical quotation marks are his). Its propounders, he says:

tend to identify the quantity of socially necessary labour with its *average quantity* used up in producing a given commodity. To maintain this amounts to repudiating all that Ricardo had done for the elucidation of the laws which rule the value of different commodities produced at different production-cost (levels). Ricardo's analysis leaves no doubt that the value of a product is determined by the quantity of labour used up in producing a given commodity *under the least* favourable, rather than average conditions of production.[4]

In recent times the new mathematical school has tried in an oblique

---

[1] Dmitriev, *op. cit.*, p. 149. Solution is obtained from three sets of equations. The first two describe quantities and values of commodities respectively in the hands of holders before and after the exchange. The third relates quantities and utilities for holders through some coefficient which appears to be akin to Walras's *rareté*.

[2] Cf. R. Auspitz and R. Lieben, *Untersuchungen ueber die Theorie des Preises*, Leipzig, 1889, especially, pp. 8 ff.

[3] It may be of interest to note parenthetically that Dmitriev's re-discoverer, Academician Nemchinov, recently referred with approval to Morishima's finding on the similarity of Marx's and Walras's models when re-stated in von Neumann terms. (Cf. Nemchinov, 'Model ekonomicheskogo rayona', p. 134; reference to A. Morishima, 'Economic Expansion and the Interest Rate in Generalised von Neumann Model', *Econometrica*, April 1960, pp. 354.) This is a pointer to the new mood in Soviet economics.

[4] Dmitriev, *op. cit.*, p. 55.

way—but not without considerable doctrinal difficulty[1]—to re-orientate Soviet thinking towards a marginalist approach as one more relevant for pursuing comparative advantage in allocational choices. This school may hope then that by establishing the authority of a re-discovered brilliant Russian it strengthens its own hand on this point.

[1] See on this A. Zauberman, 'New Winds in Soviet Planning', *Soviet Studies*, July 1960; A. Zauberman, 'Revisionism in Soviet Economics', in *Revisionism*, L. Labedz, ed., London, 1962; and R. W. Campbell, 'Marx, Kantorovich, and Novozhilov', in *Slavic Review*, October 1961. For a critique of the papers by Zauberman and Campbell see V. V. Novozhilov, *Voprosy Ekonomiki*, 1965, no. 7.
    Further discussion of Dmitriev's significance for contemporary trends in Soviet economic thinking will be found in Zauberman's *Introduction* to the forthcoming French edition of Dmitriev's work under the editorship of Marie Lavigne *et al.*

Part II: Planning Techniques

A. Pricing

6 Traditional Prices and Efficiency Prices

THE CONCEPTION AND RÔLE OF THE PRICE TOOL

A BASIC obstacle to an integration of the physical-term and money-term aspects of Soviet planning is the nature of the Soviet money-term parameters; in the first place, of its price-tool.[1] The Soviet-type economy may be thought of as belonging to the broad class of centrally planned and controlled systems which rely for allocative choice-making primarily on physical-term calculation: it belongs then to the family of systems described by Hensel as the *Planverwirklichung bei reiner Naturalrechnung*.[2] What will strike the student is that Soviet theory has never analysed the Soviet model in these terms. In its extreme version producer-good prices would be completely 'passive'—would be confined, that is, to recording functions. They would not serve choice-making as such. Conceptually then they could form but a sign-system, a system of shorthand signs, one indispensable for aggregation and for disaggregation of heterogeneous items in conveying orders along the chains of command, down to the firm manager. Looking at the lower echelons of the Soviet-type system one could say with Campbell that basically price is used here to supply cost data to controllers rather than decision data to firm managers.[3] When we move to higher echelons we find that the price is not devised, is not conceived as a parameter of decision-making either. It does not record opportunities; it does not reflect the scales of preferences.

In Soviet doctrine price had been designed over the decades as a cost-plus price reducible to wage cost (with a nominal, conventional profit margin, related to it) based on the branch average.[4] This price

[1] For the discussion of this and some other points dealt with in this chapter, see A. Zauberman, 'Principles and Methods of Price Formation for Producer-Goods', in *Plannungsprobleme im Sowjetischen Wirtschaftssystem*, E. Boettcher, K. C. Thalheim, E. Klinkmueller, P. Knirsch, eds., Freie Universitaet Berlin, 1964.

[2] K. Paul Hensel, *Einführung in die Theorie der Zentralverwaltungswirtschaft*, Stuttgart, 1954, especially pp. 170 ff.

[3] Robert W. Campbell, 'Accounting for Cost Control in the Soviet Economy', *Review of Economics and Statistics*, February 1958, pp. 59 ff. See also G. Grossman, 'Soviet Economic Planning—Industrial Prices in the USSR', *American Economic Review* May 1959, p. 57.

[4] Morris Bornstein, *American Economic Review*, March 1962. Cf. also Hans Hirsch, *Quantity Planning and Price Planning*, English translation by Karl Scholz, Philadelphia, 1961; see also my review in *Economica*, November 1963.

construct is claimed to be derived from Marx's theory of value (I have in mind the inter-industry price; the consumer-goods price—with little concern about its doctrinal filiation—is devised essentially so as to clear the market; it is insulated from the inter-industry price structure). In actual fact Soviet price structure has tended to degenerate in the sense that it has deviated from its structural principle, forming as often as not quite arbitrary price relations. (It is in this circumscribed sense that it has been irrational: I submit that it is not really legitimate to test rationality of Soviet-type prices by use of yardsticks which are alien to their conceptual nature and function—as was done by some participants in the heated debate in the West in the 1950s.)[1]

In fact the mechanism as operated does, and has to, deviate in a rather patchy way, from its conceptual ideal. With not too much concern about conceptual tidiness price is used, and increasingly so in a growingly complex economy, as a subsidiary steering instrument as well as a planning tool. On the planning level prices form the scaffolding of macro-balances which express macro-allocative decisions. The planner's choices in capital formation are made to a significant extent with the use of price-based calculation: so are to some extent choices involving foreign trade. It would appear that technological coefficients are in actual practice influenced by such calculation.

Price-relations exercise a still stronger allocative influence at the enterprise level. They do so in so far as the manager can exert a certain discretion in the choice of outputs and inputs within some, if only narrow, limits. Largely it is because of the lack of intrinsic consistency of the Soviet mechanism as operated that a cumbersome multi-angle system of performance indicators, some in physical terms, some in money terms, had to be resorted to. On the firm level they form a complicated system of incentives—negative and positive—for the management. Their purpose is partly to prevent price-relations from misguiding the manager: in other words to neutralise the impact of a price which is still too 'active' and possibly is so in the wrong direction. In actual fact this heterogeneous system of indicators pushes and pulls, as often as not, in conflicting directions, which adds to the unwieldiness of the mechanism; and the breakdowns of the internal logic of guid-

---

[1] Since this essay was written the Soviet practice has adopted the principle of a branch-averaged, full-cost-plus price. The price includes a fixed charge for capital employed (land excepted). It is akin to the concept of the *Produktionspreis*. It is not derived from any optimality (efficiency) calculus.

ance have inevitably an adverse effect on the course of economic life.

There has been, for years, a general consensus both among Soviet planners and theoreticians that the inter-industry pricing methodology requires reform. However, the great debate in Soviet economics on the subject, started around the mid-fifties,[1] has largely been revolving around the traditional price-cost concepts, with little clarity about structuring price in such a way as to conform with the nature of the Soviet economic mechanism and the role of the inter-industry price within it. Prices discussed in this 'Debate on the Law of Value' were constructed on the basis of either Marxist 'value' (Strumilin, *et al.*); or Marx's *Produktionpreis* schema (Atlas, Vaag, *et al.*); or a variant of this schema established in Soviet practice: the 'average value' concept, with 'surplus product' charged to commodities proportionally to their 'cost value' (Kondrashev and Bachurin).[2]

It was only the mathematical school—emerging towards the end of the 1950s—that put forward the rigorously argued postulate of a price as an efficiency-calculation parameter and of its structure to conform with this function. The formalisation of the efficient price in Soviet writing is due to Kantorovich. Formulated as early as the 1930s as an

---

[1] See on this my 'Law of Value and Price Formation', in G. Grossman, *Value and Plan*, Berkeley, 1960.

[2] Since this chapter was written the plenum of the Academy's Economic Institute and the learned Council for Pricing Problems met to formulate—on the basis of a report by V. P. Dyachenko—the definitive stand on price construction. The rapporteur argued that it was impossible to remain faithful to the Marxist labour theory of value whilst maintaining that the latter's magnitude was determined by capital-intensity of production or relative utilities or scarcities of commodities. Yet—in what will seem to be *non sequitur*—he argued at the same time that an allowance for capital intensity as a factor 'deflecting' price from value (defined by that theory) was compatible with it, and rational. In this he was supported by protagonists of the *Produktionspreis*, Z. V. Atlas, A. I. Pashkov (and P. S. Mstislavskiy coming out in defence of the suggested solution against the charge that it reflected the theory of three factors of production). Indeed what emerged from the session seems to be the endorsement by Soviet academic doctrine, of this type of price, its supporters remaining divided only on the question as to whether a single or a differential, interest-type, profit-coefficient was more appropriate in this kind of price for a socialist economy. The known defenders of the strict 'value-price'—S. G. Strumilin, Ya. A. Kronrod, K. V. Ostrovityanov, Sh. Ya. Turetskiy—restated their opposition on policy as well as doctrinal grounds (that a capital charge in price, additional to a wear-and-tear allowance, would inhibit technological progress favoured by capital intensity). On the other hand Academician Kantorovich opposed the rapporteur's proposal because of its failure to reflect the conception of optimal planning and the necessity to compute and employ the whole system of interdependent economic indicators, in particular a price 'conditioned' by the optimal plan. (Cf. report on the debate in *Voprosy Ekonomiki*, 1964, no. 7, pp. 147 ff.)

instrument of calculation at the firm level (which secures for it chronological primacy) it was reworked as a macro-instrument in the late
1950s and has ever since exercised a considerable influence on Soviet
planning thought, and indeed has crystallised its quest for an efficient
price.[1] It rests mathematically on Minkowski's fundamental theorem
that a point of a bounded convex polyhedron, which is defined as a
finite number of halfspaces, is expressible as a linear non-negative
combination of its extreme points; from this, proof was provided for the
existence of a system of solving multipliers.

Let us recall then Kantorovich's formulation of the plan problem,[2]
which is: given the technology matrix and the resource vector choose
the optimal intensity-vector. (As we shall see the difference from the
conventional activity analysis is in the maximand used.) Gosplan
organises its plan as a vector $\pi = (h_1, h_2, \ldots, h_r)$; its components show
the employment-intensity of respective technologies identified by a
vector $a^s = (a_1^s, a_2^s, \ldots, a_N^s)$ describing the volume of production of
each of the N 'ingredients' of the plan—of factors, and intermediate
and final goods—with each technology operated at unit level (negative a are inputs). The planner's task is now to secure a maximum
output of some ingredients—the final bill of goods—with a required
product mix. He will have to make a choice from among feasible π
which confront him, that is to choose one with non-negative components
subject, for each 'ingredient' in production, to constraints of the form
$x_i^\pi \geqslant b_i$ (the b_i are some given numbers: zero for intermediate goods
which are not to be used, negative for factors and materials constrained
by availability of resources). From alternatives faced the planner will
adopt that under which the minimum value of

$$\mu(\pi) = \min_{1 \leqslant j \leqslant n} x_j^\pi / k_j$$

[1] One should also note Novozhilov's outstanding merit in the development of the
concept of the efficiency-price in Soviet economics. His model was evolved in a series
of papers published from the late thirties onwards, and it shares the conceptual basis
with the Kantorovich construct—it would seem that they were developed independently
of each other. Its original version was not quite consistent in so far as Novozhilov
employed cost-price valuations. (Cf. 'Metody soizmerenya narodno-knoziaystvennykh
effektivnosti planovykhi i proyektnykh variantov', in *Trudy Leningradskogo Industrialnogo
Instituta*, 1939, no. 4). In subsequent revisions he explicitly adopted Kantorovich's
system of solving multipliers (see his 'Izmerenye zatrat i ikh rezultatov v sotsyalisticheskom khoziaystve', in *Primenenye Matematiki v Ekonomicheskikh Issledovanyakh*, vol. i,
V. S. Nemchinov, ed., Moscow, 1959).

[2] Cf. L. V. Kantorovich, *Ekonomicheskiy rasschet nayluchshego ispolzovanya resursov*,
Moscow, 1960, especially pp. 281 ff.

reaches its maximum: the k_j describe the $1 \leqslant j \leqslant n$ product-mix of the final bill of n goods in such a way as to make for everyone of these goods the right-hand term constant $x_j^\pi / k_j = \mu$.

The positive side of Kantorovich's message is then expressed in the valuation counterpart of this solution. Its substance is the familiar duality proposition: for a feasible π to be optimal it is necessary and sufficient that there should exist a system of solving multipliers—in Kantorovich's terminology 'objectively conditioned valuations', the 'ooos'—satisfying the following conditions, for each actually employed technology: (1) they should be non-negative: positive for a maximised valuation of at least one component of the final bill of goods, zero for factors which do not limit production and for final goods produced in excess of requirements: (2) total valuation of production for the economy should be zero, the valuation of outputs equalling exactly that of 'ingredients' absorbed, in other words profits in excess of valuation of contributing factor-services being zero. Negative profits would indicate non-optimality in allocation. The reasoning has introduced the Soviet planning thought to the concept of a Lagrange multiplier type of price, a price that is which performs a role similar to that of such a multiplier in the calculus. The solution obtained corresponds to the game-theoretical saddle point.

The negative side of Kantorovich's message has been offered in his discussion of a special case of his 'gamma' programme. This is the case of only one scarce factor: of each technology yielding only one product with other products and the factor forming inputs (the factor is the only ultimate input), and of each product being produced by one technology only. For each of the n products product (j) this technology is written as a vector $a^j = (a_0^j, a_1^j, \ldots, a_n^j)$; $a_0^j < 0$, $a_l^j > 0$, $a_l^j \leqslant 0$ if $l \neq j$. The avowed purpose of building up this case was to prove the limitations, from the planner's point of view, of the embryonic linear programme, Leontief's open input-output model, which follow from its assumptions. The first limitation stems then from the disregard of all productive factors but one (Kantorovich's proof at the same time exposes by implication the inadequacy for the efficiency-calculation of the traditional Soviet doctrine's price reducible to labour cost, designed for a world with one homogeneous factor but employed in a world where this factor is heterogeneous and one of many that are scarce). The second is accounted for by the broad averaging of technological 'ways' with imputed prices depending on the convention adopted for aggregation.[1] First and foremost one would stress—as has Professor Leontief—that in so far as technical coefficients are treated as independent parameters of the system, the underlying assumption is that they are independent of prices of respective cost factors, which eliminates the substitution effect of the marginal productivity theory.[2]

This may be the right context to note in turn some of the limitations of Kantorovich's own construct stemming from the nature of formalisation adopted. Lurye's warning may be worth mentioning here to the effect that (1) in a more general, possibly non-linear and thereby more realistic treatment, the existence of the Kantorovich 'ooos' is only a necessary but not a sufficient condition of an optimal plan; (2) the realism of Kantorovich's plan model is circumscribed by the strong assumption that it can be built up as a set of mutually independent activities (technological "ways".)[3]

In his subsequently published sketch of a dynamic model (1964) Kantorovich[4] concedes that once non-linearities and integer-valued variables and parameters come in, the finding of the optimal plan becomes more complicated: that they affect the argument on efficiency price itself. Pricing would have to be based on the calculation of differential rather than full cost—for the producing unit the 'profitability principle' would no longer hold *per se*: that would be typically the case of external economies and diseconomies[5] (analogously differ-

[1] See V. D. Belkin, *Tsyeny yedinogo urovnya i ekonomicheskiye izmerenya na ikh osnovye*, Moscow, 1963.

On additional complications (stemming from the high degree of product aggregation and differences between administrative and 'pure' product branches) experienced in Soviet empirical application of input-output matrices for price revisions see A. Komin, *Planovoye Khoziaystvo*, 1964, no. 6.

The author maintains that these matrices proved of some use only for testing broad directions of price changes.

[2] Cf. W. Leontief, (Econometrics), in H. S. Ellis, ed., *A Survey of Contemporary Economics*, vol. I, New York, 1952, p. 409.

[3] Cf. A. L. Lurye, 'Obshchaya skhema diskretnogo planirovanya', in *Problemy optimalnogo planirovanya, proyektirovanya i upravlenya proizvodstvom*, Moscow, 1963; also A. L. Lurye, *O matematicheskikh metodakh reshenya zadach na optimum pri planirovanyi sotsyalisticheskogo khoziaystva*, Moscow, 1964, pp. 241 ff. and 316.

[4] L. V. Kantorovich, 'Dinamicheskaya model optimalnogo planirovanya' in N. P. Fedorenko, ed., *Planirovanye i Ekonomiko-Matematicheskiye Metody'*, Moscow, 1964, pp. 336 ff.

[5] The question of the efficiency price for the increasing returns and indivisibility situations is discussed by Professor Baumol (*Economic Theory and Operation Analysis*,

ing prices may have to be adopted for production of this kind in current plans and in the analysis of investment efficiency, a subject to which we come later).

With all this Kantorovich is still inclined to think that the hypothesis of linearity is adequately realistic—and again the more so for a dynamic system (even if some situations might have to be dealt with by means of non-linear, integer or sometimes dynamic programming). His argument is that, when planning for the economy as a whole and for a long period ahead constancy of returns to the scale may be presumed: the scales of operation may be presumed to be 'normal'— near optimality: hence increasing the scales would not affect proportionality. The argument is an empirical one (e.g. it may be valid for an economy of the size and type of the Soviet economy, which Kantorovich seems to have here primarily in mind, rather than in general); and little can be said on this in an *a-priori* reasoning. But Kantorovich is on safer ground when arguing that, as often as not, non-linearities can be handled by treating outputs on various scales as technologically different, linear activities: especially so over time (though this may raise, in given conditions, the question of manageability of the plan-programme). By implication Kantorovich concedes the point of the critique made with regard to the 'ooos' of his original static construct concerning the zero value of commodities and resources unused in a given time segment:[1] but legitimately argues that in dynamics ways of 'storage' for carry-over from one plan period to another can be technically employed. No less defensible is his point that a dynamic treatment mitigates the instability of valuations which is likely to prevail under conditions of a current-planning model. Generally speaking Kantorovich grants in substance that 'objectively conditioned valuations' designed in his original model as short-run equilibrium prices

---

Englewood Cliffs, 1965, pp. 608 ff.). He shows how, in the *discrete* programming case, there are likely to arise efficient outputs which are not competitive (value-maximizing) outputs. The solution would be, conceptually, arbitrarily to break up the output of a homogeneous commodity into a sum of sub-outputs each assigned a different price. The snag for the central pricing authority is rightly pointed out.

[1] By V. S. Nemchinov in his Editorial Introduction to Kantorovich's *Ekonomicheskiy Raschet Nayluchshego Ispolzovanya Resursov, op. cit.*, p. 9.

See also Nemchinov's 'Teoreticheskiye voprosy mezhotraslevogo i mezhregionalnogo balansa proizvodstva i raspredelenya', in *Mezhotraslevoy Balans Proizvodstva i Raspredelenya Produtktsyi v Narodnom Khoziaystve*, Moscow 1962, pp. 31 ff.

would not necessarily agree with optimal solutions for the 'perspective' plan: it is therefore rather difficult to follow his argument—in a rejoinder to Novozhilov who made this point[1]—to the effect that sensitiveness of valuations, specifically of valuations of capital goods, to the impact of 'objectively justified disproportions connected with unforeseen technological progress [and] newly developed needs is [precisely] their virtue'.[2]

Whatever the limitations, the most important point is—and this may be stressed again here—that ever since the Kantorovich original, static model was presented, Soviet planning thought has been aware of the concept of a price as a tool of a 'sensitivity test', as a 'shadow' imputed in the optimand when made to obey given conditions with regard to resource availabilities and policy postulates. (Parenthetically, this concept has introduced Soviet planning theory to the idea of efficiency computation being analogous, in its rationale, with perfectly competitive processes.[3] We shall see in the following chapter how, by now, Soviet economic thought has adopted the concept of efficiency computation as one to be approximated by what is empirically feasible: note the analogy with the concept of perfect competition in Western thinking as a tool of reasoning.)[4]

The Soviet dialogue between the mathematical school and its opponents has focused largely on the question of the 'marginalist' versus the 'averagist' approach to price. The 'marginalist' nature of Kantorovich's solving multiplier price was the principal point brought

---

[1] Cf. V. V. Novozhilov, 'K diskusii o printsipakh planovogo tsenoobrazovanya', in *Primenenye Matematiki v Ekonomike*, Leningrad University, 1963, issue 1.

[2] *Op. cit.*, pp. 333 ff.

[3] In a recent paper J. Waelbroeck argues that by now the idea of equivalence of competitive equilibrium with the optimal use of resources is no longer the alpha and omega of the planning theory, and that further, the duality theorem which is the modern way of describing this equivalence, is an ideal which the planning and competitive economies alike should try to approach, rather than a realistic description of the way economies work ('La grande controverse sur la planification et la théorie mathematique contemporaine', in *Rationalité et Calcul Economique en URSS, Cahiers de l'ISEA*, Paris, February 1964). My stress would be on the planner's need to come as close as possible to this ideal.

[4] For an excellent discussion of the concept of perfect computation as related to the concept of perfect competition see P. J. D. Wiles, *The Political Economy of Communism*, esp. pp. 193 ff.

against his construct by Boyarskiy and others.[1,2] (Note: This is the terminology of the discussion in Soviet economics which partly reflects, and greatly adds to the conceptual confusion. Clearly what one could term marginalist programming is a particular case of *non*-linear programming where marginal calculus is applicable owing to the smoothness of the curves [differentiability of production surfaces]. What is opposed by Soviet traditionalists is a 'programming price' *sensu largo*, one corresponding to the solution of a constrained extremal problem. The label 'marginalism' is permissible in the context only if by convention it is to stand for the latter. It is employed here in this sense in so far as we adhere to confusing Soviet conventions.)

It has been argued, and I think correctly, that Marx had rejected explicitly the standpoints of Ricardo and Storch and maintained that only in exceptional cases—'ausserordentliche Kombinationen'—does the inferior producer (or for that matter the superior producer) set the price. Arguments from Marxist tradition apart, objections raised in the debate between the traditional 'averagist' and the 'marginalist' schools of thought are partly of an empirical and partly of a theoretical nature. Thus it has been contended[3] that the 'marginalist' price has no empirical support in what happens in the capitalist market, and has not been adopted as a pricing principle in Western nationalised industries (notably in Britain), an argument of little relevance for central computation of price, which would have to simulate an ideal

---

[1] Cf. Ya. A. Boyarskiy, *Planovoye Khoziaystvo*, 1960, no. 1. Particularly disturbing to critics have been the implications for wages: 'It is known that application of this marginalist conception to wages leads directly to John B. Clark's apologetic theory whose fallacy has been fully exposed by Marxist critique', *ibid*. (It may be parenthetically noted that as labour becomes increasingly a scarce factor and its regime increasingly one of a market-type a '000'-type price for it becomes increasingly a postulate of efficiency.)

On the other hand, the attitude of the traditionalist Soviet-Marxian school has some historical roots. The curiosum in the history of economic doctrines—the moralizers' attempt to 'impute virtue to partial derivatives'—is well discussed in W. J. Baumol, *Economic Theory and Operations in Analysis*, Prentice-Hall, 1965, p. 404.

[2] Academician A. N. Kolmogorov had still to argue a few years ago that 'there was no need to fear the traits of formal similarity between the mathematical apparatus of the Marxian theory of the socialist economy and, for instance, the theory of 'marginal utility' in the bourgeois political economy. This is accounted for by the generality of the mathematical apparatus for the solution of all variational problems. . . .' Cf. *Obshchiye Voprosy Primenenya Matematiki v Ekonomike i Planirovanyi*, USSR Academy of Sciences, Moscow, 1961, p. 189.

[3] Cf. Bronislaw Minc, *Zarys teorii kosztow produkcji i cen*, Warsaw, 1958, especially pp. 103 ff. and 138 ff.

rather than an imperfectly competitive system. No more relevant, and in any case open to argument, is the point that while 'marginalist' price has a definite socio-economic function under capitalism as a basis of policy of high prices, a high-price policy would not be acceptable for a dynamic socialist economy.

It has been argued further that the pace of contemporary technological progress entails a wide spread of cost differentials; that the coexistence of producing units with wide cost discrepancies is facilitated by the institutional framework of a socialist economy; and that the wider the discrepancies, the more 'capricious' and unworkable is the marginal price as the single price of the system.

The area of applicability of the 'marginalist' price has been usefully explored in Polish literature by Lipinski.[1] That to a Western economist some of his points sound like a re-statement of familiar Marshallian propositions does not detract from their relevance in the discussion.

He argues that no production costs, whether marginal or average, are of relevance *per se* for the very short run over which no adjustments are possible, due to any kind of bottlenecks under given factor conditions, and more or less rigid technologies. To this extent equilibrium prices will correspond to relative scarcities, or in so far as foreign trade can be and is resorted to, to world market relations. However, assuming a rationally working planned economy one would expect to find any capacity reserves in the inferior rather than the superior-producer area. (This is contested by some who contend that in a dynamic planned economy extra capacity should be available in the currently maturing additions, that is, in the technologically superior plant. But in any case experience seems to point to very high production unit costs in new plant, over a longish period after their commissioning.) If so, over the time-period in which the productive apparatus is a datum, it is the less efficient firm's costs that would have to be approximated. Where the production apparatus is the bottleneck, improvements may be desirable in order to expand output even at the inferior unit: a rational price policy precept would suggest then a margin over its unit cost, a margin co-measuring social gain from the expansion of its output compared with that of channelling resources to other products: for substitutes prices paid to producers would reflect relations of substitution. (The assumption throughout is linear or possibly linearised

[1] J. Lipinski, *Ekonomista*, 1958, no. 4 and 1963, no. 2.

cost functions.) The Lipinski price is conceived as a 'belt price'—a price corresponding to 'belts' of demand and located by a step-curve of successive practically feasible output increments.[1] It is then a price rather far from the smooth marginalist cost curve that has to be considered as a practical solution: as Dorfman-Samuelson-Solow succinctly remark, in the traditionalist analysis, the marginal cost-price concept stemmed from the idea of 'dosing' while in the 'programming approach it corresponds rather to a production function split into a finite number of activities, characterised by physical input-output relations of the machine age'.[2] This is the kind of reasoning which one will detect behind the price-precept formulated by the Polish Economic Council.'[3] In these recommendations what is seen as the short-run price-of-departure in manufacturing would correspond to the average unit-cost of the high-cost group of plants—totalling perhaps one-third of capacities—which have still to be operated to meet the planned demand for their output; this average would carry a charge proportionate to it and derived on a national scale so as to cover overheads, interest on fixed and working capital and some profit margin. The price structure would have a built-in check of international comparative advantage through the fixing of domestic prices of exportable raw materials—as suggested by Michal Kalecki in the mid-fifties—at world market prices converted at a rate of exchange which would be made realistic.

The point of criticism raised in Soviet literature that the programming price corresponds to a static equilibrium is valid as far as it goes (in Western writing Maurice Dobb[4] too expressed his reservation with

[1] Lipinski, *op. cit.*, pp. 781 ff.

[2] R. Dorfman, P. A. Samuelson, R. M. Solow, *Linear Programming and Economic Analysis*, New York, 1958, p. 141. In his recent exposition of the general mathematical foundations of the theory of programming Lange too, stresses the greater realism of the activity-analytical, as against the marginalist proper approach, in as much as the former abandons the assumption of differentiable production or cost functions (Oskar Lange, *Optymalne Decyzje-Zasady Programowania*, Warsaw, 1964, especially chs. IV and V).

[3] Cf. 'Tezy Rady Ekonomicznej w sprawie zasad ksztaltowania cen', in *Życie Gospodarcze*, 1957, nos. 51–52. The price-construct has never had the benefit of an empirical test.

[4] Maurice Dobb, 'The Discussion about Price-Policy Further Considered', in *Bulletin*, Centre des Pays de l'Est, Université Libre de Bruxelles, 1962, p. 165. In this paper (notable for the excellence of exposition of the problems involved) Dobb's reservations are underscored with regard to operational applicability of dynamic accounting prices. This is, I suspect, partly due to some misunderstanding caused by Kantorovich's lack of clarity on the point.

Maurice Dobb reverts to and expands his argument in a more recent paper ('Some

regard to the Kantorovich-type price on the ground that it would correspond to transitory situations). Clearly an opportunity cost-price for a *future* time-point must be one corresponding to a *future* equilibrium position.[1] The argument that the programming-type price as such is necessarily anti-dynamic rests on a misunderstanding.

Indeed the structural principle of the long-term plan price has been elaborated by now at least on the theoretical level. Broadly it is based on the idea of a time series of price-relations corresponding to efficient solutions for the successive time-intervals of the plan, and knit together by a time discount. In Drewnowski's[2] system too the long-term 'perspective' plan prices would be shaped in such a way as to equalise investment efficiency rates throughout the economy: in other words price relations would correspond to long-term relations of transformation, that is investment-efficiency relations (price relations for a future date would be obtained from the present relations through multiplying them by Drewnowski's sectoral coefficients of the 'purposefulness of investments'). Kantorovich's method[3] of reducing a dynamic 'ooos' system to a one-time basis also rests essentially on the same reasoning.[4] (The investment efficiency-rate is also employed as actualis-

Further Comments on the Discussion about Socialist Price-Policy', in *On Political Economy and Econometrics*, Warsaw, 1965). The point stressed is that the Kantorovich price system is employable only as one of the accounting prices since 'there cannot normally be two systems of actual prices coexisting for the same thing' (p. 84). But in Kantorovich operated prices are expected to coincide, as a rule, with the 'ooo's'."

[1] Since I wrote these words I found the point cogently argued by K. Porwit, 'Problem cen rachunku efektywnosci inwestycji' in M. Rakowski, ed., *Efektywnosci inwestycji*, Warsaw, 1963, p. 345. The obvious tenet is that the existing marginal, the least favourable that is, level of costs cannot be validly taken as applicable for future price relations.

The problem of the 'gap' between price and allocation theory, and between statics and dynamics in pricing, is extremely well discussed in Leif Johansen's, *Some Problems of Pricing and Optimal Choice of Factor Proportions in a Dynamic Setting* (Memo from Institute of Economics, University of Oslo, 11 August, 1966). As he shows there is in general no price system such that efficiency can be achieved when decisions are taken on the basis of *current* prices alone.

[2] J. Drewnowski, *Ekonomista*, 1962, no. 3, p. 536.

[3] Kantorovich, *op. cit.*, p. 293.

[4] The relation between prices and time discount is treated in a similar way *inter al.* by Malinvaud in an elegant analysis. The rate of interest is derived there from a 'dated' general price level. With the constant, undiscounted price $\bar{p}_{nt}$ of the last commodity taken as unity, the undiscounted price of the i-th commodity would be $\bar{p}_{it} = p_{it} - p_{nt}$.

Generally, a normalisation rule will give $p_{it} = \beta_t \bar{p}_{it}$ with the proportionality factor β_t. The rate of interest for the period will be:

$$r_t = \beta_t / \beta_{t+1} - 1$$

(E. Malinvaud, 'The Analogy between Atemporal and Inter-Temporal Theories of Resource Allocation', *Review of Economic Studies*, June 1961, p. 146).

ation rate in Kalecki's sketch of methodology of planning with variable prices.) I shall return to the matter in the context of investment-efficiency criteria (see chapter 13).

EXCURSUS ON THE UTILITY CONCEPT AND PRICE

Another point of the traditionalists' critique against Kantorovich is that he has tried to graft on to Soviet planning thought the concept of utility.[1] In fact in Kantorovich the objective function is formed by some postulated collection of commodities, postulated that is by the planner; and indeed the lack of explicitness as to the principle on which it has been formed leaves open, as it were, the question of the ultimate optimand.[2] As we shall see Nemchinov and others are trying to fill in the lacunae. This may justify a short excursus into what verges on the philosophy of the price as an instrument of the optimality-calculus in a planned economy.

If we may go rather far back into the history of the economics of socialism,[3] Lange of the thirties and the forties took upon himself the onus of demonstrating that the mechanism of a socialist economy can be put effectively, indeed more effectively than that of the capitalist economy, at the service of the welfare assumptions underlying perfect competition. (Pareto-optimality of competitive equilibrium.) The logical position on which his approach (and that of Bergson and Samuelson)[4] rested was the equality of the marginal rates of substitution and ratios of marginal utilities with the transformation rates in the input-output system. Lange at a later stage adopts the 'praxio-logical' interpretation of utility: he airs his doubts as to the validity of borrowing the principle of rational economy from the firm for the

---

[1] Cf. Ya. A. Kronrod's contribution to the discussion, *Vestnik Statistiki*, 1959, no. 9.

[2] Kantorovich's programme is optimal if no other programme secures greater consumption of *any* good (with given constraints); it is independent of either Pareto optimum or social-utility optimum, as usually defined. In Kantorovich output structure is fixed by the planner. The problem is one of choosing between output vectors $x, x', x'', \ldots$, where $x_i/x_j = x_i'/x_j' = x_i''/{}_j''x = \ldots$. The output vector x preferable to any other feasible x', if $x > x'$. Kantorovich's maximand is unique.

[3] Cf. O. Lange, *Econometrica*, 1942, pp. 215 ff. and his *Political Economy* (translation by A. H. Walker), London-Warsaw, 1963.

[4] See for reference footnote 3, p. 76. For an excellent discussion see also R. G. D. Allen, *Mathematical Economics*, London, 1963, pp. 722 ff.

consuming household, and of maximising intellectually construed magnitudes that evade empirical observation.[1,2]

Generally, the Polish and Soviet mathematical-planning schools started by strongly dissociating themselves from concepts anchored in the behaviouristic assumptions of welfare economics. The stress was that their approach does not involve them into a family relationship with any measuring of utilities, cardinal or ordinal or probabilistic: that they have nothing to do with any 'subjective' theory of value if only because theirs is a macro-approach.

Soviet 'modernists' of whom Nemchinov is representative could be located in the same class if understood sufficiently broadly. Nemchinov himself, as will be recalled, works with standards—'norms' of consumption imposed by the planner's fiat. In fixing them the planners would be expected to rely on 'scientific' principles, whatever this would mean: one would think that thereby an objective element is intended to be brought into the matter. Yet at the same time Nemchinov refers himself to households' scales of preferences (income and price elasticities of consumer's demand) for his retail market equilibrium.

The matter has found further articulation in recent Polish discussions. In earlier debates on the criteria of economic policies the production-possibilities curve in a centrally planned system was seen as confronted with the State's indifference curves determining the equilibrium position as the measure of collective welfare. Later Drewnowski[3] made explicit and analysed the co-existence and the simultaneity in operation of the two systems of preferences—those of the State and the consumers. The 'duality' of the system would be the general case, the operational areas of each of the two systems depending on social-economic institutions: under socialism the area ruled by

[1] The question of the validity domain of the basic theorem of welfare economics turns largely on that of certain exceptions on the production side (e.g. external effects and increasing returns to scale) and also, as it has been argued, on the preferences side (cf. M. Ellman, 'Individual preferences and the Market', forthcoming).

[2] As Professor Bergson notes the criterion of social welfare, in welfare economics, is today no less controversial than it was when the doctrine was in its infancy. Cf. his *Essays in Normative Economics*, Cambridge, Mass., 1966, p. 51 (the work offers an incisive *aperçu* of attempts to determine the criterion).

[3] J. Drewnowski, *Ekonomista*, 1962, no. 3. The distinction between variables of the State's preference function and those in the individual utility function is stressed also in Dr. Drewnowski's 'The Economic Theory of Socialism: a Suggestion for Reconsideration', *Journal of Political Economy*, August 1961. The crucial question to be answered is then that of the 'blending'.

consumer preferences would be a residual one. The analyst's focus is thus on the *revealed* system of preferences and little if any consideration is given to any utility concept behind it as such. (Since it is revealed *ex post*, can it form the basis of the perspective, very long-term plan?)

Moving further, Czerwinski in his inquiry into planned prices has developed[1] the concept of 'consumer's maximum choice', that is of choice operating within the output possibilities and within a residual area left when the requirements of the State for investment and collective consumption have been met. Hence consumer-goods prices are defined as optimal when they correspond to such a combination of these goods which consumers will like and be able to buy and which will satisfy their needs no less adequately than any other producible combination (the assumption is that of the weak axiom of revealed preferences, as elaborated by Samuelson and Houthakker). Mathematically stated the system of consumer-goods prices would then be this:

$\bar{p}$ would be optimal *if* and *only if*
$\mathrm{d}(\bar{p}) \in \mathcal{Z}$ (prices $\bar{p}$ are feasible equilibrium prices), and for any arbitrary $y \in \mathcal{Z}, \bar{p}'y \leqslant \Upsilon$ (the $\bar{p}'$ are prices of the 'maximum choice').

In other words the equilibrium prices $\bar{p}$ must be such that the demand expressed in the $\mathrm{d}(\bar{p})$, should be found within the $\mathcal{Z}$, the space that is of productive possibilities of the economy, allowance being made for resources earmarked by the planner to satisfy the priority claims of the public hand, including collective consumption. Further the price system $\bar{p}$ should be one of equilibrium in the sense that it should secure to the consumer the choice, from among all possible combinations, of the one most desired by him: that means that the most desired combination, some $y = \mathrm{d}(\bar{p})$ at prices $\bar{p}$ should be placed within the consumers' income Υ: it is in this sense that the prices set are those of the consumer's 'maximum choice'. (An alternative formulation for an optimal p would be that the demand at such prices $\mathrm{d}(p)$ should form the solution of a linear programme: maximise $\bar{p}'y = {}_j\Sigma_K\, p_j k_j$ subject to $y \in \mathcal{Z}$.) In this way the notion of 'consumer's sovereignty within the limits of production possibilities' has been evolved.

In the past year or two a similar train of thought has found a significant expression in Soviet literature, too: its notable formalisation has

[1] Z. Czerwinski, *Problematyka planowania cen w ujeciu matematycznem*, Poznan, 1963.

been produced by Volkonskiy.[1] The Volkonskiy construct is the criterion-maximand in efficient patterning of resources allocated by the planner to the consumption of households over a given period: it is a preference function, $u(x)$ applicable in short-term planning (on its adaptation for 'perspective planning' see below, p. 95). Volkonskiy's stress is on its 'objective' nature and validity on the macro-level only: the problem of aggregation of demand over individuals is disregarded[2]: its conceptual dissociation of the function from the utility notion is emphasised (though it displays an affinity with the stochastic-utility theory of Jacob Marschak and others). Its properties and place in planning can be briefly summarised as follows.

Let $p = (p_1, \ldots, p_n)$ be the price vector for n consumer goods and services and s the average expenditure per household or per head, satisfying the budget equation

$$\sum_{k=1}^{n} p_k x_k = s$$

which is the average money income (per household or head). By definition the actual structure of consumption, described by the vector $x = (x_1, \ldots, x_n)$, whose elements are commodity groups and possibly leisure, is a point of maximum for $u(x)$ subject to this equation. For planning purposes the $u(x)$ is conceived of as dependent on a set of parameters $a = (a_1, \ldots, a_m)$ characterising some factors likely to have a strong influence on its shape during the period under consideration: one of these parameters a_k could be simply time over which changes occur in the course of plan-fulfilment. The function thus takes the form of $u(x, a)$ (possibly it could be decomposed for specific commodity groups absorbing a fixed part of the budget, independent of the rest of the consumers' expenditure). For each consumption-unit there is then a collection (x, a) from among $(n+m)$ numbers, characterising the volumes of commodities consumed by it and the values of a which correspond to it. When each of such collections from $n+m$ numbers is represented by a point of a $(n+m)$ dimensional space (x, a) we have the

[1] V. A. Volkonskiy, 'Ob obyektivnoy matematicheskoy kharakteristike narodnogo potreblenya', in *Ekonomiko-matematicheskiye metody*, A. L. Vainshtein, ed., Moscow, 1963.
[2] The focus is on the aggregate consumption. It may be noted that W. M. Gorman ('Community Preference Fields', *Econometrica*, January 1953) has investigated the relation between the type of optimum considered and Pareto optimum. He proved that the necessary and sufficient condition for a given system of personal indifference maps to yield a unique community indifference map is that the personal Engel curves should be parallel straight lines for different individuals at the same prices.

distribution of consumers in this space. The (x, a) collections appear then as independent realisations of one random vector (ζ, α) whose distribution is the probability analogue of that of consumers in the space of points (x, a) (the (X, A)—where the symbols denote the average structure of consumption and average value of the parameter a—would be thus the mathematical expectation of the (ζ, α) vector).

In a general case the x_k would be expressed in some conventional units based, for instance, on constant prices: accordingly the price vector would possibly rest on an index of averaged prices for aggregated commodity groups. In this, use is made of Konyus's[1] ideas on the nexus between quantities of goods consumed and price-index weights; then some $U(x)$ would measure the minimised total expenditure necessary for securing consumption levels which correspond to the structure x_0 in base-year prices. When varying over time it will be written—as the 'indicator of consumption level'—in the form

$$U[x; a(t)] = \min \{\sum p_k y_k : u[y; a(t)] = u(x; a(t))]\}$$

(Here the $a(t)$ denotes parameters a at the time t, and the variable vector $y = (y_1, \ldots, y_n)$ replaces the x vector.)

In the treatment of separated homogeneous commodity groups physical-term measuring could be adopted. Then the maximum of $u(x)$ would be sought as constrained by $\sum p_k x_k$ and possibly also imposed 'scientific norms'—a matter of programming.

Worth noting may be the treatment of cases where effective demand is not met by supply. Here the x_k average is some quantity provided for the consumption unit: the consumption volume of the k-th commodity can be treated here as one of the parameters 'a' conditioning

---

[1] These ideas were first evolved by A. A. Konyus in the 1920s ('Problema istinnogo indeksa stoimosti', in the *Bulletin* of the Institute of Trade-cycle Research, 1924, nos. 9–10) and revived by him and adapted to the planning of effective demand, in the late 1950s ('Teoreticheskiy indeks tsen potreblenya i yego primenenye v planirovanyi platezhesposobnogo sprosa', in A. Vainshtein, ed., *Teoreticheskiye voprosy potreblenya*, *op. cit.*, and 'Consumer Price Index and Demand Functions', in *Revue de l'Institut International de Statistique*, vol. xxvi, 1958, 1/3).

In Konyus's argument the price index is considered as a tangential equation of the hyper-surface of indifference corresponding to consumption standards determined by the consumers' income in the base-year. With prices given for the considered plan-period, income, yielding consumption levels equal to those of the base-year, would be obtained for that period with the use of the price index. Thus hyperplanes of household budgets in different periods would appear as tangents of the same indifference hyper-surface. Hence (with constant consumption levels) the demand function, corresponding to the adopted index form, is derived.

the $u(x)$. The approach is close to that of Western inquiries of the early post-war period—especially those by Tobin and Houthakker[1] into the manner in which characteristics of demand functions, derivatives and elasticities with respect to price and income, are affected by partial, 'straight' rationing. Rationing in various forms—especially with regard to durables and housing—being a permanent socio-economic phenomenon, this approach is of considerable relevance for Soviet conditions. The consumer's preference scale thus appears 'dominated' by a constraint additional to that of basic assumption of the criterion-maximand; as noted, the criterion is conceived as operating only within the boundaries of resources set aside by the planner.[2] The assumption leaves beyond this frontier time preferences which are the absolute realm of the planner's sovereignty, not affected by whatever household saving there may be.

In trying to summarise the point reached we could say broadly that at the back of the minds of most of the new 'mathematical' schools there is some conception of a *social* welfare function (the emphasis being placed on the adjective)—a function vaguely akin to that of Bergson-Samuelson[3] type, one reflecting a consistent preference-ordering by a 'benevolent despot' (as put by Samuelson; or a 'Superman', as put by Little) which would accommodate in one way or another actual, of justifiable, preferences of households. The new Soviet articulation is particularly close to Bergson's most recent formulations of the welfare concept as applicable to the Soviet society: one

---

[1] Cf. J. Tobin and H. S. Houthakker, 'The Effect of Rationing on Demand Elasticities', *Review of Economic Studies*, 1950–51, no. 47.

[2] These and related problems are discussed by me in 'On the Objective Function for Soviet Economy' *Economica*, August 1965. I am submitting there that what the Soviet theory of demand is at this stage concerned with is the consumer's behaviour in a money economy of a particular class, one where purchasing power assigned to the consumption unit is in the nature of a generalised ration card of the type of the UK 'points' rations used in the last war.

[3] Cf. A. Bergson's 'A Reformulation of Certain Aspects of Welfare Economics'. *Quarterly Journal of Economics*, 1938, pp. 310 ff.; and 'Socialist Economics' in H. S. Ellis, ed., *Survey of Contemporary Economics*; and *Soviet National Income and Product in 1937*, New York, 1953, p. 44; P. A. Samuelson's *Foundation of Economic Analysis*, Harvard, 1957, ch. 8.

In his recent work (*The Economics of Soviet Planning*, New Haven—London, 1964), Professor Bergson adopts the proposition that consumers' welfare is supposed to be the concern where supplies of goods to current consumption may be made physically available to different households more or less independently (p. 9).

For an interesting discussion of the subject in the context of a war economy see E. Devons, *Essays in Economics*, London, 1961, p. 65.

based on utilities of individual households, allowance being made for collective preference-scales established by some political processes and possibly divergent from the former.

Indeed, a noteworthy development in the re-thinking of these problems is re-assimilation of utility concepts. The way for it has been paved by attempts to prove that the time-honoured opposition against this concept resulted from mis-reading of some of Marx's *obiter dicta*. (I shall not be concerned with this aspect.) Nemchinov's employment of the concept of use-valuation (discussed earlier) has been one of the stages of this re-assimilation.[1] Of interest here are the studies by two Soviet writers, Dudkin and Girsanov (discussed here in the chapter written jointly with Dr Mishan, pp. 39 ff). In this approach shadow prices characterise production which is optimal in the sense that they maximise social welfare.[2, 3]

COMPUTATION AND EMPLOYMENT OF THE PROGRAMMING PRICE

From our excursus we are coming back to the programming-type of price. Even some of those in Soviet economics who have accepted its logic have had doubts as to whether the 'shadows' are employable as operative prices as well as subsidiary instruments of calculation. Kantorovich himself answers this question in the affirmative. Indeed, one should think that for a planned system this answer stems from the logic of the solution. Nemchinov's answer is essentially the same though more qualified.

[1] Nemchinov accepted the Raiffa-Luce reasoning on the preference-utility logical sequence (see his 'Potrebitelnaya stoimost i potrebitelnye otsenki', in A. L. Vainshtain (ed.), *Narodnokhoziaystvennye Modeli-Teoreticheskiye Voprosy Potreblenya*, Moscow, 1963; reference to H. Raiffa and R. D. Luce, *Games and Decisions*, New York, 1957). 'Objectivizing' a course of action that is consistent with the decision-maker's own preference for 'consequences', expressed by numerical utilities and weights accorded to possible 'states of the world' expressed by numerical probabilities, would be thought of as an adequate theoretical approximation to the planner's problem (H. Raiffa and R. Schlaifer, *Applied Statistical Decision Theory*, Boston, Mass., 1961, p. vii). Cf. my 'On the Objective Function for the Soviet Economy', *op. cit.*

[2] Cf. R. Radner, *Notes on the Theory of Economic Planning*, Athens, 1963, p. 60; in his graphic argument, the feasible output with maximum welfare is the point at which an iso-welfare curve is tangent to the efficiency curve.

[3] By 1966 the differences between the average cost-plus price (in the meantime recommended for planning by the Scientific Council for Pricing Problems) and the "optimal price" inherent in "optimization planning" (as presented by N. P. Fedorenko *et. al.*) were found to be ultimately reducible to their fundamental theoretical bases: "while the former rests on the labour theory of value the latter is based on the theory of marginal utility" (Conference on the methodology of pricing as reported in *Voprosy Ekonomiki* no. 5, 1967, p. 153).

It is indeed here that the most forbidding obstacles are encountered. Kantorovich himself is certainly not unaware of the conflict between the conceptual rigour of his construct and practical possibilities. Since, so he argues, a fully fledged operational programming on the scale of national economy is still beyond the planner's reach, plan construction should start from a rough approximation to efficiency prices to be employed, imparting efficiency to the plan. And since direct evolving of a whole system of the 'ooos' is empirically inconceivable as yet, the point of departure in plan-building should be a set of basic prices for factors and a small number of key commodities obtained from a tightly aggregated linear programming macro-model and then expanded with a good dose of common sense and intuitive judgement. This suggestion is vulnerable to criticism on what seems to be an obvious point of its weakness: since the prices of the few selected commodities themselves are bound to be influenced by the whole prevailing system of price-cost relations, and thereby vitiated as it were *ab initio*, what chance is there that they will provide a basis of an optimal-price structure? The suggestion violates the principle of 'simultaneity' on which the very solution for efficiency-parameters intrinsically rests. The alternative suggested is to treat the plan in actual operation as if it were optimal and try to obtain from its analysis a set of rough approximations to the ooos, but here the snag is—how to trace the path of optimality adjustments.

On the conceptual plane it is a matter of convenience whether one chooses to solve the primal or the dual. On the empirical plane there is something to the argument of some Soviet critics of the Kantorovich 'gamma' approach—Boyarskiy[1] and others—that the planning procedures suggested suffer from circularity: efficient 'ooo'-type prices would be obtained as the imputed dual of an efficient programme and the 'best' programme would be obtained by testing it, for efficiency, with the aid of this kind of parameters. In this predicament Soviet 'planometricians' are divided against themselves. Some insist that optimal prices could and should be derived as a solution of the optimal plan model and they reject the idea of a separate 'pricing model'. Another school of thought maintains that far from obviating it, an optimal macro-plan requires an optimal system of planned price formation, connected with 'value' and through final demand, with 'use value'.

[1] Cf. A. Boyarskiy, *Matematiko-ekonomicheskiye Ocherki*, Moscow, 1962, p. 367.

The principal representative of the latter trend in thinking is Nemchinov. It was his tenet—expressed in several works[1]—that from a cybernetical point of view prices contain two 'codes' of information: one is as it were the vehicle of quantities of social-labour value and according to this code prices are formed at the 'value' (one could say labour-theory value) level; the other code carries information on 'use value' implying social assessment of scarcities. According to the latter code prices deviate from 'value', the deviations being confined to the 'surplus product' in the Marxist sense. This is then the process dealt with in the pricing model.[2] It presupposes the existence of a plan determining the optimal *physical* structure of production based on selection of technologies: Nemchinov's pricing model, or rather a sketch of its 'contours', seems to focus at this moment the Soviet debate on the 'mathematical' price. A closer look at it therefore may be profitable for our purpose. The first 'contour' starts by determining the full labour-input coefficients from the Leontief-Dmitriev iteration equation $\tau_j = \sum_i a_{ij}\, \tau_i + t_j$; in terms of matrix algebra we have for full 'labour intensity' $\tau = t\,(I-A)^{-1}$. (Notation a_{ij} = technological coefficients of current inputs, including depreciation and imports; t_j = the row of labour-intensity coefficients, τ_i = transposed row of full labour-intensity coefficients; τ_j = branch row coefficient of full labour-intensity: t = vector of labour-intensity: τ = vector of full labour-intensity.)

At the next step full labour-intensity is expressed in terms of 'simple' labour. The row-vector of labour-inputs in these terms, t'_j, would be obtained either from wage differentials or cost differentials in training for skills. Then socially necessary labour is derived with reference to a matrix $[Q_{ij}]$ describing consumption of the i-th commodity by workers employed in the j-th branch and their dependents. Nemchinov's coefficients of consumption per unit of simple labour in the j-th branch (required for the calculation of the necessary-labour expenditure) appear then as $h'_{ji} = Q_{ij}/T'_j$, the denominator showing total labour input in the j-th branch. A matrix $[h_{ij}t'_i]$ describing consumption in terms of simple labour is obtained through post-multiplying the matrix

[1] For Nemchinov's view see his *Ekonomiko-matematicheskiye metody i modeli*, Moscow, 1962, pp. 284, 285; for a recent critique of this view cf. M. Fedorovich, *Planovoye Khoziaystvo*, 1964, no. 1, p. 8.
[2] V. Nemchinov, *Voprosy Ekonomiki*, 1963, no. 12. The argument was subsequently expanded in Nemchinov's 'Osnovnyie kontury modeli planovogo tsenoobrazovanya', *Problems of Economic Dynamics and Planning*, Warsaw, 1964.

of the h_{ij} coefficients by a diagonal matrix of simple-labour expenditure. Further on (following a procedure applied by Morishima-Seton)[1] the exchange process of commodity—against-commodity and of labour—against subsistence means is mathematically expressed by an iteration formula

$$\sum_i a_{ij}\tau'_i + e_0 \sum_i h_{ij}\tau'_i = \tau_j$$

I shall say more about the e_0—the coefficient of 'surplus product', which is meant to correlate the 'physical' contents of national income —and household consumption.

The actual prices of consumer goods—retail market prices—are thought of in the same way as they are in Soviet practice as those corresponding to an overall purchasing power budget. It equates the product prices times quantities with the sum-total of elements of the population's purchasing power.

To be more specific, in Nemchinov's model consumer-goods prices are determined at the level of household budgets with reference to what he terms the use valuation [potrebitelnaya otsyenka] measured by means of each of three parameters, which are:

(1) the coefficient of 'saturation [nasyshchenye] of needs', μ_i, a ratio of actual consumption of the i-th commodity to some perspective 'norm' —saturation standards assumed to be 'objectively', 'scientifically' derived and prescribed for the plan's horizon.

(2) the coefficient of 'intensity of needs', η_{ij}, relating the price of the saturation standards of the i-th commodity to the purchasing power of the j-th consumption unit. The degree of intensity when determined at the level of economy as a whole, η_i, is being related to either total purchasing power or, if expressed in full-order labour input of the i-th commodity, to total labour resources.

(3) the coefficient of price and income elasticity of demand $E = \Delta \ln x_{ij}/\Delta \ln s_j$; the Δx_{ij} denotes the j-th consumer's incremental expenditure on the i-th need, and Δs_j the increment in price or budget-income.

The 'use' valuation would be then expressed by an exponential function with each of these parameters as exponents $u(\eta_1) = e^{1-\eta_i}$: $u(\mu_i) = e^{\mu_i - 1}$ and $u(E_i) = e^{1/E - 1}$. Its expression by means of the three

---

[1] M. Morishima and F. Seton, 'Aggregation in Leontief Matrices and the Labour Theory of Value', Econometrica, April 1961.

parameters simultaneously is suggested as a linear combination of the form

$$\theta_i = a_i + b_i\eta_i + c_i\mu_i + d_i . \mathrm{1}/E_i$$

the coefficients of this equation a, b, c, d being evaluated by the method of least squares from data of household-budget inquiries. (The θ_i is envisaged for an optimised system of production and consumption; the $u(\theta_i)$ would then be proportional to 'social cost' of the i-th commodity in terms of 'socially necessary labour'.)

Such parameters are treated as expressing deviation from 'labour-theory value'.[1] So are wholesale prices. A wholesale price, which is broadly the inter-industry price for the i-th commodity is taken to be dependent on quantities produced X_i and socially required Z_i: the coefficient of 'proportional deviation' would depend on the degree of 'saturation of the use potential' (*nasyshchenye potrebitelnoy sily*), $\eta_i = Z_i/K_i$ and have the form of $K^0 (\eta_i) = \mathrm{e}^{1-ni}$.

It will be noted that in the course of Nemchinov's exercise, the Marxist concept of socially necessary labour has itself been fundamentally revised to mean such minimised inputs of factors as would correspond to an *efficient* resource allocation. The choice of the extremal, the optimal value that is of the coefficient e_0—seen as a saddle-point—would be made for each of the plan years by reference to a programme: which, let us say, would be made to obey the postulate of a maximum living-standard subject to a minimum full-order input of 'simple' labour per unit of gross output.

In the Nemchinov process of 'transformation of value', let us add, the one factor world is being abandoned; factors other than labour

[1] The problem of this 'deviation' is treated in an original way in a chain-reaction model designed by Plyukhin and Nazarova ('Upravlayemaya tsepnaya reaktsya rasshirennogo vosproizvodstva v odnosektornoy i dvusektornoy modelyakh', in *Primenenye matematiki v ekonomicheskikh issledovanyakh*, V. S. Nemchinov, ed., vol. ii, *op. cit.*, p. 375), a model postulating a 'law of preservation of value' in the work processes. In a three-dimensional space axes denote endowment in manpower, fixed-capital stock and materials. A vector of labour-theory prices emanates from a fixed origin shared with two other factors, those of resource availability and of 'k's', kinetic prime-factor valuations for balanced growth. When the course of balanced growth, corresponding to given technological relations, is acutely upset due to manpower shortage, the k-ray becomes colinear with the manpower axis. If next the manpower bottleneck is eased while the supply of materials tightens, the resource-vector turns in space—its end-point comes close to the coordinate fixed capital-plane while that of the k's approaches the materials coordinate. It is only in the intuitively obvious case where the labour-theory price vector rests along the resource axis that it coincides with that of the k's.

appear with an explicit opportunity claim to product: profits are related to man-made resources and obtained from a matrix of full capital coefficients, after differential rents for scarce natural resources have been deducted. We are thus back in the world of Kantorovich's 'ooos'.[1] Its organising concept is that of mirroring relative scarcities, and it is this concept that forms the link between the wholesale price and the consumption price. It is indeed a feature of the pricing model that, in contrast to the traditional Soviet approach, both are integrated in one system and the system is based on consumption price. (With an eye to the theoretical background one will notice that in the fundamental contour the household consumption is conceived of, very much as in von Neumann's construct, as part of the productive cycle—the ultimate input of the system, the output being socially necessary labour.)

True, a student unaccustomed to the conventional frame and mode of Soviet thinking in these matters is likely to find the build-up of the argument around deviation from labour-theory of value a superfluous burden.[2] Yet the tradition of Soviet practice as well as theory being what it is, the approach has its purpose. This granted—and granted generally its didactic and heuristic virtues—as an indication of the

---

[1] See pp. 62 ff.

[2] In Soviet economics a good deal of effort is still being put into attempts towards reconciliation of Marx's theory of value with the efficiency-price. Academician Novozhilov devoted to such an attempt his latest paper on the 'labour theory of value and mathematics' (*Voprosy Ekonomiki*, 1964, no. 12).

Novozhilov returns to the subject in his 'Model Obshchestvenno Neobkhodimogo Truda' (*Matematiko-Ekonomicheskiye Problemy*, Leningrad, 1966). He argues that the prevailing tenet that the socially necessary labour-time is determined by the average expenditure of labour under 'socially normal' conditions does not exhaust Marx's teaching on the subject; that it fully applies to those economic conditions where prices gravitate towards value.

It is only fair to note that the futility of these exercises is now being stressed also by at least some Soviet economists. Lurie (*O Matematicheskikh Metodakh Reshenya Zadach na Optimum pri Planirovanyi Sotsyalisticheskogo Khoziaystva*, op. cit., p. 258 fn.) criticises Kantorovich's exercise in his classical work and points out that the proof of the agreement of the ooos with 'average labour cost' is obtained by resorting to an artificial *numeraire* of 'averaged labour'. The argument is expanded in A. Lurie, *Voprosy Ekonomiki*, no. 7, 1966.

There is little one can add, I think, to Leontief's words written decades ago: 'The modern theory of prices does not owe anything to the Marxist version of classical labour theory of value; nor can in my opinion profit from any attempts towards reconciliation or mediation between the two types of approaches' (W. Leontief, 'The Significance of Marxist Economics for Present-Day Economic Theory', op. cit., p. 5).

route to be followed in planning it raises serious doubts and objections.

Some of them have been put forward in support of methodology and algorithm for price calculation offered by a representative of the other school of the two schools mentioned, Zakharov.[1] The practicable base of departure in the construction of the price structure, he argues, can be only the actually-implemented rather than any 'mythical optimal' plan and he sees the rescue from the formidable difficulty in a computer-stations network linking the planning centre with enterprises (via regional, 'sovnarkhoz', authorities) and enterprises among themselves: the system would handle the multi-way information traffic flows, would process the data and provide parameters. It would start from prices as operated, and technological coefficients characterising the physical-term structure of production and distribution, including labour-input and capital coefficients. The role of the key-parameter is reserved for the latter as translated into the coefficient of efficiency of 'productive funds' or 'profit' per one rouble-worth of these funds. Once re-calculation of prices corresponding to the existing 'environment' at a given moment has been completed—that is once the series of successive approximation has brought prices and all other 'intermediate' indices to their equilibrium values—the Gosbank would fix the valuation of each enterprise's assets (and would accordingly perceive the charge for their employment). Step by step integrated systems of nation-wide single prices of factors and single product prices (*loco* consuming unit) would be evolved, the substitution effect of commodities—in production and consumption—being determined by some methods of appraisal of comparative 'use values' (the methods, it is admitted, are still in their infancy). Further series of successive approximation would be expected to yield perspective prices *pari passu* with optimisation of plan variants of development, from one period to another. The process itself of this dynamic optimisation has not been described, which is but one of several points of vagueness which inhibit an analysis in depth.

Coming back again for a moment to Kantorovich's model, for a very-long-term plan he goes still further away from his fundamental conceptual postulates: for such a plan the planner would have to do with a system of 'normal valuations' as a rough approximation to a dynamic valuation. The perspective plan, he argues, needs the lesser exactitude the more remote its horizon: it should be elaborated with

---

[1] S. Zakharov, *Voprosy Ekonomiki*, 1964, no. 5.

more and more precision as a given time-interval is approached; and this should apply also to its key economic indices, the 'ooo' prices, which should gradually be given a greater measure of 'concreteness' and precision. Indeed it is the use of such prices that would add to flexibility and help plan-adjustments. This is a tenable proposition: in fact it lies on the line of the observable shift towards the continuous —'rolling' or 'sliding'—planning, planning with a moving horizon.[1]

However, even when the 'rolling' planning method is adopted the problem of a continual issue of parameters does not appear to be solved. In so far as the Gosplan's programme should be thought of as a functional substitute for that other computing mechanism, the perfect market of the market-socialism models, it must *currently* supply equilibrium choice-parameters as effectively as the latter would do (in their theoretical blue-prints). There is doubtless a common-sense postulate of reconciling efficiency requirements with a minimum stability in the choice-calculation, and, therefore, in its price framework. But if prices are to serve as dependable instruments of efficient choice-making, while derived from the 'perspective' plan-programme, and thus being parameters of the future, they must correspond also to *current* equilibria positions. In providing them, time must be treated as a continuum—as it is 'handled' by the alternative computing mechanism, the market—rather than as made up of the usual longish plan-periods.

The accent on these aspects has led to some re-thinking in Poland— notably by Jan Lipinski[2]—of price as the economical carrier of ('external') information adequate for choices consistent with criteria of social utility, and of its thereby determined role as coordinator in decision-making. It is argued that intrinsically the theoretical model of a socialist economy reduces itself ultimately to one of monopolies, vertical and/or horizontal, which form the objective limit to decentralisation and inhibit both function of prices.[3] (It may be noted in the context that while the virtue of decentralised decision-making is the access to a greater volume and better quality of specialised information, there arises the problem of a possible conflict with prices set centrally as carriers of information available at the centre.)

[1] See p. 98.
[2] Jan Lipinski, *Ekonomista*, 1964, no. 2.
[3] This school favours an empirical examination of relative information loads entailed in obtaining efficiency prices on the one hand, and in centralised planning based on physical-term data on the other.

Another Polish school (Zielinski and Wakar)[1] in a sense draws extreme consequences from this reasoning. It too endorses the proposition of a price obtained from a 'market of shadows' as the one able to secure optimality. Its emphasis is, however, on the submission that strict observance of the rules of the game, which conditions efficiency of choices based on such prices, is not feasible, and that prices fail to provide all the information necessary for these choices. At any rate in the view of this school there is little chance that the planner will have at hand operative efficient parameters in a foreseeable future, which by itself would commend reconciling himself to a second-best solution, that of 'direct calculation'. The latter would be essentially a physical-quantity calculation working with the postulated final outputs, capacities, labour availabilities and technical coefficients. For both the planners and the firms, prices in this solution are seen as having no true parametric character: prices would be employed instead as a secondary tool of command transmission, incentive prices that are moderately active, tailored to a given system of success indicators. Parameters are defined as being 'true' if they correspond to the optimal solution and are employed in the construction of the plan and also by firms in their calculations. In the model they are essentially passive in the build-up of the plan; they do not serve the improvement of the plan in its implementation (note that one of the characteristics of the model is that there is no verification of techniques). Nor do prices permit the firms to decipher the plan's proportion. It is in the sense described that the model is considered as a non-parametric one. The non-parametric nature of the planning model predetermines the degree of devolution in decision-making.

The signal point about the Zielinski-Wakar construct is that while starting from the postulate of a 'programming' efficiency-price, it ends up by accepting what in substance is but an idealised version of the Soviet-type model in actual operation (cf. opening remarks to this chapter). This has been pointed out in fact, in the Polish discussion, by several critics (Pohorille, Hagemajer, Sulmicki, Pajestka).[2,3] At

---

[1] See R. Bauer, J. Beksiak, S. Dulski, S. Gora, S. Nowacki, A. Wakar, J. G. Zielinski, *Zarys Teorii Gospodarki Socjalistycznej*, Warsaw, 1965, esp. part II.A. See also A. Wakar and J. Zielinski, 'Socialist Operational Price System', *American Economic Review*, March 1963.

[2] On these discussions cf. Z. Bosiakowski, *Ekonomista*, 1963, no. 6, pp. 1206 ff.

[3] Jan Lipinski returns to the problem in his latest paper (*Ekonomista*, 1965, no. 1) and weighs up the virtues of the two alternatives:

least one of them emphasised what has been brought out by experience, that the quasi-parametric role of prices cannot be eliminated if only because the planner refers himself to draft-proposals from firms and, in turn, firms base themselves on price calculations as well as on physical-term directives from the centre (cf. our discussion on p. 60). None of these points, however, disposes of reservations as to the empirical obstacles to the alternative—'indirect'—calculation through the 'shadow market'. Paradoxically, while some defenders of the 'direct' calculus solution stress its Marxist elements (B. Minc), some of the critics read between the lines of the analysis implications closer to von Mises, and they do so, we believe, with at least as good reason. Whether the chances for an efficient-price tool for managing planned systems are no brighter than would appear from this analysis, I do not feel qualified to commit myself. (The father of programming in the West, Professor Dantzig, believes that students of the arts of decision making are about to witness the start of an explosion![1]) What is reasonable to think is that if pessimism at this degree is justified, the scope for devolution in decision-making of Soviet-type economies, imperative as it may be owing to the increasing complexity of choices, would be rather circumscribed.[2] (The issue of decentralisation versus centralism as related to the parametric framework and the regime of guidance is discussed in Appendix to chapter 10.)

(a) full centralisation of choice: with the existing level of planning techniques that entails reconciling oneself to the Wakar-Zielinski kind of direct calculation and giving up the verification of economic rationality of production techniques (technical coefficients);

(b) a degree of decentralisation of choice at the level of plan-drafting and ultimate decision-making: that entails relying, for choice-making, on a price which at best conveys to the basic operating unit approximate information only on external conditions.

In either case non-efficient solutions result for the economy as a whole: the employment of prices based on limited information as parameters of choice may be then justified only where the choice of technological solution thus arrived at yields larger final output than that secured by means of the direct-calculation alternative.

[1] G. B. Dantzig, 'New Methods in Mathematical Planning', *Proceedings of the Second International Conference on Operational Research, op. cit.*, p. 284.

[2] In contemporary Polish writing the market solution for the socialist system is discussed in an illuminating way by W. Brus. Cf. his *Problemy funkcjonowania gospodarki socjalistycznej*, Warsaw, 1961; see also my review of this book in *Economica*, November 1961.

A quasi-market solution, as a possible alternative for the Soviet economy, was adumbrated—for the first time over decades—by Nemchinov in *Kommunist*, 1964, no. 5.

APPENDIX I TO CHAPTER 6

Soviet theoretical work has centred on attempts, on the one hand, to generalise the Kantorovich-Lagrange type of the solving-multiplier price and, on the other, to adjust it to the role of an instrument of parametric planning and control. Following Lurye,[1] several students, notably Tyurin,[2] Golanskiy[3] and Belayev,[4] have broadly designed discrete non-linear systems and algorithms for the quantification of their solving multipliers.

The dominating contribution in the field is that by Academician Kantorovitch: he investigates—jointly with Makarov[5]—the nature of the dynamic price which he sketched out in his previous work (cf. p. 57) and the implications of the shift from the static to a dynamic price system.

Concern with the practicability of the efficiency-price construct has stimulated exploration of its relationship with the 'price of production'. In the light of experiments carried out in the Academy's computing centre, Belkin[6] maintains that the latter has proved to be the relatively closest approximation to the former among those which, at the present stage, are informationally and computationally manageable. From this angle Volkonskiy's formulation of the 'production price' *under optimum* (note our emphasis) is of immediate interest.[7] His statement can be summarised as follows. We have a plan-programme:

$$C(x) = \max, \text{ subject to}$$

$$z_t = L_t y_t + x_t; \quad t = 0, 1, \ldots, T;$$

$$z_{t+1} = z_t + A_t y_t - B_t z_t + h_t$$

$$x_t, y_t, z_t > 0$$

[1] A. L. Lurye, *O Matematicheskikh Metodakh Reshenya Zadach na Optimum pri Planirovanyi Sotsyalisticheskogo Khoziaystva, op. cit.*

[2] Yu. M. Tyurin, 'Matematicheskaya formulirovka uproshchennoy modeli proizvodstvennogo planirovanya', *Ekonomika i Matematicheskiye Metody*, no. 3, 1965.

[3] N. M. Golanskiy, 'Raschetnye otsenki i tsenoobrazovanye', *ibid.*, no. 3, 1966.

[4] L. S. Belayev, 'Model planirovanya razvitya sotsyalisticheskogo khoziaystva', *ibid.*, no. 4, 1966.

[5] L. V. Kantorovich, V. L. Makarov, 'Optimalnye modeli perspektivnogo planirovanya', *op. cit.*

[6] V. Belkin *et al.*, 'Ischislenye ratsyonalnykh tsen na osnove sovremennoy ekonomicheskoy informatsyi', in *Ekonomika i Matematicheskiye Metody*, no. 5, 1965.

[7] V. A. Volkonskiy, 'Skhema optimalnogo perspektivnogo planirovanya i otsenki resursov', in V. S. Nemchinov, ed., *Primenenye Matematiki v Ekonomicheskikh Issledovanyakh*, vol. 3, *op. cit.*, p. 100.

Then for any set of technologies, $\mathcal{J}$, we have the cost price under optimum:

$$\sum_{j \in J} (\hat{p}_{t+1}A_t)^j y^j = \sum_{j \in J} (\hat{q}_{t+1}L_t)^j y_t^j = \hat{q}_{t+1}z_t^J$$

$$= (\hat{p}_{t+1}B_t) + \hat{p}_t(v_{t+1} - v_t)/v_t + (\hat{p}_t - \hat{p}_{t+1})z_t^J$$

Notation: *Vectors:* z_t = resources employed, y_t = activity levels, x_t = consumption (households and social), h_t = exogenous increment in resources over period $(t, t+1)$; *Matrices:* L_t = resource employment with various techniques, B_t = use-up of resources including processing and wear-and-tear and obsolescence (diagonal matrix), A_t = input-output, $C(x)$ = optimand. Further $\hat{}$ denotes normalisation so that $\hat{p}_t = v_t p_t$ and $\hat{q}_t = v_t q_t$ where v_t is some scalar magnitude. Thus $z_t^J = \sum_{j \in J} L_t^j y_t^j$.

Optimality price, stated in such terms appears then to be formed of three components: (1) cost of current inputs plus amortisation; (2) 'efficiency' of capital resources employed in the economy, at a uniform rate of $\Delta v_t/v_t$, and (3) 'compensation' of gain-positive or negative—from price change over time. Where prices p_t are constant the (3) becomes zero: in that case the p_t is built up on the principle of the 'production price', and—so it is suggested by Volkonskiy—the Belkin construction becomes relevant. Two observations, however, seem to us legitimate. *First*, as far as one can see, in the Belkin experiment only a part of the price was derived from a programme: his 'production price' is then not necessarily one at optimum. *Secondly*, the Kantorovich-Makarov explorations throw significant light on the two kinds of prices. They show that while when expressed in terms of 'production prices' incremental costs are distributed in accordance with the *first*-order, when stated in 'ooos they reflect the *full*-order use-up of resources and their structure. For the two prices to coincide, a number of strong conditions would have to be met: the sets of both the plan 'ingredients' and technologies would have to be invariable over time; the system would have to be mathematically closed or its exogenous vectors would have to be identical with its growth-rate; the system would have to be in a von Neumann equilibrium—a combination which could hardly ever be expected to materialise. The production-price concept appears particularly inadequate for pricing of joint products and new products, for the calculation of depreciation and pricing of capital goods with long gestation.

Others have stressed (in agreement with the point made by us here), that to correspond to the efficiency postulate prices have to be *currently* supplied from the planning centre. To avoid a continuous cobweb-type pursuit of instantaneous equilibrium, it is argued, what at best can be expected from a pricing methodology is to secure a gravitation of prices towards the economy's optimal dynamic trajectory: a minimised deviation from it would be the criterion of their adequacy.[1] (Academician Novozhilov[2] has examined the limitations of what he defines as informational capacity of the price at the macro-level of the planned system).

Suppose, however, that the Belkin construct is—as it is claimed to be—the best that the central planner is able to provide to the micro-level, which is a plausible contention.[3] (Makarov[4] has subsequently argued though that where there is no problem of selection of an optimal plan, what he terms a 'self-recoupment price' would do better.) The question still has to be answered (empirically?) as to whether the workable second-best price is not too far from the optimal to be dependable. It is then on this answer that turns also the viability—practical as distinct from theoretical—of parametric guidance and indirect centralism.[5,6]

[1] N. M. Golanskiy, *op. cit.*

[2] V. V. Novozhilov, 'Problemy planovogo tsenoobrazovanya i reforma upravlenya promyshlennostyu' *in Ekonomika i Matematicheskiye Metody*, no. 3, 1966.

[3] For a valuable appraisal of the present possibilities in the build-up of programming-type prices, in the light of Hungarian experiments, see Gyorgy Simon 'Ex-post examination of macro-economic shadow prices', *Economics of Planning*, no. 3, 1965.

[4] Cf. Makarov's contribution to a Seminar, *Ekonomika i Matematicheskiye Metody*, no. 4, 1966, p. 625. The price construct is described as one based on the 'exchange equivalence' as between branches. The description is not clear enough to permit its appraisal.

[5] When this book was in proof I learnt, thanks to Dr Kyn, about experiments carried out in Czechoslovakia in the mid-sixties by him, Sekerka and Hejl, parallel to those by Belkin *et al.* (described and analysed in O. Kyn, B. Sekerka, L. Hejl, *A Model for Planning of Prices*, Prague, 1966?). The types experimented with include the labour-theory-of-value price, the 'production price' and what is denoted as the 'F-income price' (with a uniform rate of income as related to capital). In particular the production price has the form

$$p = v(I-A)^{-1} \{I - \rho K(I-A)^{-1}\}^{-1}$$

where the $v(I-A)^{-1}$ is the vector of full wage cost and the $K(I-A)^{-1}$ the matrix of full capital-output coefficients: the ρ parameter denotes the economy's averaged rate of profit. The production price appears as a 'mix' of the value price and the income price; the latter is determined by the equation

$$p\{I - \rho K(I-A)^{-1}\} = 0$$

(the ρ is the inverse of the characteristic root of the matrix of full-order capital-output coefficients).

As can be seen, the Czechoslovak experiments work with the simple, consistency-securing Leontief type apparatus. Indeed Dr Kyn and his associates think that sophisticated optimisation is not accessible at this stage; they refuse to share the opinion that the mathematisation of pricing techniques could 'enable such exact calculations of prices of all important products, as to make it possible to set these prices centrally as binding for all enterprises' (p. 2). Our reader will note the implications of these findings for our argument on the workability of what in our conceptual frame is indirect centralism (see Appendix to ch. 10).

[6] In a sense this is where the famous question of 'millions of equations', raised one-third of a century ago by Lord Robbins (*The Great Depression*, London, 1934) stands today for the indirect variant of centrally planned socialist economy.

APPENDIX II TO CHAPTER 6

The usefulness and meaning for a socialist planning theory of the utility notion—which, as we have seen, has returned to Soviet economics in the wake of the empirical investigation of the consumer's behaviour [1]—remains one of the areas of controversy among Soviet economists. Its protagonists and opponents can be broadly identified as those connected with the mathematical school and with the traditionalists; but, and as is only to be expected, there are varying nuances on both sides. On the traditionalist wing Maslov [2] would contend that in so far as in a Soviet-type society sharp income differentiation is absent, the theory of elasticities has little meaning for it (he reworks the elasticity index for socialism); and that continued rise in incomes and decline in prices deprive the indifference curve of significance. In the opposite camp a distinguished exponent of a utility-type concept, Konyus, [3] maintains that in fact the indifference-curve apparatus permits consumption theory to dispense with conceptions of marginal utility theory in so far as it aspires to the solution of fundamentals of the theory of value (Konyus, to recall (cf. p. 75), bases his own function on his price index applied for the construction of the indifference curve in tangential coordinates; an alternative design of the function, linking up with some Slutskiy propositions and akin to that by Tsujimura, [4] is that offered by Volkonskiy: it is based on the solution of problems of relative maximum).

On the other hand, as will be noticed, the Harrod-Frisch approach has inspired the tackling of the problem of time preference in the model experimented with in Soviet perspective planning. Harrod, to recall, works with the elasticity of diminishing marginal utility of income schedule understood by him as some weighted average for the community. [5] The authors of

[1] For a good, analytical presentation of Soviet advance in this field see V. V. Shvyrkov, *Ekonomiko-Matematicheskiy Analiz Potrebitelskogo Sprosa*, Moscow, 1966.

[2] In a paper 'Kriticheskiye zamechanya po teoreticheskim voprosam potreblenya' summarized in *Ekonomika i Matematicheskiye Metody*, no. 3, 1965, p. 467. For his concept of elasticity adjusted for the needs of a socialist society see P. P. Maslov, 'Nekotoryie puti vospolzovanya koeffitsyenta elastichnosti potreblenya', in *Primenenye Matematiki v Ekonomicheskikh Issledovanyakh*, vol. 2.

[3] A. A. Konyus, *Metodologicheskiye Voprosy Izuchenya Urovnya Zhizni Trudyashchikhsya*, Moscow, 1959, p. 180. In his recent paper, Konyus argues in terms of a dialectical process: 'It was noticed as early as the 'twenties that the marginal utility theory is the opposite (negation) of the labour theory of value. The negation of the thesis of departure (the antithesis) is a necessary stage of development. When brought to its conclusion it enriches the thesis of departure' ('Trudovaya teorya stoimosti i ekonometrika', in *On Political Economy and Econometrics, op. cit.*, p. 244.

[4] K. Tsujimura, 'Family Budget Data and the Market Analysis', The International Stat. Institute, 32nd Session, Tokyo, 1960.

[5] R. Harrod, 'Presidential Address', *The Economic Journal*, September 1963.

Soviet perspective plan model, Gavrilyets, Mikhalevskiy and Leibkind[1] employ in their objective function a concept playing the same role under the name of 'elasticity of marginal effect in the use of a final-product unit'. Can the adoption of this function, and indeed of the whole Harrod apparatus, be understood as sharing the view that a utility concept, specifically a cardinal-utility concept, is imperative in the consideration of a dynamic system?[2] (The view, of course, is far from common consensus among Western utility theorists; cf. e.g., Morishima.[3])

It is not always easy to pin down Soviet economists working with the utility-type concepts as to what kind they actually have in mind. In his paper on the rate of interest, Mikhalevskiy—a co-author of the Soviet model we have just mentioned[4]—works with his 'effect function' and refers himself to Koopmans-Diamond-Williamson[5] on the preference ordering of consumption programmes for an infinite future and quasi-cardinalist utility functions with time-perspective properties. The Mikhalevskiy function is defined as one of transformation of uncertainty of a partially ordered perspective into certainty (uncertainty is considered in terms of the risk involved in the degree of roundaboutness of technologies employed): the plan's perspective is described in terms of mathematical expectation.

As has been suggested here Soviet doctrine adopts a more or less articulate Bergson-type social welfare function (Shvyrkov: 'In planning production of consumer-values their social utility is taken into account in the first place in a socialist society'). It may be noted in the context that, before settling for the objective function adopted in the perspective-plan model mentioned, its authors have analysed several alternatives and rejected them as unsuitable for the country's economic environment and/or informationally and computationally unmanageable. It is illuminating to read, we feel, that it is on the first of the two counts that they see as inappropriate, as yet, the one otherwise accorded by them the highest rank, the 'criterion of maximized social welfare'. As understood by them, that superior criterion would be workable for an economy industrially and socially advanced enough to develop in conformity with an 'objective system of consumers' preferences', being corrected by the planner's preference only in a strictly circumscribed

---

[1] Yu. N. Gavrilyets, B. N. Mikhalevskiy, Yu. P. Leibkind, 'Lineynaya model optimalnogo rosta planovoy ekonomiki', in *Primenenye Matematiki v Ekonomicheskikh Issledovanyokh*, vol. 3. *op. cit.*

[2] R. Frisch, 'Dynamic Utility', *op. cit.*

[3] M. Morishima, 'Should Dynamic Utility be Cardinal', *Econometrica*, October 1965.

[4] B. N. Mikhalevskiy, 'Odnosektornaya dinamicheskaya model i otsenka effektivnosti kapitalovlozheniy', *op. cit.*, p. 177; cf. also his *Perspepektivnyie Raschety na Osnovye Prostykh Dinamicheskikh Modeley*, Moscow, 1964.

[5] T. C. Koopmans, P. A. Diamond, R. E. Williamson, 'Stationary Utility and Time Perspective', *Econometrica*, October 1965.

sphere (defence, major projects entailing redistribution of social risk, external economic relations). The workability and acceptance of the welfare criterion is in the view of the model's architects a fundamental corollary of a decentralised system of planning and control—a view which is shared by the present writer (see my 'Centralism and the Parametric Framework')[1]. It is in such a situation that the parameters of the calculation could be decentrally formed so as to correspond to the periphery's system of preferences.[2, 3]

[1] Paper read at the CESES Seminar, Florence 1966.

[2] Cf. in this context Dudkin's argument, pp. 43 ff.

See also his contribution in L. E. Mints *et al.*, Eds. *Statisticheskoye Izuchenye Sprosa i Potreblenya* (Moscow, 1966) on the employment of preference function in plan construction. The planner's choice is here made from among variants of dynamic 'optimal material balances' of the economy, identical in initial data but differing in postulated dynamics of earnings per head.

In the same volume V. V. Shvyrkov designs a 'multi-factor dynamic model of demand'. Demand over the plan period is calculated, in constant prices, with given total commodity turnover in constant prices and real price index. (Technically the variate-difference method is applied in the treatment of time-series).

See also in this volume an interesting comment by A. L. Vainshtein on the ways of relating the statics and dynamics of consumers' preference systems (specifically on the Fourgeau method)—in perspective planning.

[3] In his latest writings Academician Kantorovich points to what he describes as 'elemental' elements (*elementy stikhiynosti*) in the socialist economy. Their presence, he argues, calls for the build-up of mathematical models of consumers' valuations and preferences; the matter, he suggests, could be possibly tackled in the formal terms of the theory of semi-ordered spaces. See his 'Matematicheskiye problemy optimalnogo planirovanya', in L. V. Kantorovich, Ed., *Matematicheskiye Modeli i Metody Optimalnogo Planirovanya*, Novosibirsk 1966, p. 120.

7 Information Planning and Prices[1]

THE dilemma of dimensions has been with the planner ever since macro-planning has been attempted, but the advent of mathematical techniques has articulated the problem and added to its weight. To illustrate its magnitude it is enough to say that for the Soviet economy the numbers of constraints limiting capacities of enterprises and primary resources, and that of unknowns—levels of outputs and inputs of primary resources—are of the order of 5.10^6 and 5.10^7 respectively. Were the classical simplex method adopted as the tool in plan-programming the volume of calculations involved would be proportional to the number of unknowns and the square of constraints: with a linear setting of the problem it would be equivalent to $5^3.10^9$ 'standard problem units', each taken to have 10^3 constraints and 10^4 unknowns.[2]

In groping for viable ways of coping with the dilemma mathematical-planning thought has turned to the conception of information-feedback. In this it has partly drawn inspiration from Western theoretical work. To mention only a few of its sources, Theil[3] and Grunfeld and Griliches[4] have influenced investigations of certain general aspects of aggregation of macro-systems. Arrow and Hurwicz, Malinvaud[5] and others, have helped to elucidate some aspects of decentralised computation in resource allocation. Julia Robinson's and George W. Brown's[6] study of iterative procedures for solving a

---

[1] The original version of this chapter appeared in Italian under the title 'Alcuni rilievi sulle informazioni, la pianificazione e i prezzi' in R. Mieli, ed., *Le Riforme Economiche nei Paesi dell'East*, Milan, 1966.

[2] V. Pugachev, 'Ob optimalnom planirovanyi narodnogo khoziaysva', in *Voprosy Ekonomiki*, 1964, no. 7.

[3] Cf. H. Theil, *Linear Aggregation of Economic Relations*, Amsterdam, 1954; also his 'Linear Aggregation in Input-Output Analysis', *Econometrica*, January 1957.

[4] Y. Grunfeld and Z. Griliches, 'Is Aggregation Necessarily Bad?', *Review of Economics and Statistics*, 1960, no. 1.

[5] K. J. Arrow and L. Hurwicz, 'Decentralisation and Computation in Resource Allocation', in *Essays in Economics and Econometrics*, Chapel Hill, 1960; E. Malinvaud, 'On Decentralisation in National Planning', *Working Papers*, no. 36, Management Science Research Center, Berkeley, Calif., August 1961.

[6] Julia Robinson, 'An Iterative Method of Solving a Game', in *Annuals of Mathematics*, 2nd Series, vol. liv, September 1951; George W. Brown, 'Some Notes on Computation of Game's Solution', in *RAND Report*, April 1949, p. 78. V. V. Amvrosyenko ('Uskoreneye skhodimosti metoda Brauna reshenya matrichnykh gyer',

game (a method corresponding to each player choosing in turn the best pure stategy against the accumulated mixed strategy of his opponent), has carried ideas of relevance for methodology of progress towards an optimum in the 'confrontation' of the planning centre and the lower tiers of an economy. First and foremost there has been the seminal influence of the Dantzig and Wolfe[1] work on decomposition of linear programmes, with all its further ramifications and extensions. By now explorations in the Soviet Union and other planning countries have yielded some important original theoretical contributions which in turn crystallised in certain schemes envisaged for planning by exchange —by flows and counter-flows—of information.

Broadly speaking, among planning models designed for dealing with the dilemma of dimensions, three groups are discernible.

The first group embraces constructs resorting to successive aggregation and disaggregation of variables and constants of input-output systems along with what one could describe as classical lines. A good representative is the Soviet Gavrilyets construct.[2] Optimisation is carried out in an iterative process: a criterion of 'optimal error' resulting from the aggregation-disaggregation process—optimal in some defined sense—is added to whatever is adopted as the overall objective function (choosing the aggregation variant is handled as a minimax problem). In aggregation by products the micro-problems are solved by an iteration process controlled by the macro-problem: convergence of shadow prices for resources for micro-models completes the process. Symetrically aggregation by resources is carred out by means of duals of sub-problems; iterations come to an end when micro-outputs converge. In partitioning the matrix along rows and columns, in solving the programme, some parametric-programming device is employed. Examples produced seem to suggest that as far as

Ekonomika i Matematicheskiye Metody, no. 4, 1965) has suggested a procedure for accelerating convergence under the Brown method. E. P. Borisova and I. V. Magarik ('O dvukh modifikatsyakh metoda Brauna reshenya matrichnykh gyer' *ibid.*, no. 5, 1966) have published results of testing the convergence speeds, in practice, of iterative methods of solution of matrix games.

[1] G. B. Dantzig and Ph. Wolfe, 'Decomposition Principle for Linear Programmes', *Operations Research*, vol. viii, 1960, no. 1, pp. 101 ff.

[2] Yu. N. Gavrilyets, 'Problema agregirovanya i optimizatsyi ekonomiko-matematicheskikh modeley', in *Optimalnoye Planirovanye v Uslovyakh Bolshoy Razmernosti*, Moscow, 1963; and his 'Uchet vliyanya variatsyi koeffitsyentov matritsy usloviy na reshenye nekotorykh ekonomiko-matematicheskikh zadach', *ibid.*

convergence goes the model more or less compares with the simplex method.

The common feature of the second class is its close kinship to the Dantzig-Wolfe prototype. To recall, in Dantzig-Wolfe, from the solution of the master programme objective functions are formed for sub-programmes; their solution provides new columns which are being added to the master: the process is re-cycled until the optimality test is satisfied.

Of Soviet-designed models that by Volkonskiy, elaborated in the Cybernetics Institute of the Ukrainian Academy of Sciences, falls clearly into this class.[1] Here each unit of the multi-tier system obtains from the hierarchically superior unit, or elaborates in an exchange of information with its suppliers and users of its products, constraints with regard to limited resources. It also obtains from the centre its objective function assigned, according to specific features of the system, either in the shape of prices only, or also in terms of bounds and weights describing permissible limits of violation of some constraints. The objective function is then the principal instrument of control in the hands of the centre: local criteria are harmonised with the all-economy one. Schematically the centre would start plan contruction by solving its master programme based on adjusted data from past performance; it would derive and promulgate its provisionally-optimal prices of resources, and the lower echelons would report back by submitting plans of inputs and outputs subject to the rule of profit-maximisation. (Activities as programmed are of course non-profit at the optimum; Volkonskiy extends his planning model[2] by building into it a profit-incentive scheme which we leave out of consideration.) The promulgation of correct prices would set in a new round and in the process local criteria might be adjusted, and so might the matrices and constraints describing the enterprise's capabilities. The rounds would be terminated when price equilibrium, reflecting demand-supply equilibrium, would be deemed adequately approximated; values obtained in successive iterations might be averaged by the Brown-Robinson method for solving games. The main gain in the pace of

[1] V. A. Volkonskiy, 'Sistema tekushchego planirovanya s pomoshchu otsyenok resursov na osnovye matrichnykh modeley', in *Optimalnoye Planirovanye v Uslovyakh Bolshoy Razmernosti*, 1963; also in N. P. Fedorenko, ed., *Planirovanye i Ekonomiko-Matematicheskiye Metody*, Moscow, 1964.

[2] V. Volkonskiy, 'Skhema optimalnogo perspektivnogo planirovanya i otsenki resursov' in *Optimalnoye Planirovanye v Uslovyakh Bolshoy Razmernosti*, esp. p. 104.

convergence, as compared with Dantzig-Wolfe, is expected however from cutting out constraints not infringed in reaching the solution. (Under some conditions the employment of the Arrow-Hurwicz gradient is considered for the equilibrating process.)

The Hungarian Kornai-Liptak model[1] belongs to the same family: its heuristic attraction rests on the elegance of its apparatus of formalisation which conceptualises the planning process as a game-theoretical exercise. Western students have been apprised of it by its authors and only a few words will be said here about its substance. The feasible allocation patterns and the feasible shadow price systems in the duals of sectoral problems are the strategies of the centre and of the team of sectors respectively, and the pay-off function is the sum of the duals of the sectoral objective functions. The authors show that the optimum of the planning task—the 'overall central information problem'— corresponds to the maxmin of the polyhedral game, and in place of the latter apply the Brown-Robinson fictitious play method. In this schema, each sector evaluates, by means of a dual of programme, its initial allocations (possibly worked out by the centre from a plan built up on traditional methods) and reports to the centre; the centre sends down new directives; and so on until the 'overall central information problem' is found to be solved with a desired degree of accuracy. A feature which distinguishes the Kornai-Lipták construct within this class is that no prices are determined from the dual at the centre: they are set at the lower echelons while the centre confines its controls to re-adjusting the tasks so as to get product prices equalised in sectoral optimisations, prices that is, imputed in the central directives.

This is also one of the main differences in substance (as distinct from formalisation) between this model and the Polish perspective-planning scheme designed by Porwit.[2] Here the ball starts rolling when the central planner has derived from his first-approximation plan (1) sectoral targets of outputs to be supplied to outsiders—a total weighted by constant prices (point-of-departure prices), supplemented by physical-terms targets for principal products; (2) dual-type prices for each sector, for specific categories of fixed-capital assests and foreign exchange (presumably also for labour?); (3) 'material

[1] J. Kornai and Th. Liptak, *Two-Level Planning*, Computing Centre of the Hungarian Academy of Sciences, Budapest, 1962; subsequent version in *Econometrica*, January 1965.
[2] K. Porwit, *Zagadnienia Rachunku Ekonomicznego w Planie Centralnym*, Warsaw, 1964, especially ch. 4.2.

'balances' of main products from which specific sectoral input limits are obtained. Within this framework each sector derives from its own programme the 'dual' for its own products by minimising the input of labour and of factors and supplies from outside, at the centrally set prices, in pursuance of the allocated task of external deliveries. Alternatively profit would be adopted as the maximand with floors for external deliveries and ceilings for external supplies given in physical terms, and with constant prices for the sector's products.

The critique raised against the models resting on the multi-round information exchange is that while dealing with the load of dimensions they are likely to compromise manageability by the load of iterations that would be usually entailed (even assuming a handy set of block sub-programmes; no trouble with degeneracy, and so on). Equilibrium for a highly aggregated all-economy system would not necessarily secure it for a more disaggregated 'nomenclature': multi-iterative schemes would not be convenient for the control of the planning process inasmuch as correctives could be brought into the statement of the problem only after a solution had been reached. The criticism would seem to be legitimate even if to a degree different in respect of the different models considered. As we shall see, the weakness of the original decomposition technique stemming from the slow pace of convergence—from the point of view of planning—has been implicitly conceded by Dantzig.

Two constructs—apparently of independent design—try to remedy the weakness. First the Almon model, for planning without complete information at the centre, presented by Dantzig in his 1963 work.[1] It starts on the familiar Dantzig-Wolfe lines: as the first step the planning centre announces its simplex-multiplier prices obtained from the master programme (formed from memorised past data) and orders each firm's manager to propose a plan maximising his profit from sales and purchases based on them. In the light of such bids he resolves his programme and revises and announces the price vector corresponding to the quasi-optimal plan, optimal that is 'given the information possessed'. At this stage as a rule the process is cut short: further iterations are resorted to only if time permits. Together with his price-tariffs the planner announces a set of quotas: quantities of traded commodities which each firm must produce and is permitted to

[1] See ch. 23 contributed by C. Almon to G. B. Dantzig, *Linear Programming and Extensions*, Princeton, N. Jersey, 1963.

97

purchase. The principle of profit maximisation, however, is now treated as only facultative. Should it be imposed it is to be made con ditional upon meeting the quantitative targets.

The other construct in this class is the Soviet Pugachev mode elaborated in and adopted by the Central Economic-Mathematica Institute of the USSR Academy of Sciences (TSEMI).[1] The originality o its approach to cutting out the burden of iterations consists in 'aggre gation by constraints': one linear constraint is to approximate th capabilities of each 'cell' (enterprise, branch). The all-economy programme would yield, with reference to the adopted (quadratic) criterion,[2] optimal structures and volumes of branch outputs and the imputed prices. With the number of 'pure' branches of around 1,00 and totals of constraints and unknowns estimated at $5 \cdot 10^6$ and $5 \cdot 10^7$ respectively, the computational load is expected to be within the capabilities of the proposed computer-stations network, even allowing for any additional optimisations. If anything this model is one of a 'regu lated' degree of optimality. One should add that both Soviet con structs, the Volkonskyi and the Pugachev models, aspire to handling the plan dynamics. They try to formalise the concept of planning wi a 'sliding' horizon: their philosophy rests on the proposition that ' dichotomy of short- and long-term planning is largely in conflict reality, if only because in real life information flows of relevanc both the future and the present are inextricably interwoven. 'Roll planning would integrate them and take care of dynamic equilibriu in the continuous process of structural change in the economy. Thu makes the models more exacting informationally than, for instance, the Almon-Dantzig system: they have to rest to a considerable degree on information which is uncertain as well as incomplete, that is, to rely on probabilistic values for most of the relevant indices. That favours a planner's operation with information the more 'compressed' the more distant a time point, and then gradually expanding as this time-point is approached. *Pari-passu* valuations of resources would be obtained from the duals. Such shadow prices would form in turn signals for the direction of technical progress; and at the same time would act, as it were, as 'customers' ordering new production 'ways'

---

[1] V. F. Pugachev, 'Model mnogstupenchatoy sistemy optimalnogo planirovanya', in *Optimalnoye Planirovanye v Uslovyakh Bolshoy Razmernosti*, *op. cit.*

[2] The Pugachev-type of criterion is discussed by me in 'The Objective Function for Soviet Economy', *Economica*, August 1965.

—'ordering' the supply of new economic information which has to be ʲed into the planning system in subsequent cycles.

The claims put forward on behalf of the Pugachev model, and perᵑaps also the TSEMI aegis, may justify a closer look at it. Its formalisaᵗion can be summarised in these terms:

Let x_{in} and x_{ex} be vectors of the cell's inter-cell inputs and outputs ᵒf m and n dimensions respectively. Then we may take $x_{in} = f(x_{ex})$ ᵃnd consider the cell's capabilities in the space of x_{ex} only. Assume that ᵂithin the practicable range it is convex (or near-convex or divisible ᵢnto a finite number of convex components). Take in this space some L extreme points a_{ex}^l and form a convex polyhedron of $m + n$ dimenᵗions $x = \sum_l a^l \xi^l$ where all ξ are non-negative and the $\sum_l \xi_l \leqslant 1$: and the vertices a^l are determined by $a^l = a_{ex}^l - f(a_{ex}^l)$. Consider the vectors a^l as columns of some matrix $A = (a)$ of the rank $(m + n)L$, describing the cell's activities, while their levels are described by some vector $\xi = (\xi^l)$ with non-negative components. We may write then for the cell's approximating polyhedron

$$(1) \quad x = A\xi; \qquad (2) \quad I\xi \leqslant 1$$

᷍quality (2) is the constraint describing the cell's productive ᵃcities (I stands for a unit vector).

᷍he procedure starts with the construction, 'by the usual methods', ᵗhe cell's plan, x^0. Consider it as one of the vertices of a polyhedron, $a^0 = x^0$ the 'starting vertex' of approximation. Further, a series of n specialised plans of the cell's production with 'dominant' product, i, is considered as vectors x^i of $(m + n)$ dimensions, the n corresponding to the product-mix which is being varied. On this path n, linearly independent extreme points of the approximating polyhedron $a^l = x^i$ $(l = i)$ are obtained; together with a^0 there will be then $(n + 1)$ vertices sufficient for the build-up of the convex polyhedron (1)–(2). In processing information for each group of cells, k, the (1) is being related to some vector b whose negative and positive elements characterise respectively, availabilities of limited factors and the final bill of goods so that the $\sum_k A^k \xi^k \geqslant b$. At the centre the economy's optimality criterion U, a convex function of ξ^k, is brought into the macro-problem now written as

$$(3) \quad I\xi^k \leqslant 1; \qquad (4) \quad -\sum_k A^k \xi^k \leqslant -b; \qquad (5) \quad U(\xi^k) = \max$$

Simultaneously valuation is carried out: for the systems of inequalities (3) and (4) valuations are characterised respectively by some q_k

and p_k. The former, being related to productive capacities, are understood as rental charges; the latter as imputed prices of primary factors and intermediate and final products. In so far as the (3)–(5) problem is convex, the determining of the optimal plan and prices is equivalent to finding the non-negative saddle-point of the Lagrangian function

$$(6) \quad \phi(\xi^k, p, q) = U(\xi^k) + \sum_k (\mathbf{1} - I\xi^k) \cdot q_k + (\sum_k A^k \xi^k - b) \cdot p$$

The activity levels, ξ^k, and rental charges and prices q and p from (6) are the source of the flows of control information moving down the hierarchical ladder and, in the process, successively disaggregated. Here too prices are to harmonise local criteria at all tiers with the overall one for the system.

The Pugachev approach stands and falls with the effectiveness of its postulated one-constraint description of the primary cell and this begs one or two pertinent questions. In its general case the single cell constraint is arrived at, as we have seen, without reference to prices: 'inflow' and 'outflow' are characterised by vectors in the space of physical-term indices. Intra-cell optimisation is to be secured by measuring the additional gain in productivity obtainable by means of a given 'specialisation': the point at issue is precisely in what terms relative productivities of the x^i can be appraised where efficiency-valuations of factors are absent. The answer offered seems to be that the variation of the i-th product should be bounded by limits given externally. That still leaves unanswered the next question: by what criterion? A special Golden-Age-type case considered is one in which a 'stabilised functioning' of the system and availability of valuations approximates optimality prices—from the previous cycle. This case is in substance quite close to Almon-Dantzig.

From what has been said before it follows that in Almon-Dantzig the price paid for the one-exchange-of-information system is *ultimate* reliance on physical-terms guidance. For when in conflict, targets and limits set in physical terms should be obeyed rather than profitability indications which in fact may be abandoned altogether (see above, p. 97). It is argued in Almon-Dantzig that were the firms told simply to maximise their profits, the planning centre would almost certainly have difficulty with its balance constraint.[1] The point is convincing and holds also for the Pugachev special case: in fact unlike the Almon-Dantzig, the Pugachev model is not explicitly committed to any

[1] *Op. cit.*, p. 465.

specific regime of guidance although, as noted, control information is issued in it in the shape of prices and rental charges as well as quantities. To the extent that quantity data would be treated, as they are in Almon-Dantzig, as equilibrium safeguards, the question would arise as to the degree of optimality of the physical-term indicators, when divorced from price-term calculation. So much for the special case. As to the Pugachev general case, our probing into its formalisation would suggest that the basic-cell constraint is formed without any reference to an optimality price; that would vitiate the overall optimality at its root level.

These remarks are confined to a survey of the main approaches to information feedback planning, basic difficulties encountered and attempts made to overcome them. It seems safe to conclude by suggesting that while these attempts have provided considerable insight into the nature of the problem involved, the final judgement on their merits could only be empirically obtained.

APPENDIX TO CHAPTER 7

Unwieldiness of the vast dimensions of a macro plan-programme which could aspire to full realism, and loss of information inseparable from their compression, remain the two principal twin barriers to formalisation of planning, and Soviet students have persevered in seeking tolerable ways to overcome these hurdles. (There is though something in Dantzig's remark, to the effect that, generally, there are too many theoretical proposals and too few experiments in this field.[1])

Of recent developments in the theory of the problem one may note further elaboration of the Pugachev model to which some space has been devoted here.[2] He now offers, as an alternative approach, approximation by means of hyperplanes. On the all-national level the problem then is stated as:

$$ h^k y^k \leqslant 1; \quad \sum_k (x^k - A^k x^k - a^k) \geqslant d; \quad U(x^k - A^k x^k - a^k) = \text{max}. $$

(Of the additional symbols h stands for a vector of the hyperplane's normalised coefficients and indicates the share of the 'cell's' capacities absorbed by a product group (in this sense it measures substitutability of outputs);

[1] In the address to the First World Congress of the Econometric Society, Rome, 1965.
[2] V. F. Pugachev, 'Approksimatsyonnaya skhema mnogostupenchatogo optimalnogo planirowanya narodnogo khoziaystva' in S. M. Vishnev, ed., *Ekonomiko-Matematicheskiye Metody—Metody Optimalnogo Planirovanya*, vol. 2, Moscow, 1965.

x stands for the 'cell's' optimal plan, A for its full-order technological matrix). It is further assumed that the 'cell' has some optimality criterion by which its output vector, x, is related to that of input, y, so that $y = \varphi(x)$, a possible non-linear function but expected to lend itself to linearisation; and a is some vector of constant cost (so that $y = Ax + a$). This approximation is relatively handier, but its admitted trouble is that it fails to determine the limits of its own feasibility. As to the alternative 'trick', the description of the 'cell' by a single linear constraint—approximation by means of a convex polyhedron—it is made clear now that here product aggregation is carried out by physical-term coefficients of substitution at the production stage rather than by prices. This would seem to validate our doubts as to the valuation frame of technological alternatives (cf. p. 100).

Of other proposals we would point to the Dudkin-Yershov[1] scheme of an optimised all-economy material balance, for current planning, with allowance for variable technologies. It has a block-diagonal structure and block methods of programming are to be applied. The way the structure is to be related to the iterative aggregation procedure itself, however, has not been made clear as yet.

One may note also in the context an interesting shift to more classical methodology in Kornai's[2] more recent work. Here too, block-diagonal arrangement is secured for matrices of coefficients in *intra*-sectoral constraints (a feature of the model is the working with *intra*-sectoral and *inter*-sectoral matrices). The Dantzig-Wolfe decomposition principle is now employed: the theoretically attractive method of a fictitious play (cf. p. 96) has been abandoned because its non-monotonic nature revealed itself as a serious drawback: as optimum is approached the criterion values tend (strongly) to fluctuate; and, in addition to monotonic convergence, the advantage of the Dantzig-Wolfe principle is now thought to lie in certain gain from sectoral programmes—at the start of the all-economy calculation —at the beginning of iterations.

Finally, Volkonskiy[3] has tried to formulate some general propositions on the convergence of iterative processes. The point made is broadly this. Logically, so long as the process is still far away from optimum and there is little risk of 'jumping' over it, the iteration step may be long and it should be shortened as the optimum is approached. Hence a non-monotonic method should be more helpful where an approximation to optimum is

[1] L. M. Dudkin, E. V. Yershov, 'Blochnoye postroyenye optimalnogo materialnogo balansa sotsyalisticheskogo narodnogo khozyastva', *ibid.*

[2] J. Kornai, *Mathematical Programming as a Tool of Socialist Economic Planning*, Rome, 1965 (mimeo).

[3] V. A. Volkonskiy, 'Optimalnoye planirovanye v uslovyakh bolshoy razmernosti', *Ekonomika i Matematicheskiye Metody*, no. 2, 1965.

looked for. By contrast, if exact optimum is sought where a good approximation is known but the objective function or the edge of the admissible set is not smooth (such as for instance in linear programming), monotonic methods should be more effective. The conclusion drawn is then that some combination of the two methods should prove best for tackling the problem of an exact optimum of a large-dimension plan-programme: an approximative solution would be first found by means of a method of iteration proper and then it would be improved by some fixed-step method. However, the Kornai experience would not seem to bear out this proposition.[1, 2]

[1] In a contribution which I was able to read when these pages were already in proof Volkonskiy states the case for a game-theoretical approach (cf. his paper *Optimum Planning Schemes and Methods of their Conjugation* submitted to the ES/TIMS Warsaw 1966 conference). The apparatus is extended to that of a convex non-coalitional multi-person zero-sum game and the main theorems established that (a) it is possible to arrange the centre-periphery interactions on a homeostatic principle, pricing being carried out either by the centre which acts as a quasi-buyer and quasi-seller or in a decentralised fashion; (b) maximisation of the participants' win-functions leads the system towards the unique min-max equilibrium point which is optimum. (An interesting observation, made apparently in the light of Soviet experiments, is that while the classical linear-programme scheme proves suitable for current planning, integer-programming—usually of the zero-one kind—is required for the firms' long-term plans; and again linear and convex programming proves workable in national macro-planning; stochastic methods and randomisation procedures are being recommended for integer programming because of the simplicity of iterations entailed). These ideas link up with a noteworthy non-linear model of perspective planning formalized by Volkonskiy with an iterative *prima facie* manageable, algorithm by V. Byelenkiy: it is supplemented by a simplified model of calculation of the dynamics of average branch prices based on the input-output balance (cf. *Ekonomika i Matematicheskiye Metody*, no. 4, 1967, pp. 544 ff. and 496 ff.

[2] At a late stage I could acquaint myself with two further attempts of formalized coping with the problem of dimensions:

(I) Katsebelinboygen *et al.* (1966: cf. reference on p. 129) try to generalise the conception of block-programming with a multi-tier system of constraints, aggregation by products and processes, parallel optimisations within blocks with localised intra-block optimisations resting on parameters of neighbour-blocks only;

(II) Dudkin (1966: cf. reference on p. 46) offers a schema for securing consistency of his 'optimal material balance' of the economy with balances for specific commodities. For the current plan balance the aggregation algorithm relies on weighted-mean direct input 'normatives'

$$a_{gi} = \sum_{q \in M_j} a_{gq} x_q / \sum_{g \in M_j} x_q; \quad a_{ij} = \sum_{g \in M_i} \sum_{q \in M_j} a_{gq} x_q / \sum_{g \in M_j} x_q$$

(subscripts *g*, *q* and *i*, *j*, respectively denote product-indexes of the detailed and the consolidated 'nomenclatures', $M =$ set of indexes: for further notation see p. 46). Algorithms for perspective planning are built up analogously, with time-dimension brought in.

8 Planning with Variable Prices

A NOTEWORTHY theoretical attempt in Eastern European literature to escape from the rigidity of the usual assumption of price constancy over the plan period has been made by Professor Kalecki.[1] The approach hinges on his concept of 'consumption equivalents' (see above, chapter 4). By a familiar argument he shows, for a two-commodity case, that minimum cost corresponds to the point of tangency of the cost curve and his 'consumption equivalence' curve; that, for the minimum-cost consumption variant, prices of realisation would be proportionate to units costs; and that for a general n-commodity case the solution would have to be sought in establishing first the coordinates of all the equivalence points of the $(n-1)$ dimensional surface, and then by trying to find that point to which prices are proportionate to costs. Technically of interest is a short-cut suggested by Kalecki for approximation of this solution, which is broadly this: Start from some consumption structure A and households' purchasing power corresponding to income per-head postulated for the $(o+t)$ year and expressed in the zero year's ('constant') prices $p_{1A}, p_{2A}, \ldots, p_{nA}$; find corresponding unit costs (as above), E_1, $E_2, \ldots, E_n$ (there is a hint at actualisation of the cost structure by the use of a time-discount borrowed from the methodology of selection of efficient-investment variants); calculate the total value of the A set at prices $\sqrt{E_1 p_{1A}}, \sqrt{E_2 p_{2A}}, \ldots, \sqrt{E_n p_{nA}}$; find for the $(o+t)$ year a set R of commodities $q_{1R}, q_{2R}, \ldots, q_{nR}$ with the same total value at the same prices, and prices of realisation proportionate to $E_1, E_2, \ldots, E_n$; in other words the set R is being determined from

$$q_{1R}\sqrt{E_1 p_{1A}} + q_{2R}\sqrt{E_2 p_{2A}} + \cdots + q_{nR}\sqrt{E_n p_{nA}}$$

(The consumption equivalence curve containing A and R is approximated by a straight line, a chord of a vertical-axis parabola with an $-\sqrt{E_1 p_{1A}}/\sqrt{E_2 p_{2A}}$ gradient.)[2]

[1] Michal Kalecki, *Gospodarka Planowa*, 1963, no. 7, pp. 3 ff.

[2] A Polish experiment in perspective planning with variable prices is described in M. Lesz, 'Optimization of the economic plan in the conditions of price variations' (presented at ES/TIMS Warsaw 1966 conference). As it appears first a programme for optimizing consumption structure with constant price was iteratively solved (with a 20 × 20 matrix: nine years' plan period ending 1970). Next the solution was sought,

The attempt lies on the lines of a few inquiries carried out by con-
tructors of plan-models in the West, with a focus on financial flows.
One notable construct is that of the French SEEF, designed by Pro-
essor Nataf and his associates.[1] Here too, a mathematical variable-
price model is grafted on one in constant prices. Average-price indexes
of individual industrial branches are derived from their wage bills on
certain assumptions with respect to a set of parameters (the latter is
formed by taxation parameters and coefficients describing the financial
balance of each of branches considered). With relevant relationships
linearised this is obtained by the use of a Leontief-type matrix, M, and
the relative price vector appears as its inverse multiplied by a column
matrix (vector) of wages, $p = M^{-1} . n$. The aspect of optimality is left
out of consideration.

This aspect is explicitly tackled in Professor Stone's well elaborated
attempt without Kalecki's inhibition in respect of the utility concept.[2]
As in Nataf-Thionet the price vector is related to the volume of
expenditure. What is sought at the first step is the amount of money
needed in the $(o + t)$ plan-year for keeping at the utility surface of the
(o) year (with reference to a constant-utility index of living)—while
the price vector shifts from p_0 to p_{0+t}; then the consequential vector
of total demand, direct and indirect, placed on individual sectors of
the economy is formed by reference to matrices of current input coefficients and capital coefficients. At the next step a production function
of Cobb-Douglas type, is brought into the system relating factors and
technological progress; and eventually the price vector is obtained of
the form $p = (I - A)^{-1} . f$, the f expressing factor cost per unit of product.

None of the three models has been manageable enough to be applied
in plan construction, as yet.

with given price-elasticity data, for changes in equilibrium prices corresponding to the
new optimal consumption structure.

[1] Nataf et Thionet, *Le Modèle à Moyen Terme à Prix Variables S.E.E.F.*, Ministère des
Finances et des Affaires Economiques, Service des Etudes Economiques et Financières,
Paris, 1962.
Of relevance for this study is the attempt made by Professor Nataf, jointly with C.
Fourgeaud, to formulate the interdependence between the nominal and 'real' income
and price elasticities of demand. (Cf. their 'Consommation en Prix et Revenu Reels et
Theorie des Choix', in *Econometrica*, July, 1960, pp. 329 ff.) They evolved there a
'correction coefficient', $\eta = - \gamma_k(\alpha_k + \beta_k)$, the γ measures elasticity of the general price
index in respect of each price (price index and consumption having the same structure)
and the two parameters, α and β describe 'real' income and price elasticities.
[2] Richard Stone, 'A Demonstration Model for Economic Growth', *The Manchester
School of Economic and Social Studies*, January 1962.

9 Full Labour-Input Coefficients and Pricing[1]

THERE is an element in the present Soviet experiments with Leontief-type matrices which is, understandably, intellectually exciting to Soviet Marxists. It is that the promises contained in classical Marxist economics of the technical feasibility of expressing all cost, under socialism, in terms of labour appears, at last, to have materialised. The relevant point which should be made explicit in the context is that in the traditional Soviet-Marxian interpretation, that would hold for the *short*-term as well as long-term economic calculation.

In continuing its work on the first *ex-post* (1959) input-output tables the USSR Central Statistical Administration has produced a double-entry, two-quadrant *tableau economique* in terms of labour (for 1959/60), the first of its kind.[2] Thus the CSA has now linked up with its own ideas of forty years ago. Almost at its inception, as early as 1920, it decided to elaborate a methodology of calculating labour-time cost of products (as it seems that was connected with Strumilin's report on the urgency of substituting labour-time 'tariffs' for money-prices). This initiative was soon to be abandoned as impracticable.[3]

The present CSA exercise supplies information on (*a*) each branch's direct labour expenditure and (*b*) on the sum-total of labour directly used in a given branch and by each of its suppliers. Finally, full (direct and indirect) inputs of labour, throughout the system (and history) involved in fabricating the final product were calculated.[4]

[1] This is a revised version of 'Note on the Soviet Inter-Industry Labour Input Balance', published in *Soviet Studies*, July 1963.

[2] Cf. M. Eidelman in *Vestnik statistiki*, 1962, no. 10, pp. 3 ff.; see below, p. 109 ftn. 3.

[3] Cf. *Byuleten Ts.S.U.*, 12 November 1920, no. 34; and N. Morozova, *Vestnik Statistiki*, 1958, no. 4, pp. 36–7 ff.

[4] For method of calculation see *Vestnik Statistiki*, 1962, no. 10, p. 11. The formula employed was

$$\tau_j = \sum_{i=1}^{n} b_{ij} K_i X_j + T_j$$

where τ denotes labour expenditure of the j-th branch (column-wise), b_{ij} denotes full-order coefficient of the use of the i-th branch output in production of the j-th branch; K_i denotes coefficient of labour expenditure per output unit of the i-th branch, in man-years (divided by 1,000 roubles) and T_j denotes yearly average of manpower in the j-th branch.

This formula has been re-written as $\tau_j = C_{ij} t_{ij} + T_j$, where $C_{ij} = b_{ij}/a_{ij}$, i.e. the ratio of the full-order coefficient of i-th branch output used up in production of the j-th branch and the corresponding direct-input coefficient; the t_{ij} describes, in man-years, the use of output of the i-th branch in production of the j-th branch.

Labour expenditures were computed per physical unit of specific final goods and/or per 1,000 roubles' worth of output of product-groups. The experiment is of obvious and considerable practical importance. Thanks to it, for the first time the planner has been provided with fully quantified information on certain important facts of economic life which he has to order. It is indeed fascinating to delve into the data arrived at. It has been found, for example, that of 97 million man-years, rather more than a half, about 50 million, is ultimately devoted to the production of consumer goods; of this about two-thirds, 34 million man-years, go into the production of food and 9 million into that of clothes and footwear. Some 17 million man-years go into the public non-productive sphere which comprises administration and so on; and nearly 30 million into capital formation, exports and elsewhere (not surprisingly, labour inputs into armaments have not been specified in the published tables). A comparison with value-data on the distribution of the national product may be particularly tempting; in terms of labour the shares of public consumption would appear considerably higher and of household consumption lower. No doubt the fuller information obtained will enable Gosplan to pattern the uses of the nation's manpower more rationally. However, in the present remarks I propose to concentrate on certain theoretical rather than practical aspects of the CSA inquiry. The point of particular interest is its relevance for the system of socialist accounting as hinted at by Marx.

In one sense the methodology now tested in the Soviet Union does appear to bring this system nearer realisation and it does so for several reasons. *First*, it shows production as a 'phenomenal form' of labour— as one of 'living' labour being added to 'past' (or 'embodied') labour; *secondly*, it does show the historically accumulated labour 'content' of a commodity as a measurable magnitude of economic relevance; *thirdly*, it thereby does show all cost components resolving themselves into labour; *fourthly*, it does consequently permit the planner to compile a meaningful, analytical or *ex-ante*, balance-sheet of an economy in terms of labour-time available:[1] each element of this balance-sheet, as read in Marxist terms, appears on its horizontal lines as expenditure of living labour and on its vertical lines as 'embodied' labour.

---

[1] Independently of the way an economy is organised, the substance of *the* dynamic planning problem is the reaching of the goals in the efficient way, with given initial endowment in resources and the expected flow of labour (cf. J. Hicks, *Capital and Growth*, Oxford, 1965, pp. 203 ff).

While all this is granted, the methodology at the same time brings into full relief the limitations of the labour-content calculus, and in fact the elusiveness of Marx's basic concept of labour cost.

To begin with the latter: while the measuring of labour congealed in a commodity has become at least a practicable proposition, what is measured is not really the 'substance' which Marx made the corner-stone of his theory of value. In Marx, it will be recalled, the value of a commodity is defined as cost in terms of undifferentiated simple labour, simple 'socially necessary' labour.

The experiment has revived in Soviet economics the old question as to what is socially necessary labour. Marx's value theory equates 'socially necessary' with actual labour cost: a cost magnitude is 'necessary' because it has actually been incurred, and value but registers cost.[1] The concept raises quite a few issues, in particular that of the ways in which the labour cost is to be 'averaged'. Its weakness is that, as traditionally interpreted by Soviet Marxists, 'social necessity' of a labour input based on the fact of its actual expenditure is divorced from, or at least not explicitly linked up with, the postulate of efficiency. That is why some members of the new Soviet planometric school have tried to re-define social necessity as that corresponding to an optimum programme. (Nemchinov in particular has reformulated the notion of social value as the full-order input of labour per unit of output corresponding to an optimum with given resources and policy constraints.[2]) Leaving apart the technical difficulties of arriving at an optimum, this makes the ground underneath the concept somewhat safer: but it does so at the price of building into it an efficiency structure alien to Marx's valuation framework. Another vexed point is the reduction of actual to 'simple' labour. The underlying concept in Marx is a physiological one—that of expenditure of the human organism's 'labouring power' (human brain, nerve, muscle) which is hardly measurable as such. Its economic corollary too evades quantification. For lack of anything more satisfactory the idea of applying the wage-tariffs in force as indicators of prime value has once again tempted some Soviet students. We have now a published account of an industrious attempt carried out recently in Gosplan's Economic

[1] M. Wolfson (*A Reappraisal of Marxian Economics*, p. 59) argues that Marx tried to avoid value determination by demand, and correctly points to the circular question: how to know that socially necessary labour determines demand rather than that demand determines the labour necessary for the extra unit of product.

[2] See sbove, ch. 3.

Scientific-Research Institute (NIEI).[1] Average earnings of 'productive' personnel in the textile-manufacturing branch (*shveinaya promyshlennost*) were adopted as the unit of 'labour complexity' (*slozhnost truda*) and all other branch averages of Soviet industries were related to it. The system of 'labour-complexity coefficients' yielded was employed for the reduction of respective labour-time inputs to 'simple'-labour magnitudes. It is for full labour-input coefficients adjusted in this way that the claim has been made of adequately approximating 'labour valuation' (*trudovaya otsenka*), and the suggestion to build up on such 'labour norms' (*trudovye normy*) a price system, that is a system of accounting prices and largely also operational prices. (As one would expect, production of heavy industries expressed in present prices has been found under-'valued' (by seven per cent) and that of light industries over-'valued' (by nearly two-fifths). But some intra-group disparities less easily accountable have emerged in heavy industries: e.g. prices of ferrous metallurgy have appeared to be almost a quarter below, and those in chemicals nearly one-third above, 'value'.)[2] Whatever else can be said about the use of prevailing Soviet wage-tariff weights inter-industry analysis, they certainly cannot be accepted as a basis in the quest for value-expression on Marxist grounds. Indeed the approach itself would stand Marx's conception on its head. In Marx wage differentials would reflect 'simple'-labour inputs and not vice versa.[3] It is evident that those instrumental in the pioneering computation of full labour-output coefficients by the Central Statistical Administration refuse to endorse the NIEI approach as legitimate for determination of Marxist value-relations.

---

[1] I. Doroshin, 'Trudovaya otsenka narodnokhozyaistvennykh velichin i plani-rovanie', *Planovoye khozyaistvo*, 1963, no. 2.

[2] A more generalised procedure suggested would be to calculate the average wage-tariff coefficient for each, *i*-th, branch as

$$k_i = \sum k_i L_i / \sum L_i,$$

where k_i and L_i stand respectively for tariff-coefficients and employment in each tariff class. Reduction to simple labour would be then carried out through multiplication of total branch employment by such an averaged coefficient:

$$L_i^1 = (\sum L_i) . k_i$$

(M. R. Eidelman, *Mezhotraslevoy Balans Obshchestvennogo Produkta*, Moscow, 1966, p. 357).

[3] In experimenting with labour coefficients as a price-basis the Hungarians subscribe to the view that 'ratios of the wage inputs are not necessarily equal to those of the values'. Cf. P. Havas, 'Examination of the Price System by Means of the Input-Output Table', in *Input-Output Tables*, O. Lukacs, ed., Budapest, 1962, p. 197.

The sense of full-labour coefficients in pricing has been well explored within the framework of the Leontief system. It will be remembered that in the fundamental static Leontief model, too, labour is the sole social cost. It has been shown that in this framework total labour inputs would determine rates of substitution and thereby the price relations of final goods. To get 'absolute' price levels, relative content data would have to be multiplied by the prevailing wage rates. As Professor Leontief puts it, the system of full-input coefficients reflects relationship between price and value added: when price of labour is made explicit, value added is split into wages and its residuum, a certain non-wage component.[1] If we assume a perfect competitive equilibrium with zero-profits, price relations would correspond in this system to ratios of full-order labour coefficients.

All this stems from the fact that in this system labour is the numeraire and the only productive factor. How far then could prices based on what are in substance labour-productivity indicators be employed by Gosplan for allocative purposes? They would orientate the planning board with regard to commitments of manpower involved in its choices, but not with regard to that of other resources. This simply follows from the fact that in the adopted conceptual framework other scarce resources are non-existent. Indeed, prices based on the relative productivities of labour express one side of the picture, just as prices based on productivities of other factors would have done. Were capital the only scarce factor of production, prices of various products would tend to equalise capital-output ratios.[2] Prices would then reflect productivity of capital in terms of a given product: price relations would correspond to full input-ratios of capital. In an analogous way, were all factors but land free in some odd environment, the acreages involved in getting final goods would similarly form a rational basis of a price-system. In fact, for the beginning of the Soviet industrialisation era the assumption of labour being free and capital the only deficit factor would be almost realistic, and therefore capital-input prices appropriate: and even today it would be *comparatively* nearer to Soviet reality than the reverse assumption.

[1] W. W. Leontief, *The Structure of the American Economy* 1919–39, New York, 1960, p. 190. The problem of relationship between Leontief price and Marxist value has been rigorously investigated in an interesting paper by M. Morishima and F. Seton, *Econometrica, op. cit.* (cf. p. 80 above). See also reference to the literature, *ibid.*, p. 203.
[2] J. Tinbergen, H. Bos, *Mathematical Models of Economic Growth*, New York, 1962.

Were the matrix of labour input coefficients to serve Gosplan as a guide in choice-making, it would have to be supplemented by one of capital coefficients describing the commitment of capital assets. (Inputs of heterogeneous capital could be for this purpose meaningfully expressed in its reproduction costs, in terms of labour-time, but co-measuring the two factors would still require bringing in, explicitly, their marginal productivities.[1]) Each factor would be priced at its opportunity cost and each 'final' good at the cost of factors it absorbed.[2,3]

[1] Cf. R. M. Solow, *Econometrica*, October 1963.

[2] Suggestions have been made in Soviet planning literature (Yu. Yaremenko, *Planovoye Khoziaystvo*, 1963, no. 4) to elaborate a concept, and calculate a system, of full capital/labour coefficients (*koeffitsyenty fondovooruzhennosti*) per unit of final product obtained as ratios of full-order capital-output and labour-output coefficients. This leaves open the relative valuation of factors. Cf. p. 261 below.

Full-order input of labour entailed in production of the final bill of goods, of the given branch, T_i (with A_{ij}-matrix of full inputs of i per unit of j) will be described as

$$T_j Y_j = Y_j \sum_{i=1}^{n} t_i A_{ij}$$

since total output entailed in production of the final bill of goods is $\sum A_{ij} Y_j$ we have

$$\sum_{j=1}^{n} T_j Y_j = \sum_{i=1}^{n} t_i X_i$$

(cf. P. P. Litvyakov, in *Metody Planirovanya Mezhotraslevykh Proportsiy, op. cit.*, 1965).

[3] On the Soviet calculation of full capital coefficients, see ch. 7.

Part II: Planning Techniques

B. Profit Guidance

10 Rules of the Game[1]

BY COMMON consensus of students, both inside and outside the Soviet Union, the Soviet method of appraising industrial performance is highly inadequate. It is indeed generally agreed that this method is, by itself, a major handicap to industrial growth. Criticism has been voiced and a search for remedies has gone on for many years. The issue has been highlighted by proposals advocated by Professor Evsei G. Liberman and the discussion that followed.[2]

To begin with, a few words about the present methodology. The principal performance index of the Soviet enterprise—and in fact of the industry as a whole—is based on gross output. A firm's success is measured by, and incentive rewards are essentially dependent on, fulfilment and overfulfilment of the plan with regard to gross output. In particular, premia for the firm's personnel are related to gross output per man. Of the many shortcomings of this indicator, two are particularly obvious. One is that the firm has an interest in securing from the state the lowest possible output targets. The other is that the firm has an interest in maximising costly inputs. Actual policies of Soviet firms have been shaped by these considerations to the detriment of the economy. Attempts to eliminate these and other defects of the method have resulted over the decades in a patchy system of a dozen or so supplementary indices, both in money terms and *in natura*, which are allowed for in determining the firm's and its staff's entitlement to incentive payments. Of the former the index of cost reduction is the principal one: in Soviet doctrine cost is seen as 'synthesising the work of a socialist enterprise'.[3] The method of Soviet cost calculus being what it is, a firm may be considered to be highly successful even if it has paid for a cut in its costs by excessive capital intensity. Another subsidiary index is that of 'accumulation'—roughly net profit, based on and related to cost. Yet another is the average ratio of gross capital to output. (One should bear in mind that valuation of capital stock—

[1] This is a re-worked and expanded version of an article published in *Slavic Review*, December 1963.
[2] For the exposition of Liberman's proposals see in particular *Voprosy Ekonomiki*, 1962, no. 8, and *Pravda*, 9 September 1962; also a summary of his views in *Ekonomicheskaya Gazeta*, 10 November 1962. See also A. Nove, 'The Liberman Proposals', *Survey*, April 1963.
[3] *Politicheskaya ekonomia*, Moscow, 1962, p. 522.

a tricky matter everywhere—has been neglected in the Soviet Union, and only recent years have seen some progress in this field.) The *in natura* indices include, in the first place, physical-term output targets, over-all and per man, targets of output per unit of capacity, and so on. The weaknesses of each of these indices are magnified by their heterogeneity. As often as not they will be in conflict with each other.

Recently some experiments have been carried out in the Soviet Union in substituting net for gross indices.[1] A value-added index has been tried out in several industries, and, as could be expected, its merit proved to be that it discourages excessive material intensity, though not excessive processing.

Once the concept of net indices is accepted, the next logical step after the acceptance of value-added indices is the use of a profit index. This step has been taken by Liberman. It is an essential feature of his proposals that they postulate a single yardstick for appraising an enterprise's performance—net profit. Profit would form the exclusive basis of an incentive system, and by rationalising the firm manager's choices would permit a devolution in decision-making. As suggested by Liberman, the firms would be given, in addition to their profit 'normatives' (see below, p. 122), their quantity targets for output with a broadly prescribed product-mix and delivery schedules. In contrast to the present practice, the firms themselves would draft their own plans of inputs, including labour inputs—and thereby of costs—and of 'accumulation' and investment, major projects excepted.

The idea of return from capital as a significant element of calculation has by now almost a twenty years' history in Soviet economics.[2] It has gradually crystallised in the dialogue on the operation of the 'law of

---

[1] Especially in the clothing and printing industries.

[2] For an extremely interesting analysis of the history of the Soviet attitude to problems of capital see Marie L. Lavigne, *Le Capital dans l'Economie Sovietique*, Paris, 1961, especially pp. 31 ff.; and for comment see my review article in *Soviet Studies*, April 1963. Of particular interest are the suggestions for reconciliation of Soviet thinking of the era of industrialisation with Lerner's conceptions which, unlike other socialist participants in the Western debate, he had elaborated as 'pure theory' in the sense that they were abstracted from any specific institutional set-up. Dr Lavigne's point is that the apparent disagreement between Lerner's marginalist principle of calculus and the Soviet approach dissolves itself in the 'dynamics' of the concrete Soviet economic milieu of the 1930s: that is, a milieu with an emphasis on expansion of heavy industry, a sector with a long-range tendency towards falling cost strongly accentuated by the massive assimilation of advanced technology in a retarded industry. The 'negative profitability' could justify itself by the Lernerian train of thought and thus integrate itself in a superior economic rationality.

value' under socialism. It has made a strong impact on the methodology of appraisal of investment alternatives. It has had less success in establishing itself in the methodology of pricing. To an outside observer, the incongruity of the principle of a zero price of capital with the Soviet environment of acute scarcity of capital always has been patent. The resulting waste in the use of capital has caused a growing concern to Soviet economic leadership, especially the dispersion of investment resources, their long 'maturation lag', the high rate of uninstalled equipment and idleness of capacities. (I shall not enter here into the interesting question why the principle of zero price of capital proves to be even more harmful at the present stage of Soviet economy than it was in the past when capital was shorter.) But Soviet-Marxist economics has been too inhibited in regard to the notion of productivity of capital to permit anything but its gradual assimilation.[1] In Academician Strumilin's argument, the profit norm as a success indicator is suitable only under conditions of competition between capitalist entrepreneurs.[2] By now, however, there is in Soviet economics quite a strong and articulate school with a clear vision of a profit-guided economy. This school, eminently represented by Vaag, Atlas, Malyshev, Sobol, Zakharov and Cherniavsky, has persistently and consistently advocated the concept of an interest-type 'minimal rate of profit' as the integrating element of a system of parameters in cost and price and investment-efficiency calculus, and consequently the key tool of both short- and long-term guidance for the system.[3,4]

Liberman's proposals can be placed within the frame of the 'profit-guidance school'. It is his incentive scheme rather than the conceptual framework that is really novel. The main difference in approach between him and Vaag *et al.*, is that the charge on capital is inherent in Liberman's incentive scheme rather than explicitly adopted as a matter of principle. Incentive payment (per unit of capital) would be related to profitability which in turn is related to capital employed in the enterprise (see below). The awkward question of the equalisation

---

[1] A. S. Tolkachev, *Nepreryvnost' v planirovanii i pokazateli gosudarstvennogo plana*, Moscow, 1962, p. 66.

[2] S. G. Strumilin, *Planovoye Khoziaystvo*, 1963, no. 3, p. 27.

[3] For a recent systematic presentation of its stand see in particular I. Malyshev and L. Vaag, *Ekonomicheskaya Gazeta*, 16 October 1961; and L. Vaag and S. Zakharov, *Voprosy Ekonomiki*, 1963, no. 4.

[4] At present the rate would be about 20 per cent; see L. Vaag and S. Zakharov, *Voprosy Ekonomiki*, 1963, no. 4, p. 92.

of the rate of profit is also bypassed: norms of profitability are differentiated by branches and groups of enterprises.

For an analysis of Liberman's model, a useful starting-point may be the question whether and under what conditions it can secure efficiency of choices. The problem of rational choice has two logical elements.

To begin with the first problem, we may usefully approximate it here by adopting the theorem to which the Soviet economic doctrine has now been introduced by its mathematical school. It is that with given resources and demand functions an optimal solution will be uniquely determined by maximisation of output value and its 'dual'—minimisation of factor costs—if, and only if, perfect competition prevails or is ideally imitated.[1] Logically then, the same is true of maximising the difference between the two, that is, the profit margin. We thus leave aside some vexed issues that one comes up against in this context, such as the formulation of a preference function. Nor shall we pursue here the complicating problem of returns to scale. These and a few other snags disregarded, one can say that in a perfectly competitive setup the rule of profit maximisation would guide the system toward an optimal input and output mix; and that under this regime macro- and micro-economic optima would converge—the planner and the firm manager would make identical choices.

Let us turn to the other of the two elements of the central problem I have mentioned. In the Liberman debate parameters of profit calculation, prices in particular, should be centrally set. Once profit is adopted as the maximand, the consequence for pricing can be rigorously established. For there is a unique constellation of prices of factors and their products implicit in competitive equilibrium, and thereby implicit in the optimal configuration of outputs and resource uses, again with the given constraints, that is, availability of resources and demand functions.[2] It is this system of prices, and only this system of prices, that corresponds to efficiency—on macro- and micro-planes alike—through maximisation of output values and minimisation of factor costs. It is this price framework then, and only this framework, that could drive the firm in patterning its production toward the

[1] The reader may be usefully referred for rigorous proof to R. Dorfman, P. A. Samuelson, R. N. Solow, *Linear Programming and Economic Analysis*, New York—London, 1958, especially pp. 366 ff. and 404 ff.: *cf. the formal assumptions, ibid.*

[2] For proof see R. Dorfman, P. A. Samuelson, R. N. Solow, *loc. cit.*

efficiency frontier, when under the order 'maximise your profits'.[1,2]

Liberman agrees that a 'rational' price system is a precondition of the effectiveness of his model, but he stands uncommitted on any reform of pricing required. Indeed, some of his few references suggest

[1] Professor Kantorovich has defined the firm's indicator of success as

$$c_1 x_1^{\pi} + c_2 x_2^{\pi} + \cdots + c_N x_N^{\pi} = 0$$

where the c_i denotes the solving multipliers of the optimal (efficient) plan-programme and the x_i^{π} the planned volumes of output and input of the i-th sector. He assumes, however, that the sum total would be as a rule positive through cuts in inputs and expansion of outputs (as against plan indices). The success indicator would be then some *positive*

$$R = c_1 x_1^{\phi} + c_2 x_2^{\phi} + \cdots + c_N x_N^{\phi}$$

where x_i^{ϕ} denotes actual volumes of output of input (cf. L. V. Kantorovich, 'Optimalnoye planirovanye i ekonomicheskiye pokazateli', in *Obshchiye Voprosy Primenenya Matematiki v Ekonomike i Planirovanyi*, Moscow, 1961, pp. 96 ff.).

Dr A. L. Vainshtein has rightly argued that the R may become positive owing to the violation of the planned product-mix just as much as to economies on inputs per output unit. He suggests then an indicator of success of the form

$$S = r_m{}^{\pi}{}_m{}^{\phi} \sum_{i=1}^{N} c_i x_i^{\phi}$$

where the r is a correlation coefficient for the series of planned and actual output structure. It is designed in such a way that it would equal unity for $S = R$; it would be < 1 for the case of $S < R$ (violation of the plan-'assortment'). Cf. *Matematicheskaya Statistika*, Moscow, 1962, pp. 219 ff.

[2] The implications of what is technically the regime of *zero*-profit have been examined by V. F. Pugachev, ('Lokalnyi Kriteriy i Stimulirovanye Rabotnikov' in *Ekonomika i Matematicheskiye Metody* no. 5, 1966). The burden of his argument is that profit-guidance tends to create a conflict between the local and the all-economy criteria, specifically with regards to the dynamics of technical advance. This is due, so its argued, primarily to the basic cell's interest in perpetuating its benefits from any technological improvement. The corrective suggested is to adopt for the cell, as its efficiency criterion, a period-by-period profit increment written

$$\Delta W = \int_{t-1}^{t} p \cdot dx$$

(p and x are vectors of Lagrange-type prices and of outputs and inputs, respectively).

Further, Pugachev brings in a concept of 'integral valuations' of resources of the cell, k, at the time-point t_0. This is described as a vector

$$P^k(t_0) = \int_{t_0}^{t_k} p(t) \, dt$$

A prognosis for effective life-time of k and the change of optimal prices would permit computation of proportionality coefficients of the p's at t_0 and the corresponding 'integral valuations'.

The matter is essentially one of the stimulation design rather than of the optimality criterion proper.

that he would be prepared to accept the implementation of the prevailing doctrine as compatible with, and sufficient for, his model.[1] The 'profit-guidance school' in Soviet economics has called for a change in the formula, to make the normative profit margin proportionate to the capital employed and the rents charged on nonreproducible resources.[2,3] It is only the mathematical economists who, while otherwise supporting Liberman, postulate a parametric framework internally consistent with his performance criterion: a system of imputed values of Kantorovich's solving-multiplier type.

Moreover, there is the risk of a conflict between the planner's and the firm manager's choices unless these choices have been arrived at within the same parametric framework and in obedience to the same rules of the game. How can the planner expect that he and the firm manager, the latter guided solely by profit calculus, would opt for the some output and input structure? Here again, starting from opposite premises, we finish in agreement with some 'conservative' critics of the Liberman model, such as Zverev,[4] who fear that it may result in unbalancing the economy.

However, let us suppose for the sake of argument that the behaviour precept would be identical for the command and the implementation echelons. Then first, profit maximisation under non-efficiency prices could push the planner himself to choices that might possibly be located even further away from an optimum than those toward which he gropes under the existing procedures. Second, maximising profits— could as often as not yield decision-indications at variance for the planner and the manager. It could do so if only because the cost configuration of alternatives facing the firm and the national average facing the planner could look different. It is not surprising that the Academy's scientific council, while endorsing profit as one of the relevant yardsticks of efficiency, felt unable to commit itself to Liberman's

[1] *Voprosy Ekonomiki*, 1962, no. 8, p. 111.

[2] This would correspond to Marx's formula of price under competitive capitalism— *Produktionspreis*. Liberman explicitly dissociates himself from this postulate: 'relating profit to productive funds is only a way of measuring efficiency of production. This does not mean that the formula of the 'price of production' (*Produktionspreis*) must be necessarily adopted in price formation'. *Ibid.*, p. 106, footnote.

[3] On the type of price, akin to the *Produktionspreis*, adopted by now, see footnote 1 on page 60 above.

[4] A. Zverev, *Ekonomicheskaya Gazeta*, 13 October 1962; and *Voprosy Ekonomiki*, 1962, no. 11: 'one cannot subsitute an average profit rate of an enterprise for the role and power of State planning', p. 97.

conception of a single success indicator.[1] Central allocation of output targets and constraints on the choice of techniques were not found to be a sufficient safeguard.

Theoretically, the risk that the profit-maximising firm may swerve off the guide line can be avoided by appropriate 'hedging' of its choice-path, in defence of social preferences as represented by central planning agencies. The problem of this 'hedging' technically is one of the contraints for an extreme-value problem. But perhaps one or two hints can be made here about its features. Generally speaking, the model must be such that any course of operation open to the firm adds, or leaves unaffected, or reduces the firm's profitability, depending on a given activity's location in the planner's own scale of priorities.[2] All price-cost elements of the firm's calculation would have to be moulded in such a way as to elicit the firm's required reaction. Perhaps starting from the firm's own cost calculations, the centre would have to determine unit costs in detail, and order price margins, covering overheads and profits, for each commodity so as to accord with the centre's preferences.[3] A foolproof tariff of this kind seems hardly a practicable proposition.

Hence, for better safety, physical-term specifications of outputs, and possibly of inputs, recommend themselves as a subsidiary check on the choice-making by a profit-maximising firm. In his original conception, put forward in the mid-fifties, Liberman relied on production cost as the unique plan target to be conveyed down to the firm's level.[4] As pointed out, in the present model the profitability maximand

---

[1] See reports from the session of the Academy's Scientific Council for Problems of Economic Accounting and Material Incentives in *Voprosy Ekonomiki*, 1962, nos. 10 and 11, especially the concluding contribution by the Council's chairman, Professor L. Gatovskiy. Note that while the conception of profit as a single success indicator was rejected as incompatible with the socialist mode of production, the idea of a 'tax' on capital stock was found to 'deserve serious examination' (*Voprosy Ekonomiki*), 1962, no. 11, p. 138.

[2] For a discussion of this point sse J. Lipinski, *Ekonomista*, Warsaw, 1963, no. 2, pp. 256 ff.

[3] In this context see an interesting discussion by J. Kornai and T. Lipták, 'A Mathematical Investigation of Some Economic Effects of Profit Sharing in Socialist Firms', *Econometrica*, January 1962, especially p. 157. Problems of an operational price structure within the framework of profit incentives for a model approaching Soviet-type economy are analysed by A. Wakar and J. G. Zielinski, 'Incentive Systems and Operational Price Systems', *American Economic Review*, March 1963.

[4] E. Liberman, *Kommunist*, 1956, no. 10.

is subject to targets of total commodity outputs and product assort-ment—the former presumably to be given quantitative floors and ceilings. Inputs would be shaped by firms, but clearly their patterning would be inhibited by the centre's intervention on the output side.

How detailed the centre's intervention ought to be would have to depend on the area of conflict between the output-input structures—that corresponding to the optimum of a profit maximising firm and the one preferred by the planner. Since the area is likely to be very wide indeed, in so far as Liberman's proposals aim at devolution in decision-making, they might prove to be self-defeating.

A major criticism levelled against the construction of the Liberman incentive scheme is that to the extent that profit/capital ratio rather than sum total of profit, minus uniform capital charge, is its key suc-cess indicator, it may lead to a sub-optimal allocation of national resources.[1] The point is well proved; the criticised shortcoming, however, is but a consequence of Liberman's refusal to adopt an integ-rating single interest rate on capital for the economy as postulated by the profit-guidance school.

The problem of incentive guidance at the micro-level of harmonising the interests of an individual firm and its staff with those of the econ-omy as a whole has its own strong fascination for a student of the Soviet scene. The relation of extra-economic and economic stimuli is the concern of the polical scientist and sociologist rather than of the economist. The design of a purposeful and effective mechanism of incentives and disincentives lies, of course, within the purview of the economist's analysis. The incentive construct is no doubt of consider-able practical importance, but by its very nature its problems are those of technicalities subordinated to the fundamental dilemma of what place profit maximisation as such can take within the mechanism and under the institutional setup of a Soviet-type economy. [2,3,4]

---

[1] See Vaag and Zakharov, *Voprosy Ekonomiki*, 1963, no. 4, p. 100.

[2] Since this was written, I have acquainted myself with the article 'What Price Economic Reforms? Ills and Remedies', by Harry G. Shaffer in *Problems of Communism*, May–June 1963. It gives a valuable description of existing and proposed systems of incentives and procurement and supply procedures. The reader may also be usefully referred to sources quoted in that article.

I was also able to acquaint myself with a most valuable inquiry into the 'morphology' of incentives in a collectivist society, published in Poland by Aleksy Wakar, *Morfologia bodzcow ekonomicznych*, Warsaw, 1963. The author deals with incentives—in the broader sense, including the extra-economic ones—as related to prices and methods of account-

To come back to this set-up one may note that Soviet discussions have moved beyond the scope of the Liberman proposals. Several students have advanced the postulate that some inter-enterprise 'state trade' should replace the system of allocation by administrative fiat.[1] The relatively most advanced are Nemchinov's suggestions of a kind of a plan-market. Their crucial component is a change in pricing principles and procedures.[2] The insulation of the inter-industry and the retail (consumer good) price would be abandoned: an integrated price system reflecting demand-supply position would be built up. Only with regard to a limited number of key commodities would the central administration exercise its powers of fixing rigidly stabilised prices or price 'belts': a special equalisation fund would bring such prices, *for the producer*, to the equilibrium level: the bulk of prices would be flexible and fixed by producing enterprises themselves, subject to administrative supervision. The chances of such proposals will not be appraised here. Should they lead in the Soviet Union to something approaching a competitive solution, profit-guidance would form a part of its logic, but it would do so as an element of a planning mechanism different from that assumed in Liberman. Nemchinov saw price-profit guidance conceptions as a part of a compromise between the two—of a blend of two 'control mechanisms': 'a centralised purpose-directed mechanism of command (*upravlenya*) and a decentralised mechanism of self-tuning and self-regulation (*samonastroyki i samo-regulirovanya*) of the economic system'[3]. A more exact description of the

ing. He believes that on the balance a system of integrated 'synthetic' incentives is preferable to that of 'non-synthetic' incentives.

Professor Wakar's appraisal of Liberman's proposals appears to be close to mine, *ibid.*, pp. 89–90, footnote.

[3] The Liberman discussion has been brought into a new phase by Academician V. Trapeznikov's article in *Pravda*, 17 August 1964, suggesting a profit-guidance mechanism under which financial instruments—taxation, bonuses to, and penalties on firms and interest rates on capital stock—would serve as the principal levers. There is in Trapeznikov greater consistency on some points than in Liberman (particularly with respect to charges on capital) but both share the fundamental weakness with regard to the nature of the principal parameters of the efficiency calculus, especially prices. This variant of the Liberman proposals does not affect our basic argument on the correlation of the calculus at the *micro-* and *macro-*levels.

[4] Practical implications of the Liberman proposals in terms of the ruling system of preferences are discussed incisively in Nove, 'Planner's Preferences, Priorities and Reforms', *Economic Journal*, June 1966.

[1] See Vaag and Zakharov, *op. cit.*, p. 100.

[2] See *Kommunist*, March 1964, no. 5, pp. 74 ff.

[3] V. Nemchinov, *Voprosy Ekonomiki*, 1964, no. 7, p. 86.

model of such a hybrid would be needed to permit an analysis of its workability[1].

APPENDIX TO CHAPTER 10

The issue of profit-guidance of a planned system may justify a few remarks, in a more general way, on the subject of decentralisation to which I am reverting in various contexts.[2] First this issue calls for some general notional frame and I would suggest that the regime of preferences could be usefully employed as the decisive criterion.[3] The concept of decentralisation would be reserved for an economy where the periphery's system of inter- and intra-temporal preferences would rule. The dichotomy of direct and indirect centralism would then be employed with reference to socialist societies as we know them (the terminology, though not strictly the concept, is borrowed from Academician Novozhilov[4]). Under the direct variant the central planner solves more or less explicitly what can be seen as the economy's system of difference or differential equations and imposes his solution by specific, essentially physical-term orders. Under the indirect variant of centralism the executive echelons receive their orders 'coded' in the parametric system supplied by the centre, for the decision-making processes. The employment of a competitive inter-enterprise as well as consumers' markets would fall within the classes of decentralisation and indirect centralism, respectively, depending on whether parameters for the market-

[1] Under the new Charter for the Soviet industrial enterprise the manager is to be given a set of obligatory performance indicators. These include output of specified commodities *in natura*, sales, wage-funds, transfers into the State budget, volume of centrally controlled investment and the operated capacities.

The build-up of the incentive funds is to be based on deductions from profit dependent on two possible indicators: (1) incremental volume of output sold or the absolute size of profit, (2) profitability levels. Professor Liberman now argues that in the extracting, raw material, power and groups of manufacturing industries whose output is in short supply it is the output (sold) rather than profit that is to be the maximand. (Cf. E. Liberman, 'Profit as the Servant of Communism', *The Economist*, London, 26 February 1966.) Thus the conception of the unitary criterion has been abandoned. See also the statement of the Chairman of the State Committee on Prices, V. Sitnin, *Kommunist*, September 1966.

[2] The argument of this note is elaborated in my paper 'Centralism and Parametric Framework' submitted to the ceses Seminar, Florence, 1966.

[3] T. Marschak rightly notes that while in the classical debate on the viability of a socialist economy virtually all participants, from Barone onwards, were rejecting centralised controls, they failed to define what it was that they rejected. See his 'Centralization and Decentralization in Economic Organisations', *Econometrica*, July 1959.

[4] V. V. Novozhilov, 'Zakonomernosti razvitya sistemy upravlenya sotsyalisticheskim khoziaystvom', *Ekonomika i Matematicheskiye Metody*, no. 5, 1966.

participants are formed by the market itself or provided by the centre.[1] Within this definitional frame and with reference to our discussion of the parametric system (cf. p. 61 ff.) we would submit the following. So long as the *current* supply from the centre to the operating periphery of parameters, sufficiently close to those under a dynamic optimum, exceeds the centre's technical possibilities, the indirect variant of centralism is not a workable proposition. The conclusive answer as to the sufficient approximation to optimum could probably be obtained only empirically. If and so long as indirect centralism is not workable, the only operationally viable variant of 'market socialism' would be that under decentralisation. The advance in the techniques for ensuring consistency—'the marriage' of the static, and recently also the dynamic interindustry analysis to the traditional 'balance method'—is helping to secure a greater degree of consistency of plans under direct centralism with optimisation of techniques left to some un-formalised procedures. However, in so far as an effective working of such a model is considered to be dependent on the employment of a system of stimulating and counter-stimulating pseudo-parameters, it presupposes the existence of some plan suboptimal, efficient 'under circumstances': the computational gain may prove dubious.

Under direct centralism as hitherto practised the un-articulated assumption is that of the over-all plan's very imperfect consistency. It is this assumption that makes the requirement of overfulfilment—of various performance indicators—possible and desirable. In order to carry out a function of stimulants under such a system the prices must be (a) harmonised with the planner's targets and (b) satisfy at least the condition of an over-all feasibility.[2]

The relative merits of indirect and direct centralism have to be judged on grounds of informational and computational manageability[3] and advantage. The question of the relative virtues of centralism as against decentralisation —whether with the use of a competitive market or some universal computing system, a kind of a perpetual electronic plebiscite visualised in Oskar Lange's

[1] Even where parameters are provided by the centre the firm is here a 'price-taker' in a sense that carries certain analogy to Tibor Scitovsky's concept for the competitive market system: it is so in as much as the firm has to treat the price as given and can obtain, and dispose of, as much of a commodity as it likes.

[2] N. N. Vorobyev, 'Metody issledovanya operatsyi v reshenyi ekonomicheskikh zadach', *Matematiko-Ekonomicheskiye Problemy*, Leningrad, 1966.

[3] The notion of manageability could be understood in a wider sense. In a Polish discussion the relevance of such factors as time-consumption, cost and risk of distortion of information was stressed. See O. Lange, ed., *Niektore Zagadnienia Centralizacji i Decentralizacji w Zarzadzaniu*, Warsaw, 1964. A similar approach, similarly formalised, will be found in Dr W. Sadowski's 'Economic organization and planning' (P. E. Hart and others, eds., *Econometric Analysis for National Economic Planning*, London, 1964).

latest works[1]—ultimately relates to social philosphy; and on this the economist *qua* economist cannot take a stand. Our emphasis is here on the ultimate consideration for clearly a choice made must have implications of economic nature: saving for growth is their patent area.[2]

[1] Oskar Lange, *Optymalne Decyzje-Zasady Programowania*, Warsaw, 1964. Lange discusses the minimax principle in relation to collective decision-making, and concludes: 'Here we have a mathematical solution to the problem of finding the minimax of elements of some matrix: it can therefore be carried out by a mathematical machine. This opens up to a socialist society the possibility of automation of administrative processes. In agreement with the postulates of socialist democracy, all members of the society would register their preferences (this too could be mechanised), and the decision would be computed by 'electronic brains' on the minimax principle. Such decisions would be the objective logical outcome of valuations by individuals, free from arbitrariness and subjectivism, and from possible distortions by bureaucratic decision-making agencies' (p. 294). Cf. my 'Breakthrough to Economics', *Survey*, no. 56, July 1965.

(Relative virtues and drawbacks of the market and computer as the planner's 'servo-mechanisms' are assessed in an interesting way by O. Lange in the posthumously published *O Socjalizmie i Gospodarce Socjalistycznej*, Warsaw 1966, pp. 448 ff. The conclusion is that of the two the former lends itself for securing static equilibrium—in *current* planning, and the latter could be effectively used in dynamics—in *perspective* planning. The point stressed is that investment has to be 'taken out' of market mechanism: the weakness of the precept lies in the disregard of the link-up of the two spheres of planning.)

[2] These implications for a socialist society are far from explored. Among the very few attempts a noteworthy one is that by B. Horvat (see his 'The Rule of Accumulation in a Planned Economy', submitted to the ES/TIMS Warsaw 1966 conference, and other contributions by him quoted in that paper). It is largely a critique of the Phelps-Robinson-Solow Golden Rule; the central tenet is that marginal efficiency of investment is different for the firm and for the system as a whole, and that consequently growth of national economy (socialist economy) postulates two fundamental decision levels. A discussion of the tenet and of the differing macro and micro rules offered would exceed the scope of the present context.

11 Mathematical Re-statement of the Profit-Guidance Problem

A. Bergstrom and A. Zauberman

THE LIBERMAN problem can be sketched in mathematical terms as follows. The manager is under instruction to maximise his profits, subject to capacities which are allotted to his firm and technologies which are open to it, and to constraints on his production function; floors and ceilings are placed by the planner on outputs and inputs respectively. When, for the sake of convenience, the usual simplifications—additivity and constant returns to scale—are assumed, the manager is confronted with a straightforward linear-programme situation (in fact convexity assumption will suffice: the efficiency surface may have constant and/or decreasing rates of transformation). Prices which correspond to the solution are those of the dual of that programme; they are the Lagrangean-type opportunity cost prices. Such is, then, the set of prices given to the manager by the planner in order to lead the former towards the optimum.

To re-state, let x_i $(i = 1, \ldots, k)$ be the quantity of the i-th output and $-x_{k+j}$ $(j = 1, \ldots, l)$ the quantity of the j-th input. Then the production function can be written in the form

$$(1) \qquad f(x_1, \ldots, x_m) = 0 \quad \text{where} \quad m = k+l$$

Suppose that there are floors $a_1, \ldots, a_k{}^*$ on the quantitites of k^* outputs and ceilings $b_1, \ldots, b_{l*}$ on the quantitites of l^* inputs.
Then we have the additional constraints

$$(2) \qquad x_i \geqslant a_i \quad i = 1, \ldots, k^*$$

$$(3) \qquad x_{k+j} \geqslant -b_j \quad j = 1, \ldots, l^*$$

It is assumed that the manager is required to maximise $\sum_{i=1}^{m} p_i x_i$ subject to (1) to (3).
Let $x_1^0, \ldots, x_m^0$ denote the values of the x_i for which $\sum_{i=1}^{m} p_i x_i$ is maximum subject to (1) to (3). Then $x_i^0, \ldots, x_m^0$ must satisfy (1) to (3)

and, in addition, there must be non-negative numbers $\gamma, u_1, \ldots, u_{k*}$ $v_1, \ldots, v_{l*}$ such that

$$(4) \quad \left. \begin{array}{l} p_i - \gamma f_i(x_1^0, \ldots, x^0) + u_i = 0, \text{ if } x_i^0 \neq 0 \\ p_i - \gamma f_i(x_i^0, \ldots, x_m^0) + u_i < 0, \text{ if } x_i^0 = 0 \end{array} \right\} \quad i = 1, \ldots, k*$$

$$(5) \quad \left. \begin{array}{l} p_{k+j} - \gamma f_{k+j}(x_1^0, \ldots, x_m^0) + v_j = 0, \text{ if } x_{k+j}^0 \neq 0 \\ p_{k+j} - \gamma f_{k+j}(x_l^0, \ldots, x_m^0) + v_j < 0, \text{ if } x_{k+j}^0 = 0 \end{array} \right\} \quad j = 1, \ldots, l*$$

$$(6) \quad u_i = 0, \quad \text{if} \quad x_i > a_i \quad i = 1, \ldots, k*$$

$$(7) \quad v_j = 0, \quad \text{if} \quad x_k + j > -b_j \quad j = 1, \ldots, l*$$

The manager will be lead to the optimum solution by prices if he is paid $p_i + u_i$ per unit for the i-th output and required to pay $p_{k+j} + v_j$ for the j-th input.

NOTES TO CHAPTER 11

(1) Kantorovich-Makarov have brought the concept of profit into the frame of their dynamic-planning model by means of the following reasoning. Assume that the system of operating prices coincides with the vector of '000s for all the plan time-intervals, $\pi = [\pi(1), \ldots \pi(T+1)]$. Take some s technology participating in the optimal plan, (a^s, b^s) where matrices describe 'a-temporally' inputs and outputs respectively, including that is the formation and use-up of capacities, and $x^s(t)$ the employment intensity (activity scale) of this technology during the t plan-interval. Profit from the use of this technology will equal $\{(b^s, \pi(t+1) - (a^s, \pi(t))]\}x^s(t)$. Normative rate of profit for any technology employed at optimum appears then as

$$[\{b^s, \pi(t+1)\}/\{a^s, \pi(t)\}] - 1$$

and coincides with the normative efficiency rate for investment (on this see Appendix to Chapter 14). The process of finding the optimal plan is thus shown as one of equalising profit rates for participating technologies throughout the system when plan 'ingredients' are valued at optimality prices.

(2) Tyurin[1] has investigated controls of a system by means of solving-multplier prices under discrete (Lurye-type) programming. Optimality condition appears as selecting a plan of inputs and inputs such that 'national

---

[1] Yu. N. Tyurin, 'Matematicheskaya formulovka uproshchennoy modeli proizvod-stvennogo planirovanya', *Ekonomika i Matematicheskiye Metody*, no. 3, 1965.

income' is maximised in terms of corresponding prices. The implied condition is shown to require that each enterprise chooses its outputs and inputs so as—in terms of such prices—to maximise profits, written as

$$\max_{\substack{y^t \, \epsilon \, w_i^t(x_i^t) \\ x^t \, \epsilon \, a_i^t}} (p^{t+1} y_i^t - p^t x_i^t)$$

(y and x are respectively vectors of outputs and inputs; for the i-th enterprise they form respectively closed convex sets a_i^t and w_i^t; p is the vector of prices, and t denotes time).

Assuming that vectors $p^1, p^2, \ldots, p^t, \ldots$ are collinear, some scalar $\lambda^1, \lambda^2, \ldots, \lambda^t, \ldots$ can be found such that $p^t = \lambda^t . p$; the expression in brackets would appear then as $(\lambda^{t+1}/\lambda^t . p y_i^t - p x_i^t)$. The λ^t/λ^{t+1} is thus identified as the normative efficiency rate of investment carried out during t.

(3) Of considerable interest is an algorithm of block-programming in planning for a multi-tier system, designed in the Central Economic Mathematical Institute.[1] Its maximand is

$$u_w^k = - \sum_{n_{wk-1} \in N_{wk-1}} \; \sum_{\substack{wk+1 \in W_{wk}^{k+1} \\ \pi_{wk+1} \in \Pi_{wk+1}}} c^{n_w k+1} a_{\pi_w k+1}^{n_w k-1} x_{\pi_w k+1}$$

$$- \sum_{g_{wk-1} \in G_{wk-1}} \; \sum_{\substack{wk+1 \in W_{wk}^{k+1} \\ \pi_{wk+1} \in \Pi_{wk+1}}} c^{g_w k-1} a_{\pi_w k+1}^{g_w k-1} x_{\pi_w k+1}$$

(k—no. of 'tier'; w—no. of 'complex' within 'tier'; g—no. of 'internal' product; n—no. of 'external' (traded) product; π—no. of technology; x—level of employment of technology; a—input of n-th product under π; c—solving-multiplier price of external product). Variables whose values are sought are employment levels of technologies in sub-complexes w^{k+1}. The maximand is, in substance, profit of a 'complex'.

12 The Western Inquiry into Profit Guidance

THE LIBERMAN discussion, and its ramifications in Soviet 'plano-metrics' can be seen, at least in a sense, as a belated Soviet joining of the Western inquiry into the working of decentralised systems, which originated in the debate on the rationality of collectivist systems from which Soviet economics held studiously aloof.[1] The present remarks try to relate this inquiry to the Liberman problem.

Like Liberman's, the systems envisaged in the debate on collectivism are profit-controlled. But in Lange's system in particular,[2] the manager is permitted to fix the scale of his outputs and his inputs (so as to minimise the average cost and equalise marginal cost and price of the product). At least some of the systems assume—here is another analogy to Liberman—centrally promulgated prices; but, unlike in Liberman, the prices are set in a competitive framework, for the planner regulates his equilibrium prices in response to the competitors' signals

In the early fifties Koopmans provided an analysis of the efficiency of allocative decisions under a wider range of institutional systems. In his centralised variant the planning agency has all the information going into a technology matrix (assumed to be linear), and chooses the activity vector so that the output vector would be an efficient point. The decentralised alternative is a game played by the 'helmsman' and 'custodians' for each commodity (for our purposes both roles would be integrated in that of the central planning agency). In the decentralised variant the knowledge of each of the matrix columns is available only to the manager; he determines the level of activity while the price vector is being given to him. (As compared to the 'socialist discussion' of the 1930s the analytical framework is generalised in so far as, by relating it to the specific model of technology, it has been

---

[1] Since these words have been written I have read Benjamin Ward's remark that recent developments in economic analysis suggest the pertinence of re-opening the 'socialist controversy': the question of the range of feasibility and the efficiency of economic outcomes in an economy in which means of production are subject to sub-stantial central control. (Cf. Summary of his paper to the Pittsburgh meeting of the Econometric Society, *Econometrica*, October 1963, p. 741.) I would subscribe to his view that the comparative study for economic organisations continues in its infancy.

[2] O. Lange, 'On Economic Theory of Socialism', in B. Lippincot, ed., *On the Economic Theory of Socialism*, Minneapolis, 1938, *passim*.

made independent of the continuous production function.) The discussion of the 1930s established that the requirement that each commodity to be allocated in such a way as to equate value of its marginal product in each use (at a level which cannot be exceeded in potential uses) is the necessary condition of efficiency. The Koopmans analysis shows this to be also the sufficient condition. To relate it to the Liberman problem, the Koopmans efficiency rule for the firm manager is to refrain from activities with negative profitability and keep at a constant level those where it is zero, and to expand those with positive profitability, by issuing additional orders for inputs and offering outputs.[1] For the Liberman context the latter part of the rule would mean expanding profitable activities—not constrained by minimum targets and maximum inputs allotted by the planner—and applying the price vector corresponding to the necessary and sufficient condition[2] (as above).

Further investigations, extended beyond the sphere of linearity, have centred on the convergence to postulated equilibrium in a decentralised set-up. Pioneering contributions in this field have come from Kuhn and Tucker, and Arrow and Hurwicz. The latter[3] attack the problem of concave and strictly concave, i.e. non-linear, cases by a gradient method and show that it reduces to that of a game-theoretic saddle point. (Note the methodological affinity of approach to the convergence problem in the recent Hungarian optimisation model of Soviet-type planning, by Kornai and Lipták.[4]) Of special interest, from the point of view of the Liberman problem is the Arrow-Hurwicz solution of the dynamic allocational problem, spelt out in the system of differential equations[5]:

$$(1) \qquad dy_i/dt = \begin{cases} 0 \text{ if } y_i = 0 \quad \text{and} \quad (\partial U/\partial y_1) - p_1 < 0 \\ (\partial U/\partial y_1) - p_1 \text{ otherwise} \end{cases}$$

---

[1] T. C. Koopmans, 'Analysis of Production as an Efficient Combination of Activities' in *Activity Analysis of Production and Allocation*, T. C. Koopmans, ed., New York, 1951, esp. pp. 93 ff.

[2] *Ibid.*, p. 94.

[3] K. J. Arrow and L. Hurwicz, 'Decentralisation in Resource Allocation', in *Essays in Economics and Econometrics*, Chapel Hill, 1961, esp. pp. 78 ff.

[4] Since this note was written the model was published in *Econometrica*, January 1965; see also our remarks above, pp. 96, 102.

[5] Arrow and Hurwicz, *op. cit.*, p. 79.

$$(2) \qquad \mathrm{d}x_j/\mathrm{d}t = \begin{cases} 0 \text{ if } x_j = 0 \quad \text{and} \quad \mathrm{d}\pi_j/\mathrm{d}x_j < 0 \\ \mathrm{d}\pi j/\mathrm{d}x_j \text{ otherwise} \end{cases}$$

$$(3) \qquad \mathrm{d}p_i/\mathrm{d}t \begin{cases} 0 \text{ if } p_i = 0 \quad \text{and} \quad g_i > 0 \\ -g_i \text{ otherwise} \end{cases}$$

The economic interpretation of the solution is briefly this. Final demand y_i and process-scales x_j are varied in accordance with (1) and (2) respectively and prices p_i adjusted to accord with (3): π is the profit evaluated at current prices. A 'helmsman' changes each final-demand —with reference to (1)—at a rate equal to the difference between marginal utility (U) and price (except that if the final demand for a commodity is zero and marginal utility less than the price, the final demand remains at zero). For each process its 'manager', taking price as given, changes the scale of the process—with reference to (2)—at a rate proportionate to its marginal profitability, except that if the scale is zero and the marginal profitability negative, the scale remains at zero. Price adjustments are carried out by a 'custodian'—with reference to (3)—in response to excess supplies g_i. (The roles of the helmsman and custodian would correspond to those in the Koopmans system.)

The aspect of utility maximisation is left out of the present context. Of relevance for this context is rather the role of the process manager, who, as in the Liberman system, is under the instruction to maximise his profits according to[1]

$$d\bar{\pi}_j/\mathrm{d}x_j = \bar{p} - \sum \bar{p}_i \left[-g_{ij}(x_j) \right]$$

where $\left[-g_{ij}(x_j) \right]$ is the increase in the i-th input per unit increase in the j-th 'process' output. At the optimum price, for an operated 'process', would equal marginal cost. Arrow and Hurwicz argue, however, that the usual marginal-cost pricing condition would be correct with regard to individual processes but not where the decision-making unit would have the control over several processes. This is then the situation pertinent to the planner's price-fixing in the Liberman model. The point made concerns indeed the general validity of identifying cost minimisation with optimality: it is argued that the rule may lead to socially inefficient decisions by leaving some resources

[1] *Ibid.*, p. 93.

with positive usefulness unused. The argument turns on the definition of social optimality as related to this concept (of 'positive usefulness') postulating, as it would seem, maximisation of output with all potentially usable resources employed. The formal reasoning is helpful in the analysis of the Liberman system inasmuch as it establishes, *argumento a contrario*, that profit maximisation implies price equal to marginal cost and that the Arrow-Hurwicz concept of social optimality as adopted is not compatible with a generalised regime of profit guidance (the concept, in fact, may rationalise the *traditional* Soviet approach).

The problem of profit-guidance has also been tackled in the Hungarian study (re-published in the West) by Kornai and Lipták,[1] dealing specifically with a regime of 'profit-sharing' in a Soviet-type system: the institutional framework adds to it special significance for our theme. The assumptions of the model—that the firm is guided solely by the desire to achieve a maximum value for its index of profitability (either the profit sum or a certain profit ratio) and that unit prices are given to the firm—are in broad consonance with the Liberman postulates. The objective function is

$$p(x_1, \ldots, x_n) = \sum_{i=1}^{n} b_i x_i - G\left(\sum_{i=1}^{n} x_i\right)$$

(p denotes difference between the firm's revenue and costs, x's stand for output and b's for difference between unit price and cost. G is the over-all cost function taken to be strictly positive, monotonically increasing and differentiable).

Of interest from our angle is the Hungarian discussion of the authorities' profit-shaping policy. One of the alternatives considered in Hungary was adoption of an 'indifferent' price, a price that is which under the given incentive system, and with a defined total output, would be of no influence on the profitability index, whatever the commodity composition of the feasible programme. (The authors argue that indifference is logically equivalent to fixing total output at the normal capacity level: clearly this would call for additional conditions in regard to output mix at full capacity.) In the particular case of a profit-sum incentive system the indifference could be thereby secured with

$$b_1 x - G(x) = b_2 x - G(x) = \cdots = b_n x - G(x)$$

[1] J. Kornai and T. Lipták, 'A Mathematical Investigation of Some Economic Effects of Profit Sharing in Socialist Firms', *Econometrica*, vol. xxx, January 1962, no. 1, see also above p. 96, 102, 131.

The formula for the indifference price would then be $a_i = k_i + \beta$, where k is the firm's unit cost and β an arbitrary number for which all the a's are still positive. The alternative to the indifferent price system would be one with price-margins, shaped for individual products so as to make prices conform with social preferences, b_i's being always higher for the preferred article. The argument bears out our point about the necessity of the 'hedging' of prices—in the case of a non-efficiency price structure—to reach conformity of the firm's decisions with the planner's preferences.

Finally, the Soviet manager's decision-making has been incisively analysed some years ago, in the West, by Ward (with the use of a model designed by Berliner).[1] The maximum for a Soviet firm, able to fulfil its norms, has been taken to be in the form

$$G = G(\pi, Q, x_1, \ldots, x_m)$$

The allocation decision is represented here as broadly related to a possible substitution between profits $\pi = \sum_i p_i x_i$ and value-term output $Q = \sum_{i=1}^{k} p_i k_i$, and subject to the constraint of production function $F(x_1, x_2, \ldots, x_n)$, whose first k and the remaining $(m-k)$ arguments, respectively, denote outputs and inputs. (In actual fact as we have pointed out, the Soviet manager's decision function is much more complex, related as it is to a dozen or so yardsticks of performance.) Hence in so far as he does move within some area of choice and tries to maximise his G subject to his F, out of the equilibrium conditions confronting the manager, k have the form

$$1/\lambda = F_i : [p_i(G + G_Q) + G_i]$$

where $F_i = \partial F/\partial x_i$, $G_\pi = \partial G/\partial \pi$ etc., and the remaining $(m-k)$ have the form

$$1/\lambda = F_i : (p_i G_\pi + G_i) \quad \text{etc}$$

Ward suggests that in leading the firm towards the bill of goods intended by the planner, any effect achievable by adjusting p could be also obtained by adjusting the G; and that the converse is *not* true (although one will note p does appear in the G). Hence in his variant of the model, in so far as we allow for a degree of the manager's choices, out of the set of parameters under the planner's control the G

[1] B. Ward, 'The Planners Choice Variables', in G. Crossman, ed., *Value and Plan*, Berkeley, California, 1960.

is a more effective device in a partly decentralised leading of the firm towards the goals. A relevant consideration is the incidence of change of variables involved; and from this point of view too the setting of output targets appears to be handier than that of variation of price, because the former has a more concentrated effect. Presumably because prices are seen to play a secondary role only, no analysis of the efficiency price has been offered by Ward in the context of Soviet planning. However, from the angle of our discussion, a valid point is made: it is that if the planner were to rely on price, prices which would be rational in the 'realisation' phase would not be, in general, the ones that reflect the terms on which alternatives are available to the planner himself (realisation prices are defined as 'rational' if they lead to appropriate behaviour of those concerned with plan implementation).

Part II: Planning Techniques

C. Efficiency of Investment

In chapter 13 the Soviet criteria for choosing between investment projects are described and evaluated. They are shown to suffer from a number of weaknesses, the most fundamental of which is that they are not related to a methodology ensuring efficient inter-temporal allocation of resources. In chapter 14, the underlying logic of the Soviet investment appraisal calculus is discussed. Some Soviet programming models of efficiently patterned capital formation over time are described. It is argued that the appropriate rate of interest to use in investment efficiency calculations is that derived from such a programme. In chapter 15, the question of the optimal growth is considered. It is argued that rigorous thought on this matter is desirable, but a wholly 'objective' formulation not possible.

13 Investment Criteria[1]

AT THE start of the planning era, investment decisions were made by planners on the basis of qualitative assessment of engineering data. No formal criterion was used to rank investment projects.

This practice was rationalised on Marxist grounds. In a socialist society, it was argued, preferences in general and time preferences in particular, do not lend themselves to meaningful quantification; and indeed, have not necessarily a common denominator of measurement (a hypothesis revived in discussions a third of a century later). In particular, where yield on capital is rejected as the motive force of the economy, its maximisation could not serve as a guide for investment decisions.

I am inclined to submit that it was something more than mere ideological inhibitions that militated against the explicit use of criteria and the concept of return on capital. In the heroic phase of growth, time dimensions of decision making were, perhaps, affected by dialectics. Time horizons were extended beyond sight and because they were so grand and so remote the planner felt no possibility, and in a sense no need, to allow for the passage of time. In such an environment the return on investment, on individual projects, the elasticity of yield with respect to capital, appeared hardly measurable.

In actual fact, investment choices had to be made in 'real' terms in the light of the planner's very generally conceived and poorly articulated priorities, and conveyed down the administrative ladder by means of fiats also couched in physical terms. Gradually, however, as the economy expanded in width and depth, choices confronting the

---

[1] The subject of the present chapter has been treated by me *inter alia* in 'Economic Thought in the Soviet Union. I. Economic Law and The Theory of Value', *Review of Economic Studies*, vol. xvi, 1948, no. 1; 'The Prospects for Soviet Investigations into Capital Efficiency', *Soviet Studies*, April 1950; 'A Note on Soviet Capital Controversy', *Quarterly Journal of Economics*, August 1955; and 'The Soviet and Polish Quest for a Criterion of Investment Efficiency', *Economica*, August 1962. The present chapter expands, and in some points, revises the discussion of last-named article. The reader may be directed for references and bibliography to that contribution.

For a historical survey of Soviet investment strategy and calculus, see J. M. Collette, *Politique des Investissements et Calcul—L'Experience Sovietique*, Paris, 1965, and the review-article A. Zauberman, 'Forty Years of the Time-Factor in Soviet Economics', *Soviet Studies*, July 1966.

decision-makers became more and more complicated and diversified, adding to the precariousness of intuitive judgement. It was from the technical periphery[1] rather than the planning centre that pressures gradually developed for some 'synthesised' measuring of efficiency in inter-temporal resource allocation. It may not be a coincidence that it was the engineers and builders of the grandiose hydro-stations who started employing some rates (in the 1930s)[2,3]—the rates being chosen entirely at random (it is their opposite numbers who have demanded such very long-term rates in Western indicative planning). The attempts came up against resistance as being unacceptable on Marxist grounds. Since the mid forties the broad notion of an actualisation coefficient gradually rooted itself in Soviet practice as well as in theory, to find eventually in 1960 a definitive formulation in official method-ology. It was borrowed by other socialist countries, with some original elaborations in two of them, Poland and Hungary. (One could parenthetically note here yet another point of East-West convergence in economic thought. Professor Solow[4] says that he too would 'tech-nocratically' concentrate on this concept—as one independent of the

---

[1] See for instance suggestions made in the 1930s for railway projects: M. Proto-dyakonov, *Izyskanya i proyektirovanye zheleznykh dorog*, Moscow, 1932.

[2] Chronologically, the first formulation may be credited to F. F. Gubin's paper pub-lished in 1945 in a hydro-technological journal (*Gidrotekhnicheskoye Stroitelstvo*, 1945, nos. 1–2). He advocated average rate of profit as an investment-efficiency yardstick (he argued, incidentally, that the rate must be set, *caeteris paribus*, higher than is normal in capitalist economies, in consideration of more favourable conditions for productivity of capital under socialism). Academician Vedeneyev's corrective to Gubin's proposals suggested differential sectoral rates instead of a single national rate of profit. Their proposals were rejected as incompatible with socialism.

[3] In Western literature the problem of measuring the benefits of investment by 'public hand' has been investigated largely in relation to projects intended to promote efficiency of private economic and social activities. Significantly here it is the practi-tioner who tends to be sceptical about the scope for the cost-benefit and a formalised method in general. Cf. Professor Dorfman's editorial introduction to *Measuring Benefits of Government Investments*, Washington DC, 1965.

[4] R. M. Solow, *Capital Theory and the Rate of Return*, Amsterdam, 1963. In a comment Prof. Joan Robinson remarks that the notion of factor allocation in conditions of perfect competition makes sense in a normative theory for a planned economy rather than in a descriptive theory of capitalist economy, and that the notion of the marginal produc-tivity of investment makes sense in the context of socialist planning [rather than a market economy?] 'Solow on the Rate of Return', *Economic Journal*, June 1964, p. 410. This proposition is valid if meant to convey the idea that in order to be perfect the plan-ner should simulate perfect competition assuming that he could do so more perfectly than the imperfect market of real life.

nstitutional regime of the economy—rather than on observed market ates or other forms of income receipt.)[1]

The Soviet methodology[2] uses two principal indicators of return on nvestment.

One is termed the criterion of general or absolute efficiency. It is lefined as the ratio of the annual increment of the physical volume of national product (as defined in the Soviet Union, that is material gross-gross output minus depreciation and material inputs) to the total nvestment which generated it. It is the marginal output-capital ratio. The computational principles are anything but precise: it may suffice to point out that the question of gestation has long been left untouched. The purpose of this criterion appears to be, to provide broad, *ex post*, information on the course of economic life. Because of the conceptual and practical shortcomings of this yardstick, some critics (especially Lurie) have demanded, in the debates on a revised version of the methodology, that it should be abandoned. It is generally agreed that at least at the lower tiers of the economy profit rather than net product has to be related to investment owing to both definitional and computational difficulties, and that this undermines the logic of the coefficient; its sensitiveness to the distortions of the Soviet price-system has been also stressed.[3]

The other indicator is called the 'coefficient of comparative economic efficiency'. Its purpose is as follows. Assume that the plan fixes an output target for a particular sector. More than one technically feasible investment project for producing this output exists. Which

[1] After the completion of this chapter I read Professor Dorfman's illuminating discussion of problems of the appraisal of investment efficiency in a 'mixed' economy ('Econometric Analysis for Assessing the Efficacy of Public Investment', in *The Econometric Approach to Development Planning*, Amsterdam—Chicago, 1965). One of the approaches, close to the build-up of a fully-fledged social utility function would be, in his suggestion, the establishing of shadow prices for the various objectives involved. In a discussion of the paper he stressed, however, the help of the private sector's presence in the providing of the valuation frame by the market.

[2] USSR Academy of Sciences, *Tipovaya Metodika Opredelenya Ekonomicheskoy Effektivnosti Kapitalnykh Vlozheniy i Novoy Tekhniki v Narodnom Khoziaystve*, Moscow, 1960.

On recent developments in Soviet methodology and practice see *Metody i Praktika Opredelyenya Effektivnosti Kapitalnykh Vlozheniy i Novoy Tekhniki*, issues 1–6, Moscow, 1964; for a more recent discussion see T. S. Khachaturov, *Ekonomicheskaya Effektivnost Kapitalnykh Vlozheniy*, Moscow, 1964. Problems of sectoral perspective plans of investment are discussed in A. I. Mitrofanov, R. M. Merkin, *Metody Rashcheta Kapitalnykh Vlozheniy pri Perspektivnom Planirovanyi*, Moscow, 1966.

[3] See V. N. Bogachev, *Srok Okupayemosti*, Moscow, 1966, pp. 198 ff.

INVESTMENT CRITERIA

should be chosen? If one project has both a lower initial capital cost
and a lower annual running cost than the other, then clearly it should
be chosen. It may happen, however, that one project has a higher
capital cost but a lower annual running cost than the other. In
this case, the more capital-absorbing project is chosen only if the
additional investment cost can be recouped by savings on current costs
within a period equal to, or smaller than, the normative recoupment
period officially established for that sector.

Let I_1 be the capital outlay on the project with the larger initial
cost, and I_2 the capital outlay on the project with the lower initial cost,
and c_1 and c_2 be the respective annual operating costs of the two projects, then

$$\frac{I_1 - I_2}{c_2 - c_1} = T$$

where T is the recoupment period. If $T \leqslant T_n$ where T_n is the normative recoupment period, then project 1 is chosen. If $T > T_n$ then project
2 is chosen. It is customary to operate, not with T, but with its
reciprocal, E, known as the 'coefficient of comparative economic
efficiency'. The latter can be regarded as the *normative* net marginal
efficiency of capital[1] or the normative net incremental output/capital
ratio. (The sense in which this definition is used here will be qualified
in the subsequent discussion.[2])

Suppose that there are more than two technically feasible projects.

$$\frac{c_2 - c_1}{I_1 - I_2} \geqslant \frac{1}{T_n}$$

is the criterion for choosing 1 in preference to 2. This inequality can
be rewritten

$$c_1 + I_1 \cdot \frac{1}{T_n} \leqslant c_2 + I_2 \cdot \frac{1}{T_n}$$

[1] Capital outlay in the convention adhered to in Soviet planning embraces the
cost of buildings, of equipment and its installation, and of improvements to the site,
but not the cost of the site itself. This approach, conforming to the traditional view on
the socio-economic role of land, is shared also by the Hungarian and Polish methodologies. Somewhat curiously, the official Czechoslovak methodology—otherwise rather
closely patterned on the Soviet—prescribes the inclusion of land in the costs of capital
formation.

[2] As Lurie remarks (*O Matematicheskikh Metodakh Reshenya Zadach na Optimum pri
Planirovanyi Sotsyalisticheskogo Khoziaystva*, op. cit., pp. 234 ff.) there is striking confusion
in the Soviet literature of the subject between the investment-efficiency norm—a
marginalist concept—and the (average) rate of profitability, the net-product/capital
stock, and accumulated-net-product/capital stock ratios.

Generalising to the more than two project case, choose that project which minimises

$$c + I.\frac{I}{T_n}$$

(i.e. choose that project which minimises the sum of operating costs plus capital charge).

These criteria suffer from a number of weaknesses:

(1) The costs considered in the model methodology are those of the enterprise only. Indirect repercussions of its decision are ignored. For example, if the construction of a project, which appears to be advantageous on the basis of the official formulae, would require the building of an additional railway or a new mine, the cost of expansion of these latter industries could easily exceed the economies derived from the decline in unit costs of the project, so that a variant which failed the formulae might be more advantageous for the economy as a whole because it had no expensive indirect repercussions.

Now when input-output techniques are employed, the full-order effects can be read off the inverse of an inter-industry matrix. However, debates on the revised methodology[1] brought out the snags of what one participant (Chernomordik) described as the 'fool's infinity': there is the practical difficulty in attributing the extra-capacities required as the 'indirect effect' to a *given* principal plant. There seems to be a general consensus of opinion that differentiation should be made between investment in installations providing the basic plant with elements of fixed capital, and those supplying it *currently* with elements of working capital; and that it is practicable to take into account in full only the latter group. In any case no more than one 'round' of consequential investment is likely to be recommended for computation in practice; Soviet students[2] have found that generally the indirect effect tends to fade out by the third or fourth iteration. (One may note here that in Tinbergen's model, for instance, projects are grouped in 'bunches' with the complementary national and regional capacity extensions estimated with the aid of an imaginative 'semi-input-output' method.)[3]

---

[1] See the report quoted, *Voprosy Ekonomiki*, 1964, no. 11.

[2] Cf. F. Shevyakov, *Planovoye Khoziaystvo*, 1964; no. 3; also V. P. Krassovskiy in the report quoted above, *Voprosy Ekonomiki*, 1964, no. 11.

[3] The method is described in *The Appraisal of Investment Projects*, Rotterdam, November 1963, and *Regional Planning*, January 1964; it may make possible the solution of the problem by using only a portion of the total set of equations of the matrix.

(2) The existence of substitutable inputs and joint products raise difficulties. According to Shevyakov,[1] Gosplan's Scientific and Research Institute recommends the use of 'coefficients of technical equivalence'. (They are conversion factors which can, for example turn coal, oil, natural gas, uranium and waterfalls into a common unit of measurement, say tons of coal equivalent.) Not enough is known about the principles on which *technically* oriented substitution parameters are to be arrived at to dispel doubts about their full adequacy for the assessment of *economic* effects. The procedure recommended is that of successive approximation with a set of input-output matrices; the check of efficiency of the 'balance' of production is to be carried out by means of the methods of linear or dynamic programming.

(3) Another weakness of the Soviet and other methodologies is the handling of capacities as a *datum*, usually a *datum* in physical quantities, with no consideration of returns to scale and its impact on efficiency.

(4) An obvious corrective which had to be introduced into the testing procedures for investment is that for the period of the 'maturation' of the capacities: that is firstly, for the gestation period during which capital input remains sterile, and secondly, for the additional period over which the project would be brought to the fully planned output levels. The immobilisation of capital is considered an additional cost, and is computed by compounding the sum involved at the rate prescribed by the efficiency coefficient, $(1 + E)^t$. (Thus the traditional idiosyncrasies of Soviet thinking in respect of interest-like calculations has been overcome, not without hesitations.) However, debates on the revised methodology have brought out the doubts—legitimate doubts, we think—as to the validity of employing this kind of efficiency coefficient, or for that matter the average rate of profitability, for this purpose.[2] It seems that employment of some arbitrary rate finds more favour, at least until the nature of inter-temporal calculation is explored.

The problem of sterilisation of capital during the 'maturation' of the project is treated in Poland[3,4] in a way which is interesting

---

[1] *Op. cit.*

[2] See report quoted, *Voprosy Ekonomiki*, 1964, no. 11.

[3] *Instrukcja Ogolna w Sprawie Metodyki Badan Ekonomicznej Efetywnosci Inwestycji*, Warsaw, 1962.

[4] There is a good discussion of the way 'maturation' lags can be handled in planning, by S. M. Vishnev ('Ob eshelonirovanyi kapitalnykh vlozheniy vo vremeni', in *Planirovanye i Ekonomiko-Matematicheskiye Metody*, N. P. Fedorenko, ed., *op. cit.*). It has a

theoretically as well as from the point of view of practice, a way which, as will be seen, has been made possible, and indeed necessary, by the adopted macro-approach (the adopting of the single investment-efficiency rate). In brief this approach, owed to Kalecki and his associates, is this:[1] let the reciprocal of the marginal fixed capital/output ratio be a certain 'm'; then a postulated increment in national income 'd' would entail investing $m.d$; when the associated quantity of circulating capital, u, is allowed for, this would make a total of $d.(m+u)$. Assume further that factor balance, capital/labour balance prevails with a marginal ratio of reward for labour to national income being a certain r. Then providing the complementary labour force for this capital asset would entail adding $r.d$ to the national wage-bill.[2] At the same time replacing the labour channelled away from elsewhere in the economy—when the national efficiency coefficient E is taken as a yardstick—would entail extra labour-saving capital outlay of $r.d/E = r.d.T$. Hence the incremental national income as related to a unit capital-outlay required to generate it (expressed also in terms of income) appears as the 'freeze coefficient', i.e. as the

$$q_z = d/(m.d+u.d+r.d.T) = 1/(m+u+r.T).$$

Finally, the expression will become $q_z = 1(m+u+r.T) - A$, if an A is allowed for the amortisation element in gross national product.

---

suggestion of a triangularised matrix for a recursive system in the build-up of capacities over time. On this basis a non-cyclical 'directional' network would be constructed to help delineate the 'critical route' determining the cumulative lag and pattern of capital formation over time (so as to minimise the lag for a maximised 'maturation' of investment).

[1] See M. Kalecki, *Ekonomista*, 1957, no. 1, and *Ekonomista*, 1958, no. 6; and with M. Rakowski, *Gospodarka Planowa*, 1959, no. 11; *Ekonomista*, 1961, no. 5; and *Gospodarka Planowa*, 1962, no. 3; see also M. Kalecki and M. Rakowski, 'Generalized Formula of the Efficiency of Investment' in A. Nove and A. Zauberman, eds., *Studies on the Theory of Reproduction and Prices*, Warsaw, 1964.

[2] The Hungarian official methodology requires a separate appraisal of each of the two effects of investment: that is its labour-saving and its output-rising effects. At the enterprise level the first is measured as the volume of investment required for cutting-down the wage-bill; the second is taken as the ratio of incremental net output (gross output minus cost of materials) to the investment entailed in creating new capacities within a given project, plus that needed for releasing elsewhere, the labour to man them (calculated per unit of saved wages). When testing efficiency at the all-economy level consequential, indirect, capital requirements throughout the economy are to be allowed for. (For a good discussion of traditional practice cf. B. Balassa, *The Hungarian Experience in Economic Planning*, New Haven, 1959.)

The rationale of employing the two yardsticks, the $1/T$ and the q_z, has been cogently questioned in Polish writing. Their structure is, as we have seen, different. On the one hand, the q_z is designed as the actual equilibrium net rate of return on capital; on the other hand, the $1/T$ is devised as the rate corresponding to the *postulated* pay-off; it is gross of cost of repair and replacement and carries the planner's discount of the future (see p. 144). We shall not analyse now the respective merits and demerits but it is hard to see why one coefficient rather than the other should better perform the same role at the two stages of the project's cycle (its gestation and operation), a role that is of measuring opportunity cost of capital sunk in it.

A partly inter-connected problem is the treatment of durability of capital assets and the aging-process. It is one of the impact of project's life-time on efficiency, one of a conflict between the dynamics of an economy and the static nature of investment once it has been 'embodied' in a given set of capacities. Hence the question of optimality of the life-span.

In Soviet literature Novikov[1] maintains that minimisation of total cost of the economy's output could not be achieved with the use of a constant normative recoupment period T for assets with varying useful life-times. (He has further shown that this would require a Lagrangean-type multiplier—this point will be dealt with later in the presentation of Kantorovich's argument).

The solution sought in Poland for the single T rate has been the 'reduction' of efficiency of assets with different useful life expectation to 'equivalence' with that of some standard unit (the 1960 methodology). Essentially the idea is akin to that represented in Western literature by Arrow and Solow and others[2]: the idea of looking upon the stock of capital goods over time as exposed to a constant force of mortality, and the relative productivity of additions to the stock as being under pressure from older vintages. Thus each crop of productive assets embodies a more advanced technology; their efficiency is viewed as related to that of cumulative volume of the stock inherited from the past. Kalecki's geometric exposition of the approach—offered in a

[1] M. Novikov, *Voprosy Ekonomiki*, 1964, no. 4, pp. 123 ff.
[2] See in particular R. Solow, 'Investment and Technical Progress' in K. J. Arrow *et al.*, eds., *Mathematical Methods in the Social Sciences*, Stanford, California, 1962; and K. J. Arrow, 'The Implications of Learning by Doing', *Review of Economic Studies*, June 1962.

Polish controversy[1] may be sketched out perhaps fairly and, for our purposes, usefully as follows:

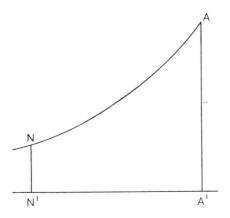

Let the abscissae and the ordinate axes measure respectively time, and the 'stream' of investment of a given type being brought into use continuously up to the moment A. Denote further the volume of investment per time unit by I, its rate of growth by some constant a and the useful life-time of a project under consideration by n. The NA curve traces the course of investment up to the point A. Then the whole stock of assests of the type considered is shown by the area NN'A'A enclosing the curve NA: by assumption the pre-N' assets have been scrapped by that time while the whole of the post-N' vintages have survived and are still at work. At any moment assets in operation are of ages between o and n years. The area can be expressed as $\{1 - 1/(1 + \alpha)^n\}$: *a caeteris paribus* output from assets of the kind considered is proportionate to this magnitude, an increasing function of n. (It could be expressed alternatively as a certain integral of time derivatives.) In other words, the expression describes the rise in investment productivity of a given kind of asset as a function of the life-span n. It follows that with the respect to its investment efficiency a project

---

[1] M. Kalecki, *Ekonomista*, 1961, no. 5.

with a given output P and a useful life-time n is equivalent to one with a standard life-span n_{con} and an output of

$$P.[1 - 1/(1+\alpha)^n] : [1 - 1/(1+\alpha)^{n_{con}}]$$

The expression following the P is denoted by the symbol $\mathcal{Z}_n$: in other words this symbol stands for the ratio of the sum total of annual outputs from a given asset actualised back to the base-year of exploitation, to the sum total of similarly actualised outputs for a project with a standard longevity. The $\mathcal{Z}_n$ coefficient serves thus for 'reducing' a given capital asset to one with a standard life-time. (It can easily be shown that the ratio of outputs from two capacity sets—varying in respect of life-spans and in respect of capital-output ratios—will equal the ratio of their respective average capital-output ratios, which in turn will equal the $\mathcal{Z}_n$, a function of the a and n.)

Symmetrically, running costs are 'reduced' to those of a standard capacity set, and a coefficient Υ_n is obtained for cost as an analogue of the $\mathcal{Z}_n$. (The sum of running costs C of assets built during a year may be taken to grow at a lower rate than the sum of investment I, due to an assumed decline in unit costs: if the rate of this decline is β we will have $\alpha > \beta$.)

Now, by 'reducing' a given asset to a standard one, i.e. one with standardised life-time and cost, we can synthesise its efficiency in terms of a cost/output index as

$$E^* = \frac{1/T.I(1 + q_z n_z)}{\mathcal{Z}_n P} + \frac{\Upsilon_n C_{con}}{\mathcal{Z}_n P}$$

This is the index whose value has to be minimised (and is relevant for the ranking of alternatives).

Both $\mathcal{Z}_n$ and $\Upsilon_n/\mathcal{Z}_n$ are increasing functions of the number of years, $f(n)$. Hence with the normal relationship of I and C_{con}, and with a rising n, E^* declines up to a point beyond which it too is rising. There would be then some optimal period of n at which the total cost/output index E^* is at a minimum. The decline in the left-hand term reflects gains from longer use of invested capital; the rise in the right-hand term reflects the loss due to the growing number of assets with rising current cost, in other words to obsolescence. The intuitively obvious point is that under conditions of faster growth it is the short-lived type of assets that would be more advantageous: but this is in conflict with the empirically observable fact that it is the more durable capital goods which are usually carriers of advanced techniques. It is the consideration of such losses and gains which forms the framework of the optimality of capital outlay in a project designed—here is the stress—for a growing economy.

Theoretical critique and experience have apparently induced a change in the treatment of the problem of varying useful life-spans.

The most recent revision[1] of the methodology prescribes the adjusting of investment outlays and current cost by means of coefficients which are some functions of the life-span n. The 'reduced outlays' appear then as $i.f(n)/T + k.\varphi(n)$, where i and k denote respectively investment and current cost. The value for n which sets this sum at minimum is taken as optimal (rather than any n rigidly set for a given kind of assets).

Thus the selection procedure rests on the formula

$$i.f(n_{\text{opt}})/T + k.\varphi(n_{\text{opt}}) \leqslant i.f(n)/T + k.\varphi(n)$$

for any life-span n.[2,3]

[1] I learned of this revision only at a very late stage—from a re-statement in M. Kalecki, *Ekonomista*, 1965, no. 1, pp. 12–13.

[2] The impact of ageing on economic efficiency is measured in Soviet investment practice with the use of δ_c, a 'coefficient of longevity' evolved by the Gosstroy's Research Institute: it is a function of two variables, T, the asset's life-span, and α, the maintenance cost-coefficient (in per cent of initial value)

$$\delta_c = [1 + (1 + \alpha)/T.\varDelta_T]$$

The $\varDelta_T$ is here a coefficient of incremental maintenance cost: it is derived from discounted cost over the useful life-time

$$\mathcal{Z} = \alpha/100.\int_0^T dT/(1+E)^T = \alpha/100.\varDelta_T$$

Here

$$\varDelta_T = 1/\ln(1+E).[1 - 1/(1+E)^T]$$

The E is the normative coefficient of investment efficiency. (V. Maltsev and A. Koretskiy, 'Dolgovechnost' i ekonomicheskaya effektivnost'' in *Planovoye Khoziaystvo*, 1965, no. 7.)

As will be noticed the impact of competition of progressive techniques is not explicitly allowed for.

[3] Problems of depreciation were, for decades, neglected in Soviet economic theory: the relevance of the question of obsolescence was in fact denied for a non-competitive system. Recent advance in this field is largely owed to Academician Kantorovich and his school. Simple models of amortisation and a discussion—in programming terms—of optimal life-time of equipment, replacement of old technology and coexistence of old and new techniques will be found in his 'Amortizatsyonnyie otchislenya i otsenka effektivnosti novoy tekhniki v sisteme optimalnogo planirovanya', V. V. Novozhilov *et al.*, eds., *Matematiko-Ekonomicheskiye Problemy*, Leningrad, 1966. Cf. also L. V. Kantorovich and I. V. Romanovskiy, 'Amortizatsyonnyie platezhi pri optimalnom ispolzovanyi oborudovanya', *Doklady*, USSR Academy of Sciences, 1966.

(5) The common major weakness of Soviet and other methodologies of investment-efficiency appraisal discussed here is that they are arrived at and operate within the framework of commodity prices, which by their very construction are *non*-efficiency parameters *par excellence* (see our remarks above, p. 61). The problem of the value-frame of the investment-efficiency scrutiny is the more complicated as it is precisely the investment processes that inevitably influence price relations themselves. The weakness pointed out here is shared by the Soviet, Polish and Hungarian T's, and by the Polish q_z and also by the coefficients of the Kalecki-Rakowski theoretical blue-print for the latter. On the empirical plane the designers of the Hungarian investment-efficiency coefficient[1] have tried to escape from the disability by taking the annual outputs into calculations of efficiency—into the numerator that is of the efficiency testing formula—as well as by taking imported materials, at world market prices, converted at the current exchange rate for the forint. This short cut towards efficiency prices is, however, hardly legitimate for an economy whose internal prices are insulated from world price relations. (*Mutatis mutandis* one would incidentally say the same of the Hungarian methods of comparing capital efficiency of projects under consideration with that of similar projects abroad—as an indicator of competitiveness.)

(6) In Soviet practice, the officially prescribed 'normative' recoupment periods are differentiated as between sectors. In this the Soviet approach differs from that adopted in both Poland and Hungary where a single rate is fixed for the economy as a whole: in those two countries methodology of investment-appraisal proceeds from the idea that the correlation of operating costs and investment outlay of projects has to be subordinated to macro-economic criteria.

The matter has been for some time a point of controversy in Soviet economics. The protagonists of the solution adopted argue that critics confuse the problem of ends and means: that the purpose of the Soviet calculus of efficiency is to discover ways of achieving objectives with the lowest cost, and not to set the objectives themselves. Indeed, it is contended that a single rate would inhibit the conscious structuring of investments according to the planner's hierarchy of aims. The

---

[1] The Hungarian formula of the efficiency appraisal is basically similar to the Soviet: one of the major differences is that its capital-cost item consists of three specified components, those of the main investment adjusted with a gestation-coefficient, of auxiliary investment (corrected in the same way) and of circulating capital required for the operation of the project. Cf. p. 145, footnote 2.

argument is valid under its assumptions (I shall return to these assumptions later on). It is evident, however, (though the authors of the construct do not seem to have accepted the conclusion) that with this approach the significance of the efficiency test—of measuring comparative advantage—by means of the E or $1/T$ is severely circumscribed. In actual fact the test is not taken to be absolute—it is supplemented by additional checks with reference to a series of indicators, most of them in physical terms.

In his latest discussion of the problem Kalecki[1] has validly argued that, under the adopted system of efficiency testing, a given pay-off period T has as its corollary a definite level of investment (I) and labour input (R) which are required for an increment of product of a given volume and pattern: and that the geometrical locus of the two, of I and R, is a falling production function curve. With a uniform T, with no allowance made for varying life-spans of projects: (1) the curve is concave and investment outlay is minimised for a given R; (2) the slope of the tangent at the point I, R, corresponding to the T, equals $-i/g$. T (where i is investment cost and g an hourly wage of 'simple' labour; labour inputs are measured here in terms of such a wage). And these properties are shown to be lost once in addition to investment and labour some other variables are brought in as is the case in the Soviet procedures of input minimisation.

As devised, the Soviet investment efficiency criterion does not lend itself as a tool for macro-choice-making. Demand for a single rate is finding a virtually unanimous support from the mathematical school. Indeed, it seems to correspond to the general trend in Soviet thinking on the subject. True, as it seems, the regime of differentiated rates is likely to be preserved in the revised version of the methodology. But in the debates on this version even the supporters of this regime conceded that for inter-sectoral (as distinct from intra-sectoral) choice-making, some 'averaged' or an all-economy single rate should be used.[2,3]

---

[1] M. Kalecki, 'Krzywa produkcji a rachunek efektywnosci inwestycji', *Ekonomista*, 1965, no. 1.

[2] See in particular the contribution by A. I. Shuster to the debate on the revised version in *Voprosy Ekonomiki*, 1964, no. 11. For the arguments of those postulating a unified rate for the economy see contributions by A. I. Lurie and V. I. Dmitriev, *ibid.*

[3] A pertinent point, on pragmatic grounds, has been made by G. S. Detkov ('Vzaimosvyaz mezhdu normativom ekonomicheskoy effektivnosti kapitalovlozheniy i tempom rasshirennogo proizvodstva', in *Effektivnost Kapitalnykh Vlozheniy*, T. S. Khachaturov, ed.,

(7) The point discussed is related to the question of the macro-maximand. Soviet efficiency criterion is meant indirectly to maximise net product, but it does so under the proviso that other elements in the calculation correspond to this optimum—let us call it a '*caeteris paribus*' proviso. In the Soviet testing procedure of a given project's efficiency, total cost is taken to be the minimand: the scrutiny does secure the lowest per unit cost, and thereby a contribution to net product—again under similar proviso *caeteris paribus*. Indeed, the minimand is not explicitly related to any optimand in the economy as a whole to which the project under consideration is expected to contribute: it is related to a constant production-capacity, and the optimisation of this production *datum* is not touched upon in the schema adopted for the measuring of comparative advantage (this matter is partly treated in our previous point). Last but not least, the optimality of choices is, in fact, not expected to be achieved exclusively by reference to criteria underlying the T: it will be recalled that a set of other yardsticks is recommended for parallel use.

The Polish methodology does adopt national income as a macro-economic maximand. This is explicit in particular in the argument proffered in support of the Kalecki-Rakowski capital-efficiency coefficient for the 'freeze' period: the q_z is (it was noted) related to the growth of national income. Indeed the path along which this parameter is being quantified may be thought of as a very rough kind of programming—as a (linear) programme with national income being maximised subject to two constraints: (1) resource availabilities—the assumed two-factor labour/capital equilibrium, under the full employment of labour (other scarce factors, such as foreign exchange, are left aside), and (2) policy postulates with regard to wage-goods consumption, the wage-bill being related to national income. However, the clarity of the optimisation approach in the Kalecki-Rakowski solution is blurred in the test of efficiency itself.[1, 2, 3]

Moscow, 1963, p. 83). While defending, in principle, differentiation of rates, he argues that it is not practicable where full-order rather than direct costs of projects are considered.

[1] Malinvaud mentions the Kalecki-Rakowski construct as one of those in which the many correctives applied to the recoupment-period criterion bring the latter into quite close vicinity with that of 'actualised value'. 'Actualised value' is defined in Malinvaud as $V = \sum_{t=1}^{h} \beta_t (B_t - A_t)$, where B and A are, respectively, values of 'benefits' discounted for, and costs to be incurred at, the moment $t = 1, 2, \ldots, h$ and β is the actualisation factor based on the rate of interest. It is argued by Malinvaud that—by contrast

Increasingly in recent years the problem of investment criteria has been treated as one aspect of the wider question of inter-temporal resource allocation. A discernible general line of progress in Soviet thinking in these matters is the successive widening of its frame. Originally it centred on the technical parameters of a project, next it was widened to allow for its immediate economic aspect, and now it tends to place project testing within the context of overall optimality in the economy.[1] Indeed, only within this context is the appraisal of an individual investment consistent with its logic.

to two other criteria, those of the rate of return and of the recoupment period—'actualised value' does provide an adequate efficiency yardstick of a project variant (the inadequacy of the rate of return is primarily ascribed—and convincingly so—to ambiguity with regard to the constancy, or otherwise, of the rate of interest over time: constant rate would make the criteria equivalent).

Note, however, that Malinvaud assumes the employment of the 'actualised value' criterion as related to an all-economy programme for which optimum had been found, and prices and rates of interest associated with this optimum determined: 'actualised value' of project variants would be calculated with the use of these parameters; only the variants retained would maximise the value of projects entered into the programme. With this qualification Malinvaud's appraisal broadly coincides with ours. Clearly the Kalecki-Rakowski construct fails to meet the Malinvaud requirement with regard to the price framework.

(Cf. E. Malinvaud, *L'Interêt comme l'indicateur de choix dans l'allocation des ressources*, a paper read at the Royaumont, 1962, Colloquium on the rate-of-interest theory, especially pp. 40 ff.: I read this important contribution only after the completion of this essay and wish to express my thanks to Professor Malinvaud for very kindly providing me with a mimeo-copy of the paper.)

[2] Academician Khachaturov criticises the Polish T and q_z *inter alia* on the ground that they are *averaged* magnitudes and hence cannot be employed in setting the limit of employable projects. (Cf. *Voprosy Ekonomiki*, 1964, no. 7, p. 133.) This criticism does not seem legitimate, at least with regard to the Polish q_z: the reasoning presented above shows that it is conceived as an extremal magnitude.

[3] Since this paragraph was written I have found in *Zagadnienia Rachunku Ekonomicznego w Planie Centralnym*, Warsaw, 1964, pp. 208 ff. by K. Porwit, a well-presented argument on the similarity of the logic underlying both the Polish normative investment-efficiency coefficient and the dual price of the 'investment limit', corresponding that is to the optimum solution of the programme for the choice of techniques.

[1] The line of development of Soviet thinking in this field emerges from the interesting paper by V. V. Novozhilov, 'Faktor Vremeni v Ekonomicheskikh Raschetakh', in *Matematiko-Ekonomicheskiye Problemy*, Leningrad University, 1963.

14 Efficient Capital Formation

THE BASIC philosophy behind the investment efficiency criterion is that propounded by Strumilin in the 1940s[1] (partly reviving ideas which had currency in Soviet economics in the 1920s). Formally Strumilin's was a one-factor world. In his construct then efficiency of investment is mirrored, and adequately expressed, in terms of productivity of labour. This is an approach congenial to Marxists. In the West it has been adopted by Dobb; and as an expositional device it is not confined to Marxists, for Kaldor[2] among others argues that in the absence of any reliable measure of quantity of capital, and in a world where moreover, technical specifications of capital goods are continuously changing, the notion of the amount of capital loses precision, and the focus in the moving equilibrium of growth must be rather on productivity of labour.

In substance, however, ever since Strumilin's famous disquisition, the rate of actualisation of investment has been seen, even if rather poorly articulated, as one of the planner's two-factors macro-production function, relating dynamically use-intensities and efficiencies of the labour-force and capital stock employed with certain assumptions as to the trend in technological advance. This is the aspect around which battles on the economic strategy to be pursued with regard to the optimal factor intensities (or, one could perhaps say, factor 'biases') have been at their fiercest in Soviet planning literature. Optimality of the factor-combination is the central aspect of the Kalecki-Rakowski approach, coming into strongest relief in the handling of the 'freeze' rate—q_z. As has been noted, the assumption— explicit in Kalecki-Rakowski, particularly in their reasoning on the q_z—is a factor equilibrium, one corresponding to full employment (or one would in fact say to the planner's 'bias', implying some optimum of factor productivities, a point of special significance for the Polish economic milieu to which the rate is to be applied).[3]

[1] S. G. Strumilin, '*Faktor vremeni v proyektirovkakh kapitalnykh vlozheniy*', *Isvestya Akademii Nauk SSSR, Otedelenye Ekonomiki i Prava*, 1946, no. 3, pp. 195 ff. '*Suggestions for a Theory of Soviet Investment Planning*' can be found in G. Grossman's important paper under this title, reprint no. 20, Univ. of California, 1956.

[2] N. Kaldor, 'Capital Accumulation and Economic Growth', in F. A. Lutz and D. C. Hague eds., *The Theory of Capital*, London, 1961, p. 203.

[3] Since this paragraph was written I found in Polish literature an explicit postulate

The normative rate of capital efficiency has been explicitly related to capital-labour intensity by Lurie.[1] His rate of 'differentiated return on assests' δ_i is a partial derivative of a function describing the dependence of maximum volume of output on the availability of labour and capital:

$$\delta_i = \partial f_i(L_i, K_i)/\partial K_i$$

Similarly Novikov[2] assumes, as do Kalecki-Rakowski, a full employment equilibrium, and puts total labour cost as dependent on capital invested per unit of output $L=f(K)$, and writes his normative efficiency rate as

$$P_t = -dC/dK = -[1 - f'(K)]$$

where C denotes total cost, and capital cost K is expressed in terms of L/K, factor intensity.

This approach could be easily translated into the language of a conventional production function. If we took as the expression of technical possibilities a dynamic linear homogeneous function of the Cobb-Douglas type, we could obtain, by differentiating it, the equilibrium price of capital for period t, expressed in terms of the economy's

of *optimum* productivity of labour and capital efficiency. The argument is that each combination of manpower and investment resources has its own optimal type of investment (optimal in the macro-scale). M. Rakowski, 'Uzasadnienie podstawowej formy wzoru wzoru wskaznika efektywnosci', in *Efektywnosc Inwestycji*, Warsaw, 1961, p. 106.

[1] A. L. Lurie, 'Sopostavlenye zatrat v prosteyshikh modelakh sotsyalitcheskogo khoziaystva', in Alb. L. Vainshtein, ed. *Narodnokhoziaystvennye modeli—Teoreticheskiye voprosy potreblenya*, Moscow, 1963, pp. 17 ff. A change in the planned 'way' of production would be efficient if the loss in output due to reduction of labour and capital by some small l and k, respectively, would be no more than p, incremental output obtained through the release of the marginal quantities of factors

$$\partial f_i(L_i, K_i)/\partial L_i . l + \partial f_i(L_i, K_i)/\partial K_i . k \leqslant p$$

Denoting further the two partial derivatives in the above expression, that is the differential productivity of labour and of capital, respectively as π_i and δ_i (investment efficiency 'norm'), and writing λ_i for the 'differential labour intensity'. Lurie defines the condition of the 'profitability' (*vygodnost*) of the 'way':

$$l + \delta_i \lambda_i c \geqslant \lambda_i p$$

Lurie has subsequently re-stated his concept of differential productivities, for the optimal perspective plan, in his 'General scheme for optimal economic processes and the generalisation of the notion of objectively conditioned estimates' (submitted to the ES/TIMS Warsaw, 1966 conference).

The argument is similar to V. V. Novozhilov's 'Izmerenye zatrat i ikh rezultatov v sotsjalisticheskom khoziaystvie', in *Primenenye matematiki v ekonomicheskikh issledovanyakh*, *op. cit.*

[2] Novikov, *Voprosy Ekonomiki*, 1964, no. 4.

relative factor intensity (the labour/capital ratio) and labour productivity, α, as a certain $r = (1-\alpha)(L_t/K^t)^\alpha$ where the two capital letters stand respectively for manpower and capital stock at the moment t (Qayum).[1]

In recent years several Soviet and Polish students, especially A. A. Konyus, J. Pajestka and L. I. Gorkov,[2] have tried to formalise the problem of a normative rate of investment efficiency by means of a two-factor macro-production function of one type or another. Gorkov's analytical attempt may be particularly noteworthy. The starting point is an optimal 'instantaneous' technological net production function $U(C, L) = \int_0^1 C^\alpha . L^{1-\alpha}\, \mathrm{d}p(\alpha)$, the $p(\alpha)$ being a certain weight. The economy is seen as a combination of technological 'cells': in the cell corresponding to the parameter α, production would equal $C^\alpha L^{1-\alpha}$. In further treatment the time-shape of capital formation is expressed as $c(t, \tau)$ showing stock with life-periods from τ to $\tau + \mathrm{d}t$ at the time t. Assuming that by the end of the life-span period assets are totally worn out, on the average over a certain period a, those in operation would amount to $1/2c(t, \tau)$. With some rate of investment γ (rate of consumption $1 - \gamma$), when dividing by $\mathrm{d}t$ we arrive at

$$c(t, 0) = \gamma \int_0^a U[1/2c(t, \tau), l(t, \tau)]\, \mathrm{d}\tau + \int_0^a c(t, \tau)/a\,.\mathrm{d}\tau$$

where the second integral denotes replacement of capital stock. In Gorkov's handling the coefficient of investment efficiency would appear then as the partial derivative $\partial U/\partial C$ measuring the increment in output per incremental unit of investment. The approach, novel in Soviet economics, has helped to exhibit the logic of the various suggestions in the Soviet debate on the investment efficiency 'norm'. There is on this point illuminating discussion in Gorkov. It well illustrates the Strumilin 'bias' (see above, p. 154). Since Strumilin takes normal investment efficiency to equal the labour-productivity increment per time-unit, it would mean

$$\mathrm{d}/\mathrm{d}t(U/L) = \partial U/\partial L.\gamma U/L + (\partial U/\partial L - U/L)\, \mathrm{d} \ln L/\mathrm{d}t$$

[1] Cf. A. Qayum, *Theory and Policy of Accounting Prices*, Amsterdam, 1960, p. 36.

[2] A. A. Konyus, 'Matematicheskiy analiz organischeskogo stroyeniya izderzhek proizvodstva' in *Matematicheskiy analiz rasshirennogo vosproizvodstva*, Moscow, 1962; J. Pajestka in *Ekonomista*, 1960, no. 6; L. I. Gorkov, 'Odnoprodutktovaya ekonomicheskaya model i analiz ekonomicheskoy efektivnosti kapitalovlozheniy' in *Matematicheskiy analiz rasshirennogo vosproizvodstva*, Moscow 1962.

In Khachaturov's approach, which underlies the official 'Model Methodology', capital efficiency would be measured as $\partial U/\partial C = dU/dt : dC/dt$. The solution is rightly shown to be correct only with constant labour resources (and no non-investment factors of change in efficiency), and thus failing to isolate the 'pure' rate of capital-efficiency. This point has been argued—with weaker apparatus—for some time by other participants of the Soviet discussion on the methodology of appraisal of capital efficiency.[1]

Moving along this line of thought—looking for a rate of actualisation of capital outlay as would correspond to an equilibrium in the two 'markets', those of labour and capital—Fiszel and Siwinski[2] give a fuller statement of the problem in a matrix frame. In the latter's reformulation, a sum of matrices of investment outlays and running costs discounted back to the moment of the commissioning of the capacities (with a given average wage-packet) would take this shape:

$$I_{11} + (C_{11}^M + L_{11}w_1)\alpha, \quad I_{12} + (C_{12}^M + L_{12}w_1)\alpha, \ldots, I_{1R} + (C_{1R}^M + L_{1R}w_1)\alpha$$

$$\cdot \quad \cdot \quad \cdot \quad \cdot \quad \cdot \quad \cdot \quad \cdot \quad \cdot \quad \cdot \quad \cdot$$

$$\cdot \quad \cdot \quad \cdot \quad \cdot \quad \cdot \quad \cdot \quad \cdot \quad \cdot \quad \cdot \quad \cdot$$

$$I_{m1} + (C_{m1}^M + L_{m1}w_m)\alpha, \quad I_{m2} + (C_{m2}^M + L_{m2}w_m)\alpha, \ldots, I_{mR} + (C_{mR}^M + L_{mR}w_m)\alpha$$

(Notation: matrices of investment, of current material cost and of manpower employed and average branch wages—I, C^M, L and w respectively, in the total of $1, 2, \ldots, m$ sectors under R variants of technology—with an output target described by a vector $p_1, p_2, \ldots, p_m$.) The actualisation coefficient $\alpha = [(1+r) - 1] : [r(1+r^n)]$, where r is the unknown rate of discount ('rate of interest'). The problem would be then to find the r, and thereby the α for

$$\sum_{n=1}^{m} [I_{nx} + (C_{nx}^M + L_{nx}w_n)] = \min$$

subject to availability of factors, i.e. $\sum_{n=1}^{m} I_{nx}$ and $\sum_{n=1}^{m} L_{nx}$. It is presumed that there is an r meeting these requirements, and it is suggested that the value of this parameter could be found, by trial and error.

[1] In particular B. N. Smekhov, *Planirovanye kapitalnykh vlozheniy*, Moscow, 1961, pp. 196 ff.

[2] H. Fiszel, *Ekonomista*, 1961, no. 5, and his *Efektywnosc inwestycji i optimum produkcji w gospodarce socjalistycznej*, Warsaw, 1963; and W. Siwinski, *Biuletyn Naukowy Wydzialu Ekonomii Politycznej*, University of Warsaw, November 1963, p. 89. The latter is an interesting discussion of my article in *Economica*, August 1962.

The relevant point (made by Rakowski[1]) is, however, the empirical evasiveness of the strategic relationship to which the planner has to refer himself when fixing his T. The value of his $m = f(d)$, that is the rise in average capital intensity (m) as a function of the average rise in labour productivity (d), has so far eluded efforts at quantification.[2]

On the other hand the apparatus of programming now being resorted to has helped conceptually to attack the problem of technological and economic inter-relationships within a fuller statement of optimality.

The classical formulation is again that by Kantorovich.[3] In the outline of his dynamic model (see above, p. 128) each commodity produced and each factor used in each time-segment of the plan becomes a separate 'ingredient'. His matrix (denoting the output volumes for each ingredient with the unit-use of a given technology) becomes 'dated' as

$$\|a\|_{it}^{s} \quad (i = 1, 2, \ldots, N; \ t = 1, 2, \ldots, T; \ s = 1, 2, \ldots, r)$$

Possibly capacities of given types are brought into this dynamised matrix along with specific factors, and technological advance is allowed for essentially by a reduction of input coefficient by means of one kind of projection or another. As to efficiency for such a dynamised system, it may be taken to mean that with given resources (say, natural resources), given, that is, either for the initial period or for all periods, and with postulated use of final goods for every time-segment, the plan would secure for the final year a maximum of the bill-of-final-goods with a specified composition, or of specified capacities. The necessary and sufficient condition for the best plan vector, the vector that is of the employment-intensities of technologies, is 'dynamised' accordingly. The efficiency condition is now the existence of a system of '*dated*' multipliers (dated shadow prices)

$$c_{it}(i = 1, 2, \ldots, N; \ t = 1, 2, \ldots, T)$$

[1] M. Rakowski, 'Uzasadnienie podstawowej formy rachunku wzoru wskaznika efektywnosci', in M. Rakowski, ed., *Efektywnosc inwestycji*, Warsaw, 1963, p. 114.

[2] Czechoslovak planning practice seems to claim a success in precise solution of the problem at least for individual industrial branches. Thus the incremental unit of labour productivity in the chemical branch is taken to be due to the following factors: investment 70 per cent, improved organisation 2·5 per cent, improved skills 10·9 per cent, others 6·6 per cent. The method by which this has been arrived at is not known to us.

[3] L. V. Kantorovich, *Ekonomicheskiy raschet nailuchshego ispolzovanya resursov*, Moscow, 1960; see in particular the mathematical appendix, pp. 291 ff.

uch as (1) all of them should be non-negative, and not all of them ero; (2) the valuation of outputs $\sum_{it} c_{it}a_{it}^s$ for each feasible technology hould not exceed the valuation of input-ingredients; and (3) for the echnology actually used this sum, the valuation of outputs, should ust equal that of inputs (the profitability principle).

The multipliers could be then normalised by means of some coefficient *lambda* as a time-sequence over the whole plan period so that aking $c_{it} = \lambda_t c_{it} (i = 1, 2, \ldots, N; t = 1, 2, \ldots, T)$ we may, say, get such a valuation of some fixed product-mix over the whole plan period hat it should equal unity:

$$c_{it_1}' + c_{it_2}' + \cdots + c_{it_n}' = 1; \qquad (t = 1, 2, \ldots, T)$$

Then the valuation sum (of inputs and outputs) becomes

$$\sum_{i=1}^{T} \lambda_t \sum_{i=1}^{T} c_{it}' a_{it}^s \, (s = 1, 2, \ldots, n)$$

whereby in evaluing a given 'technology' of outputs and inputs carried out in various time-intervals, valuations (shadow prices) are being reduced to one time-intervals by means of the *lambda*. With the adopted unit, the coefficient for the reduction of inputs of the t period to the τ period will appear as the ratio of the respective *lambdas* λ_t/λ_τ, and 'normal efficiency of investment' is obtained by subtraction of a unit from this ratio for two successive time-periods:

$$\lambda_t/\lambda_{t+1} - 1 = (\lambda_t - \lambda_{t+1})/\lambda_{t+1}$$

Here the c_{it}—accounting prices of inputs and outputs reduced to one time-interval—mirror the dynamics of the price system and the c_{it}'—the *relative* dynamics: hence two ways of calculating efficiency of a capital outlay, and the problem of its worth will depend on whether the sum

$$\sum_{i,t} c_{it}\bar{a}_{it} = \sum_t \lambda_t \sum_i c_{it}'\bar{a}_{it}$$

is positive or not. With relative accounting prices constant over the plan-period it will suffice for evaluation of the 'technology' to have the c_{it}' and the λ_t given.[1]

---

[1] In an excellent discussion of a dynamic system with technological choice the authors of the French plan model, Moustacchi and associates, show that (1) the rate of relative 'rentability' of techniques employed equals the rate of discount; (2) optimal dual prices settle down at a relative level such that for the best techniques the rate of 'rentability' equals the discount rate. Cf. Centre de Recherches Mathematiques pour la Planification, *Application d'un Modèle d'Allocation des Ressources à la Planfication Française*, 1965.

With due qualifications then it is Kantorovich's λ that we had in mind when noting in a previous context that price-valuations appear as knit together through time by means of the investment-efficiency coefficient as their rate of actualisation. Prices of future plan-periods appear as the 'discounted', and 'shadow' value as the present value c. The efficient programme is the one with the highest present value.[1]

On the empirical plane there again arises the snag of circularity, the question as to the end from which to start optimality calculation; this will not retain us at the present stage. Whatever its empirical snags, the Kantorovich analysis of 'normal efficiency of investment' provides us with a useful new scaffolding for re-examination of the efficiency criteria with which we were heretofore concerned. The fundamental inference is that for a criterion of investment efficiency to be valid it must mirror scarcities of factors committed: it must be built on and used within a system of scarcity prices. Technically the inference is that the investment-efficiency coefficient is but one of mutually related solving multipliers. Relating the issue of efficient resource allocation to the saddle-point game-theoretical problem is but one element of a system of valuations imputed in the efficient solution. (Indeed in the treatment the concept of capital 'as such' as it were dissolves itself. Professor Samuelson notes that working with a series of vectors—of inputs and outputs—one gets the concepts of interest and of prices, and thereby obtains mutually inter-dependent relationships without reference to capital as such[2]).

The problem of efficiently time-patterned capital formation over the plan period has been sketched out by V. Dadayan,[3] with the assumption of maximum total consumption throughout the period as the objective function:

$$(1) \qquad\qquad L = \sum_{t=1}^{\tau} H(t) = \max$$

---

[1] In the Soviet and Polish writing the rate of discount is usually assumed to be constant over the plan period. Actually in a general case it should rather be taken as differentiated from one time-interval to another (cf. *inter al.*, A. K. Sen, *Choice of Techniques*, Oxford, 1960). See also Malinvaud, as cited on p. 153.

[2] See Samuelson's contribution to the discussion of Hicks's paper in F. A. Lutz, D. C. Hague, eds., *The Theory of Capital, op. cit.*, p. 308.

[3] V. Dadayan, *Ekonomiko-matematicheskoye modelirovanye sotsyalisticheskogo vosproizvodstva*, Moscow, 1963, pp. 228–31.

A year's consumption is written as

$$(2) \qquad H(t) = K(t)/\gamma - \varDelta K(t)$$

where γ denotes the full-order capital coefficient for the economy, taken to be constant, and the $\varDelta K(t)$ is net yearly investment. Now, with the help of (2) the (1) is re-written as

$$(3) \quad L = (S_1^{\tau-1}/\gamma - \tau)\varDelta K_0 + (S_1^{\tau-2}/\gamma - \tau + 1)\varDelta K_1 + (S_1^{\tau-3}/\gamma - \tau + 2)\varDelta K_2$$
$$+ \cdots + (S_1^1/\gamma - 2)\varDelta K_{\tau-2} - \varDelta K_{\tau-1} + C$$

where $S_1^{\tau-i}$ is a sum of terms of an arithmetic series with a common difference $d = 1 (i = 1, 2, \ldots, \tau - 1)$. The term C denotes elements which do not influence the patterning of production over time for $L = \max$. The linear functional (3) is then shown to be reducible to the form

$$(4) \quad L = a_0\varDelta K_0 + a_1\varDelta K_1 + \cdots + a_\theta\varDelta K_\theta - a_{\theta+1}\varDelta K_{\theta+1} - a_{\theta+2}\varDelta K_{\theta+2}$$
$$- \cdots - a_{\tau-2}\varDelta K_{\tau-2} - \varDelta K_{\tau+1} + C$$

with $a_u > a_{u-1}$ holding for every positive a_u. The latter symbolises the coefficients to each of the $\varDelta K$ in (3) and can be re-written as

$$a_0 = S_1^{\tau-1-0}/\gamma - \tau + \theta.$$

and the curve of its variation can be drawn from (3). The 'regulation regime' for $\varDelta K(t)$ is obtained from (4) possibly with certain boundary conditions.

By taking a fixed time-horizon of the plan Dadayan appears to circumvent the problem of a discount rate. In fact it is evaded only in part: since his maximand is the consumption total over the whole plan period, rather than yearly increments, there does arise the question of discounting consumption within that period. Moreover, the fixing of the period implies in fact a time-discount: the problem of the length of the period substitutes itself in the maximisation of consumption for that of the level of the discount.[1,2]

An interesting analytical study of optimality of investment has been

[1] The implied rate of discount would correspond to the expansion of future production made possible by the foregone consumption. Cf. for these problems, J. Tinbergen and H. C. Bos, *Mathematical Models of Economic Growth*, London, 1962, pp. 25 ff.

[2] In his recent numerical model of optimally time-patterned accumulation S. Strumilin, (*Planovoye Khoziaystvo*, 1962, no. 6, p. 10) adopts an implied rate of discount corresponding to the coefficient of investment efficiency.

made by Mikhalevskiy.[1] He found (with Solow[2]) that a strictly deterministic dynamic system of an inter-industry balance, with the assumption of a full use of capacities and inventories, suffers from instability (*inter alia* due to instability of prices); and therefore tried an input minimisation approach as a multi-stage linear programme: min $U(t)X(t)$, subject to

$$\begin{bmatrix} a(t) \\ \alpha(t)l\,(t) \\ \left[\alpha(t) - \dfrac{1}{\hat{T}}\right] b\,(t) \end{bmatrix} X(t) \;=\; Y(t)$$

and to usual non-negativity conditions; $a(t)$ and $l(t)$ are coefficients of current non-labour and labour inputs for competing technologies, and $b(t)$ capital coefficients all varying over time; $\alpha(t) > 1$ is normative efficiency of investment, $\hat{T}$ is life-span of capital assets (characterising the replacement policy); $X(t)$ is total output and $Y(t)$ is final product.

In order to circumvent the exacting requirement of full information with regard to the structure of final product for the whole plan period, an auxiliary programme is shaped: the structure of net capital-accumulation increments over time is taken to be unknown. The data include then private and social consumption, initial capital stocks, replacement policy, sectoral weights of fixed and working capital for the last year. Now in each sector, at each stage, the level and pace of net capital formation is taken to be determined by the limitations of the existing stock of capital, alternatives of employable techniques and the prescribed volume and pattern of consumption. Optimisation, that is, minimisation of total investment by means of suitable patterning of capital formation, is obtained—with the use of a modified simplex method—through selection of competing technologies characterised by B_{ij}, the matrix of full capital coefficients involved (with built-in technological progress). It will be easily seen that the multi-stage decision process and its formal apparatus are largely those of the

[1] B. N. Mikhalevskiy, 'Osnovnye puti opredelenyia optimuma fondov novykh kapitalnykh vlozheniy v obshchey dinamicheskoy modeli' in *Matematicheskiy analiz rasshirennogo vosproizvodstva*, Soviet Academy of Sciences, Moscow, 1962, p. 188 ff.

[2] R. Solow, 'Competitive Valuation in Dynamic Input-Output System' *Econometrica*, 1959, No. 1.

Dorfman-Samuelson-Solow dynamic inter-industry model,[1] except that no concern is shown here for its 'shadow' dual. The triangular-recursive system is then complicated by abandoning the assumption of known sectoral configuration of capital assets for the final plan year. More realistically it is taken then that the planner may compromise for some variants of these proportions and broad limits of their variations. A series of solutions is thus obtained providing a maximum of a linear functional over a conveniently narrow interval, of relevance for the exercise, with given linear constraints. The objective function is then a preference functional and the problem of maximising capital formation turns into one of stochastic linear programming, the probability values of policies for sectoral allocation of the final plan-year being determined in one way or another (the problem would appear to be reducible to one of parametric programming). Finally, realism of the system is enhanced by treating the technological parameters as functions of total output (non-constant returns to scale) and by building into the system investment-production lags in a way borrowed from Ichimura.[2]

In some respects Lange's macro-programme belongs to this family inasmuch as it relies for optimisation on 'physical', sectoral, shape of investment flows. His maximand[3] is the rate of growth of national product with a posited minimum of final consumer goods. The configuration of λ's weight-coefficients of sectoral distribution of investment, is to be such as to bring about a maximum total yield with given β's coefficients of net sectoral investment efficiencies. In short we write down this programme as

$$\sum_{j=1}^{n} \beta_j \lambda j = \max$$

satisfying the constraint $\bar{C_i} \geqslant C_i$, which states the postulated consumption profile in terms of an i-th final product (and with the usual non-negativity conditions). The consumption constraint is then re-stated as the permissible maximum component of national product set aside for the support of growth (to make it determinate this maximum too is expressed at the next step in terms of λ's, and coefficients of physical

[1] R. Dorfman, P. A. Samuelson, R. S. Solow, *Linear Programming and Economic Analysis*, New York–London, 1958, especially pp. 337 ff.

[2] S. Ichimura, 'Dynamic Input-Output and Linear Programming Models', United Nations, Ap. v, February 1960.

[3] O. Lange, *Wstęp do ekonometrii*, 2nd ed., Warsaw, 1961, pp. 355 ff., cf. p. 179.

composition of investment flows and sectoral capital-output ratios). Further, a dynamised time-lagged version[1] of the programme has yet another coefficient, $\gamma_{j'st}$ of 'time-sectoral structure' of investment, a ratio denoting the share which an investment outlay with a s-year cycle, made during the t-th year within the j-th sector, takes in the total investment of the economy over the k-year plan period. Lange's maximum maximorum (weighted total of net efficiency of investments with varying cycles carried out in different sectors during different plan years) becomes then a certain

$$\sum_{t=1}^{k-1}\sum_{s=1}^{k-1}\sum_{j=1}^{n}\beta_{js,\,t-s+1},\,\gamma_{js,\,t-s+1},$$

and the principal constraint is being dynamised accordingly.

The conventional framework of investment-efficiency appraisal of the Soviet-type planning practice has been adopted by Fiszel for his programmes, with either a given or unknown rate of interest.[2] His criterion is a (time-discounted) cost function rather than an explicit contribution to national product, or net efficiency, as it is in Lange.

For a set of commodities the cost alternatives of project variants are ordered in two matrices of competing technological alternatives, one describing capital outlays $\|\mathcal{J}_{px}\|$ and the other corresponding operating cost over and above replacement $\|K_{px}\|$. Then the minimand is total cost actualised by means of an α factor, formed by the rate of interest (r).[3]

With total investment resources A, the programme would read

(1)
$$\sum_{p=1}^{m}(\mathcal{J}+K\alpha)_{px} = \min$$

subject to

(2)
$$\sum_{p=1}^{m}\mathcal{J}_{px} \leqslant A$$

As we have noted in Lange the efficiency coefficient is a purely 'objective' category. In Fiszel too, the rate of interest is related to a technical concept (it is quantified from this angle as roughly equalling half the net output-capital ratio). At the same time it is explicitly related to capital intensity of acceptable variants, and thereby to the

---

[1] *Ibid.*, pp. 370 ff.
[2] H. Fiszel, *Efektywnosc Inwestycji i Optimum Produkcji w Gospodarce Socjalistyczneh*, 2nd ed., Warsaw, 1963, pp. 41 ff.
[3] $a = [(1-r)^n - 1] : [r(1-r)^n].$

relative availability of capital, and thereby to consumption. (Suggestions are made as to the kind of function, discontinuous and non-monotonic, which relates the rate of interest to availability of resources; we shall not pursue here the argument on this point.) Unlike Lange's 'technocratic' coefficient, Fiszel's rate of interest does and can be understood by implication as equalling the proportional rate of decrease of the marginal utility of consumption over time (marginal rate of consumers' time preferences).

This is the implication which can also be read into the sketch of a dynamic version of Kantorovich's original programme,[1] even if it is somewhat obscured by his extremely laconic and compact notation. Here a project's efficiency is tested with reference to a sum

$$\sum r_t \sum_i p_i a_{it}$$

the last member is an element of a matrix $\|a_{it}\|$ describing lagged output volumes, positive and negative, of products and factors, and the p_i are prices. The r is Kantorovich's rate of 'normal' investment efficiency (see above, p. 158). It is in Kantorovich's system at the same time 'shadow' parameter employable for actualisation of a dynamic shadow-price structure and defined as incremental labour productivity obtained in an optimal programme from an investment unit per time-unit—thus a marginal product of capital derived from a two-factor production function. The rate, Kantorovich stresses time and again, is a parameter derived from the programme, depending on conditions of the given economic environment and goals posited.

In an inter-temporal efficient production programme, the rate of interest is one of the inter-related dual variables.[2] Only the actual use of a rate of interest derived from an efficient programme can ensure efficient inter-temporal resource allocation.

APPENDIX I TO CHAPTER 14

By the mid-'sixties Soviet thinking on the problem of measuring investment efficiency has crystalised in what can be seen as the general programming

[1] L. V. Kantorovich, *Ekonomicheskiy raschet nayluchshego ispolzovanya resursov*, Moscow, 1960, pp. 220 ff.
[2] Cf. Hahn and Matthews, 'The Theory of Economic Growth: A Survey', *Economic Journal*, December 1964, p. 864 and pp. 877–82.

approach. It is the overall dynamic equilibrium approach, in strong contrast to the traditionally evolved static and partial equilibrium one. In this monistic treatment, prices of products and factors—the normative efficiency rate for capital being one among the latter—are intrinsic to the optimality (efficiency) of the programme-plan. The adjective 'monistic' is borrowed here from Kantorovich[1] who uses it in a stronger sense: in the sense that as against the other principal co-founders of the contemporary Soviet mathematical-economic school, Nemchinov and Novozhilov, he now sees—we would submit, more consistently—the finding of the parameters as belonging to one operation with, and inseparable from, the build-up of the plan itself.

In Soviet writing the formal relating of the dynamised normative rate of investment efficiency to the economy's rhythm is primarily due to Academician Kantorovich's work. There is a noticeable impact of von Neumann on this mode of approach, and one would note again the convergence of Soviet thinking in this area with that in the West—in the context, specifically, with that of Morishima,[2] Malinvaud[3] and Dorfman-Samuelson-Solow;[4] also with that of Harrod[5] who indeed has had, as we shall see, a formative influence on the conceptual approach in Soviet planning experiments (cf. p. 167).

As formulated by Kantorovich-Makarov,[6] the economy's pace of growth appears, in two variants, as the technological (or 'natural') rate and the economic rate. They are respectively (1) the growth rate of the accumulation of the plan-'ingredients', as weighted with the 'ooos—some price vector $\pi = (\pi(1), \ldots, \pi(t+1))$; and (2) the rate of decrease of the π weighted by the quantities of the 'ingredients'. (Correctives brought in to allow for the degree of the openness of the system will not detain us here). The nexus with the normative investment efficiency rate, ρ_t, reveals itself then when the logic of the latter is shown as that of measuring the relative return from a small increment of resources most rationally employed in the plan's time-interval, t, by the start of $(t+1)$. For a collection of plan-ingredients, some

[1] L. V. Kantorovich, 'Amortizatsyonnye otchislenya i otsenka effektivnosti novoy tekhniki v sisteme optimalnogo planirovanya' in *Matematiko-Ekonomicheskiye Problemy*, Leningrad University, 1966.

[2] M. Morishima, 'Economic Expansion and the Interest Rate in Generalized von Neumann Model', *Econometrica*, April 1960.

[3] E. Malinvaud, 'Programmes d'Expansion et Taux d'Interêt', *Econometrica*, April 1960.

[4] R. Dorfman, P. A. Samuelson, R. M. Solow, *Linear Programming and Economic Analysis, op. cit.*

[5] R. Harrod, 'Themes in Economic Dynamics', *Economic Journal*, September 1963; also his 'Optimum Investment for Growth', in *Problems of Economic Dynamics and Planning* (Essays in honour of Michal Kalecki), Warsaw, 1964.

[6] *Op. cit.*, p. 4. For an interesting interpretation see A. L. Lurye in *Matematika i Ekonomicheskiye Metody*, no. 2, 1967, p. 178.

166

vector X, the efficiency norm appears as $\rho_t(X) = [X, \pi(t)]/[X, \pi(t+1)]$. Next the scale of the π is being brought in, in this way. Denote as $\mathcal{Z}_t$, $(t = 1, \ldots, T)$ the value of all initial resources at the beginning of t, that is the value of $X(t)$ at *operating* prices. The vector of optimality (efficiency) prices is then normalised from $[\pi(1), X(1)] = \mathcal{Z}_1$. For the remaining time-intervals $\hat{\pi}(t)$ is being substituted for $\pi(t)$, derived from $\pi(t) = \lambda_t \hat{\pi}(t)$; $[\hat{\pi}(t), X(t)] = \mathcal{Z}_t$, whence $\lambda_t = [\pi(t), X(t)]/\mathcal{Z}_t$. Now the value of ρ_t^Z can be found as one depending on the scale vector $\mathcal{Z}$ (rather than a random collection X). The norm is namely $\rho_t^Z = \lambda_{t+1}/\lambda_t - 1$.

Informational and computational difficulties have given a strong impulse to the search for more simplified solutions, notably in the production-function approach. The adoption of this approach by the socialist planning theory was bound to meet with objections. Describing the economy's production processes by a homogeneous function of the first degree, taking the first derivative as the marginal productivity of factor, has raised all the doubts well known in Western writing. Some have stressed the lack of realism in the technological aspects—in the assumed homogeneity of factors and the fundamental regime of factor substitution (Oskar Lange[1]). Traditionalists have been worried about the implications for the theory of distribution. On the other hand the observable tendency in Western thinking to view capital stock, in a *long*-run analysis, in terms of a labour-equivalent, has also helped the passage of the tool.[2]

By now Soviet planning literature displays an ever growing interest in the production-function instrument; in variants with either non-unit or unit elasticity. Among the latter the Cobb-Douglas type of function is the one usually worked with. Of the quite a few recent exercises I would mention that by Kornai-Wellisz,[3] with a dynamised function of the form $Y(t) = A_0 e^{\mu t} K(t)^\beta L(t)^{1-\beta}$ where A_0 is a constant of 'technical organisation' and μ the exponent of its change (this corresponds then to a Cobb-Douglas function with $\mu = 0$).

I would further draw attention to Mikhalevskiy's[4] latest contribution.

---

[1] O. Lange, 'Qantitative Relations in Production', in *Problems of Economic Dynamics and Planning* (Essays in honour of Michal Kalecki), Warsaw, 1964. See also M. Golanskiy, *Voprosy Ekonomiki*, no. 5, 1965, p. 107.

[2] Cf. e.g. Robert M. Solow, *Econometrica*, October 1963, p. 644.

[3] J. Kornai, P. Wellisz, 'Protsentnaya stavka v perspektivnykh raschetakh po ekonomicheskoy effektivnosti, in *On Political Economy and Econometrics* (Essays in honour of Oskar Lange), Warsaw, 1965.

[4a] B. N. Mikhalevskiy, 'Odnosektornaya model i norma effektivnosti kapitalovlozheniy', *Ekonomika i Matematicheskiye Metody*, no. 2, 1965; cf. also his 'Dve zadachi otsenki effektivnosti kapitalovlozheniy v otrasl' in *Primenenye Matematiki v Ekonomicheskikh Issledovanyakh*, vol. 3, *op. cit.*

[4b] See also appendix II to this chapter.

Its significance for the developments in Soviet thinking lies primarily in a rigorous articulation of the relationship between the normative rate of investment efficiency and the rate of interest. If we take the average useful life-time of capital goods equal to the plan period, T, and assume that over time their 'effect' depreciates at a constant rate r, the maximum long-term efficiency rate of investment ρ is obtained from:

$$R_0 = \int_0^T Q_0(\Upsilon_t)\, e^{-(\rho-r)t}\, dt + e^{-rT}.H$$

The symbols have the following significance: R_0 is initial value of capital goods, Υ is final product; Q is 'effect' function; H is present value of surviving capital goods. The normative maximum long-term investment efficiency rate appears as one approximately equalling the difference between the maximum discounted efficiency rate in the initial time-interval and maximum long term interest rate: $\bar{\rho} = e^r \rho_0 - \bar{r}$. The values are sought in a stochastic calculus and the procedures followed are these. First the 'general parameter of substitution', $\Omega_t(\Upsilon_t) = dQ_t(\Upsilon_t)/d\Upsilon_t$, is estimated, with the assumption of a strict additivity of $Q_t(\Upsilon_t)$, on the Frisch method,[1] for all the T years. Next the maximum variable growth rate of the incremental final product is found for that period. Then the ρ_t is calculated from the equation for the maximum current investment efficiency rate

$$(1+r_t)\rho_t = -\Omega_{t+1}(\Upsilon_{t+1}) \cdot (\Upsilon_{t+2} - \Upsilon_{t+1})/\Upsilon_{t+1}$$

which means that the discounted short-term efficiency equals the growth rate of the incremental physical-term magnitude of the 'effect' multiplied by the rate of its decline $-\Omega_{t+1}(\Upsilon_{t+1})$. To obtain $\bar{\rho}$ under uncertainty (remoteness of horizon, technical progress) we maximise the convex

$$Q(\rho) = 1 - e^{-i\rho}; \qquad \rho = \pi - i.\sigma^2/2$$

First then $\Omega_t(\Upsilon_t)$ is estimated over T; then ρ_t is found; thence the π and σ^2; next—$\bar{r}$; finally—the $\bar{\rho}$ itself.

Thus the Kantorovich concepts have been brought to the stage of quantification of investment efficiency and the discount rate—for the planner's use.[3]

---

[1] R. Frisch, 'A Complete Scheme for Computing all Direct and Cross Demand Elasticities in a Model with Many Sectors', *Econometrica*, April 1959.

[2] The actual Soviet ρ has been calculated from

$$\bar{\rho} \approx -\bar{g}_{max}\, \Omega(\Upsilon_t)\, e^{-\bar{g}_{max}} = -0.0659.2.655.e^{-0.656} = 0.1632 \equiv 16.32 \text{ per cent.}$$

Here g_{max} denotes the maximal growth rate of final product. When correctionns have been made the efficiency rate was estimated at about 17.6 per cent, long-term rate of interest at 4.3 per cent and profit rate at 21.8 per cent.

[3] One of the aspects of efficient capital formation neglected by Soviet traditional economics is amortisation (partly because the concept of obsolescence was considered

APPENDIX II TO CHAPTER 14

Mikhalevskiy's linear, closed, single-product dynamic perspective-plan model of a production-function type has as its optimality criterion the maximum rate of balanced growth. It rests on the basic relationship which is: the final quasi-homogeneous output (Y) is used up as an exogenously determined constant component (A_1) and as endogenously determined consumption and capital formation (C and ΔK respectively):

$$Y = C + \Delta K + A_1$$

The share of C in the final product is $1 > c > 0$, so that $C = c.Y$. Further $K = \ell.\Delta F.Y$. The $k = 1 - c$; and the ℓ is some positive multiplier. We have then a differential equation of first order

$$Y(t) = Y(0).e^{k/k.t}$$

Initial assumptions are zero gestation lags of investment and infinite durability of capital goods. Taking, at the next step, the capital assets' useful life-span as finite (period T), the surviving capital stock at any time-point, t, appears as

$$F(t) = \int_{t-T}^{t} \Delta K(\tau) \, d\tau$$

Further write

$$F(t) = f.Y(t),$$

so that

$$Y(t) = \frac{k}{f\int_{t-T}^{t} Y(\tau).d\tau}$$

for which the characteristic equation (showing the Y's growth rate) is

$$r = k/f(1 - e^{-rT});$$

the e^{-rT} describes the renovation's share in gross investment. Next the assumption of the investments' instantaneous 'maturation' is dropped and an exponentially distributed time-lag, with some λ as the speed of response, is adopted. Then:

$$\Delta K(t) = \lambda k/(\Delta F + \lambda).Y(t)$$

irrelevant for a socialist non-competitive system). This is also one of the fields of Academician Kantorovich's formative influence. In his recent writings he develops a model of amortisation, based on the life-time and use-time of equipment for cases of a constant and variable use-load, and indicates how amortisation and renovation of techniques has to be fitted into the over-all dynamic plan-programme. See his 'Amortizatsyonnye otchislenya i otsenka effektivnosti novy tekhniki v sisteme optimalnogo planirovanya', *op. cit.*; also, jointly with I. V. Romanovskiy, 'Amortizatsyonnye platezhi pri optimalnom ispolzovanyi oborudovanya', *Doklady*, USSR Academy of Sciences, 1965.

By substituting into the basic-relationship equation we have ultimately for the system's steady growth

$$A_1 = \Delta F^{T+2}.\,Y(t) + \lambda.\Delta F^{T+1}.\,Y(t) - f(1-k)/k.\Delta F.\,Y(t)$$
$$- \lambda f(1 + \ell - k).\,Y(t)$$

(Cf. B. N. Mikhalevskiy, 'Prostyie dinamicheskiye modeli dla perspektivnykh raschetov narodnogo khoziaystva'[1, 2], (mimeo), Moscow, 1966 (?).)

[1] In the context attention should be drawn to Mikhalevskiy's discussion of interdependence between the dynamics of final product and changes in sectoral outputs, and his stochastic (principal-component type) model for determining normative values of parameters—in *Perspektivnyie Raschety na Osnovye Prostykh Dinamicheskikh Modeley*, Moscow, 1964, ch. 4).

[2] B. M. Mikhalevskiy and Yu. P. Solovyev have published a first Soviet calculation of the country's production function (cf. 'Proizvodstvennaya funktsya narodnogo khoziaystva SSSR v 1951–1963 gg', *Ekonomika i Matematicheskiye Metody*, no. 6, 1966). It is of Cobb-Douglas type brought to the form:

$$\lg Y_t = \lg \delta + \psi(a_1 \lg L_t + a_2 \lg K_t + (1 - a_1 - a_2) \lg R_t) + \zeta t$$

where $\zeta = \psi\pi$. *Notation:* Y—final product: prime incomes + losses, const. prices. L—input of skill-averaged man-hours; K—capital (reproducible), const. prices; fixed capital stock net of depreciation (allowance for change in vintage). Adjustment made in L and fixed K for quality improvement (skills, embodied technology) at const. annual rate). R—land, compound rent from farm and mining land. Further, t—time; a—share in national income; parameters, δ of 'neutral efficiency', ψ—of 'return-to-scale effect', π—of autonomous technical progress.

When least-square method applied, the following obtained: $\lg Y_t = -0{\cdot}524219 + 1{\cdot}11111(0{\cdot}54118 \lg L_t + 0{\cdot}33398 \lg K_t + 0{\cdot}12484 \lg R_t + 0{\cdot}005179t)$;

$$\sigma = 0{\cdot}01526; \quad V = 0{\cdot}716 \text{ per cent};$$
$$d = 0{\cdot}41026; \quad 0{\cdot}02520 > \sigma > 0{\cdot}01095$$
$$1{\cdot}4820 > \psi > 0{\cdot}7395, \quad 0{\cdot}025043 > \pi > -0{\cdot}013540$$

(σ is standard deviation; V—coefficient of variation; d is Durbin-Watson statistic).

In a subsequent paper ("Ekonomiko-Matematicheskiye Modeli Planirovanya Obshchestvennogo Proizvodstva" in *Ekonomika i Matematicheskiye Metody*, no. 2, 1967) Mikhalevskiy argues, and shows on the basis of Soviet empirical data, that the model is usable as an effective instrument in plan construction.

Note: For the first calculation of production function for Soviet industry, see F. Seton, *American Economic Review*, no. 2, 1959.

15 The Objective Function and Optimal Growth[1]

SOME non-Soviet students have been tempted to interpret Soviet practice by assuming that economic strategy has aimed at the maximisation of some defined goal, say the rate of growth of national income or the terminal stock of capital over the horizon.[2] This interpretation helps to rationalise the intuitively pursued line. It is arguable that, with unlimited horizons, the strategy has dissolved itself into tactics of maximum speed in the development of specific sectors, identified as 'growth' sectors: maximum speed being that compatible with whatever maximum rate of saving is found tolerable. (In this sense the strategy can be described as one of 'growth for growth's sake'.[3]) Academician Strumilin's appraisal is illuminating[4]:

"So far planning practice has been proceeding essentially along the road of empirical searching (*empiricheskikh iskaniy*) on which the most important advances are mixed with awkward errors and obvious losses. In the process some tendencies of development are being discerned—by way of groping—as related to factors of one kind or another, capable of influencing them. In particular the most important problem, of optimally relating accumulation and the growth of consumption, is being posed. But how, concretely, such problems of optimal proportions in the national economy can be solved—this is not yet known in our planning practice."

---

[1] Some problems considered here have been discussed in my article 'On the Objective Function for the Soviet Economy', *Economica*, August 1965.

[2] Cf. B. Horvat, 'The Optimum Rate of Return', *Economic Journal*, 1958 (p. 755): he discusses Soviet inter-war strategy in terms of overinvestment.

[3] This dictum does not carry here any value-judgement; it leaves open the question as to whether or not the strategy was defensible. Consider for instance rationalisation—in terms of the von Neumann model and the Turnpike theorem—of the post-1928 strategy of growth with consumption kept at the subsistence level and treated as input yielding man-hours in a Veblenesque imitative advance.

[Since these words were written I have found that Professor J. Berliner has been thinking along the same lines and has analysed the strategy within the framework of von Neumann's consumption-less system. 'The peculiar appropriateness of the turnpike theorem to Soviet growth'—he remarks—'is that it deals precisely with those commodities that Stalin and Chen Yi had in mind in their justification of the motive to overtake and surpass the advanced countries, namely stocks of productive resources'. Cf. 'The Economics of Overtaking and Surpassing', in H. Rosovsky, ed., *Industrialisation in Two Systems*—Essays in honour of Alexander Gerschenkron, New York—London, 1966, p. 181. I commend to the reader's attention this stimulating paper].

[4] S. Strumilin, 'K probleme optimalnykh proportsyi', in *Planirovanye i Ekonomiko-Matematicheskiye Metody*, N. P. Fedorenko, ed., Moscow, 1964.

It is one of the services rendered by the 'planometric' school that it has offered some rigorous thinking on ends and means in the economic strategy[1]. Partly discussions on the subject have turned,[2] in more formal terms, on the question hinted at here before: is the objective of a socialist society a multi-element vectoral magnitude or a scalar one. This links with a wider question: whether efficient planning is possible at all without a single maximand or minimand. In recent Soviet discussions some have advocated a pragmatic approach to these matters in planning. Particularly those engaged in actual planning work advocate elaboration of a plan in several variants on different, perhaps conflicting criteria, and what would amount to an intuitive selection of the most desirable from among them. The reservations as to practical feasibility of the 'one model-one criterion' approach are understandably shared by those responsible for the development of the methodology of investment appraisal (esp. T. S. Khachaturov). In a more fundamental way, the traditionalists have revived the argument that a highly complex 'parallelism' of tasks and objectives is a characteristic inherent in a socialist, as contrasted with a capitalist, economy and that this property makes it impossible to synthesise social goals. This view has been forcibly put forward by Boyarskiy[3]: it is from this proposition that he deduces his tenet of the impossibility of formulating a plan as constrained-extremal problem.[4] Lurie legiti-

---

[1] The question arises here as to the substance of mathematical formalisation of the idea of an optimality criterion for growth. The question is asked and an answer offered by Professor Tjalling C. Koopmans ('On the Concept of Optimal Economic Growth', in *The Econometric Approach to Development Planning*, Pontificia Academia Scientiarum, Amsterdam-Chicago, 1965, pp. 226 ff.). The basic notion is that of a preference ordering of growth paths (with indifference, preference and preference-or-indifference usually required to be transitive).

[2] For the discussions referred to here see in particular reports in *Planovoye Khoziaystvo*, 1964, no. 5, and 1964, no. 6, on the March 1964 'round-table conference' on the theme of 'Cybernetics, planning and social system'.

[3] Cf. Ya. Boyarskiy, *Matematiko-Ekonomicheskiye Ocherki, op. cit.*, pp. 350 ff. In an interesting discussion K. Porwit (*Zagadnienia Rachunku Ekonomicznego w Planie Centralnym*, Warsaw, 1964, pp. 51 ff.) subscribes to Boyarskiy's view on the futility of looking for a 'universal' optimum, but he does not draw the latter's consequences.

[4] Cf. A. L. Lurie, *O Matematicheskikh Metodakh Reshenya Zadach na Optimum, op. cit.*, p. 23.

However, Lurie doubts whether a strictly quantitative formalisation of the optimum in the shape of a function (functional) is practicable. For a more optimistic view with regard to a sufficient approximation to the 'ideal' see a review by A. I. Katsenelinboygen, Yu. V. Ovseyenko, E. Yu. Fayerman in *Ekonomika i Matematicheskiye Metody*, no. 5, 1966; also *Metodologhicheskiye Voprosy Optimalnogo Planirovanya*, 1966, pp. 23, 172.

mately counter-argues that, in strict logic, the latter implies impossibility of rational planning as such; and, in Polish literature, Lange[1] shows convincingly that even assuming that the objective of a socialist economy is expressive only vectorally, maximisation calculus can be applied as one of finding a Pareto-like maximum: the problem can be turned into maximising a scalar magnitude.

Among those postulating a synthesised objective, in particular V. M. Glushkov, an intellectually attractive formulation suggests time as the minimand. In our Note on Control Systems (page 187) it is related to the maximand of activity-speed and Pontriagin's maximum principle. This, however, leaves still open the question of a specific social-goal function. By itself the time-minimand can well encompass the traditional Soviet planning tactics (see above, p. 171) and such goals as expanding output per man (I. S. Malyshev).[2]

Some would see national income—or perhaps value added—as the valid synthesising maximand of the system.[3,4] (We have noted that

---

[1] Cf. Oskar Lange, *Optymalne Decyzje*, *op. cit.*, p. 172; also his excellent paper, 'Il ruolo della matematica nella pianificazione economica', *Statistica*, July–September 1963, esp. 293 ff.

[2] In Hungarian discussions J. Rudolph suggested a coefficient of change in total-labour-input/total-output over the plan period as an efficiency criterion. See his 'Input-Output Table and the Optimum Production Plan of the National Economy', in *Input-Output Tables*, O. Lukacs *et al.*, eds., Budapest, 1962, p. 147; see also contributions by A. Brody *ibid.*, and by G. Simon, G. Kondor in A. Efimov, *Problemy Optimalnogo Planirovanya*, 1966.

[3] National income is the maximand in Feldman's model of the 1920s. The rate of growth of national income is in Feldman defined as:

$$T = \mathrm{d}Y/\mathrm{d}t \cdot 1/Y = \mathrm{d}(C.K)/\mathrm{d}t \cdot 1/Y = \mathrm{d}C\,\mathrm{d}t \cdot 1/C + \mathrm{d}K/\mathrm{d}t \cdot 1/K$$

where Y denotes national income, K denotes capital stocks, thence capital efficiency $C = Y/K$. The rate of growth of national income is the sum of the rates of growth of capital stock and of efficiency of its employment. The other key coefficient is one describing the patterning of K as between the spheres of 'means of production' and 'means of consumption'. (Cf. G. A. Feldman, *Voprosy Ekonomiki*, 1928, nos. 11, 12.) Several students have noted constructional similarities of the Feldman and the Mahalanobis models. (Cf. the latter's 'Perspective Planning in India', *Co-Existence*, May 1964.)

For a useful mathematical re-statement of the Feldman model, see W. Przelaskowski, 'Matematyczne Podstawy i Implikacje Modelu G. Feldmana' in *Studia Ekonomiczne* (10), Polish Academy of Sciences, Warsaw, 1963.

[4] There is a stimulating discussion of problems of optimality criteria for a central plan in *Le Concept d'Optimisation dans la Planification Economique et Sociale*, a paper presented at the Zurich 1964 conference of the Econometric Society by M. Verhulst and G. Faiveley (I wish to thank them for letting me have a mimeo copy). In their treatment the system of optimisation criteria is formed by the objective function, some $\phi(XA)$, and the constraints on objectives $(X\delta)$, the X denoting a set of variables characterising the social-economic situation, the A are 'functional constraints' delimiting the region feasible from

national income is adopted as the maximand in Polish planning literature by Kalecki and his associates in constructing the investment-
efficiency yardstick: it is also used by Lange.[1]) Those adopting the final
bill of goods, or some of its components, belong to the same school of
thought.

In substance the matter is one of strategy, but technically it reduces
to the formal structure given to the plan-programme: to distributing
strategic variables as between constraints and the criterion function
and/or ways of weighing the latter to comply with scales of preferences,
intra-temporal and inter-temporal.[2]

This is well borne out by Konyus's analysis, which is of notable
didactic merit.[3] In his framework the economy's advance over the
plan period is determined by the given initial capital stock and
capacity-use coefficients, investment flows to feed postulated beyond-
the-horizon capacities (alternatively secured by suitably set steps
of a dynamic programme), consumption functions and technology.[4]
Degrees of freedom are gained by abandoning the assumptions of

the technical-economic point of view, and δ are the 'directive parameters' (*paramètres
directives*) delimitating the region of situations admissible from the point of view of 'final
options'. Optimisation of the plan is then shown as a process of successive adjustments
in which the political decision-makers try to achieve compatability of the two sets of
constraints by re-adjusting the 'directive parameters'.

Two observations may be pertinent. One that the dichotomy of constraint is largely a
matter of convention. Secondly, that while the description of the pragmatic optimisation
process is of considerable empirical interest, especially for a French-type institutional
framework, it does not offer an explicit answer as to the articulation, in homogeneous
terms, of the ends pursued in planning, on which its rationality logically hinges.

[1] O. Lange, *loc. cit.*

[2] Cf. for instance models discussed in Part II, chapter 20.

[3] A. A. Konyus, 'Rasshirenye sistemy uravneniy mezhotraslevykh svyazey dlya
thseley perspektivnogo planirovanya' in V. S. Nemchinov, ed., *Primenenye Matematiki
v Ekonomicheskikh Issledovanyakh*, vol. ii, Moscow, 1961.

[4] Konyus's 'expanded system of intersectoral balance equations' has the following
form (*op. cit.*, p. 60):

$$\sum_{k=1}^{m} \sum_{h=0}^{j} X^{(h)} G_k^{hj} a_{ik}^{(hj)} + \sum_{k=1}^{m} X_k^{(1)} V_k^{(1j)} b_{ik}^{(1j)} = \sum_{h=0}^{j} X_i^{(h)} G_i^{(hj)} + y_i^{(j)}$$

where the X's stand for capacities; y for the final bill of goods minus investment; i for
the branch for which the balance is compiled, k for the one which absorbs current outputs; h and 1, respectively, for the year in which investment started and will start
yielding production ($i = 1, 2 \ldots, m$; $j = 1, 2 \ldots, N$; $j \leqslant 1 \leqslant N+1$). The remaining
symbols denote coefficients: the G's are coefficients of the use of capacities; a's input
coefficients (non-investment goods); b's are marginal capital coefficients. The V_k^{1j} describes gestation of capacities: the j-th year's portion of investment due to begin yielding production in the 1-th year (the V_k^1 add up to unity); the product of $X_k^1 V_k^{1j}$ might
be treated then as an independent variable.

echnological constancy (outputs coming from plants with competing echniques with the entailed patterning of capital formation), and of a closed system; what is derived is the branch outputs, national income with the consumption/accumulation ratio, consumption of specific commodities and investment in specific branches. It is demonstrated that equivalent goals can be reached by different formalisations of the objective—within the Konyus framework. Suppose the fastest growth of national income is the goal pursued. With consumption given for each plan year, the goal could be achieved by adopting as the minimand labour input into the terminal-year output, as determined by investment over the whole plan-period. Alternatively inasmuch as investment rate is fixed, the goal could be achieved by taking investment as the maximand (which might involve the inclusion into the maximand of investment ensuring desirable growth of capacities beyond the plan-period).

In his recent writings Kantorovich too, adopts a flexible approach to the formulation of the objective function. To recall, in his original model it had the form of the final bill of goods with fixed ingredients. This has been revised in his outline of a dynamic system (1964)— which, indeed, has been facilitated partly by the shift from statics to dynamics. The convincingly-made point is that setting the task in terms of both consumer and capital goods restricts the variation of the production plan; and that fixing the task with regard to capital goods is troublesome because it can be adequately determined only by the plans of subsequent development of production. Hence the objective function, as it stands now in Kantorovich, is defined in terms of consumer goods alone,[1] and the shaping of the programme with respect to capital goods is left to the dynamic plan-progress itself. Inevitably the familiar snag—the difficulty of appraising the growth potentialities of the system beyond the plan horizon—crops up.[2] Kantorovich's

---

[1] L. V. Kantorovich, 'Dinamicheskaya model optimalnogo planirovanya' in N. P. Fedorenko, ed., *Planirovanye i Ekonomiko-Matematicheskiye Metody, op. cit.*, pp. 334 ff. The maximand is consumption in certain posited proportions: the programme is optimal if no other secures greater consumption of any good.

Comments on his static formulation validly noted that any surplus consumption of any specific good violating the postulated proportions has zero value. Cf. Roy Radner, *Note on the Theory of Economic Planning*, Athens, 1963, p. 50; and also Benjamin Ward, 'Kantorovich on Economic Calculation' in *Journal of Political Economy*, December 1960, pp. 546.

[2] The problem of constraints placed on the terminal period is incisively examined by Malinvaud, *Sur la Determination des Croissances Optimales*, mimeo, Ecole Nationale de la

answer is *a posteriori* correction of the adopted criterion in the light of the results of the solution, and subsequent re-calculations of the plan. Specifically, in his treatment, capacities at the terminal time-point of the plan period would be valued possibly with the use of shadow prices conditioned by optimal plan itself, and also with those obtained from the solution for dynamic valuation of outputs and the value of the investment efficiency 'norm'. The stress is on the pragmatic consideration: that while the choice of the criterion is of strategic importance, it is of relatively limited significance for decision-making in the initial phases of the perspective plan, presumably because the system's behaviour in that phase is largely predetermined by the inherited state of resources. As to subsequent phases the perspective plan may be expected in any case to undergo revisions under the regime of 'rolling' planning (see our remarks on p. 178). In so far as one of the crucial elements of the criterion formulation pertains to the determining of the accumulation/consumption ratio Kantorovich, too, subscribes to the view that, in real life, the constructor of an optimal plan will find its practicable ranges rather narrowly circumscribed— on the one hand by what is considered to be the minimum level of consumption, and on the other by achievable, realistic, rates of growth of consumption. How defensible are his suppositions with regard to such 'ceilings' and 'floors' is a question to which an answer can only be discovered empirically. A suggestion offered by Kantorovich to the effect that the consumption constraint be determined by proceeding from the interdependence of labour productivity and real wages, is a valid technical solution rather than an answer to the substance of the question.

A noteworthy line in contemporary Soviet thought is the attempt to base the criterion of an economy's optimum development on the newly assimilated conceptions of 'consumption effect' and utility (see chapter 4 above). A half-way and rather timid formulation, based on the conception of scientific consumption 'norms', is offered by

Statistique et de l'Administration Economique, 1964? Two alternatives approaches are considered. One is to place some value on the capital stock postulated for the last time-interval; and the other, equivalent in substance, to attribute utility to the carry-over stock and bring it into the objective function of optimal growth along with that of consumption, the assumption being that it represents the consumption foregone in order to secure the extension of the optimal growth beyond the horizon (with an adopted rate of interest). It is shown that the carry-over capital is uniquely determined: solution is sought by means of dynamic programming.

A. I. Katsenelinboygen:[1] his criterion for planning economic growth is defined as the maximum integral of the 'consumption effect' (*potrebitelskiy effekt*) over the period of the movement towards a given goal. The correlation between the goal and the maximised 'effect' has not been adequately clarified.

There is more conceptual daring as well as formal elegance in an attempt by Pugachev to express the ultimate criterion of economic development in terms of a consumption-preference and time-preference functions. Pugachev's maximand[2] is written as a functional $U = \int_0^\infty Q(t)u[x(t)]\,dt$ describing inter-temporal as well as inter-commodity preferences. The latter are expressed by the $u(t)$, the objective of social consumption (the emphasis would be on the adjective). This function is seen in turn as one combining the Volkonskiy-type consumer's preference function, the Katsenelinboygen 'normative' preference function and some function of extra-economic needs, the three being weighted (technically in the form of constraints) in a way on which the author remains uncommitted. Weighting over time —the time-patterning of the maximand—is the role of the $Q(t)$.

The heart of the matter is thus the $Q(t)$ which shapes the time-sequence of consumption. Three time-functions are suggested for the box of instruments to serve in the selection process: three 'testing characteristics' of the optimal plan, α, β, γ—which are the growth rates of social consumption, and of capital stock, and the plan's 'efficiency norm' respectively. When the problem is tackled as an analogue of the 'dual' of mathematical programming, the 'efficiency norm' reduces price-measured products to one date. With P_x denoting the vector of the solving-multiplier type of prices and φ the change in their 'scale' (the 'characteristic' of the price dynamics), the 'normative efficiency' of the plan appears as[3]

$$\gamma(t) = -\frac{d}{dt}\left[\ln P_x(t)x(o) + \frac{d}{dt}\ln \varphi(t)\right]$$

---

[1] See A. I. Katsenelinboygen, 'Matematicheskiye metody v ekonomicheskikh issledovanyakh', in *Vestnik Akadermii Nauk SSSR*, vol. xxxi, 1961, no. 9, cf. p. 129.

[2] V. F. Pugachev, 'O kriterii optimalnosti ekonomiki', in Alb. L. Vainshtein, ed., *Narodnokhoziaystvennye modeli—Teoreticheskiye Voprosy Potreblienya*, Moscow, 1963.

For discussion of the Pugachev model see also Alfred Zauberman, 'On the Objective Function for the Soviet Economy', *op. cit.*

[3] *Ibid.*, p. 74. Again the best plan the one yielding maximum welfare for given 'shadow expenditure' is the one with the highest present value. (Cf. Radner, *op. cit.*, pp. 69–70.)

which, in fact does not bring us far beyond the Kantorovich analysis.
It can easily be shown that a given model's 'efficiency norm' is directly
connected with the time-preference $Q(t)$: if change of the price
'scale' is left aside, it equals the logarithmic derivative of Q, taken
with the sign minus.[1] Indeed the interdependence of all the four para-
meters α, β, γ, φ and the Q can be readily seen: it has been formalised
in the course of the exercise. But while this helps insight into choices
(as does also the linearisation, by means of fixing the gradient of the
scalar objective of social consumption), it still leaves undetermined the
choice itself. Pugachev connects it with the procedure of 'rolling'
('sliding') planning. By a continual recomputation of a set of small-
dimension variants, and through an analysis by means of the 'testing
characteristics', the numerical value for $Q(t)$ would be selected.
(Alternatively, say with some 'empirically validated' hunch with regard to the prevailing 'efficiency norm' and with the postulated
'characteristic' of consumer-goods price dynamics, φ, the Q would be
fixed.) The 'rolling planning' procedure would integrate the perspective and the current plans by adjusting the former in response to the
flow of current information: conceptually—as distinct from its present
application in Soviet practice—this assumes, parallel to continual
recalculations, the continual issuing from the centre of parameters,
including price parameters, which correspond to the optimum for a
given 'perspective' period. The Q is seen as subject to the condition
of 'least re-calculation' of the 'perspective' of the plan. It is legitimately argued that fast decline in the Q over time would permit the
planner to relax the degree of precision with time remoteness of a plan
period, and to content himself with rougher, more tightly aggregated
indicators, thereby also 'averaging' out the errors in prognosis. But
more qualifications would be required with regard to Pugachev's
tenet that the testing of plan variants with his 'characterististics' of
optimum would necessarily bring down the choice of practicable
values for Q to a narrow 'diapason'—indeed would make it uniquely
determined. True, Pugachev does demonstrate that when the time-
weighting function is given an exponential form, $Q(t) = e^{-at}$, his 'testing characteristics' display a high degree of sensitivity to variations of

[1] The 'efficiency norm' is re-written as

$$\gamma(t) = -\frac{d}{dt} \ln P_x + \frac{\varphi'(t)}{\varphi(t)} = -\frac{Q'}{Q} + \frac{\varphi'}{\varphi}$$

Ibid., p. 93.

ts parameter a: beyond some value for the a small increases in this parameter bring about relatively little gain in capital formation accompanied by a steep decline in consumption, thus restricting—in practice—the planner's choice area. However, it is still not certain what would be the planner's decisive criterion in this situation. The adoption of the exponential function itself influences the results. The narrowing of the planner's area of manœuvre in the model is also connected with the regime of 'rolling' planning as such, with shaping the future in response to *current* developments: consequently parameters relating to the future are sought in the neighbourhood of those corresponding to the current plan-implementation. For all its great technical and heuristic merits the Pugachev model seems to have led to an unduly generalised claim of having established that the process of the choice of the Q was 'subjective only in form but not in its basic content'.[1]

The planner's rate of discount is argued by Drewnowski (in a study produced about the same time in Poland) to be an 'objective fact' in a different sense. At his point of departure Drewnowski[2] follows Oskar Lange[3] who showed in a noteworthy exercise how the problem of the national rate of efficiency presents itself to the planner as one of a dynamic series of a certain mean of objectively determined magnitudes (the planner choosing the weights, the coefficients of sectoral allocation and/or those of physical composition of investment). Lange's accent is thus on technological data and he has little to say on the subject of choice-making, involving the time-shape of the growth process (Lange's avowed aim is to explode the 'myth' of productivity of capital, that is productivity of 'waiting': but the problem confronting the decision-making planner *is* one of his assessment of 'waiting' related to marginal productivity of the 'roundaboutness'). Drewnowski tries to articulate this aspect of the decision-making process.

Like Pugachev, he too tries first to elicit the nexus between the planner's decision on the rate of investment, the decision 'a'—one influencing the rate of growth of the economy, and therein reflecting his vision of the 'road towards socialism'—and his marginal rate of time-substitution, r: the r is a decreasing function of the a. Over a

[1] *Op. cit.*, p. 82.

[2] J. Drewnowski, *Ekonomista*, 1962, no. 3, p. 532.

[3] O. Lange, 'Produkcyjno-techniczne podstawy efektywnosci inwestycji', in his *Pisma ekonomiczne i spoleczne, 1930–1960*, Warsaw, 1961, p. 347; and his 'The Output-Investment Ratio and Input-Output Analysis', *Econometrica*, April 1960.

period of n years, the yearly income-increment y from an investmen increment ΔI, that is $n.y$, when discounted at the planner's r, would be reduced to some $\Delta \zeta$: and in the planner's mind the ζ is fixed at the point where total increment income over time just equals the invest ment that generated it (or consumption foregone), $\Delta I = \Delta \zeta$. On the other hand, investment efficiency rate relates incremental income to incremental investment and its productivity rate: $\Delta y = \Delta I.\beta$, which is the technological *datum* of the system. The ζ curve thus reveals itself as only what it could be expected to be, the geometric locus of equili bria of the planner's time-preference and technical possibilities.[1] The two elements are then gathered in Drewnowski's 'fundamental growth equation':

$$\Delta y \varphi [r(a)] = \Delta \zeta = \Delta I = \Delta y . 1/\beta$$

(Here the φ is a multiplier showing how many times the increment in the total stream of incomes, when discounted, ζ, is larger than the yearly income increment Δy.) With the planner's horizon extended to infinity $n \to \infty$, the $\varphi = 1/r - 1$,[2] and once the key decision, the decision 'a', has been taken by the planner, the φ is obtainable from the 'fundamental growth equation' as the reciprocal of the investment efficiency ratio, $1/\beta$. And at the further step—still with the planner's time vision stretched to infinity—we have $\varphi = 1/\beta = 1/r - 1$; or $1/r = 1/\beta + 1$; hence $r = \beta/(\beta + 1)$.[3] The decision 'a', Drewnowski argues, is 'an objective fact' which can be read from the plan, and so is the rate r in so far as it is implied in the a; but selection of the a, and thereby the r, is a political act which as such evades criteria of econ-omic calculation. The analyst has to content himself with an *ex post* revealed scale of the planner's time-preferences.[4] Drewnowski's in-quiry is helpful in bringing out the relation—not seldom misunder-stood in both Western and Eastern writing—between the 'objective' technological factor of the investment productivity and the planner's

---

[1] M. S. Feldstein ('The Social Time Preference Discount Rate in Cost Benefit Analysis', *Economic Journal*, June 1964, p. 374) has shown that society's location in the consumption space is a point of tangency between the investment productivity curve and a social indifference curve; in turn the slope of the latter is argued to reflect the social consumption-utility function, the rate of population growth and the pure time-preference rate that is applied.

[2] $\varphi = [(1-r) - (1-r)^{n+1}] : r$.

[3] Drewnowski, *op. cit.*, p. 532.

[4] It is thus not quantifiable *ex ante.* in plan construction.

subjective' pure discount rate, both hidden in the planner's normative investment efficiency rate, as promulgated in Soviet-type economies in the shape of the recoupment period.[1] (The term 'pure rate'
is being used here in a special sense of a rate in which allowance *has*
been made for the uncertainties with regard to technological developments and generally the imperfection of the planner's foresight—a
rate which, to refer to Shackle's schema, would have as a component
the risk-factor, say rising exponentially with the time-remoteness.)[2]
But the emphasis on the discrete nature of the planner's time-preference
factor tends to overstate, at least by implication, the empirical degree
of his freedom. In this respect Pugachev's explorations help towards a
balanced view (he demonstrated that *any* realistic rate of discount
brings the discounted value almost to zero over something like one-
third of a century).

There is something to the fact pointed out by Tinbergen[3] that the
country which was first to make a deliberate choice of saving rates
failed to provide any theoretical rationalisation of rates employed.[4]
For study of the literature leaves one doubtful as to the possibility
of an 'objective' determination of the optimal growth path.[5] Either
one considers a finite horizon, or an infinite horizon. In the first case
the solution is largely determined by the length of the time-period
considered and the valuation of the terminal capital stock. In the
second, two possibilities have been considered:

(1) To reduce the problem to the first one by introducing a finite

---

[1] J. Paelinck and J. Waelbroeck (*Programmation économique et modèles économétriques de croissance*, Liège, 1963) formulate the choice function of a decision-maker maximising consumption, with an infinite horizon, as

$$P = c \int_0^\infty e^{(r-g)} \, dt$$

The elements are: i=rate of investment ($1-i=c$, rate of consumption); K=gross marginal capital/output ratio; g=rate of discount of the future (measuring 'psycho-logical degradation' of future magnitudes); $r=1/K$ rate of growth of the product unit P available for consumption. For the Soviet case, the authors argue, great discrepancy between r and g (very weak r) makes $P=\infty$ (p. 51). This is at least a useful broad illustration of the problem.

[2] Cf. G. L. S. Shackle, *Time in Economics*, Amsterdam, 1958.

[3] J. Tinbergen, *Economic Journal*, December 1956, p. 603.

[4] For a discussion of a theory behind the rate of investment in the USSR, see A. Bergson, *The Economics of Soviet Planning, op. cit.*, pp. 317 ff.

[5] For a critical survey of the literature see S. Chakravarty, 'The Existence of an Optimum Savings Programme', *Econometrica*, January 1962.

horizon, consumption beyond which does not count. This has been done in two ways, by the introduction either of

(a) Ramsey's concept of 'bliss'. This is an assumption with no empirical support. Or,

(b) a discount rate to make infinite consumption streams comparable.

The logic of this, for an immortal society, is doubtful.[1] Ramsey assumed that to discount later enjoyments in comparison with earlier ones is 'a practice which is ethically indefensible and arises merely from a weakness of the imagination'.[2]

(2) To introduce a preference ordering of all the feasible consumption streams between now and infinity. The main problem with this approach is how to determine the preference ordering. The chief attraction of those orderings which have been considered in the literature is their mathematical tractability.[3] Further, on the usual assumptions, the optimal share of accumulation in the current national income is 'excessively' high (because future consumption has not been discounted).[4] Although rigorous thought cannot by itself determine the optimal growth path, it can determine the relationship between the objective technological and social factors and the political parameters. Therein lies its value.[5,6,7]

[1] Note in the context the critique of the Pugachev approach by P. Habibi ('O kriteryakh optimalnosti v skhemakh narodnokhoziaystvennogo planirovanya', *Voprosy Ekonomiki*, no. 5, 1966): it is argued that the Pugachev time-weighting function has its roots in the 'Law of Fear of Death' alien to socialist economics.

[2] Patently, the optimality criterion advanced in Western writing by the school of thought which postulates an inter-generation welfare equilibrium as implied in the living generation's non-compulsory saving decisions, is *a priori* inoperative in Soviet-type socialist society (cf. discussion in Professor P. T. Bauer's *Economic Analysis and Policy in Underdeveloped Countries*, London, 1965, pp. 122 ff. and *passim*).

[3] Cf. A. K. Sen, 'On Optimising the Rate of Saving', *Economic Journal*, 1961, p. 481.

[4] J. Tinbergen, H. Bos, *Mathematical Models of Economic Growth*, New York–London, pp. 24 ff. Tinbergen does introduce a discount rate for 'future utility' when discussing the impact of investment on national income in the USSR, in a recent paper, *The Contributions of Planning, Investment and Integration to National Product*, mimeo, date not stated.

[5] Technically, recent discussions in literature centred largely on the question of the necessary convergence of F. P. Ramsey's classical maximand, the utility-integral (cf. 'A Mathematical Theory of Savings', *Economic Journal*, December 1928). It has been shown, however, that a divergence of the integral would not indicate *per se* non-existence of an accumulation optimum (cf. C. von Weizsaecker, *Existence of Optimal Programs of Accumulation for an Infinite Time Horizon*, mimeo, 1965?).

Heuristically illuminating are Professor Tjalling Koopmans' 'logical experiments' where implications of alternative mathematical formulations of the optimand are llowed up with a model of technology and population growth ('On the Concept of Optimal Growth', in *The Econometric Approach to Development Planning*, Pontificia Academia Scientiarum, Amsterdam—Chicago, 1965). In our context, of particular interest is the analysis of Academician Kantorovich's objective—fixed ratios of the quantities of desired goods—as related to the Golden Rule of Accumulation (cf. E. S. Phelps, 'The Golden Rule of Accumulation', *American Economic Review*, September 961; Joan Robinson, 'A Neo-Classical Theorem', *Review of Economic Studies*, June 962).

Of considerable importance are recent inquiries into our subject by S. Chakravarty, 'The Existence of an Optimum Savings Programme', *op. cit*, 1962; 'Optimal Savings with Finite Planning Horizon', *International Economic Review*, September 1962; 'Optimal Programme of Capital Accumulation in a Multi-Sector Economy', *Econometrica*, July 1965. While stressing the fundamental weaknesses of the finite-horizon approach in a planning model (elements of discontinuity in the treatment of consumption preferences; arbitrariness in the choice of terminal stock of capital) he points to their mitigation where (1) optimal consumption is found relatively insensitive to the choice of terminal conditions; (2) terminal conditions may be chosen so as to minimise possible dicontinuity in the production regimes within and beyond the plan horizon. The stress is on the congeniality of the final-horizon approach to planners in real life.

Of direct interest for planning theory is the inquiry by James Mirrlees, *The Structure of Optimum Policies in a Macro-Economic Model*, a paper submitted to the Zurich 1964 conference of the Econometric Society. It suggests a strong sensitivity of the optimum investment rate to assumptions with regard to production possibilities and distribution, in our context specifically distribution as between generations. See also the same author's *Optimum Accumulation in an Economy with Fixed Capital* (mimeo., 20 February 1966).

Leif Johansen introduces into the objective function of his model a corrective-coefficient for the beyond-the-horizon implications of the plan. (Cf. *Saving and Growth in Long-Term Programming Models-Numerical Examples with a Non-linear Objective Function*, Memorandum fra Sosialokonomisk Institutt, Universitetet i Oslo, August 1964.) While agreeing that a theoretical formulation would not be easy, he believes that numerical exercises may give an idea of reasonable magnitudes.

Professor Joan Robinson discusses incisively in *Socialist Infiuence* (mimeo, 1966?), the experience of strategy for growth in socialist countries and deduces from it relativistic conclusions and pragmatic precepts.

[6] An interesting exercise in determining the rate of investment maximising consumption over a given time-period is carried out by Z. Czerwinski, *Ekonomista*, 1965, no. 1, who works with a Cobb-Douglas type of function: he investigates the relationships between the rate of investment, consumption, the length of the maximisation period, parameters reflecting capital-stock elasticity of national income and technical-equipment elasticity of employment. The tenet is that consideration of investment from the angle of consumption maximisation is meaningful both from the economic and mathematical point of view: and the point is made that the strong exaggeration of the required investment rate usually noted in such exercises is due to the tacit assumption that the impact of employment on the size of national income is independent of consumption per employed, cf. p. 73 above.

[7] Of signal didactic importance is R. Harrod's investigation into optimal investment (see his 'Second Essay', in *Economic Journal*, June 1960; 'Presidential Address', in *Economic Journal*, September 1963; and '*Optimum Investment for Growth*', in *Problems of Economic Dynamics and Planning*, Warsaw, 1964).

Here the basic concept is that of 'natural' or welfare rate of growth of output per head taken taken to be determined primarily by technical progress. From this some $pcG(con)n$ is derived with reference to marginal utility of consumption; with given e,

It is only fair to point out that the nature of the planner's judgement in these matters was well appraised by the brilliant Feldman before Soviet economic theory fell into its decades-long sterility. When analysing the impact of the planner's patterning investment, he pointedly remarked on the ultimately political substance of judgement involved: 'technicians and statisticians should indicate what coefficients of efficiency . . . can be achieved in what time. Then it is up to the social engineer to construct a plan for the economy.' Domar's comment[1] is that no amount of theorising could help us to tell the planner what the right rate of discount should be. Yet it is probably all to the good that after decades of silence, theorising à la Pugachev has been embarked upon with the purpose of elucidating the scope for the 'social engineer's' discrete judgement.

APPENDIX TO CHAPTER 15

The search for a formalised answer to the planner's problem of optimal growth, and the new acquaintance with the von Neumann order of ideas, have, understandably, directed Soviet 'planometrics' towards the Turnpike theory. Here again the Kantorovich school is path-breaking.

the investment elasticity of the curve showing the marginal utility of income over relevant range (to be sought by 'appropriately' weighting individuals) we have as the investment criterion $r_n \geqslant pcG(\text{con})n/e$ the welfare (marginal) rate of return on investment. (The e has been estimated by L. Johansen in *Multi-sectoral Study of Economic Growth*, 1963, p. 107, to equal 0·53).

Harrod validly maintains that the r_n can be thought of without necessary reference to 'interest' in the 'capitalist sense', and that indeed it is fundamental to growth theory under socialism and capitalism alike. On the other hand for the normatively planned system the 'welfare' optimum concept would have to be adjusted so as to allow for the planner's scales of preferences, including his scales of time-preferences. [These lines were written before I discovered the formative influence that Sir Roy Harrod's approach had actually exercised on recent Soviet planometric experiments.]

[1] Feldman, *op. cit.* E. D. Domar, *Essays in the Theory of Economic Growth*, London–New York, 1957, pp. 254 ff.

A. Lukaszewicz ('Charakter i znaczenie pracy G. Feldmana', *Studia Ekonomiczne*, no. 10; Polish Academy of Sciences) deduces from Feldman the strategy inference that a fall in consumption entailed in the acceleration process would be the smaller the lower the 'backwardness threshold' the economy has to pass. 'Regrettably [Lukaszewicz says], Feldman did not try to determine either the height of the threshold, or the time-phase or the time-horizon of the adaptation process' (p. 82).

Feldman's model appears to have become, around the turn of the 1920s, the basis of Kovalevskiy's programme for explosive expansion of Soviet economy, verging on phantasy (which Domar so fascinatingly discusses in the epilogue of his essay). In fairness to Feldman it is right to say that at least when building his model, his aim was to offer an analytical device rather than policy recommendations.

To begin with, Soviet mathematicians have probed into some elements of the theory as evolved in the West—of relevance for the construction of 'perspective' plans. Makarov[1] in particular has tried to weaken the Radner conditions[2] for the von Neumann path as the unique profit-maximising direction with the von Neumann equilibrium prices. His results were akin to those more or less simultaneously arrived at by Morishima[3] (which show that, while possibly fluctuating around the von Neumann ray, the very long-term optimal or efficient path—or any indefinitely long, feasible one—must keep close to it if outputs are averaged along such paths). Soviet explorations—in addition to those by Makarov also those by Romanovskiy in a related context—appear to have influenced the Kantorovich-Makarov approach[4] to optimality criteria. Their point of departure is the proposition that for a plan with a horizon tending towards infinity, intermediate plans tend towards some terminal plan almost independently of the criterion adopted. The existence and uniqueness of such a terminal plan has been established for a mathematically closed system and, moreover, (Romanovskiy[5]) it has been shown that the terminal plan for such a system gravitates in the direction of one optimal of the corresponding von Neumnan model (that is that with the time horizon tending towards infinity the directing cosini of the von Neumann plan-vector form the limit of those of the optimal terminal plans). The inference made from the assymptotic behaviour of the solution of the dynamic linear-programming problem is then that the best criterion for a dynamic 'production' model is the one by which the terminal plan is selected. Note in the context that the Kantorovich-Makarov model of perspective planning is of this type: it is so in as much as it is optimal as a production plan rather than optimal in every respect: to be more precise its optimality (efficiency)—of a quasi-Pareto type—is conceived of as one securing, with the given resources and at minimum cost, final outputs of a given structure determined outside the model (in other words maximising the number of final-product collections of a given composition).

[1] L. V. Makarov, 'Sostoyanya ravnovesya zamknutoy lineynoy modeli rasshirayushcheysya ekonomiki' in *Ekonomika i Matematicheskiye Metody*, no. 5, 1965.

[2] R. Radner, 'Paths of Economic Growth That Are Optimal With Regard to Only Final States: A Turnpike Theorem', *Review of Economic Studies*, February 1961.

[3] M. Morishima, 'On the Two Theorems of Growth Economics: A Mathematical Exercise', *Econometrica*, October 1965. See also his *Equilibrium, Stability and Growth*, *op. cit.*, especially on the generalisation of the Radner-Nikaido theorem and 'cyclical growth' around the Turnpike (pp. 174 ff.).

[4] L. V. Kantorovich, V. L. Makarov, 'Optimalnye Modeli Perspektivnogo Planirovanya', *op. cit.*, p. 50.

[5] I. V. Romanovskiy, 'Assimptoticheskoye povedenye protsessov dinamicheskogo programmirovanya s nepreryvnym mnozhestvom sostoyaniy', *Doklady Akademii Nauk SSSR*, no. 6, vol. 157.

Now, since the finding of a terminal plan is still a matter insufficiently explored, from the angle of the practice of planning, and is in any case computationally tricky, the precept Kantorovich-Makarov offer the planner is to solve his dynamic problem by means of a linear programme for a sufficiently distant terminal time-point, with the consideration that only the earlier part of the plan would be implemented.[1] (Elsewhere Makarov suggested[2] that a model determined over a finite plan-period should be extended to infinity by means of 'adjoining' a closed von Neumann-type model with constant technology: the plan optimal over the infinite horizon would be determined as the limit of a sequence of plans optimal over finite intervals).

The potentialities of the Turnpike for very long-term planning have also been investigated recently by Tsukui: the results are in certain points convergent with those arrived at by the Kantorovich school. Tsukui (who works with a computable Leontief system along McKenzie's lines) is concerned with situations where it is difficult to predetermine an economy's structure for the terminal phase of the plan.[3] The advice he gives the planner is this: since (according to the weak-type Turnpike theorem) all efficient paths *at some time* approach the von Neumann ray and spend most of the planning period in its neighbourhood, the planning agency should lead the economy efficiently towards this ray and keep it growing along this ray while leaving aside 'inter-generation' value-judgements. (Also of interest from the angle of planning theory is Tsukui's dual theorem which establishes the Turnpike-property of the shadow price with respect to the von Neumann price ray: this may carry some indications for the planner as to the technique of guidance towards and along the von Neumann ray.)

However, the question arises as to the scope of indications obtainable by the planner from the Turnpike when the pace of convergence is taken into account. Professor Hicks seems to have a similar point in mind when he says:[4] 'If there were a rapid convergence of the actual optimum to the Turnpike, it might not much matter if we failed to distinguish between them. . . . But if (as we have seen reason to believe) there is only a slow approximation, this by no means follows. The far future is vastly uncertain: it is the near future for which we are always (really) planning.'

---

[1] The question of 'targeting' in very long-range perspective planning was discussed in similar terms in the discussion of Leif Johansen's paper at the Colston Research Society's 1964 Symposium; see in particular comments by R. M. Goodwin and Professor F. H. Hahn (P. E. Hart and others, eds., *Econometric Analysis for National Economic Planning*, London, 1964, pp. 254 and 255).

[2] See report from a Seminar, *Ekonomika i Matematicheskiye Metody*, no. 4, 1966, p. 625.

[3] Jinkichi Tsukui, 'Turnpike Theorem in a Generalized Dynamic Input-Output System' in *Economrtrica*, April 1966; in the reference to L. W. McKenzie, of particular relevance is 'Turnpike Theorem for a Generalized Leontief Model', *Econometrica*, January 1963.

[4] John Hicks, *Capital and Growth*, Oxford, 1965, p. 236.

We have centered our attention on the Turnpike because of the promise of guide-lines for grand strategy of long-perspective optimal equilibrium advance. It is right to note, however, that Soviet model-builders have continued to work with alternatives, specifically with several variants of that focusing on streams of consumption outputs.[1] Conceptually more modest, they have not proved computationally easy as yet, either. Nor have they equalled the Turnpike in intellectual excitement.

A NOTE ON SOVIET WORK ON OPTIMAL CONTROL SYSTEMS[2]

The theory of optimal control systems is one of relatively young vintage. Still younger is the appreciation of its potentialities for economic planning.

Intellectual curiosity apart, the prime stimulus in the development of control theory has patently been its technological applicability: indeed it owes its origin largely to technological intuition. Almost inevitably however the kinship of an optimally controlled motion, of pursuit motion, generally of processes involving multi-stage choices subject to posited criteria, with an efficient guidance of economic systems suggests itself to the mind of the

---

[1] In addition to the contributions referred to already in these pages, see that by V. S. Dadayan (in *Ekonomtiko-Matematicheskiye Metody* vol. 1, *op. cit.*, pp. 148, 152) whose maximand is cumulative consumption over the whole plan-period subject to a 'limiting investment-norm'.

For a recent attempt to simplify the solution with consumption streams as the maximand, see L. M. Dudkin, E. V. Yershov, 'Blochnoye postroyenie optimalnogo materialnogo balansa sotsyalisticheskogo khoziaystva' in S. M. Vishnev, ed., *Ekonomiko-Matematicheskiye Metody—Metody Optimalnogo Planirovanya*, vol. ii, Moscow, 1965. Previously Konyus and Granberg suggested allowing for changes in the structure of consumption—in their expanded input-output systems—by making explicit its dependence on the consumption 'fund' in constant prices or on income levels, respectively (cf. A. A. Konyus, 'Rasshirenye sistemy uravneniy mezhotraslevykh sviazey dla tseley perspektivnogo planirovanya' in *Primenenye Matematiki v Ekonomicheskikh Issledovanyakh*, vol. 2, *op. cit.*; A. G. Granberg's contribution to *Opredelenye potrebnosti naselenya v tovarakh*, Kiev, 1962; solution suggested links up with Konyus's conceptions evolved in the 'twenties: cf. 'The Problem of the True Index of the Cost of Living', *Econometrica*, January 1939, and a comment by H. Schultz, *ibid.*). Dudkin-Yershov bring in, instead, as a criterion, the maximisation of consumption levels with a posited variable 'assortment' relations. For a vector of output of the i-th consumer-good, y_i, that is stated as finding the maximum of some parameter λ such that $y_i = Pi(\lambda)$. This function is piecewise linear, non-decreasing, continuous. Whether the curves in question are sufficiently well behaved to be adequately approximated in this fashion is not easy to say (cf. W. J. Baumol, *Economic Theory and Operations Analysis*, 1965, p. 144). Non-linearities in other models with consumption as criterion have proved tricky to handle.

[2] I wish to thank Professor A. W. Phillips who read this paper and encouraged me to publish it. He bears no responsibility for the contents.

student. This affinity extends indeed to all the broad classes of processes considered in the theory of optimal controls—deterministic, stochastic, adaptive. The link-up sought in more recent days between the theory of trajectory guidance and that of communication adds to their relevance for economics of planning. (Note in this context in particular Kalman's attempt to formulate a 'pure' theory of controls, his duality theorem in respect of 'controllability' and 'observability', and his approach to the Wiener-Kolmogorov filtering and prediction problems.)[1] Both are precisely the domains in which the 'planometrician' gropes today in the search of a theoretical basis for what is rather loosely known as information planning, or in East European parlance, cybernetical planning.[2]

The translation into English of the beautiful work by Pontriagin and associates has made the Western economist aware of the Soviet contribution in this field. These few remarks are intended *firstly* to give a somewhat more rounded, though far from full an idea of this contribution, and *secondly* to note one or two attempts to employ the theory in the field of our interest.

The general deterministically-treated control problem for some object S can be stated (in Litovchenko's formulation)[3] as a system of ordinary differential equations or a vectoral equation

$$x = f(x, u, t); \quad t_1 \leqslant t \leqslant t_2; \quad t_2 \leqslant +\infty$$

Here $x(t) = [x_1(t), \ldots, x_n(t)]$ is an n-dimensional function of the variable t describing the state of S over this time-interval; $x \in \Omega$, where the Ω denotes a certain manifold of the vectoral phase space X; the $f(x, u, t) = [f_1(x, u, t) \ldots f_n(x, u, t)]$ is an n-dimensional vectoral function of the variables x, u, t, determined for all $x \in \Omega$, $u \in U$, $t \in [t_1, t_2]$ and meeting some specified conditions such as continuity, piece-wise continuity or smoothness; the u's are parameters determining the course of the control process; $u(t) = [u_1(t) \ldots u_n(t)]$ is the control vector: $u(t) \in U$, where U is the domain of

[1] R. E. Kalman, 'On a New Approach to Filtering and Prediction Problems', *Journal of Basic Engineering*, 1960, pp. 34–5; and 'O obshchey teorii sistem upravlenya' in *Transactions of the First Congress of International Federation of Automatic Control*, vol. ii, V. A. Trapeznikov, Ya. Z. Tsypkin, eds., (hereafter referred to as *IFAC*), esp. pp. 541 ff.

[2] The reader who would like to acquaint himself, in the present and other contexts of this volume, with the Soviet developments in the theory of information, could be directed in particular to A. N. Kolmogorov, *Teorya Peredachi Informatsyi*; I. M. Gelfand, A. N. Kolmogorov, A. M. Yaglom, 'K obshchemu opredelenyu kolichestva informatsyi', USSR Academy of Sciences, *Doklady*, vol. 111, no. 4, 1956; M. S. Pinsker, *Informatsya i Informatsyonnaya Ustoichivost Sluchaynykh Velichin*, Moscow, 1960. A good bibliography will be found in A. I. Kondalev, *Preobrazovateli Formy Informatsyi*, Kiev, 1965.

[3] I. A. Litovchenko, 'Teorya optimalnykh sistem', in R. V. Gamkrelidze, ed., *Matematicheskiy Analiz; Teorya Veroyatnostey; Regulirovanye*, Moscow, 1964, p. 156. We have relied heavily here on this excellent survey.

values of control $u(t)$. The problem is to choose such a control $u(t)$ that the corresponding trajectory $x(t)$ satisfies the constraints while the functional

$$\int_{t_1}^{t_2} f_0 \left[x(t), u(t), t \right] \mathrm{d}t$$

is at minimum. For the case of non-existence of this control, minimising the integral, what is sought is the sequence of controls in which the sequence of integrals

$$\int_{t_1}^{t_2} f_0 \left[x_k(t), u_k(t), t \right] \mathrm{d}t$$

converges towards its lower limit with $k \to \infty$

Feldbaum and Lerner are among the earliest explorers of non-classical problems where the optimality notion was strictly related to the functional $\int_{t_1}^{t_2} \mathrm{d}t$. In the early fifties the problem of synthesis of optimal systems was attacked by Feldbaum by means of the phase-space. Lerner was first to focus on constrained phase-space coordinates: time-optimality of almost every control system is determined by absolute or conditional restrictions placed on the values of its coordinates: where the system of coordinates is constrained, some region of admissible positions has to be considered.[1]

On the non-classical line the dominating approach is that of Pontriagin's maximum principle. Originally presented in the mid-fifties (jointly with Boltyanskiy) only as a hypothesis, it was subsequently proved by Gamkrelidze for time-optimality in non-degenerate linear systems of the type $x = Ax + bu$; A is a constant matrix, $n \times n$; b a constant matrix $n \times r$; $u = (u_1 \ldots u_r)$, where $u_i(t) \ldots u_2(t)$ are piecewise-continuous functions with a finite number of points or any arbitrary finite interval of the time axis, $|u_1| \leqslant 1$; boundary conditions with $t = t_1$ and $t = t_2$ are two fixed points $x^{(1)}$ and $x^{(2)}$, respectively. Next the results were generalised by Boltyanskiy for the case of a time-optimal, non-linear autonomous system $x = f(x, u)$, where f and $\mathrm{d}f/\mathrm{d}x$ are continuous on x and u, U is an arbitrary topological space, in particular a closed manifold of the r-dimensional space of the variable $u = (u_1 \ldots u_r)$. Gamkrelidze brought in a functional of a more general form $\int_{t_1}^{t_2} f_0 (x, u) \mathrm{d}t$ and widened the class of admissible control functions to embrace bounded measurable—and not merely piecewise-continuous—functions $u(t)$ with values in an arbitrary subset of some topological Hausdorff space. Then a Pontriagin paper of 1959 treated the case of U being a bounded convex closed polyhedron in a linear r-dimensional vector space E^r with coordinates $u_1 \ldots u_r$, the non-degeneracy conditions becoming the 'general position condition' imposed on coefficients of differential equations

---

[1] Especially A. A. Feldbaum, 'Optimalnye protsessy v sistemakh avtomaticheskogo regulirovanya', *Avtomatika i Telemekhanika*, 1953, no. 6, and A. Ya. Lerner, 'O predelnom bystrodeystvii sistem avtomaticheskogo upravlenya', *ibid.*, 1954, no. 6.

which describe the law of motion and the form of the polyhedron U. Further, Gamkrelidze explored the case where the set Ω, the set of all points of the X space from which an optimal transition of x is possible, is closed in X.[1] All these results were consolidated in the celebrated work by Pontriagin, Boltianskiy, Gamkrelidze and Mishchenko of 1961 (now available in the admirable English Trirogoff-Neustadt translation).[2]

When continuing on a deterministic maximum-principle path several Soviet students evolved further models of considerable interest. Kharatishvili brought the aspect of retardation into the optimal process.[3] Here the point in the phase-space reacts to control signals with some delay θ which involves continuous prognosis, and the final equation of the control object's motion becomes a differential-difference one. In vector form the motion of an object in the phase-space X of the variables $x_1 \ldots x_n$ is described as

$$\mathrm{d}x(t)/\mathrm{d}t = f[x(t), x(t-\theta), u(t)]$$

the delayed argument appearing in phase coordinates and not in the control. (Kharatishvili's reasoning and results are re-stated in Pontriagin et al.)[4]

Butkovskiy and Lerner investigated the case where for the course of the control process the distribution of parameters is of relevance.[5] Their model is of this structure:[6] let n coordinates of the vector

$$Q = Q(t) = \{Q_1(t) \ldots [Q_n(t)]\}$$

be subject to

$$Q_1 = Q_i(t) = \int_{t_0}^{t_1} K_i[t, \tau, u(t)] \, \mathrm{d}t; \qquad i = 1, 2 \ldots n$$

where $K_i[t, \tau, u(t)]$ is a certain function of its arguments; $u=u(\tau)$ piecewise continuous control vector, which for any τ, $t_0 \leqslant \tau \leqslant t_1$ belongs to some closed domain Ω. The sought control is such $u=u(\tau)\Omega$, $t_0 \leqslant t \leqslant t_1$ that $Q(t_1)=Q^*$ which is a given vector and the functional

$$Q_0 = \int_{t_0}^{t_1} F[\tau, Q(t), u(\tau)] \, \mathrm{d}t$$

[1] Cf. Litovchenko, *op. cit.*, p. 159, and sources referred to therein.
[2] L. S. Pontriagin, V. G. Boltianskii, R. V. Gamkrelidze and E. F. Mishchenko, *The Mathematical Theory of Optimal Processes*, (Eng. translation by K. N. Trigoroff), L. W. Neustadt, ed., New York–London, 1962.
[3] G. L. Kharatishvili, 'Printsip maksimuma v teorii optimalnykh protsesov s zapazdyvanyem' in *Doklady* of the Academy of Sciences of the USSR, 1961, no. 1, pp. 39 ff.
[4] *Op. cit.*, p. 213.
[5] A. G. Butkovskiy, A. Ya. Lerner, 'Ob optimalnom upravlenyi sistemami c raspredelyennymi parametrami', *Avtomatika i Telemekhanika*, 1960, no. 6.
[6] See A. G. Butkovskiy's intervention in *IFAC*, pp. 518 ff.

is minimised. The solution arrived at for the problem stated in this form is of the maximum-principle type. At the same time conditions of transversality for the variable of the trajectory endpoint, $Q(t)$, $\in M$ are formulated, where M is some set of arbitrary dimensions not exceeding $(n-1)$. (It may be noted however that the general problem of optimal controls of objects with distributed parameters is among those still unsolved.)

Pursuit has been studied with significant results by Kelendzheridze. This is the motion of two controlled points, the 'pursuing' and the 'pursued' in an n-dimensional phase-space which is ruled for each of them by a system of differential equations with specific parameters. With the control of the pursued $v(t)$, the problem is to find the pursuing control $u(t)$ such that pursuit-time $T_{u,v}$ be at its minimum. It is assumed that for every admissible $v(t)$ an admissible $u(t)$ minimises the pursuit time $\min_u T_{u,v} = T_v$ and that there exists an admissible $v(t)$ which maximises T_v. The choice of u and of v is made so as to get their 'encounter', respectively, as early and as late as possible. The solution is then sought for the optimal pair of controls as a minimax problem $\max_u T_v = \max_v (\min_u T_{u,v})$. For the case of a linear pursuing object the proof offered by means of the maximum principle is incorporated into the work by Pontriagin and associates. Note however, that subsequently, for a general case, it was carried out by Kelendzheridze by way of the dynamic programme method on the assumption that the Bellman function is twice continuously differentiable on its arguments.[1]

Rozonoer has investigated the problems of 'qualitative conditions' imposed on the basic parameters of the controlled processes: usually these are the properties of stability and/or optimality of the system's quality index. The problem is attacked by variational methods: a quality index of a control system can be set as a functional of the control process and the solution of stability and optimality leads to extremals of functionals determining direct quality indices. Similarly treated is the case with limited information on a system: a purely statistical approach apart, the only reasonable policy left is to aim at the 'poorest' quality index—minimum or maximum—which again is a variational problem.[2]

On parallel lines attempts at a classical treatment of the optimal control problem have continued by several Soviet students. As Pontriagin and others have pointed out, the difference between the classical and the non-classical

---

[1] See D. L. Kelendzheridze, 'K teorii optimalnogo presledovanya', in *Doklady* of the Academy of Sciences, USSR 1961, no. 3; and also 'Ob odnoy zadache optimalnogo presledovanya', *Avtomatika i Telemekhanika*, 1962, no. 8; same argument re-stated in Pontriagin *et al., op. cit.*, pp. 226 ff.

[2] L. I. Rozonoer, 'Printsip maksimuma L. S. Pontriagina v teorii optimalnykh sistem', *Avtomatika i Telemekhanika*, 1959, no. 12; also his intervention in *IFAC*, p. 517.

approach lies essentially in that with the classical statement the set of admissible values of the control, u, is taken as arbitrary: yet in the applicational problems the U would be normally closed. However several students have tried to employ, by resorting to some devices, the classical calculus of variations to the case of a closed U; in particular in dealing with analogous problems in flight mechanics (Breakwell, Leitman, Miele).[1] Pontriagin and his associates examined the relationship between the theory of optimal processes and classical calculus of variations, and have demonstrated that the optimal problem as approached by them on the maximum principle lines is a generalisation of the Lagrange problem in the calculus of variations: that it is equivalent to the Lagrange problem where the control region U is an open set in an r-dimensional vector space E_r.[2]

Miele's parametric transformation of the closed U has been applied by some Soviet students in their explorations of the problem. (Letov, though, applied this transformation in a dynamic programming approach.)[3] Butkovskiy arrived at the maximum principle by a method close to the classical one, and Lurie and Troitskiy[4] presented the general optimality problem as one of the classical Meier-Bolza type, where the class of 'free' functions is extended to a piecewise continuous one and the open U region is given by a differentiable relation of the type

$$\varphi = \varphi(u, x, t) = 0; \quad \varphi = (\varphi_1 \ldots \varphi_l); \quad l < n+r$$

In exploration of constrained linear and non-linear optimal control systems several Soviet students have followed the functional analysis path. Krassovskiy has pioneered in these efforts; when turning from the classical method he applied (as did Kulikowski) the method of the 'L problem' in the abstract functional space, borrowed from M. G. Kreyn's theory of moments.[5]

Krassovskiy's work—parallel to that of LaSalle's[6] on the principle of optimal relay control, the 'bang-bang' problem—yielded results akin to the latter's. One should note here Krassovskiy's contribution to the approximation theory.

[1] Cf. Leitman, ed., *Optimization Techniques*, New York, 1962, and translators' note in Pontriagin *et al.*, *op. cit.*, p. 240.

[2] Pontriagin *et al.*, *op. cit.*, pp. 239 ff.

[3] A. M. Letov, 'Analiticheskoye konstruirovanye regulyatorov', *Avtomatika i Telemekhanika*, 1960, nos. 4, 5, 6; 1961, no. 4; 1962, no. 11.

[4] Cf. I. A. Litovchenko, *op. cit.*, p. 165.

[5] N. N. Krassovskiy, 'K teorii optimalnogo regulirovanya', *Avtomatika i Telemekhanika*, 1957; no. 11, R. Kulikowski, 'K optimalnym protsessam i sintezu optimalnykh sistem s lineynymi i nielineynymi nieizmienyayemymi elemntami', *IFAC*, pp. 491 ff.

[6] J. P. LaSalle, *The Time Optimal Control Problems*, Princeton, 1959.

Krassovskiy has also explored, with Lidskiy, the methods of an analytical build-up of regulators where random changes of the object's parameters are considered. The parametric variability is treated here as a random Markovian process.[1]

Substantial contribution has been made by Soviet students to the problem of the synthesis; of the existence of the synthesising function and of finding it—a question which still evades a general solution. Feldbaum employed here the method of the break-up of the phase-space for a class of linear time-optimal controls based on the theroem of n intervals.[2] In Pontriagin-Boltyanskiy-Gamkrelidze-Mishchenko the synthesising function is a piecewise continuous one, $v(x)$ given on the phase-space X, with range in the control region U such that equation $dx/dt = f[x, v(x)]$ determines all the optimal trajectories leading to the origin.[3] Lerner elaborated a method of an isochron domain: it is defined as an ensemble of points in an S domain describing the possible initial positions from which the object can be transferred to a point a_0—the 'pole' of the domain—over some finite time interval t_i along a trajectory in the interior of S: the position of the isochron domain is then a function of the coordinates of a_0, the boundaries of S and the t_i; for any finite t_i the region is shown to be finite and non-zero in all dimensions of the space if the value of at least one of the system's coordinates is constrained.[4] The close connection of the Lernerian isochron domain with dynamic programming was subsequently noticed by several students, in particular Krassovskiy and Sun Tsiang.

In Soviet work on dynamic programming one may note the interesting inquiries establishing its nexus with the Lyapunov functions and functionals: Krassovskiy was the first to show that for some problems with specified optimality criteria and under certain conditions the problem of optimal control reduces to an optimised Lyapunov function—in Lyapunov theory of asymptotic stability.[5] (Similar propositions will be found in the Kalman-Bertram inquiry into the control-system analysis and design via Lyapunov's 'second method'.)[6]

---

[1] Cf. I. A. Litovchenko, *op. cit.*, p. 169.

[2] A. A. Feldbaum, 'O sinteze optimalnykh sistem s pomoshyu fazovogo prostranstva', *Avtomatika i Telemekhanika*, 1955, no. 2.

[3] Pontriagin *et al.*, *op. cit.*, p. 44.

[4] A. Ya. Lerner, *Prinstipy Postroyenya Bystrodeystvuyushchikh Sledyashchikh Sistem i Regulyatorov*, Moscow, 1961, pp. 23–4, 28.

[5] N. N. Krassovskiy, 'Vybor parametrov optimalnykh ustoychivykh sistem', *IFAC*, pp. 482 ff., and further sources quoted therein.

See also A. M. Lyapunov, *Obshchaya Zadacha ob Ustoichivosti Dvizhenya*, Kharkov, 1892; and his 'Issledovanye odnogo iz osobennykh sluchayev zadachi ob ustoichivosti dvizhenya', *Matematicheskiy Sbornik*, 1893, vol. xvii, issue 2, pp. 253-333.

[6] R. E. Kalman, J. E. Bertram, 'Control System Analysis and Design via the Second Method of Lyapunov', *Journal of Basic Engineering*, 1960, pp. 371 ff. Cf. also J. LaSalle, S. Lefschetz, *Stability by Liapunov's Direct Method*, London, 1961.

The main direction of Soviet inquiry being that of maximum principle, its relationship with Bellman's dynamic programming has, understandably, been given considerable attention. Thus Rozonoer has convincingly argued that the two principal directions of the theory of optimal systems are intimately related by a link analogous to that in analytical mechanics between canonical Hamiltonian equations and the Hamilton-Jacobi equations in partial derivatives.[1]

The mutual relationship of the two dominating directions has been in fact discussed by both Pontriagin and associates and Bellman.

Pontriagin and associates are inclined to concede to Bellman's method primarily heuristic virtues. They stress that in Bellman an assumption of differentiability of the functions is added to the 'natural' conditions of the optimal control problems, an assumption which, so it is argued, fails to be legitimate even in the simplest cases.[2] Another advantage emphasised is that the Pontriagin method entails only the solution of differential equations rather than of one in partial derivatives.

In Bellman in turn emphasis is on that the dynamic-programming approach does tackle all three classes of control problems—deterministic, stochastic and additive; further, that at this stage it is desirable to have a computational algorithm based on the use of the digital computer, and this commends the formulation of control processes—from the start—in discrete terms: on this path fundamental problems of numerical solution and of the structure of optimal policies can be directly dealt with. As to the maximum principle, Berkovitz is invoked in arguing that the principle itself and more general results are in fact obtainable from Valentine's work of the thirties— on the Lagrangean problem with differential inequalities as added side-conditions. Again it is mainly the didactic and exploratory advantages that seem to be conceded to the Pontriagin model.[3]

It is not proposed to discuss here the seminal influence Bellman's work has had on contemporary economic thought (traces of it in Soviet planning thought can be found in this volume: we have seen that Bellman's apparatus is being used by several Soviet students—in particular by Romanovskiy and Makarov—in their explorations of the optimum-growth problem). On the other hand within a few years of the publication of the English translation of the work of Pontriagin and

---

[1] L. I. Rozonoer, 'O variatsyonnykh metodakh issledovanya kachestva sistem avtomaticheskogo upravlenya', in *IFAC*, p. 507.

[2] Pontriagin *et al.*, *op. cit.*, pp. 7, 69; also E. F. Mishchenko, 'Nekotorye voprosy teorii optimalnogo upravlenya i presledovanya', in *Vtoraya Letnyaya Matematicheskaya Shkola*, Academy of Sciences of the Ukrainian SSR, Kiev, 1965.

[3] Cf. R. Bellman, review of Pontriagin *et al.*, *op. cit.*, in *Econometrica*, January, 1963, p. 253.

his associates the employability of the method offered in seeking explicit solutions of time-optimal control problems of economic systems has been noted in Western writing, in particular by Kurz and Chakravarty (Chakravarty has also pointed to some desirable lines of extension of the Pontriagin switching rules'; especially an extension to the maximisation of an integral involving concave utility functions).[1] The Pontriagin apparatus has been found to show promise in the treatment of development strategies: in explorations of various types of advance 'in a hurry' towards economic maturity, considered as a problem of a maximum activity-speed or minimum activity-time. Kurz has worked with the Pontriagin principle in investigating the attainment of the von Neumann path by a developing economy: he has made use of the switching rules in a stage-wise, optimal, relating capital formation in the capital goods and the consumer goods producing sectors of the economy (interpretation of such divergent types of advance as Soviet industrialisation on the one hand and German post-1945 reconstruction on the other has been not implausibly attempted in these terms).[2] The Pontriagin principle has been actually made use of in trying to trace out, and solve numerically, optimal investment allocation as between capital goods and consumer goods industries for at least one underdeveloped country, under a combined criterion of maximum feasible consumption and full employment.[3]

ADDENDA TO CHAPTER 15

I. A simplified dynamized programming plan model has been offered with an algorithm by L. S. Belayev ('Matematicheskaya model planirovanya razvitya sotsyalisticheskogo khoziaystva', *Ekonomika i Matematicheskiye Metody*, No. 4, 1966).

The assumed information data embrace:

(1) Capacities operated at the start of the plan-period and their economic-technical coefficients: $x_{is0}, u_{is0}, r_{is}^u, a_{ijs}, v_{is}^u; i = 1, 2, \ldots, I; s = 1, 2, \ldots, S_i^0$ (Symbols: x_{ist} denotes volume of output of i-th product and s-th enterprise (with s-th technique) in t-th plan-year; u is unit cost of output; r_{is} is depreciation; a_{ij} is input/output coefficient; v^u is labour unit cost.

(2) Schedule of projects for plan-period indicating the earliest permissible start of construction of each of them and its technical-economic coefficients $x_{si}, r_{is}^u, a_{ijs}, v_{is}^u, r_{is}^h, b_{ijs}, v_{is}^h, (b_{ijs}$ denotes physical-terms input of i in

---

[1] S. Chakravarty, 'Optimal Programme of Capital Accumulation in Multi-Sector Economy', *Econometrica*, July 1965.

[2] M. Kurz, 'Optimal Paths of Capital Accumulation Under the Minimum Time Objective', *Econometrica*, January 1965.

[3] L. G. Stoleru, 'An Optimal Policy for Economic Growth', *Econometrica*, April 1965.

construction of capacity unit, s, producing j; h in superscript denotes construction industry).

(3) Volume of non-productive consumption for each plan year, w_{it}; $(t=1, 2, \ldots, T)$ and the $(T+1)$ year.

(4) Total yearly money-term labour input, V_t.

The problem is then one of finding the plan variant which minimises operating costs of existing enterprises

$$\sum_{t=1}^{T} \sum_{i=1}^{I} \sum_{s=1}^{S_i} u_{ist} x_{ist}$$

subject to material balances for each plan-year

$$\sum_{s=1}^{S_i} x_{ist} = w_{it} + \sum_{j=1}^{I} \sum_{s=1}^{S_j} (a_{ijs} x_{ist} + b_{ijs} \dot{x}_{jst+1} + a_{ijs} \dot{x}_{jst+1})$$

and to conditions that money-term investment volume for each year

$$\sum_{i=1}^{I} \sum_{s=1}^{S_i} k_{ist} \dot{x}_{ist+1} = V_t + \sum_{i=1}^{I} \sum_{s=1}^{S_i} (r_{is}^u x_{ist} + r_{is}^k \dot{x}_{ist+1})$$
$$+ \sum_{i=1}^{I} (u_{it-1} - u_{it}) \sum_{j=1}^{I} \sum_{s=1}^{S_j} a_{ijs} x_{jst} - \sum_{i=1}^{I} u_{it} w_{it} - \sum_{j=1}^{I} \sum_{s=1}^{S} a_{ijs} \dot{x}_{jst+1}$$

and that the time schedule is adhered to (k_{is} denotes investment cost per capacity unit, s, producing i; and $\dot{x} = dx/dt$).

Solution is sought by means of a Lagrangean function. The solving multipliers λ_{kt} and λ_{it} would be then employable as shadow prices of capital and products. The apparatus would be helpful in sensitivity analysis of plan variants. Less refined as it is, the model is easier in handling than that of either Pontriagin or Bellman. It is less adequate in dealing with remote horizons of perspective plans. Whether at this price sufficient degree of manageability is bought, this is not certain.

II. Gavrilyets (*Matematika i Ekonomicheskiye Metody*, no. 2, 1967) argues that the question of existence as well as that of the shape of the objective function is related to what he sees as the cybernetical nature of an economy. In his approach the mechanism of homeostasis would insure compromise values for the conflicting elements of the function. The author suggests a method which would permit tracing the path of optimal development over the "perspective" horizon from optimal indexes of shorter-term plans.

16 Soviet Reflection of Western Thought on Efficiency of Investment

DURING the last few years Soviet economic thought has moved rather a long way from its routine treatment of investment-efficiency problems of the capitalist economy in Western economics. The long-established tenet that the fundamental, qualitative differences of investment decisions and processes, under capitalism and socialism, preclude any community of theoretical problems, seems to have been tacitly abandoned. Indeed some of the most recent Soviet contributions to the literature of the subject may be of interest to the Western economist in so far as they try to extract, at least by implication, certain elements of general relevance for the quest of criteria, independent that is of social-economic institutions and mechanisms, and to deliminate areas of agreement and disagreement with Western thinking.

On the methodological side one will note a change in attitude towards the Keynesian and post-Keynesian macro-dynamic analysis, and its apparatus. Not long ago the Harrod-Domar models used to be dismissed as a mere exercise in apologetic.[1] True, there is still a good deal of emphasis on differences in the Soviet and Western approach; clearly this is valid with regard to some elements of analyses such as propensities to save and consume, or inducement and response, and so on. But one will now find in Soviet economics a readiness to concede certain basic, though qualified, similarities, especially between the Soviet approach and that of multiplier.[2] This is being qualified by the contention that while contemporary Western economics is pre-occupied with growth, the Soviet planning theory is concerned with development, a distinction which must be rather puzzling to the Western student. It is interpreted to mean that in Soviet theory the rates and the nature of development depend on the initial structure of the economy: that the focus is on the potential structural elements of its dynamics. Yet it is precisely the structural analysis that is being borrowed at present by Soviet economics from the West. And indeed it is in the course of the reception of contemporary Western inter-industry analysis with

---

[1] Cf. *Kritika sovremennykh burzhuaznykh, reformistkikh i revizyonistskikh ekonomicheskikh teoriy*, Moscow, 1960, *passim*.

[2] *Ibid.* V. S. Nemchinov, 'Statistical and Mathematical Methods in Soviet Planning', in T. Barna, *Structural Interdependence and Economic Development*, London, 1963, p. 183.

the consequential—even if only partial and reluctant—of its theoretical background, that Soviet economics must have been helped to see its affinities with the Keynesian-type analysis and its apparatus.[1]

Objection to the Harrod-Domar and Kaldor models concern the assumed trend rather than their apparatus or the employability of marginal and average capital coefficients. In particular it is argued that on the macro-plane the conventional constancy of the average capital coefficient over short periods would be a more valid approximation to reality in an analysis of the planned socialist system than of the capitalist. As to the long-term analysis, it is stressed that, inductively, changes in the value of the coefficient could be expected to reflect changes in its numerator, due to shifts in capital intensity of technical innovations, in the scales of production and skills; and that indeed the findings of Goldsmith, Abramovits, Kuznets and others for the capitalist world are corroborated by the empirically established decreasing trend of capital-coefficients in the Soviet economy. (This may invite a comment by way of digression. The snags to measuring returns to additional capital outputs hardly need to be stressed; and they were due in the case of the USSR, over long periods of the past, to both the shakiness of valuation and insufficiency of data. The excellent inquiry carried out by the ECE[2] for the decade of the 1950s would suggest that the Soviet incremental capital-output ratio during the 1950s was rather high, i.e. 2·9; and that, with capital intensity for the economy roughly unchanged, 'capital productivity' growth rate fell during the second half of the 1950s from 1·7 to 0·2 per cent compound annually. Further, according to computations by one of the principal Soviet authorities on the subject, Academician Khachaturov,[3] over the 1958–63 quinquennium productive capacities in the USSR economy increased by 56 per cent while their output, as measured by material national income, rose by 36 per cent; Khachaturov's diagnosis is that it

[1] See on this illuminating remarks by H. B. Chenery in '*Interindustry Economics*', H. B. Chenery and P. B. Clark, eds., 1959, pp. 5 ff.; on the technical analogy between Keynes's multiplier and approximation of inverse matrix by expansion in powers, *ibid.*, p. 52, fn. For this and further points discussed below see an article on 'Criteria of Investment Efficiency in Contemporary Bourgeois Econometrics', by Shlyapentokh, *Planovoye Khoziaystvo*, November 1963, pp. 74 ff.

[2] United Nations, ECE, *Some Factors in Economic Growth in Europe during the 1950s*, Geneva, 1964, ch. ii, pp. 36 ff.

[3] Report to the joint meeting of the Learned Councils of the USSR Academy of Sciences of May 1964 in *Planovoye Khoziaystvo*, 1964, no. 7; see also my note in *World Today*, Chatham House, October 1964.

is the lowered efficiency of capital investment that tends to slow-down the pace of growth of the economy.)

On the micro-plane there is a critique of some Western analyses of propulsion in the processes of capital formation. This critique is concerned largely with schools of thought connected in one way or another with the acceleration principle, with the Baumol treatment[1] of motivation in capital accumulation and the impact of the rate of profit, and with the Duesenberry model of investment embodying a parameter akin to the capital coefficient.[2] *First*, the point made is that there is no necessary contradiction in the acceptance of both the capital coefficient and the rate of profit as factors influencing the firm's investment decisions, since there is a certain nexus between the two, a nexus, in fact, recognised by some Western students (and that moreover the capital coefficient also measures the risk entailed in obsolescence). The *second* point made is that under conditions of continuous technological advance, the entrepreneur will be guided, in appraising the efficiency of planned investment, by future yields rather than either the present or past profitability (hence the phenomenon of heavy investment in some sectors affected by a high degree of idleness of capacities, a point on which agreement is expressed with Lundberg[3] and other Western students). While in the Soviet analysis emphasis is placed on the tendency for production to run ahead of demand under the capitalist mechanism (on 'production for production's sake'), the reader will bear in mind that, admittedly owing to different institutional properties, the link between direct demand and production plans tends to be severed in the Soviet economy because it is strongly future-oriented.

Even more pointed are implications for the Soviet-type economy and economics of the general inference drawn. There is in Western thinking on the subject, so it is argued, some confusion between two

---

[1] W. Baumol, *Business Behaviour, Value and Growth*, New York, 1959. Cf. in particular the discussion on the implications of the acceleration principle in the Harrod-Domar model: also on the long-run determinants of investment (the limited effect of changes in the rate of profit on the motive for accumulation), pp. 102 ff.

[2] Reference is to the parameter α in the investment equation in I. Duesenberry, *Business Cycle and Economic Growth*, New York, 1958. This parameter prepresents the double effect of changes in income on investment.

[3] E. Lundberg, 'The Profitability of Investment', in *Economic Journal*, December 1959. Discussion of the Kaldor model of growth and the contention on the lack of relation between actual *ex-post* profitability of investment and social as well as private efficiency of investment, pp. 664 ff.

questions. One concerns the general stimuli—positive and negative—of investment activity in the given institutional framework: under this heading come various elements of welfare economics, social-psychological factors, and so on. The other question is: what is the guiding criterion in the choices of investment alternatives under given conditions? Here the answer is the rate of profit, whichever way the first question has been answered. The stress on this dichotomy and the answer offered to the second question are precisely the points on which the Soviet search for investment criteria centres.[1]

[1] In his recent work, *Ekonometrika i Problemy Ekonomicheskogo Rosta* (Moscow, 1966), V. E. Shlyapentokh expands his previous inquiry (cf. above p. 198 ftn. 1) into a historical and critical survey of Western macro-models for growth. The focus is on neo-Keynsians, on the Harrod and the Smithies models and on the neo-classical models (Kaldor, Meade, multi-factor types and production-function types of models). Of interest to the Western reader may be, in particular, remarks on the significance of Western models for Soviet planning theory and practice; also comments on the assimilation of certain Western constructs by Soviet planometrics.

Part II: Planning Techniques

D. Efficiency of Foreign Trade

17 Quest for Criterion of Efficient Trade

As HAS been remarked in an incisive Hungarian study, the original Soviet doctrine of foreign trade, carried to its logical conclusion, equated autarchy with socialism.[1] It is therefore hardly surprising that for years Soviet theory was signally unconcerned about criteria for policy choices involving foreign trade. However, since the last war the creation around the USSR of what is termed the 'socialist world market' has brought such issues increasingly to the attention of Soviet economists. Moreover, the inclusion in this market of Central European countries, organically more dependent on foreign commerce and much more 'extrovert' by nature,[2] has further enhanced their importance. (A contributing factor has been the new appreciation, since the late 1950s, of the importance of trade with capitalist countries and expanded commerce with underdeveloped areas.) This is indeed a field in the economics of socialism in which Soviet students and Soviet practice avowedly look today to Central Europe for theoretical enlightenment and empirical lessons. The most recent trend towards fuller integration of the economies associated within the Council for Mutual Economic Aid (CMEA) has made imperative the development of principles of comparative advantage within the group, for the 'socialist international division of labour'.

In Soviet-type economies the State's foreign trade monopoly forms, as it were, a clearing house for the imputation of foreign-currency expenditures and receipts in terms of domestic prices. Its agencies buy goods at home for export, and sell imported goods at domestic transfer prices. Differences between these prices and foreign prices, at the official rate of exchange, give rise to budgetary levies and subsidies. The resulting insulation of domestic price and cost relationships has been seen as a vital element in the framework for planned and rapid

This is a revised version of an article under the title 'The Criterion of Efficiency of Foreign Trade in Soviet-type Economies', published in *Economica*, February 1964.

[1] Tibor Liska and Antal Marias, *Kozgazdasagi Szemle*, 1954, no. 1, pp. 75 ff. Translation of excerpts can be found in *United Nations Economic Survey of Europe in 1954*, appendix to chapter 5.

[2] The volume of Hungary's foreign trade (export plus imports) roughly equals half the net material national product: the ratio was doubled between the early fifties and the mid-sixties (I. Vajda, *The Role of Foreign Trade in a Socialist Economy*, Budapest, 1965).

203

economic growth. It is only very recently, as the economy has approached maturity, that the 'independence' of the rate of exchange in this sense has ceased to be treated in the Soviet Union itself as an unqualified virtue: comments on the 1960–1 currency reform seem to point to some change of attitude. It may be noted that in the second half of the 1950s a strong current in Polish economics, inspired by Professor Kalecki, advocated a pegging of the internal price structure on the prices of raw materials in world markets (i.e. main exports). It did so on two grounds: first, to provide a short-cut to rationality[1] in the determination of domestic price-relationships; and second, to provide a scaffolding for an opportunity-cost calculation which would take into account the potentialities of foreign trade.[2]

Similar suggestions, in a more radical variant, are now represented in Hungary by Liska; in his proposals prices of all goods which actually or potentially enter foreign trade should oscillate around those prevailing in world markets.[3] Liska argues that, in the light of experience, this appears to be the only dependable and practicable solution left for the twin problem of efficiency and competitiveness of the economy.

[1] The concept of rationality of foreign trade is analysed in the chapter 'Micro-rationality and foreign trade criteria' in Professor Wiles's forthcoming book which I commend to the reader's attention. Wiles's inquiry is particularly illuminating in the attempt to relate this concept of rationality to the planning countries' behaviour in the trade among themselves and in competitive world markets. Also of considerable interest are remarks on the chain effect of efforts to rationalise foreign trading on domestic economic policies.

[2] M. Kalecki and S. Polaczek, Gospodarka Planowa, 1951, no. 9. M. Kalecki Ekonomista, 1958, no. 3. H. Fiszel suggests integrating foreign-trade prices into the domestic price structure by means of a rate of exchange corresponding to an export-import balance for a plan-year: $V = (E_k - J_k) : (J_p - E_p)$, the J's with subscripts p and k denoting imports, respectively, of producer goods in dollars and consumer goods in zlotys; and the E's with subscripts p and k, denoting exports respectively of producer goods in dollars and consumer goods in zlotys. The import would then be inserted into the input-output matrix at prices obtained with the use of the V. Cf. Biuletyn Naukowy, 1963, no. 12, Department of Political Economy, University of Warsaw, p. 36.

[3] Correctives by means of a turnover tax, positive or negative, would allow in Liska's system for short-term disturbances in imports and exports, for difficulties in re-adjusting production patterns due to shortages of factors, and generally for requirements of demand-supply equilibrium in domestic markets. The suggestions have at this stage a rather general shape and inevitably raise quite a few questions of techniques and policies; among the latter the problem of levels, or wage-good prices and wages, is among the trickiest.

Dr Liska's ideas have been elaborated in his paper 'Wirtschaftlicher Mechanismus und Preissystem' not yet published. I wish to thank him for permission to study this paper. From discussion with him I gather that his ideas were evolved independently of those of Kalecki (of the 1950s), which were unknown to him.

Liska's present scepticism with regard to alternative solutions is the more noteworthy as it was a decade ago that a paper by him and Marias pioneered in Central European writing the elaboration of a tool—'a coefficient of efficiency of foreign trade'—to assist the planner in decision-taking in a more or less automatic way.[1]

The oldest 'tool' and a rather crude tool, is a coefficient which relates the average domestic wholesale price of an exported good (f.o.b., or franco national frontier) net of profit elements to foreign currency earnings. The most patent among its shortcomings is that it fails to answer the question whether from the purely foreign-currency point of view it pays to develop export production based on a foreign raw material. Hence its more elaborate version focuses on net gain in terms of foreign exchange: the cost of imported raw material used in production is eliminated from both the numerator and the denominator in the ratio (expressed, that is, in the foreign currency and the domestic currency, respectively).

The usefulness of the *net* rather than the *gross* calculation was demonstrated when it revealed some striking cases of negative efficiency—of foreign materials being processed and exported at a currency loss. A further variant of this indicator allows for the possible loss of foreign exchange where some domestic but potentially exportable raw material is used in production of exported commodities. This approach is particularly appropriate for a country's staple export raw materials, and more generally for those with ready outlets in world markets.[2]

Refinement of the indicator has continued along the same line, and eventually has led to the concept of net currency earnings from 'pure' manufacturing. Here the cost of *all* materials, raw and semi-processed, domestic and foreign, is eliminated: in deference to the ruling theory of value the resulting yardstick is usually termed the 'coefficient of the foreign-currency equivalent of *live* labour'.[3] In fact, in most cases all cost elements are eliminated except wages, depreciation of fixed assets

---

[1] T. Liska and A. Marias, *op. cit.*

[2] For quite a time Czechoslovak advance in this field was perhaps most significant, largely due to the pioneering work of Professor Cerniansky. The most recent presentation of his views is in V. Cerniansky, *Ekonomika socialistickehozahranicniho obchodu*, Prague, 1961. There is an interesting discussion in German written jointly by him with R. Brauer, in *Wirtschaftswissenschaft*, 1960, no. 7, pp. 977 ff.

[3] This development was anticipated in the paper by Liska and Marias, referred to above (p. 203).

and certain overheads. (However, in some variants the latter two cost components also are eliminated, so that currency gains are related solely to wage costs, or, via wages, to costs of 'baskets' of wage-goods.) The implied assumption is that the part of foreign-exchange proceeds which corresponds to the processed material is constant: in other words, that the foreign-currency proceeds would be the same if the raw materials were exported as they are. This indicator is employed for testing the relative advantage of exporting materials at different stages of processing, say pig-iron, raw steel, or rolled products. In Czechoslovakia and East Germany it is used for such *intra-branch* comparisons. By contrast, it finds general application in Poland.

Along these lines rank indices of foreign-exchange worthiness—in East German terminology *Rangfolgekennziffern*—of commodities have been compiled. Other things being equal, preference is given to the export of a commodity with the highest currency-profitability rate; in other words, with the lowest 'own' rate of exchange. This leads logically to the Kalecki-Polaczek concept of a limiting rate of foreign exchange, a concept originally connected with the Kalecki world-market peg mentioned earlier.[1] It was thought of as an equilibrium rate, one corresponding to a balance in foreign payments under the prevailing level of real wages. (One of its functions would be to counteract inflationary tendencies in the economic system.) The concept first met with a good deal of suspicion because of its marginalist flavour; but now it has gained wide theoretical recognition, and, detached from some of its original underlying propositions, it is in general use.

As things stand, the original sin from which all members of this family of coefficients suffer is the inadequate framework of domestic prices in all the countries in question. True, one of the peculiar biases in the Soviet-type price structure—the concentration of the profit component (profits so-called, and turnover tax) essentially on consumer goods only—is allowed for in more realistic variants of the coefficient. Profits and tax are deducted from internal prices, and subsidies are added to them. But even when corrected in this way the Soviet-type prices, which fail to reflect opportunity costs, do not provide an adequate frame for decision-making both generally and also in foreign trade. A parallel complication on the foreign-exchange side stems from the prevalence of bilateral and barter-type trading, and from the very high proportion of trade with countries which have

[1] M. Kalecki and S. Polaczek, *op. cit.*, pp. 67 ff.

inconvertible currencies. Typical of some of the thorny situations likely to be encountered would be that of materials bought by one centrally-planned economy from another for 'bilateral' roubles, and, after processing, sold to a third centrally-planned economy or in another market for dollars or sterling.

More generally, the methods outlined above provide answers to *specific* questions of choice with regard to foreign trade: they are specific in that they are detached from the general context of the economic life of the country. To remedy this defect, sets of coefficients are applied. But only by sheer coincidence would all of them provide the planner with the same answer. The use, additionally, of various physical-term yardsticks such as the raw-material intensity of exports or the productivity per man-hour in export branches, can hardly rescue him from his predicament. Finally, none of the indicators discussed so far is of relevance by itself where choice alternatives connected with foreign trade entail expansion of productive capacities. The assumption of given capacities, which has not always been made explicit or perhaps even been realised sufficiently clearly, limits the use of the tools to short-term appraisals and decisions.

The assumption of given capacities is also one of the reasons why in most centrally-planned economies the development and use of yardsticks for foreign-trade decisions have largely been confined to exports, with imports left to take care of themselves. Imports are treated, in fact, as a *malum necessarium*, an attitude partly reflecting the philosophy which was dominant until recently and which dies hard.[1] In practice, what has to be imported—the minimum of imports—is derived from the set of 'material balances' on which plans are built up.

Very recently efforts have been made to widen profitability checks on foreign trade by dropping the assumption of constant capacities. This introduces the time-dimension into the calculation, and thereby increases the range of alternatives and so complicates decision-making. What is measured now is the incremental investment entailed in increasing export or import-saving production.[2,3] (The coefficient used

---

[1] In some of the countries efficiency yardsticks for imports have been constructed by analogy to those serving export decisions. Their rationale is dubious.

[2] The subject is discussed in general terms by V. Komarek. *Ekonomicka effektivnost investic a nove techniky v CSSR*, Prague, 1961, pp. 19 ff. See also H. Koctuch, *Planovanie reprodukcie zakladnych fondov v CSSR*, Bratislava, 1963.

[3] There is a considerable degree of consensus among students that some elements of

here can be defined as the marginal capital/net-currency-output ratio.) The static indicators we have discussed are being dynamised by building into their formulae the element of investment efficiency. Foreign-exchange revenue, or the foreign-exchange saving on imports to be replaced, is related, over a given time-horizon, to the relevant total cost of production, including an appropriate allowance for the capital invested. But it is only those countries where established doctrine subscribes to the principle of a single rate of discount (the quasi rate of interest) for all sectors in the entire economy that meaningful conclusions can be drawn from such calculations (see above, chapter 12).

This view has found support in recent Soviet literature (Smirnov, Zotov, Shagalov).[1] The valid point made is that, whatever the virtue of a branch investment-efficiency rate, there is no room for it in the appraisal of foreign trade because, as far as foreign trade is concerned, products of all branches of the economy are potential substitutes (hence for Soviet conditions the use of some weighted mean of branch rates is proposed). In these suggestions the familiar Soviet formula of time reduction $(C + EK)$ (see pp. 142 ff.), for testing investment efficiency, would be applicable for this purpose as well, and in order to escape from the distortive impact of Soviet price relations, all cost would be reduced to wages.[2] Full cost would be obtained from the inversion of technological matrices. This would apply also to the capital-cost component, computed on the Gosplan's formula for full-order capital cost per unit of final production, $K_j = \sum_{i=1}^{n} K_i . A_{ij}$, $(j = 1, \ldots, n)$, where K_i is the capital coefficient of the i-th branch and A_{ij} full input of the i-th branch product per unit of final production of the j-th branch.[3,4,5]

---

advantage from foreign trade do defy quantification; and that this is particularly true of import-competing investment. Cf. for a discussion of such dynamic considerations G. Haberler, *International Trade and Economic Development*, Cairo, 1959. The matter is incisively discussed with special reference to the USSR by F. D. Holzman, 'Foreign Trade' in A. Bergson, S. Kuznets, eds., *Economic Trends in the Soviet Union*, Cambridge, Mass., 1963, pp. 312 ff.

[1] G. Smirnov, B. Zotov, G. Shagalov, *Planovoye Khoziaystvo*, 1964, no. 8.

[2] The distortive impact on foreign-trade decisions of the failure of Soviet-type prices adequately to reflect capital cost, may be judged from an estimate suggesting that Soviet exports are, on the average, one and a half times more 'capital-intensive' than Soviet imports; *ibid.*, p. 29.

[3] Gosplan's calculations show striking disparities in the relative export efficiency of commodities when prevailing wholesale prices, the costs of enterprises in terms of these prices, and the Smirnov-Zotov-Shagalov yardstick, are adopted as alternative cases.

The matrix calculus is used by Fiszel for a systematic analysis of relations between the balance of trade and capital formation. The problem of improving this balance by investing in export or 'anti-import' production is set by him as a programme with matrices of domestic cost and of net foreign-exchange revenue: the former is the minimand, the latter the maximand. Fiszel's cost matrix has the shape $K_{ij}\alpha + C_{ii}$, where the two component-matrices describe investment outlay and current cost (the subscripts i and j denoting respectively products and technological variants), and α is an 'actualisation' rate based on the adopted rate of interest. One will notice the similarity of certain elements of Fiszel's more refined conceptual framework to that of Smirnov-Zotov-Shagalov, but the latter's stronger points are its focus on full, rather than direct cost and its attempt to mitigate the shortcomings of Soviet-type pricing (although its wage valuation does not reflect opportunity cost adequately either).

Finally programming techniques have been resorted to, for the last few years, in centrally-planning countries in attempts to find an answer to the question as to how, in the absence of an automatic market mechanism, the commodity and geographical structure of foreign trade can be efficiently patterned, and how the differential rates of exchange corresponding to an optimum can be found. This question has been tackled directly in some Polish and Hungarian

Here are a few examples (export-efficiency of iron ore = 100):

	Export efficiency based on:		
	prevailing wholesale prices	cost in terms of same prices	full-order costs (Smirnov-Zotov-Shagalov formula)
Iron ore	100	100	100
Metallurgical coke	28	36	45
Steel	64	68	88
Electr. dynamo	55	92	177
Machine-tool	93	119	246

(*ibid.*, p. 31).

[4] The concept of the 'foreign-exchange efficiency of national labour' is expanded in G. L. Shagalov's recent work *Ekonomicheskaya Effektivnost Obmena mezhdu Sotsyalisticheskimi Stranami*, Moscow, 1966, especially pp. 84 ff.

[5] On interesting Hungarian experiments in this field see the discussion in Gy. Cukor, 'Use of Input-Output Tables in Long-term Planning—Planning of the Relations between Industry and Foreign Trade,' in O. Lukacs *et al.*, eds., *op. cit.*

models displaying certain affinities with Frisch's 'Oslo' model, Chenery's model for Southern Italy, and with Kronsjö's programmes with variable exports and imports. (Kronsjö's original idea of resorting to mathematical programming in handling problems of foreign trade in centrally planned economies has had a seminal influence on Eastern European thinking in this field.)[1] As in Kronsjö's system, the variables would be determined in a system taking account of their interdependence with domestic preference-functions and bounds in respect of the foreign market position. Broadly speaking domestic economy would become as it were, one of the currency regions taking part in the allocational 'bidding'. Here, too, with given constraints foreign trade would take such a commodity and geographic pattern as to maximise export revenue and minimise import expenditure.

Chronological primacy in these attempts belongs to the Polish Trzeciakowski construct[2] designed with the view to providing operational parameters of the levels, structure and direction of foreign trade. These are marginal rates of exchange, his M^r, ratios that is of the domestic price of marginal commodity and its price in the r-th market. The commodity is marginal in the sense that it is the one with the least advantageous ratio yet still necessary for meeting the foreign-exchange requirements of postulated imports from the r-th market and for securing a postulated balance with it (positive, negative or zero). It will be readily seen that the proposition brings to its ultimate conclusion in a more formalised shape the Kalecki-Polaczek 'limiting rate' (see p. 206). The vector of the Trzeciakowski parameters is derived from an overall programme embracing production and foreign trade and embodying a system of equations and inequalities which describe (1) technological inter-dependencies (Leontief's matrices), (2) postulated balances in transactions with specific foreign-currency regions and (3) specific constraints such as minimum employment level or living standards or national self-sufficiency in some lines of production. The optimality criterion is aggregate domestic cost, to be minimised,

---

[1] T. Kronsjö, *Optimization of Foreign Trade Policy for a Planned Economy by Mathematical Programmes*, first edition, Lund, 1960.

[2] W. Trzeciakowski, 'Problemy Kompleksowego systemu analizy efektywnosci biezacej handlu zagranicznego', in J. Drewnowski, ed., *Problemy optymizacji handlu zagranicznego*, Polish Academy of Sciences, vol. ii, Warsaw, 1961; also W. Trzeciakowski, *Gospodarka Planowa*, 1961, nos. 4 and 5; and *Przeglad Statystyczny*, 1962, no. 2. For interesting discussion of the model see also J. Jurkiewicz, *Gospodarka Planowa*, 1960, nos. 6 and 7; and W. Piaszczynski, *ibid.*, 1961, no. 7.

with boundary conditions to keep foreign trade within the demand and supply limits for individual markets, and the outputs within the limits of existing capacities. Capacities are taken to be constant: the model is a short-run one *par excellence*. Neither wear-and-tear nor other capital cost is taken into account and all cost accounted for is taken to be reducible to wages: the minimand is thus the total wage-bill. The focus can be seen then on optimising exports, while the appraisal of efficiency of imports is reduced to comparing cost entailed in domestic 'anti-import' production with that of producing the minimum of export goods needed to pay for corresponding imports.

The original Trzeciakowski conception suggested a procedure of 'indirect' optimisation rather than a direct approximation one through aggregation: by means of centrally fixed parameters partial optima would be arrived at for commodity groups formed under some strong simplifying assumptions. (One technology for each product; no commodity produced in any of the inter-dependent groups serves as input outside this group; raw materials brought from outside and used in each group are domestically produced, and capacity for producing them exceeds that for processing them or export possibilities.) In the Trzeciakowski subsequent model variant—designed jointly with Rey and Mycielski[1]—an attempt is made to escape from these severe restrictions by resorting to a system of accounting prices based on a decomposition principle (for a Kantorovich model). The optimum for a given group of goods is obtained here with reference to these prices for basic raw and intermediate materials and individual currencies that is the M^r; simultaneously the global solution is being optimised. Starting from an arbitrary solution for 'outside' subsets, the optimum for the given sector is pursued in an iterative process in the course of which the values for the levels of activities, the physical-term, size of foreign trade with the r-th market and the shadow prices are adjusted, and the M^r adjusted so as to meet the foreign-payment requirements.

While escaping from the severity of some of the restrictive assumptions, the model—as revised—still suffers from quite a few limitations and weaknesses. It seems that the commodity groups obtained in practicable decomposition are still not sensitive enough to opportuni-

---

[1] J. Mycielski, K. Rey and W. Trzeciakowski, 'Decomposition and Optimization of Short-Run Planning in a Planned Economy' in T. Barna, ed., *Structural Interdependence and Economic Development*, London, 1963, ch. 2.

ties of individual commodities in individual markets.[1] An obvious weakness stems from the assumption of perfect knowledge of relevant data, in particular of complete knowledge of potential trade-partners' policies as well as foreign market situations. To be sure, in real conditions the bulk of trade between the centrally-planning countries is usually fixed years ahead in long-term agreements: hence in respect of that part of trade there is little scope for a short-term optimisation. In respect of the rest of trade the policy-maker would have to content himself with some probability functions, and the effect of his depending on maximisation (or minimisation) of the mathematical expectation of the choice criterion has still to be tested in practice.

Coming down to structural shortcomings, even in a static construct, with constancy of capacities legitimately assumed, the zero-cost of their employment does not seem defensible: the pattern of the use of capacities does influence opportunity costs and therefore should influence the choice of foreign-trade alternatives. More generally, the adopted reduction of all cost to wage cost even in the short-run is of dubious validity.

Further linearity of technological and behavioural relationships assumed throughout—though perhaps at this stage mathematically almost inevitable—affects the realism of the model. So does, in particular, the assumption of constant returns to scale of exportable outputs.[2,3]

---

[1] As a second-best solution, computationally less exacting but less ambitious from the optimality point of view, Polish economists are considering a formula of efficiency of exports of the k-th commodity to the r-th market $E_k^r = C_k / k^r . d_k^r$, where C_k stands for production cost, that is wage cost at the last stage of production plus cost of materials; the k^r is the efficiency rate of exports to the r-th market measured as ratio of the marginal rate-of-exchange in exports (to that market) to the marginal rate of exchange adopted as the *numeraire* $k^r = M^r / M_0$; the d_k^r is average foreign exchange price, f.o.b., of the k-th commodity in export to the r-th market or price, c.i.f., paid in import. Conceptually the yardstick is affected by all the weaknesses of the present practice.

[2] Since this essay was written the new methods of optimisation of foreign trade have been actually employed in Polish perspective planning—in the construction of the plan for 1966–70. The theoretical frame adopted is broadly that discussed in our essay. With the usual balance equations, the maximand in the primal for a typical export commodity is

$$M \sum_r \sum_k y_k . d_k^r K^r + \sum_k P_k . w_k - \sum_j c_j x_j$$

where x_j is level of productive activity j supplying product k; y_k^r are exports of product k to market r; P_k is domestic demand for k; d_k^r is foreign-exchange price of k in market r; M is 'limiting' rate of exchange; K^r is index of relative value of the r market's currency;

The lines of analysis traced out by Kronsjö and Trzeciakowski and his associates have been followed subsequently by several students in Hungary. In Marton and Tardos,[1] the focus is on the most efficient advantage-taking of price differentials in foreign markets, rather than on export-import commodity pattern representing an overall optimum for the economy: the complexity and significance of this problem is increased where the bulk of foreign trade is 'tied' in bilateral trade with non-convertible proceeds from exports, which is the prevalent case in the C.M.E.A. commerce.

The maximand of the programme is here foreign exchange returns; a price index (q^r) built into this function reflects the commodity pattern under which the decision-maker would purchase incremental imports in the r-th market: it helps thereby to rank and relate currencies in different markets from the point of view of a given policy postulate. Technically the model relies on a Dantzig-Wolfe type of decomposition and offers an algorithm elaborated for a generalised

w_k is domestic price of k, c_j is the the unit cost of production for k. The corresponding dual has been resorted to in decision-making.

Some conventional rate of interest—20 per cent per annum—has been used as an additional parameter in the calculation of cost entailed in investment: only 'supplementary' investment, i.e. investment not exceeding the value of a year's output has been considered.

As it appears the currency rates for specific markets have been determined in practice along these lines: (a) calculate the value of exports and imports for each trade-partner in terms of free, that is convertible currency; (b) calculate the price-level index for the given market as a weighted average of Pasche's indexes of exports and imports; (c) derive the 'index of relative value of currency'—the 'geographical index of terms of trade'—as the quotient of index of exports/index of imports. (Cf. J. Glowacki, *Problems of Optimizing the Directions of International Trade in a Planned Economy*, 1964; also papers by J. Glowacki and E. Harasim and J. Basiuk and W. Piaszczynski in *Z Zagadnien Eksportu Artykulow Rolno-Spozywczcych*, Warsaw, 1965.)

It would seem that computational difficulties apart, the main snags in the Polish exercise are: (a) the difficulty of identification of commodities traded in the 'compartmentised' markets with those of 'free' markets; (b) the wide deviations of the domestic cost-pricing framework from efficiency prices; (c) the non-dynamic approach in what is essentially a problem in dynamics: as noted only very limited changes in capacities have been considered. Nonetheless the Polish experiment is of considerable theoretical and practical interest and worth watching.

[3] In Soviet literature a linear optimisation model of foreign trade has been outlined by B. S. Fomin, G. Z. Davidovich and B. I. Aleinikov ('K analizu vneshney torgovli v optimalnom plane', *Ekonomika i Matematicheskiye Metody*, no. 5, 1966). A variant of the model sketches out the case of markets with differing prices and transactions carried out in non-convertible currencies of each of the markets.

[1] A. Marton and M. Tardos, *Short-run Optimization of the Commodity Pattern by Markets of Foreign Trade*, Budapest, 1964.

transportation problem. A more ambitious Hungarian construct is the Kornai-Lipták 'two-level planning'[1] model. Its theoretical concept is one of an information-flow problem turning into a polyhedral game, which is carried out between the centre and a team of sectors in the light of available information. The centre's strategies are the feasible allocation patterns, and the strategies of the sectors are the feasible shadow-price systems, in the duals of the sectoral problems: the pay-off function is the sum of the sectoral dual objective functions. What is then arrived at is the saddle-point solution for the game. The maximand tentatively adopted is the foreign-trade balance, but the question of an alternative economic interpretation of the objective function has been left open by the architects of the model. Unlike the constructs previously discussed the Kornai-Lipták model aspires to optimisation over time: the standard programme is dynamised in the familiar fashion by prescribing external consumption separately for each plan period, and the carry-over investment. The question of explicit time-preference has not been attacked. (On this see also chapter 7, p. 96, and appendix, p. 102.)

The crux of the matter remains the manageability of dimensions of a foreign-trade plan-programme. The originator of the mathematical methodology in this field, Kronsjö, has re-examined the matter of its decomposition, with a focus on equations describing relationships of foreign trade and the internal production variables. His results will be found in chapter 18.

I. NOTE ON EFFICIENT PATTERNING
OF THE CMEA TRADE

The problem of criteria presents itself in a particularly complicated form with respect to the intra-CMEA exchange of commodities, and still more so with respect to efficient long-range patterning of member-economies. At present the intra-CMEA trade is organised as a largely bilateral trade between national monopolies, based on world market prices subject to certain correctives and guarantees of stability. It is being argued, however, that centralised supra-national planning would be more consonant with the logic

---

[1] J. Kornai and Th. Lipták, *Two-Level Planning*, Budapest, 1963. I wish to thank the Economics Institute of the Hungarian Academy of Sciences for kindly offering me a pre-publication copy.

of a family of centrally planned and controlled economies; this reasoning carries considerable weight.[1]

As to the efficiency criterion itself, there seems to be a good deal of consensus that it should essentially rest on differentials in national full inputs of labour per unit of given output (obtained from technological matrices).[2,3] The ratio of such coefficients would provide at least the starting point for shaping the commodity flows; and, when duly 'dynamised', also for shaping investment and thus influencing the long-range division of labour. That then would be the basic methodological approach to economic integration of the area. By its nature this solution shares its shortcomings with the conceptions of building internal efficiency criteria on a one-factor basis (we leave out of account the technical difficulties of optimisation of full-input matrices). Moreover, the shortcomings of the criterion would be aggravated if it were applied to a group of economies which considerably differ

---

[1] O. Bogomolov, *Voprosy Ekonomiki*, 1963, no. 11.

[2] Fiszel's one-nation matrix system (*Efektywosc Inwestycji i Optimum Produkcji w Gospodarce Socjalistycznej*, Warsaw, 1963) has been extended to deal also more comprehensively and more systematically with the problem of centrally planned specialisation of m commodities between n countries. Suppose we start with relating unit cost, μ, of the first and second countries to those of the third:

(1)
$$\frac{J_{11}\rho + K_{11}}{\Delta P_{11}} : \frac{J_{31}\rho + K_{31}}{\Delta P_{31}} = \mu_1^{(1)}; \quad \cdots = \mu_2^{(1)}; \quad \cdots = \mu^{(1)}{}_m$$

(2)
$$\frac{J_{21}\rho + K_{21}}{\Delta P_{21}} : \frac{J_{21}\rho + K_{31}}{\Delta P_{21}} = \mu_1^{(2)}; \quad \cdots = \mu_2^{(2)}; \quad \cdots = \mu^{(2)}{}_m$$

(Notation: J is the matrix of capital outlays; K is the matrix of operating cost over and above replacement; P the matrix of planned output increments; ρ the rate of 'actualisation'; the "$\cdots$" denote analogous ratios).

Then the supra-national planner will allot to each country, one by one, products with the lowest μ's. At the next step specialisation assignments for each member-country of the group are checked against its availabilities of resources and these are adjusted accordingly. In addition to computational difficulties of the kind mentioned above—and they are indeed magnified in this case—the suggestion leaves open the problem of the framework of prices and rates of exchange within which the planned inter-country trade would be carried out and each trade-partner's advantages could be internally assessed.

[3] Formalisation of the problem of 'optimal division of labour' among socialist countries has been attempted by P. Glikman (see *Gospodarka Planowa*, no. 11, 1961; also *Voprosy Ekonomiki*, no. 11, 1964). The point of departure is some consistent perspective plan, and successive approximation is sought to an optimum volume of foreign trade *through investment*. Efficiency of exports in a plan variant is assessed as

$$[(Z+P)(I-A)^{-1}E] : [D_e E - D_{\mathrm{im}} M (I-A)^{-1} . E]$$

(A and M are physical-term matrices of input-output and of 'import-intensity'; the remaining symbols stand for vectors: Z=wage cost per output unit, P=normative rate of return on investment, E=exports (branch-wise, physical-terms), D_e and D_{im} are world market prices of exports and imports).

This is a broad sketch which hardly deals with the crucial computational aspect.

with regard to structure and levels of development, and therefore factor relations, and with virtually no intra-group mobility of factors.

The same basic idea appears to underlie conceptions adopted for intra-CMEA pricing and possibly also for a unified common internal price system —a cost-price reducible to an averaged cumulative wage cost.[1] According to some suggestions this average would be weighted by national volumes of output. Such parameters would fail, however, to indicate opportunity costs for the same reason as do at present national price systems of individual countries. Some, rather vaguely formulated, correctives are considered though. Thus the cost of the inferior producer-country would be adopted where expansion of output of vital commodities in short supply was desirable; prices would be adjusted so as to stimulate the use of certain materials or processes in order to encourage innovations and promote technological advance; some adjustment would be made to support higher capital intensity of production and encourage substitution of certain CMEA products for imports from the capitalist world.

Conflicts of national interests[2]—for example, weighting of the average with actual national outputs would favour the larger producers—and questions of the discipline of plans and their implementation will not be pursued here.

II. NOTE ON OPTIMAL LOCATION AND SPECIALISATION MODELS

While formalisation of foreign-trade problems has attracted relatively little attention in Soviet planometrics, considerable effort has been invested into that of optimal (efficient) location. The work has been carried out largely in the Siberian section of the Academy of Sciences and is related to development problems in Siberia and the Soviet Far East. Several programming models have been designed with an eye to practical application. (For a discussion of these models see N. N. Nekrasov, L. E. Mints and Yu. Yu. Finkelshtein Eds., *Primenenye Matematiki pri Razmeshchenyi Proizvoditelnykh Sil*, Moscow, 1964.)

Experience has suggested that most problems of location and specialisation are reducible to integer-programming models. For the linear case, the assignment model would be of the form: Find $x_{ij} \geqslant 0$ such that $\sum_j x_{ij} \leqslant a_i$;

$$\sum_i \lambda_{ij} x_{ij} = b_j \quad \text{and} \quad \sum_i \sum_j c_{ij} \lambda_{ij} x_{ij} = \text{min}.$$

where $\sum_j x_{ij} = 0$ *or* a_i.

---

[1] A. Alexeyev, A. Belayev, O. Tarnovskiy, *Ekonomicheskaya Gazeta*, 1963, no. 46.

[2] See on this *inter alia* O. Bogomolov, *op. cit.*, and I. Vaja in *Tarsadalmi Szemle* December 1963.

Transportation model would have $\lambda = 1$. Experiments have apparently shown the usefulness of the *delta* method. By this method first a quasi-optimal plan is built where demand is fully met (equality $\sum_i x_{ij} = b_j$ is satisfied) with minimum cost, while the output condition $\sum_j x_{ij} \leqslant a_i$ is disregarded. At the second stage this condition is being satisfied through iteration.

The general locational problem has been stated as follows (A. G. Aganbegyan, 'Ekonomiko-matematicheskoye modelirovanye i reshenye otraslevykh zadach' *ibid.*, pp. 33 ff.):

Determine $x_i^{ks} \geqslant 0$, the delivery volume of the i-th commodity from region k to s, subject to:

$$(1) \qquad P_i^k \leqslant x_s^{ks} \leqslant d_i^k$$

where p_i^k and d_i^k denote respectively capacity and output volumes in the initial and terminal plan-years;

$$(2) \qquad \sum_k \sum_s x_i^{ks} - \sum_j \sum_k \sum_s a_{ij}^{ks} \sum_s x_j^{ks} \geqslant \sum_k n_i^k \sum_k f_i^k$$

where a_{ij}^{ks} are input coefficients of i-th product of region k in the production of the j-th product unit in region s; n_i^k denotes non-productive consumption of the i-th product in region k, and f_i^k the volume of stock-building in this product;

$$(3) \qquad \sum_j t_j^k \sum_s x_j^{ks} \leqslant T^k$$

where t_j^k stands for labour-input ratio for the j-th product in region k and T^k for regional labour resources;

$$(4) \qquad \sum_i \sum_k \left(\sum_s x_i^{ks} - P_i^k \right) . h_i^k \leqslant H$$

where h_i^k denotes incremental capital-output ratio in region k for i-th product, and H the total investment volume in the national economy over the plan period.

The minimand is

$$\sum_i \sum_k \sum_s c_i^{ks} x_i^{ks} + \sum_i \sum_k r_i^k (_s x_i^{ks} - P_i^k)$$

where c_i^{ks} are current costs, c.i.f. use-region, s in the production of i-th commodity in region k (costs of production plus transportation) and r_i^k discounted cost of investment per incremental output unit of i in region k.[1, 2]

[1] An intresting algorithm for an iterative solution of a non-linear problem, with the objective function totalling production and transportation cost, has been designed in this form:

$$\min \left\{ \sum_{i=1}^{m} \sum_{j=1}^{n} c_{ij}x_{ij} + \sum_{i=1}^{m} \varphi_i(y_i) \right\}$$

$$x_{ij} \geqslant 0; \quad y_i \geqslant 0; \quad \sum_{i=1}^{m} x_{ij} = A_j$$

$$\sum_{j=1}^{n} x_{ij} = y_i; \quad b_i \leqslant y_i \leqslant B$$

where,

A_j is demand in the j-th point of consumption

B_i, b_i are respectively, the upper and lower capacity limits of the i-th enterprise,

c_{ij} is the transportation cost of the product from point 'i' to 'j',

x_{ij} is the annual volume of transport,

$\varphi_i(y_i)$ is the accounting-price cost at the i-th enterprise as a function of capacity.

The algorithm is for a case of all $\varphi_i(y_i)$ being convex from below, continuously differentiable. It is handled by means of linear approximations. (Cf. G. D. Rakhmanin, 'Algoritm posledovatelnogo uluchsheniya v odnoy nelineynoyi zadache', in *Primenenye Matematiki v Ekonomike*, vo.. ii, Leningrad University, 1964.)

Finkelshtein has examined the problem of location with a cost minimand additionally constrained by the assigned investment total. In a subsequent paper he analysed, jointly with Mints, what in substance is an integer programming problem with the capacity variable permitted to assume discrete values (and the connected parametric programme problem). It is argued that to each variant there corresponds, in a sense, a given coefficient of investment efficiency. In the proposed treatment a set of cost matrices is considered with some posited coefficients. (Cf. Yu. Yu. Finkelshtein, 'Prosteyshaya zadacha razmeshchenya pri nalichii ogranichenya na razmer kapitalovzheniy' in *Primenenye matematicheskikh metodov k probleme razmeshchenya*, Moscow, 1963, and the same with L. E. Mints, 'Primenenye matematicheskikh metodov i elektronnovychislitelnykh mashin dla reshenya zadach po razmeshchenyu otdelnykh otrasley promyshlennosti' in *Planirovanye i ekonomiko-matematicheskiye metody, op. cit.*).

M. Barbakadze *et al.* (*Planovoye Khoziaystvo*, no. 12, 1966) offer a non-linear gain-and-loss model for location of homogenous production. Suggested method of solution is based on properties of deviation from mean.

[2] The reader will find certain convergence of approach in models discussed here—as far as consistency of inter-regional transactions is concerned—with that of Professor Leontief's multi-regional scheme (in W. Leontief, in collaboration with A. Strout, 'Multi-regional Input-Output Analysis', in T. Barna, ed., *Structural Interdependence and Economic Development, op. cit.*; cf. also W. Isard, E. Smolensky, 'Application of Input-Output Techniques to Regional Science', *ibid.*)

18 Foreign Trade Planning

DECOMPOSITION OF A LINEAR PROGRAMME FOR SHORT-TERM
PLANNING OF FOREIGN TRADE AND INTERNAL ACTIVITIES

Tom Kronsjö[1]

ECONOMIC interrelations of importance for short-run planning of internal activities and foreign trade may, as a first approximation, be described by a very large linear programming model. The great size of this model necessitates, if it should become manageable for practical use, special analysis of its equational structure and exploitation of its special features. This study will be focused on the utilisation of the *structural* properties of the equations describing the relationships of foreign trade and internal activities. The internal activities consist of production, consumption, investment and stock and are called briefly production variables.

This chapter may be seen as a continuation of the discussion by W. Trzeciakowski, J. Mycielski, K. Rey, J. Glowacki, W. Piaszczyński in Poland, by A. Nagy, T. Liptak, A. Marton, M. Tardos in Hungary, by V. Pugachev, V. Volkonskiy, Yu. Chernyak, A. Modin in the Soviet Union, by D. Pigot in France and by R. Frisch in Norway as well as of earlier contributions by the author (cf. section 11 and literature references on p. 242).

A SURVEY OF THE MODEL ANALYSED

The elements of the vectors and matrices mentioned below are not denoted by the index i but by some other index symbols with different meanings and range of values but for simplicity everywhere indicated by the same symbol j.

[1] The author wishes to express his sincere gratitude to Dr Alfred Zauberman for stimulating discussions and proposals in regard to the elaboration of this mathematical appendix, and to Dr Salah Hamid, Director of the Operations Research Centre of the Institute of National Planning, Cairo, for enabling the undertaking of this study as part of the Centre's research activities for the preparation of the Egyptian Five-Year Plan.

The original draft was made in the author's *Iterative Price and Quantity Determination for Short-Term Production and Foreign Trade Planning*, UAR Institute of National Planning, Memo. no. 397, Cairo, 10 February 1964. The author is at present with the Centre for Russian and East European Studies, Faculty of Commerce and Social Science, University of Birmingham, Great Britain.

1. Variables

Primal Quantity variables are denoted as follows:

Production in various industrial branches (i) with internal processes (j) are denoted by the vectors x_i (with elements x_{ij}).

$$x_i \qquad\qquad (i = 0, 1, \ldots, m)$$

Export and import variables are denoted by the vectors y_i, each of which embraces certain commodity numbers and the relevant markets for the commodities in question (thus with elements y_{ij})

$$y_i \qquad\qquad (i = 0, 1, \ldots, m)$$

Dual Price variables are denoted as follows:

The (dual) feasible prices of the various foreign currency resources are denoted by the vector v (with elements v_j).

$$v$$

The feasible prices of the various commodities used or produced by the industrial branches (i) are denoted by the vectors u_i (with elements u_{ij})

$$u_i \qquad\qquad (i = 0, 1, \ldots, m)$$

The feasible prices of the production capacity vectors (cf. $-\bar{x}_i$ in section 3 below) are denoted by k_i (with elements k_{ij})

$$k_i \qquad\qquad (i = 0, 1, \ldots, m)$$

The feasible prices of the export and import bound vectors (cf. $-\bar{y}_i$ in section 3 below) are denoted by h_i (with elements h_{ij})

$$h_i \qquad\qquad (i = 0, 1, \ldots, m)$$

The iteration is denoted by the variables r, s, t. Subiterations (s) within an iteration (r) by rs, etc.

Auxiliary variables in master (i.e. coordinating) problems are denoted by z. Though the same name (z) is used in various masters they are not identical, z_r, z_{irs}, z_t, etc.

2. Equations or Inequality Constraints

The *balance of payments* constraints

$$(1) \qquad C_0 y_0 + \cdots + C_i y_i + \cdots + C_m y_m = bp$$

where $C_i (i = 0, 1, \ldots, m)$ are matrices of the foreign prices obtained or paid for export or import quantities to various markets (and possibly including certain conditions for the commodity structure as determined by trade agreements). bp is the vector of net requirement of foreign currency holdings (and possibly of the trade composition). Its elements are bp_j.

The *commodity balances* which state that import—export + production —use in production should equal the requirement vectors b_i with elements b_{ij}:

$$
(2)\quad
\begin{aligned}
B_{00}y_0 &\quad &+A_{01}x_1+\cdots+A_{0i}x_i+\cdots+A_{0m}x_m &+A_{00}x_0 &= b_0 \\
B_{11}y_1 &\quad &+A_{11}x_1 &+A_{10}x_0 &= b_1 \\
B_{ii}y_i &\quad &+A_{ii}x_i &+A_{i0}x_0 &= b_i \\
B_{mm}y_m &\quad & &+A_{mm}x_m+A_{m0}x_0 &= b_m
\end{aligned}
$$

The important assumption has been made here that the *production structure* may be characterised by the following four features: (i) *certain commodities*, e.g. labour, electricity and water, are *inputs to or outputs from all branches of production*, as depicted by the first row in (2) of the o-group of equations. (ii) *Certain production processes require inputs from almost all branches of production*, as may be the case for the chemical industry. Such production processes are grouped together in the penultimate column of the x_0 activities. (iii) Except for the common input or output commodities defined above and those processes which use inputs from almost all industrial branches, the *industries* are supposed to be *groupable in branches which only use or produce mutually exclusive groups of commodities*, e.g. the textile industries producing only commodities belonging to a 'textile' commodity group, the mechanical industry only those belonging to a 'mechanical' group as depicted by the matrices A_{ii}. (iv) *Special constraints on the export and import variables* such as balance of payments (and possibly on the balancing of certain commodities as determined by trade agreements) are supposed to be included *in the matrices* C_i.

3. Bounds

The *production level* vectors have to be within the capacity *bounds*

$$(1)\qquad\qquad 0 \leqslant x_i \leqslant \bar{x}_i \qquad\qquad (i = 0, 1, \ldots, m)$$

Similarly, the *export and import* vectors have to be within their corresponding marketing *bounds*

$$(2)\qquad\qquad 0 \leqslant y_i \leqslant \bar{y}_i \qquad\qquad (i = 0, 1, \ldots, m)$$

We wish to state all the conditions of the original problem in the form of $\geqslant$ (or $=$) as we will then obtain all feasible price solutions to the corresponding dual as non negative (or unrestricted) magnitudes. We therefore multiply the right-hand part of the above conditions by (-1) and get

$$(3) \qquad\qquad -x_i \geqslant -\bar{x}_i \qquad\qquad (i = 0, 1, \ldots, m)$$

and

$$(4) \qquad\qquad -y_i \geqslant -\bar{y}_i \qquad\qquad (i = 0, 1, \ldots, m)$$

4. Preference Function

The *preference function* is formally defined by the expression[1]

$$(1) \quad \text{Min } g_0 y_0 + \cdots + g_i y_i + \cdots + g_m y_m + f_1 x_1 + \cdots + f_i x_i$$
$$+ \cdots + f_m x_m + f_0 x_0$$

5. Summary of the Model

$$
\begin{aligned}
g_0 y_0 + g_1 y_1 + \cdots + g_i y_i + \cdots + g_m y_m + f_1 x_1 &+ \cdots + f_i x_i + \cdots + f_m x_m + f_0 x_0 = \text{Min} \\
C_0 y_0 + C_1 y_1 + \cdots + C_i y_i + \cdots + C_m y_m & = bp \\
B_{00} y_0 \qquad\qquad\qquad + A_{01} x_1 + \cdots + A_{0i} x_i + \cdots + A_{0m} x_m + A_{00} x_0 &= b_0 \\
B_{11} y_1 \qquad\qquad + A_{11} x_1 \qquad\qquad\qquad + A_{10} x_0 &= b_1 \\
+ B_{ii} y_i \qquad\qquad + A_{ii} x_i \qquad + A_{i0} x_0 &= b_i \\
B_{mm} y_m \qquad\qquad + A_{mm} x_m + A_{m0} x_0 &= b_m \\
-y_0 \qquad\qquad\qquad\qquad\qquad\qquad &\geqslant -\bar{y}_0 \\
-y_1 \qquad\qquad\qquad\qquad\qquad &\geqslant -\bar{y}_1 \\
-y_i \qquad\qquad\qquad\qquad &\geqslant -\bar{y}_i \\
-y_m \qquad\qquad\qquad &\geqslant -\bar{y}_m \\
-x_1 \qquad\qquad &\geqslant -\bar{x}_1 \\
-x_i \qquad &\geqslant -\bar{x}_i \\
-x_m \qquad &\geqslant -\bar{x}_m \\
-x_0 &\geqslant -\bar{x}_0 \\
x_i \geqslant 0, \; y_i \geqslant 0 \qquad\qquad (i = 0, 1, \ldots, m)
\end{aligned}
$$

[1] Detailed consideration of the problem of formulating the preference function is given in Ragnar Frisch, *Practical Rules for Interview Determination of One-Sided and Two-Sided Preference Coefficients in Macro-economic Decision Problems*, Memorandum of 25 June 1959, from the Oslo University Institute of Economics; and in Ragnar Frisch, *The Smoothing of an Inter-preference Table*, Memorandum of 18 December 1959, from the Oslo University Institute of Economics.

6. The Dual Formulation

Instead of considering the original formulation, it will be useful at various calculation stages to deal with the dual:

$$b_p'v + b_0'u_0 + b_1'u_1 + \cdots + b_i'u_i + \cdots + b_m'u_m - \bar{y}_0'h_0 - \bar{y}_1'h_1 - \cdots - \bar{y}_i'h_i - \cdots - \bar{y}_m'h_m - \bar{x}_1'k_1 - \cdots - \bar{x}_i'k_i - \cdots - \bar{x}_m'k_m - \bar{x}_0'k_0 = \text{Max}$$

$$A_{00}'u_0 + A_{10}'u_1 + \cdots + A_{i0}'u_i + \cdots + A_{m0}'u_m - k_0 \leqslant f_0'$$

$$A_{0m}'u_0 + A_{mm}'u_m - k_m \leqslant f_m'$$

$$A_{0i}'u_0 + A_{ii}'u_i - k_i \leqslant f_i'$$

$$A_{01}'u_0 + A_{11}'u_1 - k_1 \leqslant f_1'$$

$$C_m'v + B_{mm}'u_m - h_m \leqslant g_m'$$

$$C_i'v + B_{ii}'u_i - h_i \leqslant g_i'$$

$$C_1'v + B_{11}'u_1 - h_1 \leqslant g_1'$$

$$C_0'v + B_{00}'u_0 - h_0 \leqslant g_0'$$

$$v \lessgtr 0, \; u_i \gtrless 0 \quad (i = 0, 1, \ldots, m)$$

$$h_i \geqslant 0, \; k_i \geqslant 0 \quad (i = 0, 1, \ldots, m)$$

(' denotes transposition of a vector or a matrix)

7. Main Principles of Solution

A fundamental thought underlying this study is that an efficient large-scale planning system should be based upon (1) an *interconnecting plan frame*, coordinating (2) *fairly independent blocks* of widely differentiated internal structure, which will permit application of specialised computation techniques to every one of them; (3) the coordinating work being undertaken with full attention to the *sensitivity of various blocks to price and quantity changes.*

The main purpose of this paper is to demonstrate how the *foreign trade and production variables* are subject to very *different structural constraints.* It should therefore be useful to treat them as having *computationally different qualitative properties* and partition them into different types of blocks, to which specialised computation techniques may be developed. Stress is also given to the *importance of dividing the problem into smaller, more rapidly solved sub-problems*, the solutions of which are coordinated at various levels.

One of the main tools will be the decomposition principle, of Dantzig and Wolfe [17, 18][1] and the double decomposition method proposed by Pigot [4].

8. The Decomposition of the Short-run Production and Foreign Trade System

(8.1) *Combination of partial solutions (y^r, x^r) to enable the fulfilment of all quantity equations.*

Knowing various sets (r) of feasible y, x solutions to all bounds and all equation groups *except the balance of payment and the 0-group*, we attempt to find a combination of solution vectors which satisfies all constraints. *In principle* we are interested in solving the master:

(1) $\quad$ Min $\sum_r (gy^r + fx^r) z_r$

$$\sum_r (Cy^r + 0x^r) z_r = bp \qquad (0 = \text{a zero matrix})$$

$$\sum_r (B_0 y^r + A_0 x^r) z_r = b_0 \qquad (B_0 = B_{00} + \text{a zero matrix})$$

$$\sum_r z_r = 1$$

$$z_r \geqslant 0 \qquad (r = \text{all})$$

---

[1] For an introductory account pertaining to foreign trade, cf. [11]. Numerical illustrations are rendered in [9–10]: see numbered references to literature on page 242.

In practice we will use a slightly more sophisticated formula, which may be expected to be more effective as it solves problem (1) (*a*) in several stages, and (*b*) for a given number of auxiliary variables *z* increases the range of possible combinations, though at the cost of increasing the number of equations.

(8. 1A). *The y_i, x_i sets are first combined to satisfy the o-group of equations*

$$(2) \ \text{Min} \sum_t [(g_0 - vC_0)y_0^t]z_t + \sum_{i=1}^{m} \sum_r \sum_s [(g_i - vC_i)y_i^{rs} + f_i x_i^{rs}]z_{irs} + \sum_r (f_0 x_0^r)z_r$$

$$\sum_t (B_{00}y_0^t)z_t + \sum_{i=1}^{m} \sum_r \sum_s (A_{0i}x_i^{rs})z_{irs} + \sum_r (A_{00}x_0^r)z_r = b_0$$

$$\sum_t z_t = 1$$

$$\sum_r z_r = 1$$

$$\sum_s z_{irs} = z_r \qquad (i = 1, 2, \ldots, m; \ r = \text{all})$$

$$z_t, z_r, z_{irs} \geqslant 0 \qquad (i = 1, 2, \ldots, m; \ t, r, s = \text{all})$$

This formulation will permit us to use one solution x_0 together with many different solutions of each x_i group and with various y_0 solutions. This is of great importance as the number of equations of the o-group which have to be satisfied may be supposed to be fairly large (for instance, of the order of 200). If we have one x_0 solution and, for instance, in average five solutions for every one of 50 x_i groups and 10 to the y_0 group, we will have obtained $1 + 50 \times 5 + 10 = 261$ vectors fairly easily. These may be combined to satisfy the $200 + 1 + 50 + 1 = 252$ equations.

It should be noted that this introduction of more than one auxiliary equation is not necessary from a formal point of view. The same overall solution may be obtained by making all possible extreme combinations of group solutions and including the corresponding column in the master:

$$(3) \qquad \text{Min} \sum_r [(g - vC)y^r + fx^r]z_r$$

$$\sum_r (B_0 y^r + A_0 x^r)z_r = b_0$$

$$\sum_r z_r = 1$$

$$z_r \geqslant 0 \qquad (r = \text{all})$$

An equivalent programme would then consist of $5^{50} \times 10 > 10^{36}$ variables and $200 + 1$ equations.

If the computational work required to solve a linear programme increases approximately according to the formula[1]

$$(4) \qquad\qquad T_{lp} = M^2 \times N \times \theta$$

in which M equals the number of equational constraints, N the number of variables and θ a constant, we may expect the following total computational time for solving the above mentioned problem using (2).

$$(5) \qquad\qquad 252^2 \times 261 \times \theta \approx 10^7 \times \theta$$

while for the equivalent formulation of (3) we might expect

$$(6) \qquad\qquad 201^2 \times 10^{36} \times \theta \approx 10^{41} \times \theta$$

The formulation (2) may therefore be expected to be more effective than (3).[2] A further improvement in the formulation of the master (2) may probably be achieved by not decomposing with respect to the upper bounds of the y_0 variables. The conditions $-y_0 \geqslant -\bar{y}_0$, $y_0 \geqslant 0$ would then have to be introduced into the master and the z_t variables and conditions together with the solution index of y_0, the superscript t, to be excluded from the master.

(8. 1B). *The resulting (y, x) sets are then combined to satisfy all quantity equations*

Having found a solution $(y, x = y_0^t z_t, y_i^{rs} z_{irs}, x_i^{rs} z_{irs}, x_0^r z_r)$ which satisfies all constraints except the balance of payment ones, we wish to find

---

[1] Cf. Leola Cutler and Philip Wolfe, 'Some Experiments in Linear Programming', in *Actes de la 3ème Conférence Internationale de Recherche Opérationnelle (Proceedings of the Third International Conference on Operational Research* held in Oslo, 1–5 July 1963), Paris, 1964. The number of operations per iteration is for the most effective algorithm, the product form, equal to

$$\theta_2(M+K)(N-M) + \theta_5(M+K)^2 + \theta_6(M+K)^2$$

where K equals the number of preference functions and θ_i are constants, (table 6.1). The number of iterations is given as approximately proportional to the number of constraints (section 5).

[2] The latter approach would probably only be preferable if there were comparatively few z_t and z_{irs} variables in relation to z_r ones, which presumably would be fairly inefficient owing to the considerable difference in computational work necessary to obtain a x_0 or a x_i^{rs}, y_i^{rs} solution.

one which will *also* satisfy the latter. *In principle* we do it by solving a still higher master

$$(7) \qquad \text{Min} \sum_r (g y^r + f x^r) z_r$$

$$\sum_r (C y^r + 0 x^r) z_r = b p$$

$$\sum_r z_r = 1$$

$$z_r \geqslant 0$$

In solving the previous master (2) as many of the z_r, z_{irs}, z_t will differ from 0 as there were equations. The various possible y_i vectors would in turn be a combination of the original y_i^r vectors multiplied by the nonnegative z_{irs} terms and added together. If the masters (2) and (7) embrace a great number of equations, it may perhaps be more effective to establish the net bounds for the $B_{ii} y_i$ problems, and solve them anew for given quantities, i.e. solve the subproblems $(i = \text{all})$:

$$(8) \qquad \text{Min} \ (g_i - v C_i) y_i$$

$$B_{ii} y_i = b_i - A_i x$$

$$-y_i \geqslant -\bar{y}_i$$

$$y_i \geqslant 0$$

(where the matrix $A_i = A_{i1}, \ldots, A_{ij}, \ldots, A_{im}, A_{i0}$, the submatrices A_{ij} are zero matrices, when $i \neq 0$ and $j \neq i$, 0, and where x is a solution satisfying the (2) master) using the procedure dealt with in section 8.5 and sequel).

In analogy with (2) we solve the master (7) by formulating it as

$$(9) \qquad \text{Min} \sum_{i=0}^{m} \sum_r \sum_s (g_i y_i^{rs}) z_{irs} + \sum_r (f x^r) z_r$$

$$\sum_{i=0}^{m} \sum_r \sum_s (C_i y_i^{rs}) z_{irs} \qquad = b p$$

$$\sum_r z_r \qquad = 1$$

$$\sum_s z_{irs} \qquad = z_r \qquad (i, r = \text{all})$$

$$z_r, z_{irs} \qquad \geqslant 0 \qquad (i, r, s = \text{all})$$

(x^r being a feasible solution to the (2) master).

It should be noted that *the partition into subproblems* (i) *need not be identical with the earlier partition used in respect to production and may vary from iteration to iteration.* We may also iterate between (9) and (8) as many times as we like, and in doing that we are free to choose a finer or coarser subproblem division (i) in order to obtain the optimal *structure* and *size* of subproblems of export and import quantities as well as the *swiftest routing* of their solution (cf. section 10).

(8. 2). *Feasible prices v, u_0 obtained from the highest quantity masters*

As a result of solving (9) we have obtained the value of the primal preference function, feasible prices v of the rows bp, from the renewed solution of (2) feasible prices u_0 of the rows b_0.

(8. 3). *Calculation of the u_i, h_i and k_i on the basis of given v, u_0*

Our attention is now turned to the dual problem. The selected v, u_0 are feasible price solutions to part of the price constraints. *In principle* we are now interested in complementing them by feasible $u_1, \ldots, u_m$; $h_0, \ldots, h_m$ and $k_1, \ldots, k_0$ in such a way that the dual preference function (cf. section 6) is maximised. In other words, we wish to obtain an improved solution to the dual problem (section 6), using our knowledge of earlier partly feasible price solutions and the newly attained price solutions v, u_0. As the number of equations is supposed to be extremely large, we will gain by solving the u_i, h_i and k_i in a two- or three-stage process, which will mainly depend upon the form of the matrix A_{ii}. In principle, we attempt to solve the dual problem by dividing it into a price master of the type:

$$(10) \quad \text{Max} \sum_r \left(bpv^r + \sum_{i=0}^m b_i' u_i^r - \sum_{i=0}^m \bar{y}_i' h_i^r - \sum_{i=1}^m \bar{x}_i' k_i^r \right) z_r - \bar{x}_0' k_0$$

$$\sum_r \left(\sum_{i=0}^m A_{i0}' u_i^r \right) z_r - k_0 \leqslant f_0'$$

$$\sum_r z_r = 1$$

$$z_r \geqslant 0 \quad (r = \text{all})$$

$$k_0 \geqslant 0$$

(a more effective formulation will be considered in (32)) and the sub-problem of finding u_i vectors, unrestricted in regard to sign as they correspond to equations in the primal problem, which will maximise a modified preference function

228

(11) $\quad$ Max $bp'v + (b_0 - A_{00}x_0)'u_0$

$$+ \sum_{i=1}^{m} (b_i - A_{i0}x_0)'u_i - \bar{y}_0'h_0 - \sum_{i=1}^{m} \bar{y}_i'h_i - \sum_{i=1}^{m} \bar{x}_i'k_i$$

$$A_{0i}'u_0 + A_{ii}'u_i \qquad -k_i \leq f_i' \qquad (i = 1, \ldots, m)$$

$$C_i'v \qquad + B_{ii}'u_i \quad -h_i \quad \leq g_i' \qquad (i = 1, \ldots, m)$$

$$C_0'v + B_{00}'u_0 \quad -h_0 \qquad \leq g_0'$$

$$v, u_i \gtrless 0 \qquad\qquad (i = 0, 1, \ldots, m)$$

$$h_i \geq 0 \qquad\qquad (i = 0, 1, \ldots, m)$$

$$k_i \geq 0 \qquad\qquad (i = 1, \ldots, m)$$

This subproblem may be made separable, by inserting the last feasible v, u_0 price solution obtained from the quantity masters (9) and (2). This will give: *one* subproblem of the type

(12) $\qquad\qquad$ Max $-\bar{y}_0'h_0$

$$-h_0 \leq g_0' - C_0'v - B_{00}'u_0$$

$$h_0 \geq 0$$

and m subproblems of the type

(13) $\qquad\qquad$ Max $(b_i - A_{i0}x_0)'u_i - \bar{y}_i'h_i - \bar{x}_i'k_i$

$$A_{ii}'u_i \qquad -k_i \leq f_i' - A_{0i}'u_0$$

$$B_{ii}'u_i - h_i \qquad \leq g_i' - C_i'v$$

$$u_i \gtrless 0$$

$$h_i, k_i \geq 0$$

The problem (12) is equivalent to the following problem (obtained by multiplying by minus one):

(14) $\qquad\qquad$ $- $ Min $\bar{y}_0'h_0$

$$h_0 \geq -(g_0' - C_0'v - B_{00}'u_0) = -g_0^{*\prime}$$

$$h_0 \geq 0$$

The minimum of this expression is readily found as

(15) $\qquad\qquad h_{0j} = \left\{ \begin{matrix} 0 \\ -g_{0j}^* \end{matrix} \right\}$ if $g_{0j}^* \left\{ \begin{matrix} \geq 0 \\ < 0 \end{matrix} \right\}$

The subproblem (13) may probably with advantage be solved by *developing a special simplex algorithm for problems of this structure* as elaborated by the author in a forthcoming study or by decomposing it in various ways depending upon the dimensions of the A_{ii} and the B_{ii} matrices as in the continuation.

If A'_{ii} is of the narrow lying rectangle form it may be useful to solve the problem (13) by formulating it as a master of the type:

$$\text{(16)} \qquad \text{Max} \sum_r [(b_i - A_{i0}x_0)'u_i^r - \bar{y}_i'h_i^r]z_r - \bar{x}_i'k_i$$

$$\sum_r (A'_{ii}u_i^r)z_r - k_i \leqslant f_i' - A'_{0i}u_0$$

$$\sum_r z_r = 1$$

$$z_r \geqslant 0 \qquad (r = \text{all})$$

$$k_i \geqslant 0$$

(which will give x_i values as 'shadow' quantities) and the subproblem

$$\text{(17)} \qquad \text{Max} \, (b_i - A_{i0}x_0 - A_{ii}x_i)'u_i - \bar{y}_i'h_i$$

$$B'_{ii}u_i - h_i \leqslant g_i' - C_i'v$$

$$u_i \geqslant 0$$

$$h_i \geqslant 0$$

Remembering that the B_{ii} matrices only consist of band matrices of $+$ or $-$ one, for expressing imported minus exported quantities and introducing the indexes c for *c*ommodity, d for currency block or *d*istrict, and a for trade *a*ctivity (export E or import I), we may formulate (17), omitting the index i, as

$$\text{(18)} \qquad \text{Max} \sum_c (b_c^* u_c - \sum_d \sum_a \bar{y}_{cda}h_{cda})$$

$$\text{sign} \, (a)u_c - h_{cda} \leqslant g_{cda}^* \qquad (c, d, a = \text{all})$$

$$h_{cda} \geqslant 0 \qquad (c, d, a = \text{all})$$

$$u_c \geqslant 0 \qquad (c = \text{all})$$

$$\text{sign} \, (a) = \left\{ \begin{matrix} - \\ + \end{matrix} \right\} \quad \text{if} \quad a = \left\{ \begin{matrix} E \\ I \end{matrix} \right\}$$

$$(b_i^* = b_i - A_{i0}x_0 - A_{ii}x_i)$$

$$(g_i^{*'} = g_i' - C_i'v)$$

It is evident that this maximisation problem may be separated into one for every u_c. If in each of these we transfer the u_c variable to the right side and multiply by -1, we get the problems

(19) $$\text{Max} \quad -\sum_d \sum_a \bar{y}_{cda} h_{cda} + b_c^* u_c$$

$$h_{cda} \geqslant -g_{cda}^* + \text{sign } (a) u_c \quad (d, a = \text{all})$$

$$h_{cda} \geqslant 0 \qquad\qquad (d, a = \text{all})$$

$$u_c \gtrless 0$$

For any fixed value of u_c it will always be best to select the lowest possible value of h_{cda} which fulfils the two inequalities above, which is

(20) $$h_{cda} = \text{Max } (-g_{cda}^* + \text{sign } (a) u_c; \text{ o}) \qquad (c, d, a = \text{all})$$

If we insert these expressions for h_{cda} in the preference function of (19) it will be expressed as a function of the single variable u_c

(21) $$z(u_c) = \text{Max} -\sum_d \sum_a \bar{y}_{cda} [\text{Max } (-g_{cda}^* + \text{sign } (a) u_c; \text{o})] + b_c^* u_c$$

$$\text{sign } (a) = \left\{ \begin{matrix} - \\ + \end{matrix} \right\} \quad \text{if} \quad a = \left\{ \begin{matrix} E \\ I \end{matrix} \right\}$$

$$u_c \gtrless 0$$

To find the maximum of this expression we have only to determine for which u_c value or range of values *the derivative*

(22) $$\frac{dz}{du_c} = -\sum_d \sum_a (\text{if } -g_{cda}^* + \text{sign } (a) u_c \geqslant 0$$

$$\text{then} \quad \bar{y}_{cda} \text{ sign } (a) \text{ else o}) + b_c^*$$

changes sign or becomes zero. We may start with the correct expression for some arbitrary value of u_c and successively increase (or decrease) the value of u_c to the nearest g_{cda}^* $(d, a = \text{all})$ complementing with the appropriate $\bar{y}_{cda}$ term, if the expression is positive (or negative). When the optimal u_c prices have been determined the h_{cda} ones follow from expression (20).

Thus the feasible prices of the subproblem (17) may be obtained in a very swift way.

As the problem (17) will not determine unique u_i values for commodities not subject to foreign trade, the master above (16) will have to be formulated on the following lines

$$(23) \quad \text{Max} \sum_r [(b_{i)} - A_{i0)}x_0)'u_{i)}^r - \bar{y}_{i)}'h_{i)}^r]z_r + (b_{i(} - A_{i0(}x_0)'u_{i(} - \bar{x}_i'k_i$$

$$\sum_r (A_{ii)}'u_{i)}^r)z_r \qquad + A_{ii(}'u_{i(} - k_i \leqslant f_i' - A_{0i}'u_0$$

$$\sum_r z_r = 1$$

$$z_r \geqslant 0 \qquad (r = \text{all})$$

$$u_{i(} \gtrless 0$$

$$k_i \geqslant 0$$

By the vector $u_{i)}^r$ is meant the solution to (17) but excluding all the $u_{i(}$ prices which correspond to commodities not subject to foreign trade. The closing parenthesis may be memorised as 'already committed to', the opening as 'open for determination'. The matrices $A_{ii)}$ and $A_{i0)}$ have been obtained from the A_{ii} and A_{i0} matrices by depriving them of the rows $A_{ii(}$ and $A_{i0(}$ corresponding to the commodities not subject to foreign trade. The $b_{i)}$ and $b_{i(}$ vectors have been obtained in a similar way.

If A_{ii}' is of the narrow standing rectangle form the solution of (13) by solving its dual may be considered

$$(24) \quad \text{Min} \ (g_i - v'C_i)y_i + (f_i - u_0'A_{0i})x_i$$

$$B_{ii}y_i \qquad + A_{ii}x_i = b_i - A_{i0}x_0$$

$$-y_i \qquad \qquad \geqslant -\bar{y}_i$$

$$-x_i \geqslant -\bar{x}_i$$

$$y_i \geqslant 0, \qquad x_i \geqslant 0$$

When the number of y_i variables is very great it may perhaps be solved with advantage as a master programme of the type:

$$(25) \quad \text{Min} \sum_r [(g_i - v'C_i)y_i^r]z_r + (f_i - u_0'A_{0i})x_i$$

$$\sum_r (B_{ii}y_i^r)z_r \qquad + A_{ii}x_i = b_i - A_{i0}x_0$$

$$-x_i \geqslant -\bar{x}_i$$

$$\sum_r z_r \qquad = 1$$

$$z_r \geqslant 0, \qquad x_i \geqslant 0$$

(this problem gives the feasible prices u_i and k_i and the subproblem

(26) $\text{Min } (g_i - v'C_i - u_i'B_{ii})y_i$

$$-y_i \geqslant -\bar{y}_i$$

$$y_i \geqslant 0$$

By reformulating (26) as

(27) $\text{Min } (g_i - v'C_i - u_i'B_{ii})y_i = g_i^* y_i$

$$y_i \leqslant \bar{y}_i$$

$$y_i \geqslant 0$$

it is readily seen that its solution is extremely simple

(28) $y_{ij} = \begin{Bmatrix} 0 \\ \bar{y}_{ij} \end{Bmatrix} \quad \text{if} \quad g_{ij}^* \begin{Bmatrix} \geqslant 0 \\ < 0 \end{Bmatrix}$

but we note that in addition to sending a y_i vector into (25) we have, after having found an acceptable u_i, k_i dual solution to (25), to send the latter together with the appropriate h_i prices to the overall price master (10). These dual prices h_i may be obtained by formulating (26) as

(29) $\text{Max } -\bar{y}_i'h_i$

$$-h_i \leqslant g_i' - C_i'v - B_{ii}'u_i$$

$$h_i \geqslant 0$$

which is equivalent to

(30) $-\text{Min } \bar{y}_i'h_i$

$$h_i \geqslant -(g_i' - C_i'v - B_{ii}'u_i) = -g_i^{*'}$$

$$h_i \geqslant 0$$

thus

(31) $h_{ij} = \begin{Bmatrix} 0 \\ -g_{ij}^* \end{Bmatrix} \quad \text{if} \quad g_{ij}^* \begin{Bmatrix} \geqslant 0 \\ < 0 \end{Bmatrix}$

(8. 4). *Obtaining feasible prices, v, u_i, h_i, k_i, an estimate of the dual preference function and an x_0 solution*

As the result of the result of the above calculations we have found sets of prices v, u_i, h_i $(i=0, 1, \ldots, m)$ and k_i $(i=1, \ldots, m)$, every one of which only fulfils the equations of (11). In analogy to what was done with the partial quantity solutions (2), we may now attempt to solve the overall price master (10) by formulating it as

$$(32) \ \text{Max} \sum_r (b\hat{p}v^r + b_0'u_0^r - \bar{y}_0'h_0^r)z_r + \sum_{i=1}^m \sum_r \sum_s (b_i'u_i^{rs} - \bar{y}_i'h_i^{rs} - \bar{x}_i'k_i^{rs})z_{irs} - \bar{x}_0'k_0$$

$$\sum_r (A'_{00}u_0^r)z_r + \sum_{i=1}^m \sum_r \sum_s (A'_{i0}u_i^{rs})z_{irs} - k_0 \leqslant f_0'$$

$$\sum_r z_r = 1$$

$$\sum_s z_{irs} = z_r \qquad (i = 1, \ldots, m, r = \text{all})$$

$$z_r, z_{irs}, k_0 \geqslant 0 \qquad (i = 1, \ldots, m; r, s = \text{all})$$

As a result we obtain the 'shadow' quantities x_0 of the above price problem and a value of the dual preference function.

(8. 5). *Determination of y_i, x_i for fixed x_0, v, u_0*

If we insert the last x_0 values obtained from the master (32) into our primal equation system, section 5, we may readily obtain a new partial quantity solution (y, x) if we disregard *the balance of payments and the 0-group of commodity constraints and use a modified preference function.*

$$(33) \quad \text{Min}(g_0 - v'C_0 - u'_0 B_{00})y_0$$

$$+ \sum_{i=1}^m (g_i - v'C_i)y_i + \sum_{i=1}^m (f_i - u_0'A_{0i})x_i$$

$$B_{ii}y_i + A_{ii}x_i = b_i - A_{i0}x_0 \qquad (i = 1, \ldots, m)$$

$$-y_0 \qquad\qquad\qquad \geqslant -\bar{y}_0$$

$$-y_i \qquad \geqslant -\bar{y}_i \qquad (i = 1, \ldots, m)$$

$$-x_i \geqslant -\bar{x}_i \qquad (i = 1, \ldots, m)$$

$$y_i \geqslant 0 \qquad (i = 0, \ldots, m)$$

$$x_i \geqslant 0 \qquad (i = 1, \ldots, m)$$

This problem is separable into *one* of the type

(34)
$$\text{Min } (g_0 - v'C_0 - u'_0 B_{00})y_0 = g_0^* y_0$$
$$-y_0 \geqslant -\bar{y}_0$$
$$y_0 \geqslant 0$$

with the obvious solution

(35)
$$y_{0j} = \left\{ \begin{array}{c} 0 \\ \bar{y}_{0j} \end{array} \right\} \quad \text{if} \quad g_{0j}^* \left\{ \begin{array}{c} \geqslant 0 \\ < 0 \end{array} \right\}$$

and *m* of the type

(36)
$$\text{Min } (g_i - v'C_i)y_i + (f_i - u'_0 A_{0i})x_i$$
$$B_{ii}y_i + \qquad A_{ii}x_i = b_i - A_{i0}x_0$$
$$-y_i \qquad \geqslant -\bar{y}_i$$
$$-x_i \geqslant -\bar{x}_i$$
$$y_i \geqslant 0 \qquad x_i \geqslant 0$$

As was the case in dealing with the corresponding price problems in (13), we may consider solving these quantity problems by *developing a special simplex algorithm* as elaborated in a forthcoming study or by decomposing it in various ways depending upon the dimensions of the matrix A_{ii}.

If A_{ii} is of the standing rectangle type it may be appropriate to consider the dual of problem (36) which is just (13) and decompose it into the master (23) and the subproblem (17). We note that we know a feasible solution to this problem, as it is only the preference coefficients which have changed. The x_i quantities will then be obtained as 'shadow quantities' from the master (23) and the y_i quantities from solving the dual of (17) which is

(37)
$$\text{Min } (g_i - v'C_i)y_i$$
$$B_{ii}y_i = b_i - A_{i0}x_0 - A_{ii}x_i$$
$$-y_i \geqslant -\bar{y}_i$$
$$y_i \geqslant 0$$

Again remembering that the matrix B_{ii} consists of band matrices of $+$ and $-$ ones, corresponding to import and export quantities of a commodity and introducing, as in section 8. 3—(18)–(22), the indexes c for commodity, d for currency block or district and a for trade activity (export E or import I) we may formulate (37), omitting the index i, as follows

(38) $\quad$ Min $\sum_c \sum_d \sum_a g^*_{cda} y_{cda}$ $\qquad$ $(g^*_i = g_i - v'C_i)$

$$\sum_d \sum_a \text{sign } (a) y_{cda} = b^*_c \qquad (c = \text{all})$$

$$-y_{cda} \geqslant -\bar{y}_{cda} \qquad (c, d, a = \text{all})$$

$$y_{cda} \geqslant 0 \qquad (c, d, a = \text{all})$$

$$\text{sign } (a) = \begin{Bmatrix} - \\ + \end{Bmatrix} \text{ if } a = \begin{Bmatrix} E \\ I \end{Bmatrix}$$

$$(b^*_i = b_i - A_{i0}x_0 - A_{ii}x_i)$$

This problem is separable into independent problems, every one of which only embracing one commodity, and *one* equation and upper bounds of the variables. In order to solve the c-th problem of this type, we order the corresponding g^*_{cdE} and the g^*_{cdI} terms in raising order. Using the variables with the smallest g^*_{cdE} (or g^*_{cdI}) values we satisfy the $b^*_c (b^*_c < 0)$ constraint (or $b^*_c > 0$). When this has been achieved, we pair the most favourable export and import activities $(g^*_{cdE} + g^*_{cdI} \leqslant 0)$, the next favourable, etc., until all profitable trade deals have been exhausted.

In solving the subproblems involving the y_i and u_i variables, it should be noted that these subproblems may in turn be partitioned into smaller ones and so on until we have as many subproblems as there are commodities. Appropriate changes will then have to be made in the masters above. This possibility may be used to speed up calculations. This will be briefly dealt with in section 10.

If A_{ii} is of the lying rectangle type it may be appropriate to use a master identical with (25) and a subproblem (27). We note that the earlier optimal solution will no longer be a feasible solution, as the right-hand constants have changed. But its former dual solution will be feasible and we may therefore apply the Dual Simplex method for obtaining a feasible and optimal solution.

As a result of these calculations we will have obtained a new partial (y, x) solution and may again combine it with the other known ones in (2) which was the point of departure of this chapter.

9. The Successive Contraction of the Possible Range of the Optimum Value of the Preference Function

The successive solutions of the highest quantity master (9) will give a falling sequence of possible values of the preference function. The successive solutions of the highest price master (32) will give a rising sequence of values of the dual preference function. In the optimum the values of these two functions will be equal. A useful estimate of the possibilities of still further decreasing the preference function will be obtained, as the greatest possible improvement cannot lead to a value that is lower than the last and highest value of the dual preference function.

10. The Optimal Structure, Size and Number of Subproblems and the Routing of Iterations

The most important factors for the swift solution of the linear programming problem dealt with will probably be the selection of the most effective structure, size, number of subproblems and the routing of the iterations. Some of the most interesting possibilities which seem to appear here will be mentioned below.

Sensitivity of a subproblem

In dealing with, for instance, the export and import problems we may notice that for certain commodities the *comparable prices* (g^*_{cda}) in various markets *only slightly* differ; very *large unused import or export possibilities* are existent and the value of the export or import is relatively large in relation to that of other commodities. The solution of the subproblem will then be extremely dependent upon small changes in the currency exchange rates (iterative prices v). The balance of payment vector which enters the corresponding master problem, will in turn strongly change its character, which will influence the new currency prices.

In solving the problem it may then be most efficient to *partition* it, for instance *into one subproblem embracing very many insensitive and unimportant commodities and one embracing very few but sensitive and in value important commodities.*

To obtain a feasible solution to the whole problem we repeatedly solve the relatively *small* but most *important* subproblem, and only some very few times the less important though very large in number of commodities. The advantages of this principle are readily seen. Suppose we have a master of 100 equations. If we introduce only *one* formal subproblem we will usually have to solve the subproblem at least 101 times to get a feasible solution of the master. If we assume that we have one large-sized subproblem embracing 99 per cent of the commodity numbers and one very small but sensitive and important embracing 1 per cent of the commodity numbers, we may solve the small at least 98 times and the large 4 times to obtain a feasible solution to the master of $100+2$ equations. The effort spent in solving the foreign trade quantity subproblem will then be equal to 98 per cent$+4 \times 99$ per cent ≈ 5 solutions of the entire subproblem. This would lead to a 95 per cent reduction of computational work in regard to the straightforward approach which used only one subproblem.

The sensitivity of a subproblem in respect to particular price changes

If, for instance, the foreign trade subproblems may be so constructed that they include only those commodities which are traded with *some particular currency regions*, then the resulting subproblem will only be sensitive in regard to iterative price changes of the corresponding currencies. If in an iteration no appreciable iterative price changes of some currencies but fairly large changes of certain other currencies have taken place, it may then be most effective to solve subproblems which embrace regions for which large iterative price changes have taken place.

The extremality of a subproblem

In dividing a subproblem into, for instance, two subproblems (each of which are assumed to be equally sensitive to price changes) it seems to be probable that a division into one with *predominant positive effects* (e.g. containing mainly export commodities) on the master problem and another with *predominant negative effects* (e.g. mainly import commodities) will be more effective than two with more mixed effects (e.g. each one including both export and import commodities in equal proportions). In the first case we are likely to obtain more extreme vectors in the master programme, which may permit the formation of more advantageous solutions.

The size of a subproblem

Even though we may have succeeded in partitioning the problem into some subproblems embracing approximately equally sensitive commodities, the problem of whether the size of the subproblem is the most appropriate one remains. If we, for instance, would divide one of them into two and employ the policy of immediately revising the master after the solution of each, we may make use of the improvement of the iterative prices gained from solving the first half of the original subproblem, for solving the second half. This will lead to an increase in the *relative* number of times which we will solve the master, but may lead to a decrease in the total computational work required to reach the optimal solution. Even if we will not revise the master after the solution of each of the two new subproblems, we may still have a decrease in the number of times we will have to solve the master as we have a greater number of partial solutions that may be combined in the master.

The routing of the iteration process

If we have several subproblems to one master problem, a considerable saving of computational work may often be made by immediately revising the master after the solution of a subproblem and then *selecting that subproblem for solution, which may be expected to have the greatest influence on the general solution so far obtained.* This will mean that we will *repeatedly* solve the most sensitive subproblem, then at one time or another switch over to a less sensitive one, and again work repeatedly with the more sensitive ones, etc. We will then have to introduce a *special mathematical programme a Policy Problem, the solution of which gives the subproblem which has to be solved in the current iteration.*

The topics mentioned in this paragraph would for their detailed analysis require much the same space as this mathematical appendix. Their discussion will therefore have to wait for another opportunity.

11. Relations to Certain East-European Investigations

One of the aims of this chapter has been the further development of some formulations for both production and foreign trade planning made by J. Mycielski, K. Rey, W. Trzeciakowski, [1, 2] and A. Nagy, T. Liptak [3] (see references to literature on p. 242). The conceptions of the first-mentioned authors have mainly to be developed in regard to the following aspects:

(i) the proposed procedure will not necessarily give a series of solutions converging to the optimal solution[1]; (ii) the restricted use of the knowledge gained about other possible solutions, but have the advantage of (iii) *implicitly raising* the question of whether a swifter road to the optimal prices and quantities may be found than that which is derived by combinations of known solutions.[2] To implement such an idea various approaches are possible. We may make an attempt by introducing the principle of over- and under-relaxation or in economic interpretation of 'speculation' and 'inertia', as has been done in certain studies in the Soviet Union.

The production and foreign trade model of this paper attempts to use the method of D. Pigot [4] for solving systems with some filled rows and columns in an otherwise separable problem, and analyses how the interaction of foreign trade and production may be treated.

---

[1] The thought expressed in 'Decomposition and Optimization of Short-Run Planning', [2], p. 135, that:

'On the given step of iteration the inequality $\sum_{j=1}^{v} A_{k_i j} z_j > B_{k_i}$ suggests that l_{k_i} must be lowered, and the opposite one that it must be raised,' will by itself not guarantee convergence. The simplest way of showing this seems to be by inspecting Table 3, rows 3 and 4 in the author's study 'Iterative Pricing for Planning Foreign Trade' [9]. Using the terminology of Mycielski-Rey-Trzeciakowski and adding superscripts to indicate iteration we find that

$$l_1^3 = M_1^3 = 1{\cdot}300 \quad \text{contributes to} \quad \sum_{j=1}^{v} A_{1j} z_j = -0{\cdot}85 < B_1 = 0,$$

thus in accordance with the said principle it may be raised to $l_1^4 = M_1^4 = 2{\cdot}900$;

$$l_2^3 = M_2^3 = 0{\cdot}210 \quad \text{contributes to} \quad \sum_{j=1}^{v} A_{2j} z_j = -22{\cdot}85 < B_2 = +1,$$

thus in accordance with the said principle it may be raised to $l_2^4 = M_2^4 = 1{\cdot}000$;

$$l_3^3 = M_3^3 = 0{\cdot}160 \quad \text{contributes to} \quad \sum_{j=1}^{v} A_{3j} z_j = 60{\cdot}00 > B_3 = -16.$$

thus still in accordance with the said principle it may be decreased to $l_3^4 = M_3^4 = 0{\cdot}095$;

If we study the balances of trade which correspond to the M_1^4, M_2^4 and M_3^4 thus chosen we see that while still adhering to the above principle we may set $M_1^5 = M_1^3$, $M_2^5 = M_2^3$ and $M_3^5 = M_3^3$ and continue in this way, always putting the iterative prices of an *even* iteration equal to those of the fourth iteration, and those of an *uneven* iteration equal to those of the third, *without ever reaching the optimal solution.*

[2] This possibility may be felt by inspecting Table 4 in the author's study 'Iterative Pricing for Planning Foreign Trade' [9], where certain price sets as in iteration 8 seem to deviate strongly from what in the end will turn out to be the optimal prices.

An interesting conclusion of the present study is that the problem of optimal allocation of export and import quantities to incompletely convertible currency territories may become a subproblem in the over-all system of economic planning. This will enhance the importance of empirical studies of this subproblem which are being undertaken by A. Marton and M. Tardos [6] in Hungary, by W. Trzeciakowski, W. Piaszczyński [12], J. Głowacki [13] in Poland, and by G. Grote and G. Otto [14] in GDR. Aspects of these developments are analysed in A. Zauberman [15].

This study deviates also from some Russian concepts of employing one auxiliary constraint at each level of a pyramidal economic planning system, and considers that in general it will be more effective to employ several inequalities (cf. the discussion in sections 8 and 10).

Complementary views on how blocks of different levels of planning models may be integrated to form an all-embracing planning system are contained in Yu. I. Chernyak [7] and A. Modin [8].

It seems further that the elaborated method should require less computational work and give greater convergence than the method by Kornai-Liptak as outlined in A. Nagy and T. Liptak [3]. The *a priori* reason for this is that, in general, we will have to solve greater subproblems in Nagy-Liptak: *as constraints equal in number the common constraints will have to be added to every one of the subproblems.* In the present method these common constraints will be dealt with for themselves. Unless the number of iterations is not much lower for the Kornai-Liptak method this would lead to greater computational work. But it seems as if the number of iterations required for a certain tolerance may become equal to a $\left(\dfrac{\text{constant}}{\text{tolerance}}\right)$ which seems rather large.[1]

12. Further Extension to International Co-operation, Generalization and Proof of Convergence of the Double Decomposition Method

The approach of this chapter is extended by the author in a later

---

[1] This could occur for one common constraint and two subproblems, when the optimal sharing of the common constraint would be $0 + b = b$ while the initial allocation was the reverse $b + 0 = b$. We may then expect the series of allocations

$$\left(\begin{array}{l} b \cdot \dfrac{1}{2} + 0 \cdot \dfrac{1}{2} = \dfrac{b}{2}; \quad \dfrac{b}{2} \cdot \dfrac{2}{3} + 0 \cdot \dfrac{1}{3} = \dfrac{b}{3}; \quad \ldots, \dfrac{b}{n} \\[2ex] 0 \cdot \dfrac{1}{2} + b \cdot \dfrac{1}{2} = \dfrac{b}{2}; \quad \dfrac{b}{2} \cdot \dfrac{2}{3} + b \cdot \dfrac{1}{3} = \dfrac{2}{3} b; \quad \ldots, \dfrac{n-1}{n} b \end{array} \right)$$

paper to consider the modifications of the economic model if financial stimulous and not command is to be used for implementing the plan, and for creating an efficient system for international co-operation as well as a generalization and conditions of convergence of the above outlined method of decomposition [16].

13. Literature

A production and foreign trade planning model is elaborated in:

1. Jerzy Mycielski, Krzysztof Rey and Witold Trzeciakowski, 'Decomposition and Optimization of Short-Run Planning', in Tibor Barna, ed., *Structural Interdependence and Economic Development*, London, 1963;
as well as in an extended Polish version:

2. 'Optimum całościowe a optima cząstkowe w planowaniu handlu zagranicznego' in *Przegląd Statystyczny*, 1963, no. 1, pp. 119–137.
Important questions of decomposition of linear programmes in regard to foreign trade planning are considered in:

3. A. Nagy and T. Liptak, 'A Short-Run Optimization Model of Hungarian Cotton Fabric Exports', *Economics of Planning*, Oslo, September 1963, no. 2, pp. 117–140.
The decomposition of a linear programming problem in both primal and dual directions is proposed by:

4. D. Pigot, 'Double décomposition d'un programme linéaire', in *Actes de la 3ème Conférence Internationale de Recherche Opérationelle* (*Proceedings of the 3rd International Conference on Operational Research held in Oslo*, 1–5 July 1963), Paris, 1964.
Important experiences of the efficiency of various solution policies in decomposed linear programming problems are rendered in:

5. J.-M. Gauthier and F. Genuys, 'Expériences sur le principe de décomposition des programmes linéaires', 1er *Congrès de l'AFCALTI*, 1960.
Some discussion on the preference function is given in:

6. Adam Marton and Marton Tardos, 'On optimizing the commodity pattern on foreign trade markets', *Közgazdasági Szemle*, Budapest, August 1963, pp. 932–944.
Concepts of a pyramidal system of planning models simulating the planning process of the Soviet Union are evolved in:

7. Yu. I. Chernyak, 'The Electronic Simulation of Information Systems for Central Planning', *Economics of Planning*, Oslo, April 1963, no. 1, pp. 23–40;

8. A. Modin, 'Developing Interbranch Balances for Economic Simulation', *Economics of Planning*, Oslo, September 1963, no. 2, pp. 104–116.

A numerically illustrated account of the optimisation procedure for distribution of given exports and imports (re-exports excluded), on incompletely convertible currency territories is rendered in:

9. Tom Kronsjö, 'Iterative Pricing for Planning Foreign Trade', *Economics of Planning*, Oslo, April 1963, no. 1, pp. 1–22; as well as in an extended Russian version

10. Tom Kronsjö, '*Postroenie optimalnych planov vneshne-torgovykh raspredelenij po metodu iterativnogo tsenoobrazovaniya*, Institute for International Economic Studies, Stockholm, 1963, 23 pp.
A more formal mathematical exposition is made in:

11. Tom Kronsjö, 'Decomposition of Large Linear Programmes, illustrated with an example from the foreign trade theory of a planned economy', in the first volume of the proceedings of the *Nord SAM 63* (*Nordic Symposium on the Application of Computing Machinery*, Helsinki, 15–20 August 1963), Helsinki 1964.

12. Wacław Piaszczyński and Witold Trzeciakowski, 'Optymalizacja w planowaniu bieżącym handlu zagranicznego' in Mieczysław Lesz, ed., *Ekonometria a praktyka planowania*, Warsaw, 1965, pp. 32–55.

13. Jerzy Głowacki, 'Problems of Optimizing the Directions of International Trade in a Planned Economy', *Economics of Planning*, Oslo, 1966, no. 1, pp. 27–42.

14. Gerhard Grote, 'Problems of Foreign Trade in the German Democratic Republic', *Economics of Planning*, Oslo, 1966, no. 1, pp. 68–82.

15. Alfred Zauberman, 'The Criterion of Efficiency of Foreign Trade in Soviet Type Economics', *Economica*, February 1964.

16. Tom Kronsjö, '*Mathematical Programming Model for International Economic Co-operation*', Discussion Paper of the Centre for Russian and East European Studies, University of Birmingham, Great Britain, September 1966, 68 pp.

17. George B. Dantzig, *Linear Programming and Extensions*, Princeton, New Jersey, 1963, pp. 448–70.

18. E. M. L. Beale, P. A. B. Hughes, and R. E. Small, Experiences in Using a Decomposition Program', *The Computer Journal*, April 1965, no. 1, pp. 13–18.

Part II: Planning Techniques

**E. A Comparison of Planning Techniques
under Imperative and Indicative Planning**

19 Notes on French-type and Soviet-type Planning

I

IT HAS become customary to classify planning, as practised, in two broad families, the 'indicative' or 'indirect', and the 'imperative' or 'normative' or 'direct'. This dichotomy is usually treated as one stemming primarily from differences in the economic system and mechanism, the imperative kind being identified with a 'command' economy and its institutional framework. Patently, institutional environment is relevant, and indeed decisive, for the number and effectiveness of the instrument-variables the planning State has at hand, and for its degrees of freedom in solving the underlying system of equations. This may be expected to influence the choice of certain approaches to, and tools of, plan construction and plan implementation in preference to others. While not ignoring the significance of the institutional framework, attention will be focused in these notes on techniques, and an attempt will be made to elucidate some differences and common features of planning under different institutional arrangements from this specific angle. This limitation materially circumscribes the area of this very tentative inquiry into reality, but nevertheless it may bring out a few points of interest.

The scope of these notes is also narrowed by confining them to two selected cases. This too will admittedly affect its significance. The choice of the Soviet case, the first in history and imperative *par excellence*, hardly needs justification. The choice of the French type of planning is far more arbitrary. It is arguable that some other private-enterprise countries, especially Norway and Holland, may lay a valid claim to greater refinement of some planning devices and procedures.[1] (Private enterprise, rather than market, economies are referred to here. The latter would also include Yugoslavia on some definitions, and that country in many respects forms a category of its own.) Nevertheless, the French experiment is most relevant to the present purpose because its past record, and the influence it exerts on the

[1] When this book was completed Professor Henri Theil published his *Applied Economic Forecasting* (Amsterdam, 1966). It contains a description and discussion of econometric macro-models and input-output models employed in Dutch central planning. The student will find this work invaluable for the general survey it offers of the possibilities of the prediction methods on the empirical as well as theoretical plane.

planning thought of the West, make it representative of quite ambitious indicative, or as some would prefer to label it, 'intentional' planning.[1,2]

2

Both Soviet and French plans are essentially 'verbally' framed, in the expressive French parlance, 'en termes littéraires', but both increasingly resort to, or at least experiment with, some formalised instruments. Clearly, the underlying logic of both kinds of plan, the logic that is of the procedures and of the institutional, behavioural and technological nexus of their variables and interaction coefficients, can be 'translated' into an, inevitably more or less generalised, all-economy mathematical model *sensu proprio*. Tendencies towards such an articulation will be discussed.

Soviet planners have been conservative in their methodologies, which were devised in the first experiment of its kind, and before the conception of 'modelling' for practical policy, as distinct from analytical purposes, was evolved. Subsequently, intellectual resistance to this novel conception was rationalised by the traditionalist school on doctrinal grounds as well as on grounds of practicability. On the other hand, the French, the younger practice, has consciously designed its system as one of synthesised and ordered reasoning and calculus within which hypotheses are made explicit and coherence and probability of numerical conclusions tested through iterative procedures.

The road of successive approximations and rounds of scrutiny at successive stages is a common feature of Soviet and French methods.

3

In neither case is any formal calculus applied exclusively or decisively in optimising the economy's advance over time. (In this respect practice is in accord with the scepticism of the theorists as to

---

[1] 'The Plan, however, is not purely *indicative*. The play of certain forces tends to ensure that it is put into effect. . . . Thus the Plan is in principle normative, the projection is partly normative and partly predictional.' P. Massé, 'The French Plan and Economic Theory', *Econometrica*, April 1965, pp. 266 and 267.

[2] Since this chapter was written Professor Jan Tinbergen's excellent book *Central Planning*, New Haven—London, 1964, has appeared. The reader of this chapter will find particularly useful its appendix 'An International Comparison of Planning Practices', pp. 104 ff.

the possibility of an 'objective', 'scientific', formulation of the optimum rate of growth, see p. 171, above.) In real life decision-making is very much a matter of routine, relying largely on an empirically established rule-of-thumb as to the desirable and feasible rate of investment. This is particularly true of the Soviet case. In the USSR the rate of investment has displayed a remarkable degree of constancy over decades, oscillating around a quarter of net material product.

The French planner however does at least think in terms of a quite strictly defined criterion of technical optimisation. Originally it was the minimum of investment for given values of 'political variables' (see below), as in the Chenery-Kretschmer Mezzogiorno programme. Subsequently final consumption has been adopted as the optimand instead. The problem has been put in very broad formal terms in this way.[1] Denote by K all 'political variables' except final consumption, a certain vector C_2. (Note that the K thus becomes the portmanteau which hides the most awkward obstacles in the way of a definition of the optimum rate of growth.) What is sought is a certain $C_2 = C_1 + \alpha \Delta C$, where C_1 is consumption of the last year preceding the plan, the ΔC is the incremental consumption of a given structure, and α a maximand parameter, The 'technical' optimisation consists of maximising α, given K and certain constraints, in particular regarding investment in the target year (which should be such as to preserve a desirable rhythm of growth beyond that year), and to a safety level of the balance of payments.[2]

The Soviet approach to the goal of planning is rather ambiguous. Some tend to interpret its planning strategy as pursuing the goal of maximisation of national income with the implied and inter-related maxima for productivity of labour, and consumption. The postulated rate of saving is logically related to the latter. Yet in fact, the central target in planning the economy is gross production rather than net product.

It should be noted, however, that the conception of centring planning on final consumption does gain ground in Soviet thinking, at least for very long-term planning. Consumption targets appear to have been the basis of the 1980 plan for the 'threshold of full

---

[1] P. Massé, *Programmation formalisée et programmation discrétionnaire*, mimeo, 13 August 1963.
[2] On the maximand adopted in formalised planning see below, fn. to p. 268.

communism'. (The French practice too has moved gradually towards this conception.) Attempts are being made to formalise this approach in some models recently evolved in Soviet literature.[1] In particular, the model elaborated by Pugachev and Volkonskyi adopts as a criterion of optimal development a function of the type

$$V = \sum_{m=0}^{m} Q^{(m)} U^{(m)} S^{(m)},$$

where $S^{(m)}$ is the final consumption vector for the m-th year (S_1^m, $S_2^m, \ldots, S_n^m$), U^m the objective function of consumption and the $Q^{(m)}$ a time-weighting function.[2] The form of the latter is a matter for discussion. Some would suggest, at least as a first approximation, a Q describing 'depreciation of commodities' over time. Nemchinov has suggested for this purpose a return to Strumilin's conception, formulated in 1946, of the impact of time on economic life; of the depreciation through time of material products owing to the rise in labour productivity. (This is the conceptual basis of the investment-efficiency coefficient.) The time-weighting function would then be some $Q^m = e^{-vm}$, where v would measure the change in average social labour productivity. (We shall see in the next chapter how the problem has been tackled in the first formalized long-term planning experiment.)

4

The construction of both the French and the Soviet plans proceeds from a broad exploration and charting of the path of society's economic progress over the time-horizon in terms of a few strategic macro-aggregates. Little is known about the actual processes by which the political-economic directives, specifically the postulated overall rates of development of the economy, are determined in the Soviet Union. It seems safe to say that while there is the obvious and profound difference in the institutional frame of the process, there is, and can be, little difference in substance. In both cases the optimum pace is arrived at by intuition rather than by any systematic calculation.

Very broadly, French plan-construction starts from the projecting

---

[1] This matter is discussed at greater length in ch. 15 above.

[2] See above, p. 177, and the reference to V. A. Volkonskyi's and V. F. Pugachev's approach in V. S. Nemchinov, *Ekonomiko-matematicheskiye metody i modeli*, Moscow, 1962, pp. 390 ff.

of final demands for the terminal year, that is private and public consumption, foreign trade and capital formation. (In the past it is the last that tended to be the starting-point.) Thence outputs required from productive sectors to meet the demands are estimated, and they are related to the entailed needs in manpower and capital. Soviet traditional planning practice focuses on gross outputs. Targets are set for various specific products satisfying final and intermediate demands and framing a set of 'funds'[1], including 'consumption-good funds' and 'investment-good funds'[1]. An increasingly influential school in Soviet planning thought (cf. e.g. Belkin et al.[2]) is inclined to accept the logic of moving in plan-construction from the final bill of goods via intermediate outputs involved (and the implied requirements for capital and labour) to global outputs, broadly as is typified by the French practice. These tendencies are connected with the assimilation in Soviet planning of the matrix calculus (as are the very long-term prognostications—see below).

The gist of the Belkin argument on planning procedures is this. In Soviet methodology, as historically evolved, the point of departure in plan-construction is a set of exogenously fixed goals for a mixed bag of goods, mixed in the sense that it includes both 'final' and 'intermediate' commodities. Various causes may have contributed to this approach. The low level of computational methodologies available, which Belkin singles out, has most probably been one of them. What should probably also be taken into account is the legacy from the period of initial growth, the period when production of certain commodities, the 'leading links', mainly raw and intermediate materials together with some manufactures, and in the first place some engineering products, was pursued (and perhaps under the circumstances *had* to be pursued) almost as an end in itself. Production plans for

---

[1] Cf. the argument in J. Pajestka 'Methods of Long-Term Projections for the Centrally Plannned Economies', *Studies in Long-Term Economic Projections for the World Economy*, United Nations, New York, 1964. It rests on the proposition that production in centrally planned economies cannot be limited by insufficient effective demand. Although the aggregated production functions are not utilised, it corresponds with the practical planning method to think of it as based on a function:

$$P = P_0 + \Delta P(I, E, T)$$

where P_0 is the output in the base year, I is investment, E is increase of employment, T is technical progress.

[2] V. D. Belkin, 'Natsyonalnyi dokhod i mezhotraslevyi balans' in A. G. Aganbegyan, V. D. Belkin, eds., *Primenenye matematiki i elektronnoy tekhniki*, Moscow, 1961, pp. 16 ff.

other commodities were built up around the targets for these goods. As this period draws to its close, end-uses come naturally into their own. At the same time, and here we return to Belkin's reasoning, new and powerful computational methodologies make a more rational approach possible. Logically one would have to begin plan construction from its *ultimate* objective. This is nothing other than to provide society, given the prevailing or accessible technology, and given the resource endowment, with a maximum of goods for individual and collective *consumption*. Logical as this route would be, it is blocked by forbidding hurdles of both a practical and a theoretical kind. These arise, in a growing economy, from the difficulty of adequately determining the (lagged) functional relationship between capital accumulation and consumption in successive periods. Considering the very modest achievement in the theoretical, and still more in the practical, construction of dynamic models, a less exacting and more realistic desideratum would be to adopt as a point of departure given objectives in capital formation as well as in consumption.[1] Even this implies a fundamental change in Soviet planning, a shift in the basic approach from 'gross-gross' output to national income.

On the other hand, the difference between the Soviet and French methods is perhaps not as wide as would appear on the surface, in particular when it comes to detailed 'targeting' for lower echelons, sectors and branches. Here the French planner, too, thinks primarily in terms of gross production.

5

Parenthetically, it is interesting to note that the point of departure in the British NEDC plan construction is a certain hypothetical acceleration in the growth *prima facie* believed to be achievable.[2] Its feasibility is then investigated by means of an industrial inquiry with a rather

---

[1] A recent paper in *Planovoye Khoziaystvo* (by G. Sorokin; 1966, no. 9) argues that the build-up of the plan from the final bill-of-goods tends to create a consumption 'bias'; that, moreover, when combined with extrapolation of raw-material inputs and use-normatives of equipment tends to ignore disparities of technical advance. It is hard to see why this should be so.

[2] The following remarks are based mainly on the report published by the National Economic Development Council, *Growth of the United Kingdom Economy to 1966*, London, 1963, and my conversation with Mr M. F. G. Scott whom I wish to thank; he is not to be held responsible in any way for my treatment of the subject or views expressed.

wide sample; what the industries are asked to do is to make a forecast for the end-year, under the assumptions of their own programmes and the postulated faster rate of growth, of their outputs, exports and imports, employment of labour and capacities (some of the estimates being in 'physical' and others in money terms—in constant prices). In the light of this inquiry resources and demands placed on them are confronted. The former are treated as reducible to labour availabilities and productivity; the focus is on size and distribution of manpower and expectations of technical advance. The procedure of setting ends against means following very broadly the French lines. First elements of final demand are estimated (though on the whole with less precision than is the case in France: its main component, household consumption, is projected without investigations of trends for individual groups of goods and services). Requirements in gross productive investment, in fixed capital and inventories, are derived from the target for gross domestic product; investment in housing is derived from a desirable rate of replacement plus reasonable increment. The sequence in the prognosis of external relations is somewhat different from the French. First, implications of the postulated improvement in the current balance of payments, from a deficit to a surplus, are explored. As in the French method developments in foreign trade are based on some broad predictions as to the behaviour of markets (the assumptions are *inter alia* the constancy of terms of trade for primary producers and manufacturing countries and the continuation of the rhythm of growth of the last few years in the rest of the world). Financial equilibrium is then checked under certain assumptions as to a continuing trend for changes in the distribution of factor incomes and for relative prices with a constant general national level of costs. The savings-investment equilibrium is worked out, allowance made for the postulated shift in the balance of payments on current account. Thus the macro-economic supply-use balance of resources is being approximated for the plan end-year at the postulated rate of growth of the GNP.

To use Professor Frisch's classification, the NEDC approach is typical of the 'on-looker' rather than 'decisional' category. Nevertheless, as far as the basic 'balancing' method goes, it is quite a close relation of the Soviet and French plans. Its procedures are in embryo those of the latter (though the inquiry into the industrial branches' gross production as the first step reminds one of the Soviet methodological doctrine). The NEDC technical armoury is, also in embryo, that of the French and

Soviet planner. The kinship of the British with the French planning is very likely to be better discernible as it develops and gains in sophistication. One could also say probably that its underlying philosophy is that of the Cambridge model—that this model can be seen as its formalised 'ideal' and path-finder (see below, p. 297).

6

The Soviet planning procedure, as 'idealised', is one of a dialogue between the various echelons, of 'planning' and 'counter-planning'. It moves up and down the ladder of the economic administration (time is but one of the various factors which inhibit the process in reality), till ultimately macro-magnitudes are disaggregated into enterprises' operational, 'technical-financial' programmes, *tekhprom-finplans*. The first phase of plan construction results in the promulgation of a set of preliminary guide-line indicators, 'control figures' (*kontrol-nyie tsifry*). The essential approach in building up the plan is one of working from individual branches upwards, towards a synthesis. This, it may be noted, has been criticised on the ground that as often as not the initial branch-plans are in a conflict beyond practical reconciliation.[1] Traditional procedure is to 'chop' the 'vicious circle'[2] at some key branch and then try to get consistency by a cycle of adjustments. The present tendency is to treat—in the first approximation—existing capacities as yielding constant outputs and iteratively adjust branch requirements of investment (usually 50–100 per cent in excess of alloted resources) so as to reach postulated increments.[3] (Note affinity of approach with solution of a dynamic Leontief system.)

The French grand orientation is elaborated by a process of trial and error leading to a set of feasible alternatives from which the most desirable one is selected. Each is characterised by its rate of expansion (in terms of gross domestic final output).

The possible rates are considered, account is taken of historical and international analogy and allowance is made for demographic growth, expectations of the direction and pace of technical advance, the stimu-

---

[1] M. Z. Bor, *Voprosy metodologii planovogo balansa narodnogo khoziaystva USSR*, Moscow, 1960, pp. 199 ff.

[2] G. Sorokin, *Planirovanye Narodnogo Khoziaystva*, Moscow, 1966.

[3] L. Dudkin, *Optimalnyi Materialnyi Balans Narodnogo Khoziaystva*, op. cit.

lation or damping-down impact from the outside world and so on. Certain variables are recognised as 'political' (see above, p. 249) reflecting elements to be finally appraised by the political decision-makers. (The dividing line between political and technical variables is no doubt relative. It has been remarked, perhaps with good reason, that quite a few of those regarded as 'technical' in France, would be considered 'political' in Britain.) Consequently, the technical solution area for the planner is rather narrowly delimited, which helps quicken convergence of iterations. What is eventually formulated is a certain set of marginal or quasi-marginal variants ordered according to a political hierarchy and placed in reasonably close neighbourhood of each other. The basic alternatives left within the margin of choice would be those determining the rate of investment, capital intensity and the degree of 'openness' of the economy, or when translated into explicitly 'political' consequences, the length of the working day, and the size and composition of final consumption.[1] Once choice of the variant is made it is then elaborated in depth.

7

What is sought for each development alternative is the consonance of adopted hypotheses with the means which can be mobilised for achieving the ends. The system of scrutiny refers to consistency and likelihood. The French plan is organised round three global 'balance equations', of goods and services, of manpower and of finance.[2] The French approach, just as much as the Soviet, is fundamentally, to use

---

[1] P. Massé, *op. cit.*, and his contribution to the discussion at the Vienna 1962 Congress, mimeo, 3 September 1962.

[2] J. E. Hackert, A. M. Hackert, *Economic Planning in France*, London, 1963, p. 121.
The three equations are: (1) Production of goods and services = private consumption + public consumption + fixed capital formation + exports less imports + stocks change + intermediate consumption; (2) Available manpower (taking account of demographic trends, immigration, retirement, school-leaving age and activity rates for women) = manpower required in agriculture + other productive branches + administration + financial institutions + domestic service; (3) Finance: financing needs of firms and public administrations = financing capacity of households.
Compare this with V. Dadayan (*Ekonomiko-matematicheskoye modelirovanye sotsyalisticheskogo vosproizvodstva*, Moscow, 1963, pp. 174 ff.) whose model broadly formalises the existing Soviet planning practice. He harmonises the 'real' and the financial plans by means of three coefficients which relate final outputs, as 'physically' composed, respectively to net national product, to rewards to labour in the 'productive' sphere (material production), and to re-distributed income with given taxation and posited savings by the population.

the accepted Russian terminology, one of 'balances'. Simple as the idea is, it is perhaps the greatest single Soviet conceptual contribution to planning.

8

The main Soviet instrument used for securing the dynamic balance of the economy is the 'material balance', undoubtedly an invention of first-class importance. Nevertheless, employed as it still is in its original form (it was devised in the 1920s) it is very crude indeed. Its obsolescence is rapidly progressing as inter-relationships in the maturing and increasingly diversified system become more complex. Material balances are compiled for various commodities, 'final' and 'intermediate' alike, by various echelons of the planning machinery (depending on the importance of the given commodity). Each material balance sets in quantity terms, more recently also with a partly regional as well as branch breakdown, all the proposed uses, both intermediate and final, of the commodity throughout the economy against availabilities from all sources, i.e. production, inventories and imports. A material balance can be represented as follows:

Product X

Sources

1 Production
   Subdivided by republics
2 Imports
3 Other sources
4 Stocks with suppliers at beginning
   of plan period
   Subdivided by republics

Distribution

1 Production needs
   (a) Current inputs into other
       sectors
   (b) Capital repairs in other
       sectors
   (c) Other uses
   (d) Needs of the construction
       industry for investment
2 Free market allocation
3 State Reserves[1]
4 Reserves of the Council of Ministers
5 Increases in stocks
6 Exports

[1] The problem of reserves—of patent importance for the smooth course of the economy—has been formalised in an interesting way by S. M. Vishnev (*Ekonomika i Matematicheskiye Metody*, no. 3, 1966). For each commodity, j, the balance equation has the form

$$r_j^T = r_j^0 + \int_0^T [a(t) - b(t)] \, dt$$

where r denotes the reserve, a and b, respectively, inflows and outflows over the plan period $(o - T)$. With $c(t)$ denoting the requirements changing over time $Q = Q[a(t), b(t), c(t)]$ is the maximand.

The entries are reasonably self-explanatory. On the right-hand side, item $1(a)$ is computed by multiplying the planned production targets for the other sectors by their input norms. In addition to material-input balances, balances of centrally allocated equipment—in money and physical terms—and of manpower, are being compiled.

The input-output relations which underlie a 'balance' are computed by the use of 'progressive' technological standards, derived from practice or technical calculations and projected, one way or another, for the plan-period. A major weakness of the tool is that the material balances do not provide explicit, complete information as to the inputs required for postulated outputs; hence they form a loose collection rather than an organic system. Neither do they provide any 'automatic' way for the computation of full inputs. In practice, adequate coherence can hardly be attained. For some years attempts have been made to integrate material balances in rough 'chess-board' tabulations, and more recently, into a table of inter-industry flows, and thus to make explicit the system of implied balance equations.

Conceptually, to be sure, any inter-industry flow system, such as that of material balances, can be harmonised by successive approximations. The choice of iterative procedure would depend on its arrangement and the computational equipment. In particular the Gauss-Seidel method of iteration may commend itself. Indeed, iteration can be pursued up to any degree of accuracy, and it is intuitively evident that the length of an adequate series of iterations depends on the tightness of the network of interrelationships in a given economy. (The rate of convergence depends on the dominant root or eigen value of the system. If the matrix can be perfectly triangularised, consistency can be arrived at in a single iteration.) A simple but convincing model of the Soviet type planning procedure has been suggested by Levine.[1] Confronted with a deficit of some commodity, j, the Gosplan would resort to two kinds of adjustments. Typical of one of them would be to raise the output of commodity i used in production of j, or to reduce

---

[1] Cf. of the doctoral thesis: Herbert S. Levine, *A Study in Economic Planning—The Soviet Industrial Supply System*, Harvard University, February 1961.

See also H. Levine, 'The Centralised Planning of Supply in Soviet Industry' in the *U.S. Congress Joint Economic Committee Comparisons of the United States and Soviet Economies*, pt. I, Washington, 1959, p. 165; A. Zauberman, *Soviet Studies*, July 1962; for an admirable discussion of iteration methodology see W. D. Evans, 'Input-Output Computations', in *The Structural Interdependence of the Economy*, 1956.

the output of commodity k for which the i is an input; the other kind of adjustments would be to make technological savings—to cut down the input coefficients, a_{ij} and a_{jk}. The US Bureau of Labour Statistics has evolved a procedure of approximating the path of $(I-A)^{-1}.\Upsilon$ by iterations followed by an extrapolation, and has found that five to eleven iterations would provide an acceptable degree of precision. Considering the degree of sophistication of the two economies and other elements involved, Professor Levine concludes that in the Soviet case the lower figure would be sufficient. He seems to suggest that the Gosplan practice cannot afford the minimum number of iterations and in any case is far from any systematic procedure. We should think, however, that advance in computational techniques and equipment would tend to improve its possibilities.

9

The use of material balances to ensure consistency is simplified where bottlenecks exist, which, I think, is relevant for its success in the phase of unbalanced growth. This has been studied by Montias.[1] He showed that if there are a number of sectors with capacity bottlenecks, and if the gross outputs of the unlimited sectors are known, then the net outputs of the bottleneck sectors can be determined at a single iteration by subtracting the input requirements on the part of all sectors from the gross outputs of the capacity-limited sectors. If the net outputs so derived make up an acceptable bill of goods, consistency has been achieved. Otherwise the net outputs of the capacity-free sectors have to be cut back. It also follows from Samuelson's extension of the Le Chatelier Principle,[2] that inconsistencies due to feedback effects are smaller, the larger is the number of bottleneck sectors. Thus the planners may, under certain conditions, reach a consistent plan without matrix inversion, through iterations—provided that the outputs in the capacity-free sectors are adapted to the potentials of the

---

[1] J. M. Montias, 'Central Planning in Poland', pp. 339–45, and J. M. Montias, 'On the Consistency and Efficiency of Central Plans', in *Review of Economic Studies*, October 1962, especially pp. 282–85.

[2] P. Samuelson in 'An Extension of the Le Chatelier Principle', *Econometrica*, April 1960, deals with the applicability of this principle generally to what he describes as the Minkowski type of systems.

bottleneck sectors. (Montias examined the Polish input-output table from this point of view, and found empirical support for this argument.)

During the early phase of the planning era, the use of material balances had a certain logic to commend it, both on account of the milieu and of the strategy pursued. The country was underdeveloped with a primitive economy, and sophisticated planning techniques were scarcely relevant. The strategy pursued was one of concentration on a few leading sectors; if the use of material balances led to inconsistencies and imbalances, then the non-priority sectors could release the necessary resources. As the economy has become more diversified, and formerly non-priority sectors have received attention, so the need for more refined techniques has grown.

In practice, the main defect in the use of material balances to ensure consistency is that it is immensely time- and labour-consuming (which is why, hitherto, two or more iterations have been very seldom practised, when following up the effects of target re-adjustments). As the economy becomes more complex, it will become ever more so. If planning is to survive, consistency will have to be achieved by a technique which can be mechanised.

10

As a result of the inadequacies of the material balance technique, it has increasingly been supplemented in recent years by the input-output model. The original (1959) Soviet input-output tables were compiled in both value and physical terms. The dimensions of the value table was 83×83.[1] The physical table embraced 157 commodities The experiments have brought out the striking narrowness of the present informational basis of central planning: they have had to rely on a 20 per cent sample; nor has the available statistical material proved sufficient to assess the sampling errors by a dependable way. The *ex-post* tables have been up-dated for successive years: it has been apparently discovered that current adjusting of about one in every six coefficients would in practice suffice for the purpose.[2]

---

[1] 3-quadr. version (7×7) first published in A. Efimov *et al.*, eds., *Metody Planirovanya Mazhotraslevykh Proportsiy*, Moscow, 1965.

[2] One may note in this context the apparently promising Soviet experiments in triangularisation of all-economy input-output matrices. Procedure followed is first to select essential input-output flows or coefficients and next to arrange them in a block-triangular form. The method of such processing of information flows has been adopted

A major break-through seems to be now in sight: in the course of the elaboration of the 1970 plan a fully-fledged technological *ex-ante* matrix of sizeable dimensions (129 branches—7,089 coefficients) has been produced, the first of the kind in the history of Soviet perspective planning. It seems to have been built up on a 1970 projection of direct material coefficients, per unit of finished goods and per 1,000 roubles of gross production.

The 'inter-industry balance' in money terms is an open, static, four-quadrant flow matrix with a more or less classical lay-out, and organised by the 'pure'-branch, that is, homogeneous output, principle. One of its peculiarities is that following the Soviet-Marxist doctrine, and Soviet planning practice, it accepts the dichotomy of services. Those considered 'non-productive' fail to appear in the first quadrant, and material inputs which support them are channelled straight into the second quadrant as final consumption. In contrast, 'productive', or material, services are treated as fully-fledged branches or sectors. Nor is depreciation reflected in the quadrant of inter-mediate flows. Instead, it is inserted into the vector of material pro-duction used up for replacement, repair and formation of new capital assets—in the second quadrant—without any specification of the receiving sectors (a corresponding summary vector is placed in the third quadrant). Transactions are recorded at 'delivery prices', i.e. prices to final users, including trade and transport margins. This helps to reconcile the table with Soviet national accounts, but the Soviet method of pricing patently affects its meaningfulness.

Some of the changes in the lay-out of the 1970 matrices include incorporating amortisation in the first quadrant as the part of the output of the building industry which corresponds to replacement of

as a basis of an iterative procedure for the computation of the *planned* balance, accord-ing to a statistical model. Cf. E. V. Yershov in *Ekonomika i Matematicheskiye Metody*, no. 2, 1966. On possibilities offered to planners by special structures of matrices see also V. A. Volkonskiy, *ibid.*

The promise seems to have support also in Dr Treml's interesting testing—on Soviet 83 × 83 tables—of the Simpson-Tsukui hypothesis on block-triangular inner structures for industrial economies—strong intra-block relations and inter-block independence. For the three groups, final metal products, processed foods and other non-metal pro-ducts, the intra-block use of total interindustry consumption was found to be 62, 92 and 65 per cent respectively, and the shares of total inter-block flows on and below the main diagonal 96, 99 and 95 per cent respectively. (*Structural Similarities of the U.S. and the Soviet Economies*—paper read at a Seminar, at the London School of Economics, October 1966.)

capital stock: generally in order to reflect inter-industry flows of capital goods, output of that industry is to include the value of equipment installed. The fourth quadrant is to describe the formation of final incomes of the State, of enterprises and of the population (the row 'incomes of workers and employees' would show individual and collective consumption; 'net income of State enterprises' its distribution as between formation of fixed and working capital; and 'centralised net income' distribution between capital formation and social consumption). Soviet practice does not seem to have been successful in the build-up of that quadrant. It has found out that while the matrix does portray the direct financing of each branch's output from its own means, the financing of the use of the final product is mirrored only from the angle of the general volume of the required resources; the movement of these resources itself falls out of the picture. Technically the trouble arises at the intersection of the two flows—of the flow from the third to the first via the fourth quadrant with that from the first to the second quadrant.[1]

II

The highly aggregated matrix for preliminary testing of plan variants, mentioned by Yaremenko, appears to cover nine industrial branches, construction, agriculture, transport and trade. The magnitude of fixed-capital stock and manpower absorbed by a given component of final product are obtained in this exercise as weighted capital and labour intensities:

$$B_s = \sum_j \sum_i A_{ij} f_i y_j^s$$

where,

A_{ij} is the matrix of full-order input coefficients,

f_i is the branch factor-intensity of net product,

y_j^s the weight of the j-th branch in the given element of final output.

---

[1] Cf. B. L. Isayev, 'Balansy finansirovanya oborota obshchestvennogo produkta' in *Primenenye Matematiki v Ekonomicheskikh Issledovanyakh* vol. 3, p. 240. The author suggests certain readjustments in the design of the matrix to help harmonising the flows.

In the Hungarian practice Dr Maria Augustinovic has suggested a model in which the role of direct input-output coefficients is taken over by coefficients of receipts. Her mathematical sketch of cash-credit flows indicates a 'bridge' for circulation of social product, investment, pricing.

A noteworthy use of the matrix is also computation of a duplication coefficient of gross output.[1]

12

Among the 'ready reckoners' which the input-output methodology has offered the planner, the Leontief inverse is one of the most powerful. Once the $(I-A)^{-1}$ has been obtained, the required branch outputs can be found without undue trouble by multiplying scalar-wise each of the row-vectors of the matrix of coefficients by the column-vector of the final bill of goods. Soviet planners have apparently employed the Gauss–Jordan method of elimination.[2] The snag is that (certain inherent difficulties apart, such as those relating to joint products and by-products) the standard procedure of getting the inverse is highly laborious—ways of evading or easing the 'ritual' are being sought.[3, 4]

13

The French practice has assimilated the instrument of material balances which are being drawn up for certain key commodities, in physical terms, in limited detail. It has also adopted, and gradually

---

[1] For the Soviet inter-industry balances see *inter alia*, A. N. Efimov, *Perestroyka upravlenya promyshlennostyu i stroitelstvom*, Moscow, 1957, p. 106 ff.; G. I. Grebtsov and P. P. Karpov (eds.), *Materialnyie balansy v narodno-khoziaystvennom plane*, Moscow, 1960, pp. 225 ff.; M. Edelman, *Vestnik Statistiki*, 1961, no. 7; L. Berri, F. Klotsvog, S. Shatalin, *Planovoye Khoziaystvo*, 1962, no. 2; L. Berri, *Planovoye Khoziaystvo*, 1962, no. 9; Yu. Yaramenko, *Planovoye Khoziaystvo*, 1963, no. 4; report from the research conference on methodology of inter-industry balances in *Planovoye Khoziaystvo*, 1963, no. 5; A. Efimov, *Planovoye Khoziaystvo*, 1963 no. 5; M. Kaser, *Soviet Studies*, October 1962.

[2] Successive elimination of unknowns, outputs X's, from inter-industry equations. With postulated final output Y, we eliminate

$$X_1 = \sum_{j=2} a_{ij}/(1-a_{11}) . X_j + Y_1/(1-a_{11})$$

and so on. It is applied to matrices broken up into blocks of equal rank.

[3] Cf. R. G. D. Allen, *Mathematical Economics*, London, 1963, pp. 442 ff.

[4] Thus e.g. in Soviet literature I. Z. Kaganovich (*Ekonomika i Matematicheskiye Metody*, no. 5, 1965) suggests the following procedure: Determine first-order, or first- and second-order, input-output coefficients; form of them a matrix C_0 which is taken as first approximation to the Leontief inverse if the norm of $[I-(I-A).C_0] < 1$; then through systematic correcting (say by the Hotelling procedure) bring elements of the C_0 to a postulated degree of approximation to values of full-order coefficients. The method is stated to have shown satisfactory convergence.

262

expanded, the employment of the Leontief-type inter-industry matrix: originally the matrix was used there too, in *ex post* analysis and short-term forecasts and subsequently also for experimental, medium and long-run projections (the basis is the 28×28, 1959 input-output matrix).

L. Gouni[1] singles out two differences between the French and the Soviet procedures of relevance for the consistency of plans. First, while the French plan rests essentially on a money-term *tableau-économique*, although expressed in prices supposed to be constant, the Soviet coherence tests rely on material balances in physical quantities with the advantage of translating with greater exactness the techniques of fabrication and progress envisaged. Secondly, while in France the plan perspective—a very schematic one—is being built up by twenty-eight branches from national accounts, the number of Soviet balances is greater.

14

In both countries experience has revealed the limitations as well as the advantages of the input-output analysis. A major difficulty stems from disparity between the 'pure' branches which it depicts and those of real life and, thus, of the plan. Another difficulty—and a familiar one—concerns the triple aggregation: over time, organisational units and commodities. Those concerned with the Soviet implementation of the model appear to veer between what is conventionally termed the economic and the mathematical approaches to this issue.[2] Of the later school Yamada's ideas[3] seem to influence thinking: patently the most dependable among his aggregation criteria would be his coefficient of 'invariability of repercussions'; no less obviously this is, at present, too exacting for the planning practice. The weaker one—of stability of input coefficients, which relies on probability calculus—is taken to

[1] *Aspects de la Planification Indicative et de la Planification Imperative*, mimeo, CERMAP, Paris, 1964, a paper previously delivered at the seminar on 'Economic Problems of the Communist World' at the London School of Economics.

[2] Cf. Mathilda Holzman, 'Problems of Classification and Aggregation' in W. Leontief, *et al.*, *Studies in the Structure of the American Economy, op. cit.* See also E. Malinvaud, 'Aggregation Problems in Input-Output Models', T. Barna, ed., *The Structural Interdependence of the Economy*, 1954.

[3] Isamu Yamada, *Theory and Application of Inter-industry Analysis*, Tokyo, 1961.

stand the relatively best chance of implementation in planning. (Note that it is also in harmony with the Thilamus-Theil[1] suggestion of treating coefficients—for the purpose of indicative forecasting-planning —as probabilities).

It has been discovered in Soviet experiments that, as things are now, the inter-industry model is not really employable at the stage of the elaboration of the plan *in depth*. While at that stage the plan is built up on a branch-wise calculation of capacity availabilities, an inter-industry analysis relies on averaged input coefficients without reference to capabilities. That in fact tends to confine applicability of the Soviet inter-industry analysis primarily to the initial stage of plan-construction, that of fixing 'controlling indicators' (*kontrolnyie tsifry*). This again makes for similarity in the uses of the method under both normative and indicative planning.

It is believed now, in the light of experience, that the traditional material balance and input-output analysis should be treated as complementary rather than competitive planning instruments. This view is strengthened by advances in computation, which also help to improve the traditional material-balance technique.[2]

Be that as it may, Soviet experiments now in progress do suggest an improvement in the scope for choice, thanks to the advance both in input-output methodology and in computation techniques. Suffice it to say that the 1970 matrices (see above, p. 260) have been compiled without precedent, in 20 variants differing in volume and structure of final product.

The French practice also subscribing to the multivariant approach has followed, from a rather early stage of its development, what would be the classical procedures in using Leontief-type matrices for planning. It consists broadly in calculating first the final demand bill from an initial approximation of gross national product and its components, and then multiplying the vector of final demand by the inverted technological matrix (account taken of foreign trade) and trying to reach consistency in an iterative way.[3]

---

[1] C. B. Thilamus, H. Theil, 'The information approach to the Evaluation of Input-Output Forecast', *Econometrica*, October 1965. An interesting Czechoslovak model of aggregation relies on the 'measure of information content' (cf. I. Skolka, in A. N. Efimov, *Problemy Optimalnogo Planirovanya*, 1966).

[2] S. S. Ahluwalia, 'Ensuring the Internal Consistency of the Plan', in *Essays on Planning and Economic Development*, Warsaw, 1965.

[3] See also Note on p. 290.

15

The trend in Soviet thinking, away from the traditional 'resource' planning towards 'demand' planning, has already been pointed out.[1] Indeed what is known at the time of writing about the course of present experiments would suggest that a similar road is being embarked upon. In the sequence followed by Gosplan's research institute too, first the volume and structure of national income and then of the final bill of goods (70 per cent of which consists of personal and social consumption) are computed. Next a set of hypotheses with regard to the latter's volume and branch-structure of its main elements is examined, with reference to the matrix variants. Conceptually, the route adopted in perspective planning would be then broadly this:

(1) Determine yearly volumes and structure of consumption plus investment in the non-productive sphere, exports and imports.

(2) Determine (with reference to gestation lags) volumes of capital formation for postulated growth beyond the plan horizon.

(3) Solve a system of difference-differential equations in order to determine year to year targets for outputs and investment over the plan period.

The potentialities of the system in pursuance of objectives are then determined by initial investment-sector capacity and labour-flow.[2]

In a simpler Gosplan model capital formation and output are planned year by year, allowance made for targets beyond the year. It rests on averaged yearly capital coefficients and lags.

This is in substance then, the dynamic inter-industry analysis

---

[1] It appears that by now a final-product index has been brought into the *ex post* 'balance of national economy'. Note, however, in this context, the snag discovered in *ex ante* calculation for the plan drafts. The point is that while the final-product volume can be derived from the calculation of national-income uses, determining its branch structure comes up against serious difficulties: plan indicators do not correspond to those of the final product (national-income uses are determined by their broad directions and highly aggregated component groups). Cf. V. A. Volchkov,'Mezhotraslevoy balans i narodnokhoziaystvennyi plan', *Ekonomika i Matematicheskiye Metody*, no. 3, 1966, p. 432.

[2] Cf. A. N. Efimov, in *Metody Planirovanya Mezhotraslevykh Proportsiy, op. cit.* Model of lags in investment planning can be found in Eva Mueller's contribution to *Problemy Optimalnogo Planirovanya* (framework borrowed from R. G. D. Allen). See also her paper on capital-formation balance, *Wirtschaftswissenschaft*, no. 3, 1965.

approach. To begin with, the planning practice has become confronted with the task of building up adequate *ex-post* time series of final product for modelling, over time, the nexus between the product and labour resources, investment and capacities.[1] (Again, informationally Soviet practice has had to rely on sampling: as to valuation over time, the Laspèyres index form has been employed.) The next stage has been the attempts of hyper-aggregated *ex ante* dynamic 'modelling' of the system (see the following chapter).

As has been rightly noticed, bringing in time dimension 'unlocks' the inter-industry model: in a dynamic Leontief system choice must be made at each plan-interval.[2] In this sense the planner's efficiency problem has become formalised.

16

It has been persuasively argued (Porwit), looking back over the forty years of Soviet planning, that the Russians were, and in fact had to be, concerned in their post-take-off phase with a very broadly conceived consistency problem. In fact in an environment with acute bottlenecks and very limited information, in particular—technological information, the problem of efficiency presents itself in any case in a circumscribed form. In a rigorous argument of striking incisiveness Montias shows that[3]:

(1) If the technology matrix contains no joint products, and is indecomposable, then if the entire supply of at least one exogenously given factor of production, some positive amount of which is needed to make every producible good, is used up; then the plan is efficient.

(2) If the technology matrix contains no joint products, but is decomposable (as will generally be the case in planning practice), the requirements for efficiency must be framed in terms of the indecom-

---

[1] V. S. Nemchinov (*Ekonomiko-Matematicheskiye Modeli*, Moscow, 1962, p. 380) argues that dynamising the inter-industry plan-model calls for bringing in the following vectors: average yearly manpower, capital resources, capacities (=maximum output under given conditions), investment and incremental capacities, all branch-wise.

[2] R. Dorfman, P. A. Samuelson, R. M. Solow, *Linear Programming and Economic Analysis*, pp. 265 ff.

[3] J. M. Montias, 'On the Consistency and Efficiency of Central Plans', *Review of Economic Studies*, October 1962, pp. 287–90; J. M. Montias, 'Central Planning in Poland', appendix A.

posable sub-matrices. The plan will be efficient if at least one exogenous factor (e.g. one type of capacity) is fully utilised in making one or more products from each indecomposable sub-matrix.

(3) If there are joint products, but there are no alternative techniques of production, the (1) and (2) remain valid.

(4) If there are both joint products and alternative techniques of production, a plan which simply uses up all available factor supplies may still be inefficient.

In the process of the change of the environment, conditions of what we may denote for short as the Montias Paradox (on a higher degree of efficiency owed to bottlenecks and limitations of technological alternatives) have been relaxed. Soviet planning thought has gradually moved to the problem of partial efficiency, specifically to the partial efficiency of investment, and has now arrived at the problem of the overall efficient equilibrium: it is increasingly conscious of the problem's significance.

17

Although this field is rather new to Soviet economics, the scope and elan of the theoretical and empirical effort, made in the last few years, to use formal choice-selection methods is remarkable. It extends to combinations of linear and dynamic programming, practicable integer and non-linear programming, and asymptotic analysis of dynamic programmes[1]. Ways of maximising concave multi-variable functions within convex regions of constraints are being investigated. Dynamic feed-back systems subject to stochastic processes, and their stability conditions, are being explored (by means of the Monte-Carlo method). Algorithms of a generalised optimisation problem for an inter-flow system are being elaborated (of obvious interest inasmuch as

---

[1] Of the by now vast Soviet writing on non-linear programming I would mention in particular a contribution by S. I. Zukhovitskiy, L. Ya. Leifman, offering an algorithm for quadratic programme with Jordan-type elimination, in L. V. Kantorovich, *Matematicheskiye Modeli, op. cit.*; also a contribution relating non-linear programming to control systems by E. I. Filipovich, *ibid.* Of contributions on integer programming—those by Yu. I. Volkov, V. I. Khokhluk, R. A. Polyak, *ibid.*, by G. I. Mischchenko in *Matematiko-Ekonomicheskiye Problemy, op. cit.*, by R. A. Sarchemelyan in *Ekonomika i Matematicheskiye Metody*, no. 5, 1965 and B. V. Finkelshtein (Boolean variables), *ibid.* On accelerated convergence of Brown's solution for matrix games by V. V. Amvrosyenko, *ibid.*, no. 4, 1965.

concrete definition of the objective function for a centrally planned economy is the awkward hurdle). Short-circuiting procedures for re-planning with changed objectives, through adequate approximations, are being devised.

In spite of this impressive effort—likely to bear important fruit in the future—immediate practical help from programming in the Soviet economy is still circumscribed.[1]

18

The French planners too are assimilating the fundamentals of the programming approach in their method of thinking out the overall strategy of the plans. In fact they are making formal attempts to programme their global 'esquisses'—i.e. to optimise each of them 'technically' for a given combination of 'political' variables (see above, p. 249).

At present the CERMAP macro-construct used for this purpose is a model of four sectors only—agriculture, capital goods, consumer goods and transport and other services. Its system of equations relates equilibrium of flows of goods and services, of productive capacities, labour productivities, shifts in manpower and *marginal* variations of foreign trade, all relationships being approximated by linearised func-tions. The maximand[2] is the household's consumption, or to be more

---

[1] The reader will find a valuable survey of the development of mathematical metho-dology in Academician N. P. Fedorenko's paper 'Développement des Methodes Economico-Mathématiques en URSS', presented at the ES/TIMS Warsaw 1966 conference.

[2] In the latest, the 1965 version of the CERMAP model the maximand has been formalised as

$$Z = \max \left[(1+\alpha)t_1 + t_2 + \sum_i \mu_i(\alpha)f_i + \sum_i \mu_i^*(\alpha)f_i^* \right]$$

The symbols denote: α = the rate of discount (actualisation); $\mu_i(\alpha)$, and $\mu_i^*(\alpha)$ are the residual (recuperation) values of capacities, f_i, f_i^* in the i-th branch.

Here the $(1+\alpha)$ is the price the planner attaches, at the beginning of the plan, to a unit consumption basket, t, for the first sub-period and 1 = the price of the basket in the second sub-period, whatever the price relations: the $\mu_i(\alpha)$ and $\mu_i^*(\alpha)$ measure values attached to unit capacities, f_i, f_i^* at the end of the second sub-period.

The star denotes 'modern technology': in each period there are two technologies determined by technical parameters (capital, labour current input-coefficients). In the first sub-period in addition to what is termed the 'average technique', there is an 'over-strain technique' limited only by labour availabilities. In the second sub-period, in addition to the average technique there is a 'modern' one, more capitalist and efficient, embodied in investment carried out in the first sub-period.

In so far as the objective function embraces residual capacities as well as household consumption it is not treated as a utility function; however with regard to inter-temporal preferences it is seen as equivalent to inter-temporal social utility function.

precise, the plan's time-horizon is broken down into two sub-periods, and the postulated minimum consumption—of a given structure— is programmed to be achieved during the second of the two, compatible with the required productive-capital formation. The link between the two is formed by flows of investment over the first sub-period which, with the concomitant deployment of labour over both sub-periods, builds up capacities during the second sub-period to the level sufficient for the achievement of the goals; it is then for that sub-period that alternative technologies, the 'classical' and the 'modern', are considered.[1] It is encouraging for the authors of this ingenious model

The formalised model is postulated to fit in with a 'discretionary outline' (*l'esquisse discrétionnaire*); the latter was formed by an inter-industry matrix with a branch-wise break-down of the final bill of goods into consumption and investment. It is from this outline that the coefficients of the technique termed 'average' were obtained (those for the over-strain and the modern techniques were yielded by estimates and duality analysis).

In so far as residual values of capacities the μ's, are non-linear functions of the *alpha*, the objective function too is non-linear; it is taken to be concave (see also footnote below). Cf. Centre de Recherches Mathematiques pour la Planification, *Application d'un Modèle d'Allocation des Ressources à la Planification Française*, presented by A. Moustacchi, elaborated by M. Desport and associates, for the Rome 1965 Congress of the Econometric Society.

I gratefully acknowledge my debt to Professor Nataf for letting me have the prepublication exposition of the model. Regrettably it reached me too late to permit giving in the present Notes full justice to the important new model version.

[1] The system of constraints in the 1965 version of the CERMAP model is formed of three sets of inequalities:

(1) Resources $\geqslant$ use in each of the two sub-periods. In the first sub-period output from the 'average' technique and that of the 'over-strain', x_i and y_i respectively, must at least equal total use which is composed of:

$\sum_j a_{ij}x_j + \sum_j a_{ij}y_j$ —intermediate inputs (a's are current input-output coefficients);

$\sum_j b_{ij}f_j + \sum_j b_{ij}^*f_j^*$ —investment for the average and the 'modern' techniques of the second period (b's are capital coefficients);

$\gamma_i t_i$ —increment in household consumption with fixed structure ($\sum\gamma_i = 1$);

d_i —government consumption, foreign trade balance, posited minimum of household consumption, all exogenously given.

This constraint is analogous for the second sub-period: output from the 'average' and the 'modern' techniques should at least equal the uses: the latter now includes the exogenously given investment which is to mature beyond the plan period.

(2) Outputs $\leqslant$ capacities. In the first sub-period output from the 'average' techniques cannot exceed capacities installed which are exogenously given: the technique of over-strain is, by definition, constrained only in respect of labour availability. In the second sub-period output from the average techniques is limited by capacities given,

that, hyper-aggregated and simplified as it is, it appears to have with-stood the test of realism, at least as a tool for probing into courses of policies open to the planner.

For strategic choice-making, the Soviet planners, too, have con-structed a (16 sector) programming model for the period 1965–70: it may prove a milestone in the history of normative planning (see p. 291).

19

Manpower balance is one of the main pivots equally of the French and of the Soviet plan. It forms the key element of the 'physical' equilibrium, and through reward to labour provides, at least concep-tually, the principal linkage between the 'real' and the 'money' sides of the system (see below, p. 278). The problems facing both the 'indica-tive' and the 'normative' planners are the more similar since in the Soviet-type economy labour supply and demand operate in a rela-tively free market (much as differ certain institutional arrangements, especially the systems of training and recruitment, and the mechanism of wage fixing). The starting-point in both kinds of planning is some demographic projection over the plan horizon of a more or less traditional type. Then demand and supply is worked out by project-ing the labour force and its structure, and setting against it the required labour inputs, both broken down industrially and territorially.

In Soviet practice the projected supply-demand equilibrium for manpower takes the form of one of the material balances. (For the first time the Soviet central statistical administration has now pro-duced a matrix of full labour input coefficients (see above, p. 106). Inevitably this matrix shares the general deficiencies of the input-output method, but it is likely to develop as at least an auxiliary check on the empirical productivity standards employed in planning prac-tice.) The French devices are very similar. Both the French and the

---

$C_i^2 = C_i^1 (1 - \delta)(1 + \beta_1)$ plus capacities f_i installed in the first sub-period; the two coefficients δ and β denote respectively the rates of depreciation and of autonomous technical progress. A specific constraint limits the output under 'modern' technique by the value for f_i^*, i.e. 'modern' capacity produced during the first sub-period.

(3) Labour required for output under given techniques $\leqslant$ total labour availabilities.

The system of the primal constraints has its counterparts in the dual: for constraint (1) the dual is the equilibrium price of the i-th commodity for each of the sub-periods; for (2) it is the rent charges on capacities employed; for (3) it is sectoral wage rates for each sub-period. For techniques employed in the same sub-period rate of return over cost = rate of discount (α).

Soviet planner base themselves in their projection of labour-input coefficients over the plan horizon on a prognosis of the evolution of labour productivity.

20

9. Relative factor intensities of productive processes can be determined, conceptually, by reference to the industries' technical possibilities. With given data on factor elasticities of output, on the supply of labour, capital stock in existence and capital formation, investment allocation could be patterned by the planner so as to yield postulated outputs. As noted, Soviet planning thought has familiarised itself over the last decade or so with this approach. French and Soviet planning thought meet here too, however, in attempts at expressing plan-balances of the economy in terms of inputs of labour/hours.

Indeed it is arguable that such a tableau would help towards a comparatively better insight into the French rather than the Soviet environment. In fact the CERMAP strategy model[1] correlates directly the planned increment in the optimality criterion, the households' consumption, to labour supply; for the assumed case of 'saturation' of the manpower constraint this increment has been arrived at as a certain

$$ Y = \frac{1}{\alpha_i} \cdot (\theta . B_i - K_i + D_i) $$

where,

α_i is the i-th component commodity of the consumption increment,

θ is the length of the working year,

B is a certain constant,

K_i is minimum of final consumption,

D is describing allocational adjustments of manpower.

[1] Centre de Recherches Mathématiques pour la Planification Française, *Resultats Actuels d'un Modèle d'Etude de Variantes*, March 1963, p. 21.
Of considerable technical interest is the *parametrage* carried out—numerically—with the use of the CERMAP models for investigating the effects on the system of shortening the working day. The mechanism of substitution followed is one by which as the working day shrinks the system tries to make up for it by a shift towards modern technology. The ultimate impact on consumption of households has been tested.
Cf. also A. Moustacchi's interesting paper on 'The interpretation of shadow prices in a parametric linear economic programme', in P. E. Hart and others, eds., *Econometric Analysis for National Economic Planning*. The author indicates that the model proved adequate in practical terms to obtain—in *parametric* studies—results regarding the physical organisation of production.

With $(\theta.B_i - K_i)$ assumed to fall as a function of a decreasing θ, it is the variable D_i that remains the principal policy-instrument.

The handling of the problem of relative factor-intensities based on some not over-complicated production function, say one of the familiar shape

$$x = (\mathbf{1} + \epsilon)^t e^\lambda c^\mu$$

where,

    x is output, e is labour and c is capital,

    λ and μ respectively are elasticities of output with respect to the two factors, and

    ϵ is the rate of residual increase in efficiency

is attractive to planners.[1] It may be adequate for analysis where input can be taken to be confined to two prime factors, and its substance underlies both Soviet and French broad estimates.

21

The first full-order *ex ante* capital coefficients (average and marginal) are now being computed in the Soviet Union through inversion of matrices relating capital stock and outputs.[2,3] Their inadequacy for detailed planning work is being pointed out by students. One of their

---

[1] See on this in particular the report of the 'Luxembourg group', 'Methodes de Prevision du Development Economique', in *Information Statistiques*, 1960, no. 6, Office Statistique des Communautés Européenes. See also Paelinck and Waelbroeck, *op. cit.*

[2] M. R. Eidelman (*Mezhotraslevoy Balans Obshchestvennogo Produkta*, Moscow, 1966) indicates the path of pre-multiplication of the full-order input-output matrix by the vector of direct capital coefficients:

$$B_c = K_c(I-A)^{-1} = K_c B$$

where K_c denotes the vector of first-order capital coefficients, and B the matrix of full-order current material input-output coefficients.

It would seem that *ex-ante* coefficients are being obtained from extrapolation of *ex-post* series.

Dr Eidelman has designed a schema of an *ex-post* dynamic inter-industry matrix of the economy. Columns and rows of its first and second quadrants give the intermediate and final products—by branches and plan-years. The third quadrant includes vectors of labour inputs, availabilities of fixed-capital stock (yearly average) and productive capital formation, also by branches and plan-years. Capital accumulation is summarised as some vector

$$a = (K_{\Delta f} + K_{\Delta c}).\Delta X + \bar{a}$$

where K_f and K_c are matrices, respectively of incremental fixed and circulating capital

shortcomings is their failure to reflect the time structure of investment and to relate the latter to additions to the capital stock and
replacement for wear and tear.[1] In fact the problem of 'lagged' flows
confronts the planner as a circular one. Suppose that it has been
agreed to adopt as a point of departure for a plan the final bill of goods,
we move from the final bill of goods to global outputs; but at the same
time it is these outputs that contain all the various goods which
physically form investment in fixed and working capital, which is an
element of the final bill of goods. The way out of the circle is obvious—
in principle. It is to resort to dynamic matrices and solve the system
of difference or differential equations.

22

In practice French and Soviet planners have recourse to various
simplifying shortcuts and routine rules of thumb. Thus the French
practice bases itself on an empirically noted rough constancy of the
shares taken by the two principal investment industries, engineering
and construction, in global gross fixed capital formation. That ratio is
therefore used as a rough allocational guidance[2] (with the global
marginal gross capital coefficient only very approximately computed[3]).

What has been said here so far concerns productive capital formation. Non-productive investment is considered in both French and

coefficients, ΔX is the vector of increase in output, and $\bar{a}$ is the vector of non-productive
accumulation.

[3] The first *ex-post* tables of 'capital-intensity' of production have been published in
Vestnik Statistiki, no. 9, 1966. They were calculated for 130 capital-goods producing
branches, aggregated in the published version to 21 branches, and for 84 user-branches.
The coefficient of 'capital intensity' is defined so as to measure requirements in capital
stock of the given kind per unit of output. Full-order coefficients are obtained by means
of multiplying the matrix of direct 'capital-intensity' coefficients by the matrix of full-
order current inputs per unit of final product.

[1] See on this and related matters Ya. Kvasha and V. Krassovskiy, *Voprosy Ekonomiki*,
1963, no. 7.

[2] J. Benard, *op. cit.*, p. 98.

[3] In the preparation of the Belgian 1962–65 plan marginal capital coefficients were
calculated with the assumption that value added by additional labour units equals the
branch average. Cf. Paelinck and Waelbroeck, *op. cit.* Although obviously rough, these
coefficients proved to be adequate in most cases: only in some cases, i.e. where the
period of capacity maturation is particularly long, was it found necessary to modify
results obtained by use of these coefficients to take account of the timing of investment
envisaged by industries (private communication from Professor Waelbroeck).

Soviet practice as an endogenous variable: in French practice it is in fact, and with good logic, taken as a component of final consumption.

When factor relations and patterning of investment are under discussion one has to bear in mind certain strategic 'biases'. Actual choices of technology in the USSR have been avowedly influenced by a bias in favour of capital intensity, taken to be the carrier of technological advance, and the inter-connected strategy of the 'leading links' in the development of the economy (see above, ch. 13). In differing social-economic environments the problem of desired levels of employment faces the French and Soviet planners in a different way. It is probably safe to say that in France, too, a certain (spontaneous) preference for capital intensity is at work in industrial choice-making. As to the Soviet 'leading links' principle, it is closely paralleled by the French planner's conception of 'leading industries': in fact, the composition of the French priority group—power generation, oil production and refining, chemicals and engineering[1]—is signally close to that in the Soviet industrializaton era.

23

In formulating the investment programme the Soviet planner will normally refer himself to a set of key projects of crucial importance to the national economy. In fact this is also true, though to a lesser degree, of the French planner.

In so far as inter-project choices have to be made, they have to be, and are, largely based on technical criteria. Of necessity this is the field where money-term calculus has to play a major, even if not decisive, role. For this purpose Soviet practice has developed a technique of commeasuring and ordering alternatives with equivalent outputs but different capital outlays and operating costs over the projects' life span.[2]

The complex problem of choice-making by the investor in a private-enterprise market economy will not detain us here. We will note, however, that at least in regard to some categories of investment the French public project-maker does employ tools similar to those in use in the USSR. The actualisation rate is as a rule identical with the rate

---

[1] J. Benard, op. cit., p. 97.
[2] See Chapter 13 above.

which sets the general 'threshold of profitability' for investment embraced by planning programmes[1]: it broadly equals the interest-rate on public loans. In the CERMAP models of macro-planning, too, normative profitability is taken as equal to the over-all single discount (α).[2] Current (average) and advanced ('modern') technologies are commeasured by setting against each other the differences (in current prices) in the initial investment cost and intermediate inputs—both discounted with the use of this *alpha* ('recuperation' values of capital stock beyond the plan-horizon are taken as a function of *alpha* and capital coefficients).[3]

Affinities of the French and Soviet investment-efficiency and re-coupment calculation are apparent. Precarious as the ground may be in these calculations, the French planner, unlike his Soviet opposite number, may at least get a cue for his *alpha* from the market.[4]

24

For decades 'socialism in one country' had as its corollary

---

[1] See UN, ECE, *Economic Methods and Criteria in the Selection of Investments in the Electric Power Industry*, Geneva, 1963.

[2]

Difference in cost of investment in current prices	$\left[\pi_i^* \sum_j b_{ji}^* p_j^1 - \pi_i \sum b_{ji} p_j^1\right].(1+\alpha)$
=	=
Difference in inter-mediate inputs in current prices	$\sum_{t=0}^{n-1} 1/(1+\alpha)^t[\pi_i^*(u_j^2 - \sum \alpha_{ji}^* u_j^2) - \pi_i(u_j^2 - \sum \alpha_{ji} u_j^2)]$

Cf. *Application d'un Modèle d'Allocation des Ressources á la Planification Française*, 1965, *op. cit.*, p. 16.

Here the price of the first plan sub-period, u_j^1 is 'disactualised' as $p_j^1 = u_j^1/(1+\alpha)$. For the rest of notation see footnotes on pp. 268 and 269.

[3] In an alternative formulation the dual variable associated with a capacity constraint measures the value increment of the objective function due to a marginal increment in productive capacity: the employment value of the marginal unit of capacity.

The recuperation value for the i-th branch is then the sum of future rents, i.e. rents beyond the two sub-periods of the plan, $\mu_i = r_i^3 + r_i^4 + \cdots$.

Assuming price constancy we have the actualised $r_i^n = r_i^2 . 1/(1+\alpha)^{n-2}$.

[4] In the CERMAP plan exercise, the α was given the value of 8 per cent (cf. fn. on the objective function of the 1965 model, on p. 268). This value appears to not have secured, however, the postulated agreement with the *esquisse discretionnaire* (owing to the level of technology assumed for agriculture and transport). In an iterative procedure (in which the concave objective function was approximated by linear segments) convergence was reached for a value in the neighbourhood of 14 per cent.

what was a seminar case of planning for a nearly-closed system. Neither any longer corresponds to reality. Even now, with the high degree of self-sufficiency of the USSR in raw materials and due to her policy also in consumer goods, the problem of foreign commerce appears to the Soviet planner mainly as that of import-investment substitution. This is in practice weighed up by various considerations only partly quantified or indeed, quantifiable. Exports are, basically, planned at the level required to pay for the necessary imports: comparative advantage is assessed by means of a coefficient of foreign trade efficiency.[1] In physical terms foreign trade enters both sides of the material balance for each commodity, and in addition the foreign trade components of the material balances are assembled in separate balances of external relations, in both physical and foreign exchange terms.

The French treatment of foreign trade is, technically, not dissimilar.[2] (The CERMAP strategic model considers foreign trade as an exogenous variable; only marginal oscillations are permitted around the level assumed by the central 'esquisse' and only on the assumption that they would leave the balance of trade unaffected.) Broadly speaking, import requirements in raw and semi-finished materials, and complementary imports in general, are derived from global estimates of outputs (by means of a set of 'balances matières'). Estimates of imports of finished goods, and competitive imports in general, are obtained from calculations of the import-intensity of final demand. Like his French opposite number, the Soviet planner tries to harmonise foreign trade flows by grand geographic and currency zones, and then to balance out trade with the rest of the world.

Foreign trade is to every planner the sphere of relatively the greatest uncertainty whether his planning is normative or not. Planning foreign trade is inevitably based on more or less shaky forecasts. The Soviet planner owes very probably his relatively greater degree of safety to the marginal role of trade in the economy, to the largely bilateral, barter type of Soviet foreign trade, and to the fact that as much as two-thirds of it is based on long-term delivery arrangements

---

[1] See p. 203 above.
[2] See Hackert and Hackert, *op. cit.*, pp. 126 ff.; and Commissariat Général du Plan, *Réponse à un Questionnaire des Nations Unis sur la Planification et le Développement de l'industrie*, Paris, April 1963, p. 41.

with other planned economies, as much as to the normative nature of Soviet planning.

25

The translation of the 'physical' into a financial equilibrium is a formidable task under any kind of planning. Patently, the safe-guarding of financial discipline is of far greater importance in a market than a non-market economy. The interaction of physical and financial flows is more complex, and less predictable, in a private-enterprise market system than in a Soviet-type command system, if only because in the latter behaviour relations are simpler to formulate, depending as they do, to a large extent, on the government's direct intervention.

Technically, in French planning the finance-balance equation is tackled by proceeding from grand macro-aggregates, those of enter-prises, households, public administration and external accounts, via individual production branches, towards specific 'circuits'.[1] The aim is to harmonise transaction circuits—finance of trade, wages, taxes, dividends, etc.—with those of goods and services, with assumed behaviour functions. With assumed entrepreneurial and households' propensities, undistributed profits and households' gross savings are estimated. Demand for savings implied in the postulated growth rates of the economy is assessed. Then the savings-investment balance is examined, account taken of the 'public hand's' activities and of the accepted hypothesis with regard to the balance of payments. Over-all equilibrium is sought by bringing in postulates of the State's budgetary policies, particularly with regard to public consumption and to financ-ing the economy. Then the grand streams are re-adjusted so as to reconcile specific types of saving with specific types of investment as derived from 'physical' equilibrium (i.e. the balance equations of capital formation). This involves projections of the accounts of the principal intermediaries between savers and investors—the treasury and the banking system.

At least conceptually, the Soviet approach to consolidation of the 'physical' and financial sides of the plan is not dissimilar to that of the French. It aims at an equilibrium through reconciliation of the income-expenditure balances of enterprises and households, the banks'

[1] *Réponse à un Questionnaire des Nations Unis sur la Planification et le Développement de l'industrie*, Paris, April 1963, p. 41.

monetary circulation and credit plans, and the State budget. The latter is in fact the principal vehicle in this process. Equalling about half the net national product, it has a correspondingly greater weight in plan-construction than the French. It channels the bulk of the finance of capital formation, as well as the current-account expenditures of public administration, and it finances the enterprises' operational deficits and absorbs their profits.

26

It is worth digressing to consider the relationship between the plan for final consumption and the financial plan. Household consumption is to the French planner an independent variable in a somewhat different sense than it is to his Soviet opposite number. Indeed, to the latter it is to a high degree a manœuvrable magnitude, a residuum of national product. Hence to the French planner precision of projections in this field is of fundamental importance. Not surprisingly, this is the field where French planning has resorted, from its early phase, to the relatively most sophisticated econometric tools. As we have noted, at the preliminary 'political' stage of the construction of the plan, growth of consumption is fixed in an over-all model. From this starting-point proceed projections of consumer demand for specific groups of goods, which rely on empirically established consumption functions, general and specific (for most commodities simple constant income elasticity is taken to correspond to reality; for some goods declining time or income elasticity or a simple chronological trend is assumed).[1] The Soviet planner has relied hitherto for consumption projections essentially on 'norms-per-capita' (termed 'scientific norms' and very closely akin to Houthakker's 'technology of consumption'), especially on nutritional standards. As for financial equilibrium, it is largely taken care of by indirect taxation. This is, in the hands of the planner, the effective 'insulator' of the two spheres—of production and consumption. (This does not mean that Soviet planning, unlike French planning, exhibits an ideal precision in this field. The recurring disequilibria and inflationary strains provide evidence to the contrary.) The evolution of the Soviet economic environment and new tendencies in planning (see above, p. 90) have drawn the planner's attention to the study of consumer's behaviour, until recently an

[1] J. Benard, *op. cit.*

almost virgin field. The Soviet planner is now drawing closer to French techniques both in empirical investigations and in 'modelling'. A complex model (constructed by Aganbegyan[1]) embodies demographic projections, formation of household incomes in money and kind, and correlated consumption. (The ultimate objective to which effort is now being directed is the construction of a 'differentiated balance sheet' of the population's income and consumption, devised to integrate a whole system of sub-models mirroring interdependencies of consumption with incomes and the process of their generation. Some of these partial models appear to be experimentally employed by the State Committee for Labour in tackling problems of wage structure and interconnected matters of manpower allocation.)

27

Soviet practice has evolved what is termed the 'balance sheet of the economy' *ex post* and *ex ante*. It is composed of a balance of gross material output, with supplementing balances of capital stock, of capital formation and of trade; a balance of national income with supplementing balances of social product and the population's incomes, and a manpower balance. A 'summary balance' is supposed to provide the synthesis. Planning doctrine stresses the inherent unity of the system. Conceptually, indeed, with a given set of prices, material balances link up with output plans in money terms, and thus with the transaction balance as mirrored in the financial plan. Moreover, the production side of the material balances is linked, via the wage bill, with the manpower balance. In turn wage-type incomes and money dividends of farm collectives' members, which determine the requirements for monetary circulation, are the core of householders' purchasing power originating in the financial plan and flowing back into it. Yet in actual fact, the 'balance sheet of the economy' in only a heterogeneous collection of 'balances' in various terms. Efimov has defined

---

[1] A. G. Aganbegyan, 'Ispolzovanye ekonomiko-matematicheskikh modeley i elektronnykh vychislitelnykh mashin dla perspetktivynykh rasschetov po zarabotnoy plate, dokhodam i potreblenyu trudyashchikhsya', in *Primenenye matematiki i elektronnoy i tekhniki, op. cit.* There is a reference to the model in V. S. Nemchinov, 'The Use of Statistical and Mathematical Methods in Soviet Planning', T. Barna, ed., in *Structural Interdependence and Economic Development*, London, 1963, p. 174.
Some problems of the consumption function in Soviet planning are discussed in V. V. Shvyrkov, *Zakonomernosti Potreblenya Promyshlennykh i Prodovolstvennykh Tovarov* Moscow, 1965.

it as 'an independent chapter of the plan (compiling) calculations of general economic proportions', isolated from the system of material balances.

The need for an over-all consolidation of accounts is now generally recognised in Soviet planning thought.[1] The primacy in Soviet planning of physical-term calculation, as opposed to value-term calculation, has reduced the harm of the divorce between the two faces of the plan. The growing complexity and diversification of the economy, however, now push Soviet planning thought towards a greater concern for, and reliance on, financial instruments. This adds urgency to the problem of harmonising and integrating the social accounts balances. Some Soviet students believe that the solution lies in building up the system of material balances in money as well as in quantity terms. Strumilin for one, proposes to integrate, in one matrix, income and product by sector origin and end uses. No technical solution has been found so far for this problem (see above p. 261). There is no strict tie-up between the inter-industry matrix of the economy and its financial plan. Hence there is no systematic way for determining, at the planning stage, the financial implications of changing the volume and/or the structure of the material product.[2]

28

The problem of balancing the system hinges on its price framework, on the pricing of factors, services and products. The Soviet pricing structure however, is not designed to serve this purpose, and indeed is peculiarly inadequate for it.[3] The French planner 'sponsors and supports efforts which are made to come closer to a policy of truth in prices'. '. . . one of the most constant activities of the General Planning Comissariat consists of opposing state intervention that distorts the normal price fixing mechanism without undue reason.'[4] The French planner however, unlike his Soviet counterpart, has the advantage while building his plan of reference to the market for his parameters. (Professor Perroux has remarked: 'le marche fonctionne d'autant mieux qu'il prend place dans les programmes mieux établis

[1] See M. Z. Bor, *op. cit.*, pp. 59 ff., 193 ff.; A. N. Efimov, *op. cit.*, p. 108.
[2] B. L. Isayev, *op. cit.*
[3] See chapter 6 above.
[4] P. Massé, *Econometrica*, April 1965.

et mieux surveillés'.[1] In a sense the reverse is also true.) The French planner too, however, works throughout with a system of constant prices,[2] and on this account his plans share the weakness of the Soviet plans.[3] The assumption of constancy is clearly a handicap because of the inter-dependence of technical and value coefficients. It abstracts from technical and economic evolution over the plan period, but changing the plan-framework would entail re-balancing the system. Attempts have been made in France, in a SEEF model, to bring in variable prices—a function of wage rates, investments (which are themselves a function of growth objectives) and entrepreneurial behaviour.[4] One will follow with considerable interest its empirical employment.[5] To be sure, conceptually the problem of relative prices

---

[1] Quoted in P. Massé, *Programmation formalisée et programmation discrétionnaire, op. cit.,* p. 7, fn.

[2] Clearly the system of national accounts for the target year requires a shift from constant prices to 'current' prices of that year.

[3] The complicating element in the CERMAP experiments with the 1965 model appears to be the assumption that shadow prices equal those of the discretionary outline. With $\sum \gamma_i = 1$ the dual price of the i-th commodity in the two sub-periods of the plan would be $u_i = (1 + \alpha)$ and $u_i^2 = 1$ respectively, where alpha is the discount rate adopted. The unit price of the dual would be such as to satisfy:

$$u_i - \sum_j a_{ji} u_j = r_i - w/\pi_i$$

where r_i denotes unit rent for use of equipment in producing the i-th commodity, w is the wage cost per man and π_i per-man output. The accounting price as employed in the discretionary outline would be such as to satisfy:

$$p_i - \sum_j a_{ji} p_j = \text{value added}$$

In so far as value added is formed basically of rent charges on capital and wages, the two unit prices should close to each other, assuming that those of the discretionary outline correspond to the optimum. Considering the arbitrariness of assumptions, it was inevitable that disparities between the two sets of prices should appear.

The authors of the model stress the contradiction inherent in the approach: its substance is that all the coefficients of the model are based on a calculation in terms of the accounting prices; the economy is 'modelled' as a perfectly competitive system with choices resting on shadow prices over a production set which is defined, however, with reference to the accounting prices. Cf. *Application d'un Modèle d'Allocation des Ressources à la Planification Française, op. cit.,* esp. p. 24.

[4] A. Nataf and P. Thionet, *Le modèle à moyen terme à prix variables,* Les Etudes de Comptabilité National, 1962, no. 3, Paris.

[5] In the Belgian experiment some re-adjustments were made in the system to allow for the effect of probable relative prices on substitution in certain fields. Thus, for energy this was done intuitively; for consumption, with the use of econometric techniques. The results were used to modify the coefficients of the constant price model (communication from Professor Waelbroeck).

for the target-plan years has been tackled by several students of both indicative and normative planning. The solution would be to evolve a system of shadow prices equalising marginal products of factors, with given constraints; but a practicable procedure is not yet at hand. (Incidentally the authors of the CERMAP programme argue persuasively that, for a variety of reasons, for a free-enterprise market system its dual variables cannot be interpreted as a realistic system of prices. One of the complications encountered is the regime of zero-profit which prevails under a linear programme. Although capital charges are imputed to the operational accounts, a 'physical' macro-model of the kind devised cannot allow for the firms' self-financing which involves commodity prices, and generally fails to reflect adequately phenomena of finance.)

29

There are some dissimilarities in the treatment of the time dimension in French and Soviet planning. French planning is focused on attaining policy objectives by target years rather than moving towards them. This mitigates for the planner difficulties posed, under the capitalist system, in particular by cyclical fluctuations. On the other hand, the very nature of administrative implementation of a Soviet-type plan requires greater specification in mapping out the route to be followed.

Where the Soviet and French treatment of time tends now to meet is in their adoption of very long-run horizons, as a broad frame within which long-run processes work themselves out, and their directions become better perceptible. While shorter-term plans are being fitted into the horizon, the longer-term ones are being currently re-adjusted in the light of current progress. This idea was evolved years ago in Poland and Yugoslavia by Lange and Horvat, but considered incompatible at that time with the 'law' of planned development of the economy.[1] Soviet disappointments with 'targeting' for distant hori-

---

[1] On 'cyclical echoes' in a socialist system, see O. Lange, *Teoria reprodukcji i akumulacji*, Warsaw, 1963, p. 120. In Lange they are generated by cumulated renovation of equipment; cf. also reference on p. 149 n.3. In his admirable study, 'Role of Econometrics in Socialist Economics' (*Problems of Economic Dynamics and Planning, op. cit.*) Professor L. R. Klein argues that there is considerable scope—in a socialist economy—for techniques dealing with the effect of propagated shocks, techniques employed in the business-cycle analysis.

zons, together with the empirically observed fact that rigidly fixed final-year targets tend to generate a kind of quasi-cycle, damping down and reviving the pulse of the economy, have prompted the change of attitude.[1]

It seems that the conception of continually 'rolling' horizons is receiving the attention of indicative planners.[2,3]

30

The time dimension is but one of the stochastic elements of the plan, no matter what its species. Here again, the theorist may tell the planner to try to determine the risks involved in the course of action considered, say by 'playing' a strategic game against his opponent—chance—and trying to find the saddle-point of its pay-off matrix. Whether by

[1] Cyclical fluctuations in the growth-rates of socialist economies are pointed out, in Josef Goldman's 'Fluctuations and Trend in Econmic Growth', *Economics of Planning*, no. 4, 1964. They are attributed to 'insufficient knowledge of the economic laws of socialism' and shortcomings in their application (p. 94).

[2] The theory of sliding plans is still in its infancy. One of the few important investigations is owed to J. Habr ('A Contribution to the Theory of Sliding Plans', in *Problems of Economic Dynamics and Planning*, Warsaw, 1964) and is based on the idea of alternative trajectories. The dominant trajectory within a considered spectrum is the 'planned trajectory'. The width of the spectrum is given by the deviations of boundary trajectories from the planned one: these represent lines along which the economy might develop should the conditions for planned development fail to materialise: the planned trajectory would be conceived as one corresponding to the *ex ante* optimisation and boundary trajectories as optimistic or pessimistic alternatives. The shifting of the plan from the initial to the next planning horizon is again carried out within a certain spectrum. The length (period) of the shift and the distance (interval) of the planning horizon will depend on such factors as production and investment cycles. When the shift period comes to its end—say at the end of the plan year—the planner finds a ready spectrum of trajectories to link up with the stage passed: and with the shift of the planning horizon the basic trajectories will be partitioned again. Cf. p. 178 above.

[3] I now understand that sliding horizons are built into one of the two multi-annual plan models which have been designed in Czechoslovakia and are to be experimented with numerically for the second half of the sixties. The model—the 'Bratislava Model' —is tightly aggregated, to 17×17 sectors; it is linear, quasi-dynamic with the households' income-utility a maximand (utility on J. Marschak's definition as a quantity whose mathematical expectation is maximised by a 'rational man'). The model is broken up into three parts: of these the first and the second reflect a one year's period each and each of them forms one 'shifting' block; the third part is composed of the five-years' plan, forming one block, and the 'starting period'. The side constraints of the starting period are the basis of the subsequent five years' plan; this is the apparatus of 'continuous planning' with the shifting horizon. (Cf. A. Lasciak. J. Rendek, J. Danco, *Czechoslovak Multistage Long-Term Planning Models in Centralised and Decentralised Management*, submitted to the ES/TIMS Warsaw 1966 conference.)

rigorous techniques or intuitive judgement, the planner, 'imperative' and 'indicative' alike, has to assess the probability of his expectations. He has also to insure himself one way or another against adverse chance. One can in fact detect in contemporary Soviet planning something akin to the French idea of 'polyvalence', of building into the plan the possibility of re-adjustment of ends and means, particularly as random variables harden into fixed data and constants.[1] As incisively noted by the Luxembourg team, playing safe, securing a greater amount of manœuvre, will usually exact its price in terms of growth rates, whatever the kind of planning.[2,3,4,5]

[1] See P. Massé, *Réponse aux Interventions*, at the Vienna 1962 Congress of the International Economic Association, mimeo.

[2] See *Méthodes de Prévision du Développement Economique, op. cit.*

[3] The general problem of an optimal plan-prognosis for the point-of-departure stage of macro-planning is broadly stated by A. D. Smirnov (in 'K probleme optimalnogo ekonomicheskogo prognozirovanya', *Ekonomika i Matematicheskiye Metody*, no. 5, 1966) in this way. Future values ξ_{t+L} of the known past process ξ_t are determinable with a non-zero autocorrelation betwen the values of ξ_{t+L} and ξ_t for $t-i \leqslant t$; this is analytically solvable where the random process is stationary or reducible to stationarity, the criterion of error is mean-square and the forecasting operator is linear. Under stationarity, for the first two moments of ξ_t the following would be satisfied

$$m_\xi(t) = M[\xi_t] = m = \text{const.}$$
$$D_\xi(t) = M[\xi_t]^2 = d = \text{const.}$$
$$B_\xi(t, t+\tau) = M[\xi_t \xi_{t+\tau}] = B(\tau)$$

where M denotes mathematical expectation, $D(t)$ dispersion, $B(t)$ the autocorrelation function. The values of the ξ_t are centred. The $B_\xi(t)$ is supposed to be empirically determinable for a practicable prediction from

$$B_\xi(t) = 1/N \cdot \sum_{t=1}^{N} \xi_t \xi_{t+1} \quad (\tau = 0, 1, 2, \ldots, N-1)$$

Preferably in practice a normalised autocorrelation function would be employed, determined as $\rho_\xi(\tau) = B_\xi(t)/B_\xi(0)$, $(\geqslant 0; \leqslant 1)$. Some weights a_i are accorded to past values of the process observed ξ_{t-i}. For a normalised system, for the vector of weight-coefficients of observations included into the forecast, we obtain a vector-matrix equation

$$R(\tau)\bar{a} = \bar{\rho}(\tau+L); \quad \tau = 0, 1, 2, \ldots, n-1$$

which has a unique solution. The article has an indication on experiments in forecasting tendencies of change in basic parameters of Soviet economy, carried out by G. Brown's method of smoothing the time-series.

[4] An embryonic outline of a stochastic plan-problem, in Soviet literature, will be found in Kantorovich-Makarov, *op. cit.*, p. 57: What is sought is output volumes, in m points, with known production functions $F_i(x)$, $G_i(x)$ $(i = 1, \ldots, m)$ current inputs and investment with output volume x; also, present consumption and its prognosis in n other points in the form of distribution laws $P(x)$ (probability that consumption does not exceed x). The problem is to determine investment for the build-up of capacities such that mathematical expectation of total discounted cost of production, transport and loss entailed in failure to meet requirements, is minimised.

[5] For an excellent discussion of the 'passive' and 'active' approaches to stochastic

We have noted in various contexts the considerable effort both in the USSR and France that is put into the formalisation of planning. It is worth noting that there is a striking similarity in the dialogues on this subject in both countries.[1] True, their points of departure were different. In the USSR, the country of the original conceptual development of some of the most important 'planometric' tools, their practical employment came up against certain doctrinal hurdles as well as technical limitations. The dose of scepticism of the French 'projectionistes' had a more empirical character. By now however, arguments put forward in the dialogues for and against the wider use of 'formalised' techniques meet on the same plane.

From the point of view of both the indicative and the normative planner, the basic argument *against* formalisation is that it tends to create an illusion of dependability. Furthermore, the required informational basis is not sufficient as yet, nor likely to be sufficient in the near future, to feed it, either in French-type or Soviet-type economies.[2] Moreover, formal statement and quantification of some elements of a plan, such as social-psychological constraints, is hardly possible; and more generally, the formal handling of economic life exceeds, at least at the present stage, the planner's econometric and computational resources. In addition, the conventional moulding of technical and behavioural relationships to fit these resources undermines their realism—this is particularly true of such usual simplifying assumptions as homogeneity and linearity of functions to be tackled. Moreover, whichever way the planner projects the parameters of his calculus into

plan-programming see G. Tintner, J. K. Sengupta, 'Stochastic Linear Programming and its Application to Economic Planning' in *On Political Economy and Econometrics, op. cit.,* pp. 601 ff.

[1] The literature of the dialogue is by now too vast to be listed here. For Soviet voices the reader may be referred to sources quoted in my 'New winds in Soviet planning', *Soviet Studies,* July 1960.

The French sources quoted here in various contexts reflect the dialogue. No list would be complete without two more important contributions, which I wish to acknowledge. One is by P. Massé, *Suggestions Préliminaires pour un Essai de Programmation Mathématique,* Paris, October 1962, mimeo. The other is by F. Perroux, *Le IV-e Plan Française,* Paris, 1962. Professor Perroux's work—with P. Massé's introduction—is also important for its treatment of general problems of the role of an indicative plan as an 'instrument of orientation' of the Western type of decentralised economy.

[2] On the inadequacy of the Soviet informational system see *inter alia* the contribution by L. Mints at the conference reported in *Voprosy Ekonomiki,* 1963, no. 1.

the future, their roots lie in the past, and therefore they impart a static 'bias' (see on this in particular p. 98, above); any formal dynamisation is inevitably arbitrary. Also, no rigorous treatment of the probabilistic aspects can adequately cope with uncertainties. Mathematical formulation of the planner's problems tends to give the system a specious appearance of exactness and dependability.

The case *for* formalisation rests basically on the argument that the mathematical idiom provides better safeguards for the systematic handling of economic processes than 'verbal' reasoning, that it requires a greater explicitness of adopted hypotheses, that it brings into the planner's work stricter checks on the logic of his procedures, and that it provides self-verification—an automatic scrutiny of coherence. In addition, the incidence of error is, to say the least, not increased by mathematical formulation, even if this formulation is drastically simplified (as opposed to receiving loose treatment), and indeed, it can be quantified. (Soviet mathematical economists, Kantorovich in particular, define the traditional methods of planning in the USSR as largely 'qualitative' rather than quantitative.) There is no reason why, to use Massé's expression, *peril des précisions illusoires* should be greater in formal than in non-formal planning. (Does not Soviet experience testify to this peril?) In addition to all these arguments is the scope for taking advantage of the fast progress in computational techniques and equipment.

This list of *pro*'s and *con*'s is far from exhaustive. But it does suggest that the dichotomy of planning into 'indicative' and 'imperative' is of limited significance for the conclusions which can be drawn for planning practice, even when allowance is made for the 'imperative' planner controlling a greater set of variables and parameters. This is also true of the dialogue on the advisability or otherwise of the use of any over-all 'complete' econometric model for planning purposes, as against the employment of instruments for handling elements of the plan.

The pragmatic answer to the problem faced is veering both in Western and in Eastern planning thought between an integrated decision model with automatic consistency checks, and a set of balances on various 'aspiration levels' (Frisch). On the whole the emphasis would be on 'planning by stages' (Tinbergen) rather than constructing complicated models to handle all the problems faced. In any case the pragmatic approach of the architects of the models used in both kinds of planning finds expression in a preference for the method of iterations, with the retracing of steps and revising of assumptions, time consuming and tedious as it may be, rather than the solution of simultaneous equations (an additional disadvantage of the former however, is the necessity of fixing some preliminary values of variables). This approach helps us to deal with the mathematically more complex relationships. It marks a rationalisation of, and an evolutionary advance from, the prevailing under-formalised practices relying on iterative procedures.

'French planning', Massé has written[1] 'has, up to the present, been of the discretionary type, whilst including certain formalised elements (the variable-price global model of Nataf and the sector-sequential model of the French National Electricity Authority).' Massé quotes with approval Bénard's analysis[2] of the reasons for choosing this type of procedure: 'Considerable uncertainty weighs upon a large number of relationships and parameters . . . and it seems preferable to proceed by iteration. In this way the projectionist is at all times in control of the computation process and can make corrections in mid-operation and when he receives better information . . . Economic stresses, inflationary and deflationary, and more especially political and social stresses, which may jeopardise growth, cannot always be expressed quantitatively. It is preferable to have a more flexible method of reasoning and computation than a system of equations and inequalities.'[3]

32

Having said this much one may perhaps risk a tentative thought that time seems to be on the side of the 'formalisers'. There is certainly a growing school in Soviet planning theory inclined to treat its problems in what is somewhat loosely termed the 'cybernetical' way. There is a new-found readiness to see the economy as a probabilistic 'machine' handling information, and to draw the consequences from

---

[1] P. Massé, 'The French Plan and Economic Theory', *Econometrica*, April 1965.

[2] In *Europe's Future in Figures*, R. C. Geary, ed., 1962, Amsterdam.

[3] In the present context the reader may be referred to a stimulating paper by Professor Herman Wold 'Toward a Verdict on Macro-economic Simultaneous Equations' (in *The Econometric Approach to Development Planning, op. cit.*, especially to the section on ends and means in the transition from deterministic to stochastic approaches (pp. 134 ff.).

the inexorable limitation of the planner's knowledge of both data and the causatory system. Symptomatically there is the planometrician's interest in what in substance is the 'black-box' approach (as adjusted by Beer for the purposes of economic analysis).[1] 'The feedback regulator', Academician Novozhilov postulates in his latest writings,[2] 'should take care of values of certain variables, such as for instance output volumes of each product or profitability of production, and so to operate on the system as to prevent undue deviation from their given, normative values'. Note then the interest in Phillips-type stabilisers;[3] and on the theoretical plane, in problems of informational stability of random processes.[4] The student will easily discover the parallel with elements of Stone's method in indicative planning.[5]

The ultimate aim of a school in Soviet planometrics is the build-up of something approaching homeostasis: to organise, that is, the economy in a way making use of its potentialities to 'tune' itself, to teach itself behaviour minimising the risk of error and the distance to optimality. (Note here again the impact of von Neumann, specifically of his general theory of automata.)

The conceptual scaffolding of the ideas of self-steering is borrowed by several students of planned economic systems from the theory of ergodic processes, processes that is which tend to grow independent of initial states, and 'ergodicity' is being given a meaning similar to that which it has in the theory of Markov chains (thus in Oskar Lange).[6,7,8]

---

[1] Stafford Beer, *Cybernetics and Management*, London, 1959.

[2] V. V. Novozhilov, 'Zakonomernosti Razvitya Sistemy Upravlenya Sotsyalisti-cheskim Khoziaystvom', *Ekonomika i Matematicheskiye Metody*, no. 5, 1965, p. 643. Note Beer's strong influence. Similarly E. Z. Mayminas, *ibid.* no. 2, 1966.

[3] A. W. Phillips, 'La Cybernétique et le Contrôle des Systèmes Economiques', in *Cahiers de l'Institut de Science Economique Appliquée*, series N, no. 2, Paris, 1958, also his 'Stabilization Policy in a Closed Economy', *Economic Journal*, June 1954 and 'Stabilization Policy and Time-Forms of Lagged Responses', *ibid.*, June 1957.

[4] Cf. M. S. Pinsker, *Informatsya i Informatsyonnaya Ustoichivost Sluchaynykh Velichin i Protsesov*, Moscow, 1960.

[5] R. Stone, *A Programme for Growth—The Model in its Environment*, Department of Applied Economics, University of Cambridge, July 1964.

[6] See O. Lange, *Wholes and Parts*, London, 1965, esp. pp. 58 ff.; this is an attempt to formalise the theory and also to interpret it in terms of dialectical materialism. See also his *Wstęp do Cybernetyki Ekonomicznej*, Warsaw, 1965.

[7] Cf. V. M. Glushkov, *Vvedenye v Kibernetiku*, Kiev, 1964.

[8] For a mathematically non-exacting exposition of the 'cybernetical' approach in the economics of normatively planned systems cf. O. Kyn and P. Pelikan, *Kibernetika v Ekonomii*, Prague, 1965 (especially ch. 6 on the cybernetical model).

The tendencies hinted at here have at this stage a primarily heuristic significance. But they do shape the attitudes; and they do influence the broad tracing of the development lines of the planning system which entail the build-up of an expanded and integrated set of models, couched essentially in a stochastic language, and of the information-feedback network (see in particular Chapter 7).[1] We referred ourselves in previous contexts to Soviet work in that field; our references do not even approach a complete list of fundamental contributions. Indeed, such a list would have to go back as far as the Markovian chains and up to Kolmogorov's world, to include in particular, say, the Kolmogorov-Uspenskiy schema of algorithms, and Tshebyshev's inequalities.

To sum up, this certainly is an area of East–West confluence of planning thought.

33

In conclusion one ought perhaps to express the hope that the many indications of convergence in planning techniques noted here do not over-state the case. A *caveat* may usefully be entered by emphasising the tentative and very preliminary nature of the present remarks, and by referring the reader again to their limitations, mentioned at the outset. Although they have not been written *à la thèse* they may help to redress the balance against too strong an emphasis so often placed on implications for techniques of differences in the roles which planning plays under different systems, and in so doing they may point to some areas of mutual cross-fertilisation.[2,3]

---

[1] For outlines of a 'cybernetical' development of the Soviet information and planning thought see in particular (a) N. P. Fedorenko, 'O Razrabotke Nauchnykh Metodov Upravlenya Narodnym Khoziaystvom', *Ekonomika i Matematicheskiye Metody* no. 3, 1965; (b) A. I. Berg, A. I. Kitov, A. A. Lyapunov, 'O Vozmozhonstyakh Avtomatizatsyi Upravlenya Narodnym Khoziaystvom', *Problemy Kibernetki* (issue no. 6); (c) V. S. Dadayan, 'Optimalnoye Rukovodstvo Narodnym Khoziaystvom i Zadachi Ekonomicheskoy Kibernetiki', *Vestnik Moskovskogo Universiteta*, no. 1, 1966. The latter offers a schema for a feedback system of planning and control.

[2] L. Gouni, *op. cit.*, writes:

'Planification française et planification soviétique s'efforcent de resoudre le difficile problème de la réalisation d'une économie meilleure dans un monde complexe où les problèmes humaines sont essentiels et difficiles à mesurer. Il n'y a, semble-t-il, pas lieu de les opposer dans les principes généraux; les différences résident, on l'a vu, davantage dans les pratiques; elles s'expliquent par l'écart des "âges" économiques et par la plus grands efficacité d'un systeme impératif dans une économie où les orientations sont encores guidées le développement de la production des activités de base. Aussi ne faudrait-il pas s'étonner qu'un jour ces différences se réduisent a des "nuances" . . .'

While I would be inclined to qualify some points of the reasoning, the reader will notice the degree of agreement in our final conclusion.

[3] The most recent tendencies in Soviet thinking seem to give new support to such expectations. It has been an established tenet of Soviet social-economic philosophy that planning as such is a category indentifiable only with socialism. The inclination to revise this tenet is discernible, for instance, in proposals put forward by Academician Trapeznikov which place emphasis on a guidance mechanism borrowed from indicative planning. Academician Nemchinov has spelt out the postulate of marrying the Soviet planning model—with its traditional centralism—with elements of the indirect and self-regulating guidance developed in French-type planning (*Voprosy Ekonomiki*, 1964, no. 7, p. 86).

NOTE TO SECTION 14

SOVIET planning doctrine has evolved a noteworthy model of 'economising planning'—optimised inter-industry balance—when in addition to limits on labour and capacities those on specified resources are considered (D. B. Yudin, E. G. Golshtein, 'Ob odnom metodie kolichestvennogo analiza uproshchennykh ekonomicheskikh modeley', in *Primenenye Matematiki v Ekonomicheskikh Issledovanyakh*, vol. 2, *op. cit.*, restated by E. V. Yershov in *Metody Planirovanya Mezhotraslevykh Proportsiy*, ch. III, p. 51 *op. cit.*). The problem is stated as finding non-negative vectors $X, Z^{(1)}, \ldots Z^{(2)}$, minimising

$$\sum_{j=1}^{n} c_j X_j + \sum_{j=1}^{n} \sum_{k=1}^{q} H_j^k Z_j^k$$

subject to

$$X_i - \sum_{j=1}^{n} a_{ij} X_j \geqslant Y_i + \sum_{j=1}^{n} \sum_{k=1}^{q} B_{ij}^k Z_j^k; \qquad \sum_{j=1}^{n} u_{sj} X_j \leqslant V_s$$

$$X_j \leqslant D_j^k + Z_j^k$$

Notation: s and k—limited resources, non-reproducible and reproducible respectively, within the plan period; u_{sj}—quantity of s required per unit of j; V_s—limit on s; D_j^k—limit on output volume of j entailed in the use of k; B_{ij}^k—quantity of i required per incremental unit of j, over the limit on k; c_j—inputs per unit of j with output volumes within limits on reproducible resources; H_j^k—incremental inputs per unit of j with output volumes exceeding limits on k.

The 'economising planning' model, while not a programming model *sensu stricto*, permits one to start from the vector Y, which may not include a substantial part of productive capital formation, and to build up an 'input-output balance' focused on specified resources limiting production. It is however, one will note, an essentially static model which does not explicitly allow for gestation lags of investment.

20 Techniques in Normative and Indicative Planning

IN THIS chapter I shall try to compare certain key elements in models designed for a Soviet-type normative plan on the one hand and those built up for an indicative plan of a private-enterprise market system on the other. The parallel has some obvious limitations, but it does bring out at least a few general indications of similarities in employable apparatus as well as differences imposed by environments and purposes, indications which may be of some interest to a student of the theory of model-building. The Soviet model for the perspective plan of 1965–70 is being used here as representative of the normative family, and the Stone (Cambridge) model as that of the indicative family.

I

As noted in the previous chapter the Soviet model was designed in the Central Economic Mathematical Institute of the Soviet Academy of Sciences (denoted hereafter as 'Ts'[1]). Neither its numerical solutions nor its fate have been revealed. Nonetheless, it deserves our attention as an important stage in the history of formalised planning techniques.

What has been revealed indicates that the experiment followed—in two phases—the logic of a plan construction: first consistency was secured for the terminal and the intermediate yearly plan-intervals, then optimisation was sought with some adopted objectives. In the first phase a dynamised inter-industry model was employed; in the second, a linear programme.

---

[1] The following discussion is based on *Model dla Rascheta Sbalansirovanogo i Optimalnogo Perspektivnogo Plana na 1965–70 gg;* this paper—as its title and text show—was produced to provide a model for the construction of the Soviet plan covering the second half of the sixties: a copy was generously offered to the present writer by the Director, Academician Fedorenko. Subsequently a chapter appeared under the names of Yu. N. Gavrilyets, B. N. Mikhalevskiy and Yu.P. Leibkind in *Primenenye Matematiki v Ekonomicheskikh Issledovanyakh,* vol. 3, *op. cit.* ('Lineynaya model optimalnogo rosta planovoy ekonomiki'). It has been identified by the present writer as an exposition of the programming model contained in the paper quoted and has helped him to expand certain parts of the discussion. It may be noted, however, that the Gavrilyets-Mikhalevskiy-Leibkind version has no reference to the 1965–70 plan; nor does it work with the dynamic inter-industry model contained in the quoted paper.

Troubles in attempts to apply the classical, Leontief dynamic inter-industry construct in planning have been by now investigated: disappointments are, at least in part, due to some misunderstandings as to the indications which the model can offer for an economy's equilibrium growth. Partly they are due to limitations of the apparatus.[1]

The Leontief dynamic equation system—when put in the finite-difference terms—has the form

$$\bar{x}_t = A_t\bar{x}_t + K_t\Delta\bar{x}_t + \bar{y}_t$$

where, for the year t, the $\bar{x}_t$, $\Delta\bar{x}_t$ and $\bar{y}_t$ are, respectively, vectors of gross outputs, of incremental gross product and of 'net' final product; the A_t and K_t are, respectively, matrices of current input coefficients and of incremental capital coefficients. With constant coefficients the system

$$\Delta\bar{x}_t = K^{-1}(I-A)\bar{x}_t - K^{-1}\bar{y}_t$$

has, as its solution, the vector

$$\bar{x}_t = (I+S)^t x_0 + \sum_{n=0}^{t-1}[(I+S)^n K^{-1}]y_{t-n-1}$$

where $S = K^{-1}(I-A)$. The general solution of the non-homogeneous system depends on the existence of this S. However, in the general case the S will be degenerate (since K will be degenerate and, consequently, its inverse non-existent). Moreover, there is no a priori harmonisation of the dynamics of x and y.

As far as one can see the Soviet experiment follows the Almon-Dorfman method for a system described by means of differential equations

$$x = Ax + B\dot{x} + y$$

Here

$$y(t) = y_0 + y_1 t + y_2 t^2 + \cdots + y_m t^m$$

or

$$y(t) = e^{rt}(y_0 + y_1 t + y_2 t^2 + \cdots + y_m t^m).$$

[1] Cf. W. W. Leontief and others, *Studies in the Structure of the American Economy*, New York, 1953. For a discussion of choice-making elements in a dynamic input-output analysis see Dorfman-Samuelson-Solow, *Linear Programming and Economic Analysis*, op. cit. ch. 11.

We follow here A. D. Smirnov, 'Dinamicheskaya Mezhotraslevaya Model i Planovyie Raschety', in *Ekonomika i Matematicheskiye Metody*, no. 3, 1965. Smirnov's is a noteworthy attempt to reformulate the particular solution of the dynamic inter-industry problem in a way most suitable and applicable in strategic-economic planning. In the context see A. Konyus, 'Metody postroyenya dinamicheskoy modeli mezhotraslevogo balansa' in A. Efimov, L. Berri, op. cit.

The procedure is outlined in Almon[1] who also explains the lack of realism of the standard solution. The Almon solution is of the form

$$x = (I-A)^{-1}y + (I-A)^{-1}B(I-A)^{-1}y$$
$$+ \cdots + [(I-A)^{-1}B]^n(I-A)^{-1}y^{(n)} + \cdots$$

It has been shown (by Almon) that the right-hand series does give a particular solution where the $y(t)$ has the first of the two alternative forms indicated above; further that with $y(t)$ having the second of these forms, the series is absolutely convergent if there is some norm of $(I-A)^{-1}B$ such that $\| (I-A)^{-1}B \| . | r | < 1$. The economic mechanism of the solution is this: the first term of the series describes gross output with zero growth of final product: in the second term the element $(I-A)^{-1}_y$ shows the full-order current inputs entailed in the increment of final product, the $B(I-A)^{-1}_y$ reflects full-order capital inputs for the final product increment, the $(I-A)^{-1}B(I-A)^{-1}$ full-order inputs entailed in the build-up of productive capacities $B(I-A)^{-1}$, and so on.

On such a basis, and still by the Almon procedure, a consistent, balanced perspective plan is found in the Soviet model with coefficients variable over time, time-lags, growing efficiency of constant and variable capital and a fixed minimum share of household consumption in final product. From here—in the second phase—the operation moves to a very austere programming exercise. In this each of the tightly aggregated sixteen branches is assumed to produce a single product (expressed in 'real value terms'—constant prices). Products are taken to be infinitely divisible and additive. So are the three factors—labour, fixed capital, inventories. They are the exogenously given elements of system. Fixed capital and inventories are so only at the initial time-point: they are subsequently endogenously formed. The system yields its final outputs: of which some parts are discretely fixed. Competitive technologies are assumed away. All degrees of freedom are created by the control variables. Moreover, total increment in capital stock is related to that in productive capital stock and consumption—to labour resources. To be more specific the data fed into the programme consist of: technology-matrices of current input-output coefficients

[1] C. Almon, 'Consistent Forecasting in a Dynamic Multisector Model', in *Review of Economics and Statistics*, May 1963; cf. also his 'Numerical Solution of a Modified Leontief Dynamic System for Consistent Forecasting or Indicative Planning', in *Econometrica*, October 1963.

and of capital and labour efficiency coefficients; depreciation norms; periods of construction and maturation of capacities; State consumption; non-productive investment and balance of trade; non-completed investment in the base year; minimum volume—branchwise—and changes in the structure of household consumption; labour-force and changes—by year and branch—in the real income per man. What is obtained from the programme is: distribution, by year and branch, of (a) net investment and amortisation, allowance made for technological progress and capital freeze; (b) incremental household consumption and change in social consumption and inventories; (c) the structure of additions to labour force; further we obtain the dynamics of capacities and of total outputs; also the population's money incomes in balance with supply of consumer goods by producing branches. In order to see the mechanism of the model it may be of help to have a closer look at its formal handling of investment and consumption.

Investment and its maturation—growth of capacities—are described in this way. If net capital investment, $\Delta S^{j,\,t+\tau_j}$, has matured by the year $t+\tau_j$ in the j-th branch, that would imply that $(\varphi^{j,\,t+\tau_j})\Delta S^{j,\,t+\tau_j}$ was invested during t, followed by $(\varphi_{t+1}^{j,\,t+\tau_j})\Delta S^{j,\,t+\tau_j}$ during $t+1$, and so on. For the economy's investment producing sector, aggregated in three branches, the diagonal matrices $(\varphi_k^{j,\,t+\tau_j})$ show the maturation of net investment over τ_j so that

$$\sum_{k=t}^{t+\tau_j} \varphi_k^{j,\,t+\tau_j} \begin{pmatrix} \mathrm{I} & 0 & 0 \\ 0 & \mathrm{I} & 0 \\ 0 & 0 & \mathrm{I} \end{pmatrix}; \quad \varphi_k^{j,\,l} = \begin{pmatrix} \varphi_{k1}^{j,l} & 0 & 0 \\ 0 & \varphi_{k2}^{j,l} & 0 \\ 0 & 0 & \varphi_{k3}^{j,l} \end{pmatrix}$$

(Here j denotes the investment receiving branch, k is the year of investment, l is the maturation year of investment started in $l-\tau_j$ and $(i=1, 2, 3)$ is the investment producing branch.)

The maximand chosen is a cumulative sum total of final production. Its component of household consumption is formed of a minimum part, variable over time—a 'floor' constraint—plus an increment to be optimised, $C^t = C_0^t + C^t$. The former's structure is assumed to be somehow at optimum (a clearly shaky supposition): hence, to get equilibrium, C^t must be expected to move along the gradient of the objective function of total consumption, $v(C^t)$. In fact to escape from nonlinearity, what is postulated is only the optimal number of *fixed* 'sets' of consumables (*komplektnost*), determined by that gradient at the

294

not be exceeded by the use of labour in different industries; when f^* and q denote vectors of labour requirements per unit of output and total output respectively, we have

$$E^\theta \lambda \geqslant E^\theta f^{*\prime} \cdot q$$

output l_j^t and branch output x_j^t—cannot exceed the national labour force L_j^t

$$\sum_{j=1}^{16} l_j^t . x_j^t \leqslant \mathscr{L}_j^t$$

Ultimately the labour constraint is reformulated analogously to (I) above: full-order inputs of labour, in the year t into the increments in private consumption and social consumption and inventories and capacities (time-lagged as above) cannot exceed the increment in total labour force:

$$\Delta L \geqslant \sum_{j=1}^{16} \sum_{r=0}^{tj} \mathscr{L}^t \mathscr{L}_j . M_j^{t+1}$$

$$+ \sum_{j=1}^{16} \mathscr{L}^t \mathscr{L}_j (D_j^t - D_j^{t-1})$$

$$+ f^t \sum_{j-1}^{16} \mathscr{L}^t \mathscr{L}_j \lambda_j^t$$

where the $\mathscr{L}^t \mathscr{L}_j$ describes full-input coefficients of labour.

PRIMARY INPUTS AND PRICES

The price vector in 'St', is obtained from a full-order primary inputs, f, or value added per unit of output

$$p = (I - A)^{\prime -1} . f$$

where ($'$) denotes transposition. To get prices of the year θ—in relation to those of the zero year, $p_{0\theta}$, the transpose of the input-output matrix for that year is used and a vector with elements describing reciprocals of changes in productivity $r_{0\theta}$ brought in so that

$$p_{0\theta} = (I - A_\theta')^{-1} r_{0\theta} f_0$$

A generalised variant of the Cobb-Douglas function is then employed for relating outputs to inputs of capital and labour.

The approach to pricing in 'Ts' is essentially similar to that in 'St'. With rewards to factors corresponding to their marginal efficiencies, i.e. with the π^t being the vector of annual average wages per employee and ρ^t the vector of normative investment efficiency, the price vector for the t year is

$$p^t = [(\pi^t)' . l^t + (\rho^t)'(b^t)] . [I - (a^t)]^{-1}$$

The l^t stands for the vector of labour input coefficients, and (b^t) and (a^t) for matrices of capital and current input coefficients respectively (as above).

CONSUMPTION AND DEMAND FUNCTIONS

The 'St' model of consumption is based on the system of prices and price-sensitive demand functions, with postulated non-decreasing 'basic' living standards. In this system expenditure on private consumption per head is written:

$$\hat{p}e = bm + (I - bi')\hat{c}p$$
$$= \hat{p}c + b(m - p'c)$$

Here symbols employed mean: p is the vector of prices ($\triangle$ denotes a diagonal matrix formed from it); e the vector of quantities demanded; $m = p'e$ total expenditure per head.

The b and c take care of the condition of non-decreasing standards of living: c are components of such average standards; thus only what is left after they have been paid for, that is $m - p'c$, is allocated to different commodities and this has been done so in proportion to the elements of b. The 'St' demand equations clearly form only a segment of the market economy's finance circuit (now being explored with the view to formalisation).

Unlike 'St' the 'Ts' formulates the equilibrium condition for the finance of the consumption sphere: clearly a simpler task for a system where the decisive part of the population's income may be treated as being of a wage-type, related to employment dynamics and outputs. Taking Ω^t as the 'multiplier' for correcting the wage total for what in Soviet doctrine and practice is the 'non-productive' sphere plus the population's savings and as the posited ceiling on consumer-good stocks ξ^t this condition is written as

$$\sum_{j-1}^{16} C^{jt} - \Omega^t \cdot \sum_{j-1}^{16} \pi^{jt} \cdot l^{jt} \cdot x^{jt} \geqslant \xi^t > 0$$

The general form of the household-consumption vector will be then

$$C^t = C_0^t + \operatorname{grad} v^t(C_0) \cdot f$$

and in the particular case

$$C_j^t = C_0^t + \lambda_j^t \cdot f$$

as discussed above.

While more ambitious in respect of the finance circuit than the 'St', the 'Ts' leaves unformulated the whole of the circuit beyond the consumption sphere. That may be not inadequate for the traditional planning of the inter-industry system basically in real rather than financial terms.

OBJECTIVE FUNCTIONS

In 'St' the policy aim is maximising the utility of consumption subject to constraints stated. Taking the utility of consumption in year o as E^θ_x and

The maximand in 'Ts' is the final bill of goods weighted by means of the vector of preference-coefficients P^t, (subject to constraints stated):

the community's rate of time-discount as ρ the maximand is written

$$\sum_{\theta=0}^{t-1} E^{\theta}\chi = \sum_{\theta=0}^{t-1} e^{-\rho\theta}\,\phi[\eta_{\zeta}(E^{\theta}e_{\zeta}-c_{\zeta})^{b\zeta}]$$

the ϕ is some arbitrary monotonic function, the ζ is a typical commodity and the remaining symbols have the same meaning as before. Putting $\phi\equiv$ log what is maximised is a weighted sum of the logarithms of the excesses of consumption over the quantities in the basic standard of living.

Alternatively, as a simple aternative the maximising of consumption η rather than its utility is considered. A constant-utility price index-number, π_{θ}, will be constructed such that $\pi_{\theta}=\eta_{\theta}/\eta_{0}$. The maximand will be then written as $\sum_{\theta}(\eta_{\theta}/\pi_{\theta})$.

$$\sum_{t,j}^{10,16}\left\{e^{-\beta t}[C^{t}+D^{t}+\Upsilon^{t}]\right.$$
$$\left.+\frac{T.e^{-2\beta}}{T-t+1}\Delta S\right\}P^{t}=\max$$

(as discussed above)
Between them gross capital formation and incremental private consumption are the primary control variables, while social consumption and stocks and reserves (and possibily unutilised capacity potential) are the secondary control variables. This formulation corresponds to the strategy controls of the centrally planned system.

NOTE TO CHAPTERS 19 AND 20

The Ts.E.M.I. (Central Economic-Mathematical Institute) school of thought, tends towards the view that the centrally planned economy is an 'inertial' system. Hence the recommendation to resort to extrapolation as the principal method of prediction of the broad lines of development, subject to certain error to be minimised (*Theses* of the December 1966 conference on methodology of economic plan-prognosis, in particular contribution by A. D. Smirnov). It is maintained that an empirically borne out trend in the scientific-technological progress would support the hypothesis of similarity (*skhodstvo*) of growth conditions in the past and the foreseeable future.

To be more precise, a school of thought takes as tenable, in a plan-prognosis, the assumption of constancy of the average rate of change in the incremental values of relevant economic indexes over time-intervals observed. That in a sense would generalise Konyus's hypothesis on the investment time-series (cf. his 'Perspektivnoye planirovanye v predpolozhenii ravnomernogo rosta kapitalovlozheniy', in *Planirovanye i Ekonomiko-Matematicheskiye Metody*, 1964, *op. cit.*). In the mathematical formulation of optimal plan-prognosis, the invariability of conditions of growth, resulting from the postulate of stationarity of the point-of-departure process could be relaxed—replaced by that of the k-th increments of the process analysed.

(Smirnov, cf. p. 284, ftn. 3 above.) (In the present discussions some are inclined to argue in terms of a 'law of geometric progression', others rather in terms of an empirical 'hyperbolic law' of growth (*Theses*; N. F. Shatilov, V. V. Pomerantsev).

Index of Subjects

Acceleration phase in Kalecki model, 25
Accounting price, *see* Price
Actualised value: Malinvaud criteria, 153; recoupment period criteria, 152; *see also* Discount Rate, Interest Rate
Aggregation: Almon-Dantzig model, 97; Dantzig-Wolfe decomposition principle, 94; Dudkin-Yershov, in, 102; Gome theoretical approach for Leontief matrix, 263; Gavrilyets model, 94; iterative procedures, 93; Kornai-Liptak, 96; Leontief system, in, 80; mathematical vs. economic approach, 263; optimal error in, 94; Porwit, 96; Pugachev, 98, 101; Volkonskiy, 95, 102
Algorithms: block-programming multi-tier system (Katsenelinboygen), 129; Brown-Robinson, iterative, 93; Dantzig-Wolfe, 94; general schema, *see* Kolmogorov-Uspenskiy, 289; Kantorovich, 62; simplex, 93, 97
Almon paths in dynamic multi-sectoral analysis, 293
Almon-Dantzig construct, 98
Almon-Dorfman method in Soviet experiments, 292
Alpha-beta system in Nemchinov, 31
Arrow-Hurwicz construct: dynamic allocation problem, 131; iteration, 97; Volkonskiy decomposition system, 95; *see also* Gradient
Asymptotic stability, 193
Automata theory, 288
Auto-regressive process, *see* Markov process

Balance-coefficients in Nemchinov, 36
Balance method: 'balance of national economy' with final product index, 265; French plan construct, 255; Soviet plan construct, 255, 260, 279
Bang-bang problem (LaSalle's), 192
Belkin-Grobman-Lunts theorem, 49
Bellman model, related to Pontriagin *et al.*, 194
Bergson social welfare concept, 74, 76, 91
Bernoulli theorem, 54
Black-box approach, 288
Block triangular systems, 129
Bratislava model, 283
Brown-Robinson method, 95

Calculus of variations: classical, in optimal controls, 192; maximum principle, 192
Cambridge model, 254; *see also* Stone model
Capital coefficients, 23, 162; Belgian calculations, 273; Eidelman schema, 272; Kyn *et al.* system, 89; related to investment efficiency, 141; Soviet calculations, 273; von Neumann model, 30
Capital formation, efficient: Gorkov model, 156; Kalecki-Rakowski model, 154; Kantorovich-Makarov dynamic system, 166; Kantorovich-planning model, 158, 165; Lange model, 163; Lurie model, 155; macro-production function as tool, 156; Mikhalevskiy model, 162, 167; Neumann, von, 31; optimal factor combination, and, 154; Strumilin 'bias', 156

INDEX OF SUBJECTS

Index of Names

Abramovits, M., 198
Adelman, Irma, 19
Aganbegyan, A. G., 39, 49, 217, 251, 279
Ahluwalia, S. S., 264
Aleinikov, B. I., 213
Alexandrov, G. F., 7
Alexeyev, A., 216
Allen, R. G. D., 71, 262, 265
Almon, C., 97, 98, 100, 293
Amvrosyenko, V. V., 93, 267
Anchishkin, I., 4
Arrow, K. J., 93, 131, 133, 146
Atlas, Z. V., 61
Augustinovic, Maria, 261
Auspitz, R., 54

Bachurin, 61
Balassa, B., 145
Barbakadze, M., 218
Barna, T., 39, 197, 211, 218, 263
Basiuk, J., 213
Bauer, P. T., 182
Bauer, R., 85
Baumol, W. J., 65, 67, 187, 199
Beer, S., 288
Beksiak, J., 85
Belayev, L. S., 87, 195, 216
Belkin, V. D., 39, 49, 64, 87, 251
Bellman, R., 191, 194, 196
Benard, J., 273, 274, 278
Berg, A. I., 289
Bergson, A., 71, 72, 76, 91, 181, 208
Bergstrom, A., 127
Berliner, J., 134, 171
Bernoulli, J., 54
Berri, L., 259
Boettcher, E., 59

Bogachev, V., 155
Bogomolov, O., 215, 216
Böhm-Bawerk, E. von, 48
Boltianskii, V. G., 190
Bolza, H., 192
Bor, M. Z., 254, 280
Borisova, E. P., 94
Bornstein, M., 59
Bortkiewicz, L. von., 49
Bos, H. C., 161, 182
Bosiakowski, Z., 85
Boyarskiy, Ya, A., 12, 67, 78, 172
Brauer, R., 205
Brody, A., 173
Brown, G. W., 93, 96, 267, 284
Brus, W., 12, 86
Bukharin, N., 3
Butkovskiy, A. G., 190
Byelenkiy, V., 103

Campbell, R. W., 55, 59
Cassel, G., 43
Cerniansky, V., 205
Chakravarty, S., 181, 183, 195
Chambre, H., 10
Champernowne, D. G., 27
Chen Yi, 171
Chenery, H. B., 198, 249
Chernyak, Yu. I., 219, 241, 242
Clark, J. B., 12, 67
Clark, P. B., 198
Cobb, C. W., 105, 155, 167, 183, 299
Collette, J. M., 139
Cournot, A., 48
Crossman, G., 134
Cukor, Gy., 209
Cutler, Leola, 226
Czerwinski, Z., 73, 183

313

Halabuk, L., 297
Harasim, E., 213
Harrod, R., 90, 166, 183, 184, 197, 199, 200, 295
Hart, P. E., 125, 186, 271
Havas, P., 109
Hejl, L., 89
Hensel, K. P., 59
Hicks, J., 53, 160, 186
Hirsch, H., 59
Holzman, F. D., 208
Holzman, Mathilda, 263
Horvat, B., 126, 171
Hotelling, H., 262
Houthakker, H. S., 73, 76, 278
Hurwicz, L., 93, 131, 133

Ichimura, S., 163
Isard, W., 218
Isayev, B. L., 261, 280

Jevons, W. S., 48
Johansen, L., 70, 183, 184, 186
Jordan, G., 262, 267
Jurkiewicz, J., 210

Kaganovich, I. Z., 262
Kaldor, N., 154, 199, 200
Kalecki, M., 22, 25, 45, 69, 104, 145, 147, 149, 151, 174, 204
Kalman, R. E., 188, 193
Kantorovich, L. V., 7, 8, 33, 62, 63, 66, 70, 71, 77, 87, 92, 119, 120, 128, 149, 158, 160, 165, 166, 169, 175, 183, 185, 186, 284
Karpov, P. P., 262
Kaser, M., 262
Katsenelinboygen, A. I., 103, 129, 172, 177
Kelendzheridze, D. L., 191
Kemeny, J. G., 28, 32
Kenessy, Z., 297
Keynes, J. M., 17, 197, 198
Khachaturov, T. S., 141, 151, 153, 172
Kharatishvili, G. L., 190
Khmielnitskaya, B., 3

Khokhluk, V. I., 267
Kitov, A. I., 289
Klein, L. R., 282
Klinkmueller, E., 59
Klotsvog, F., 262
Knirsch, P., 59
Koctuch, H., 207
Kolmogorov, A. N., 67, 188, 289
Komarek, V., 207
Kondalev, A. I., 188
Kondor, G., 173
Kondrashev, D. D., 61
Konyus, A. A., 75, 90, 156, 174, 187, 292
Koopmans, T. C., 91, 131, 132, 172, 182
Koretskiy, A., 149
Kornai, J., 96, 102, 121, 133, 167, 214
Kosiatchenko, G. G., 1
Krassovskiy, N. N., 192, 193
Krassovskiy, V. P., 143, 273
Kretschmer, 249
Kreyn, M. G., 192
Kronrod, Ya. K., 11, 61, 71
Kronsjö, T., 210, 240, 243
Kuhn, H. W., 131
Kulikowski, R., 192
Kurz, M., 195
Kuznets, S., 198, 208
Kvasha, Ya., 273
Kyn, O., 89, 288

Labedz, L., 55
Lagrange, J. L., 63, 127, 192, 194, 196
Landauer, C., 2
Lange, O., 2, 4, 23, 34, 43, 69, 71, 125, 126, 130, 149, 163, 167, 173, 179, 282, 288
LaSalle, J. P., 192, 193
Lasciak, A., 283
Lavigne, Marie L., 55, 116
Lefschetz, S., 193
Leibkind, Yu. P., 91, 291
Leifman, L. Ya., 267
Leitman, G., 192

315